Jay Stu

TAMING THE
VIOLENCE
OF FAITH

WIN-WIN SOLUTIONS FOR
OUR WORLD IN CRISIS

Copyright 2011 by Jay Stuart Snelson
All rights reserved
Printed in the United States of America
Library of Congress Cataloging in Publication Data
Snelson, Jay Stuart (1936 – 2011)
Taming the Violence of Faith: Win-Win Solutions for Our World in Crisis
First Edition
Jay Stuart Snelson

ISBN: 145371720X
ISBN-13: 9781453717202
Library of Congress Control Number: 2010910942

CreateSpace, North Charleston, SC

To Sarah Belle Dosser
Eliza Jane Dosser
&
Nancy Mae Rhyme

A Losing Fight

The world today is not so gay,
Fighting and bickering all the way.
Who knows when war may start
And tear this mad old world apart.
Some men fight to show their might;
Others still for the want to kill.
If countries shall make war again,
I promise you, no one will win.

Jay Stuart Snelson
Eighth Grade Creative Writing
John James Audubon Junior High School
Los Angeles, California
July 24, 1950

Table of Contents

Preface

Since the origins of civilization, striking evidence confirms a long and tragic history of institutionalized violence for religious and political gain. Over time, imposing institutions of organized oppression would become the most lethal inventions of human ingenuity. Their coercive policies have fueled the engines of murder, torture, and assault across the span of every nation. Religious and political leaders have led their faithful followers to inflict unspeakable crimes against humanity. Yet, the irony is profound. Most organized destruction of human life, wealth, and freedom has been forced upon society by respected people who intended little or no harm to anyone. Nonetheless, with noble intentions, earnest believers have fashioned our most deadly institutions of violence. Their aim was to reach religious and political goals by organizing institutions of force. Religious and political leaders sought to control the people through the status and prestige of sanctified, legitimized power for coercive gain. Of course, it is relevant to ask, if true, does any of this really matter? And, if so, what can or should be done about it?

Every literate person knows that we live in the Nuclear Age—not the Stone Age or the Bronze Age. Yet, millions, while rejecting *disorganized* violence, still cling to their faith in the merit and virtue of *organized* violence. Many decent people of good faith, openly or silently, condone the development, deployment, and potential use of weapons of mass destruction to reach their religious or political aims. However, to make such a reckless sanction is to risk an irreversible disaster. The growing threat of a collateral catastrophe from even a limited or local use of these fatal weapons could end in the ruination of every nation on earth. Moreover, the real peril of self-extinction could terminate our species.

Because the risk is critical and still rising, we must end the tradition and retire the ritual of imposing religious and political coercion on unwilling victims through violent means in the name of god, nation, or leader. Fortunately, to find nonviolent means to the worthy ends of peace, prosperity, and freedom, we do not have to change *human nature*. But, we do have to change *human paradigms* that are based on flawed doctrines of cause-and-effect, especially those doctrines that misidentify and obscure the true means to peace, prosperity, and freedom for all people of all faiths.

Our world's libraries are crammed with records of respected people who reached for peace, prosperity and freedom, by enforcing religious and political violence — violence, which inflicted war, poverty, and servitude. Again, the irony is as dramatic as it is tragic. To end these failed policies, their flawed premises and conclusions must be falsified and repudiated beyond redemption. In so doing, two widely respected paradigms of faith must fall from grace.

From ancient times, these win-lose paradigms, based on lethal models of social cause-and-effect, have deluded decent people into praising the glory of institutionalized violence for religious and political gain. These familiar paradigms of faith, which are usually accepted by default without critical analysis, are both simple and ominous. They assert the supposed truth and validity of two familiar and deadly doctrines of social causality: *For our religion to gain, your religion must be forced to lose.* And, its companion in violence is closely related: *For our nation to gain, your nation must be forced to lose.* As long as these win-lose paradigms are held as true and valid — especially among the educated classes — the risk of our demise will continue to rise.

Since Galileo and Newton introduced the strategic method of modern science with its stunning discoveries of natural law, various attempts have been made to unify science and religion as well as science and economics. The challenge of unifying any elements of science, religion, and economics is how to stay within the realm of scientific *observation* of causation, without crossing the boundary into the realm of religious or economic *imagination* of causation.

Where the fidelity and integrity of science is valued, to move away from scientific observation, toward religious or economic imagination, is to convert science into the non-science of metaphysics. Without observation to verify scientific predictions, there is no science. Observation is the keystone of science, and it is essential to all scientific unification. In meeting this challenge, *Taming the Violence of Faith* brings together and unifies certain principles of religion, economics, and science without compromising the rigid standards of the scientific method.

Unifying religion, economics, and science confirms the practicality and efficacy of applying *principles of nonviolence* in creating win-win solutions to the win-lose problems of war, poverty, and servitude that, in our time, threaten human survival. A key part of the solution is to show and verify the equity, utility, and morality of making paradigm shifts away from *win-lose religion* toward *win-win religion* for the enrichment of all believers as well as nonbelievers. Building on the discovery of social causation through independent observation and verification this book presents a viable strategy for taming the violence unleashed on innocent people by religious and political institutions, and introduces the reader to a wealth of *Win-Win Solutions for Our World in Crisis.*

Introduction

For thousands of years, spiritual leaders have praised a creed that has ignited more organized violence, more systemized terror, more legalized murder, than any other idea in religious history. This ancient tenet makes a promise to every believer: "Our faith is the one true belief in the one true god." Although this hallowed promise may sound pious to some, and ominous to others, how can belief in a unique god, a singular god, a universal god evoke violence, ignite terror, and incite murder on every settled continent? How can respected people of true faith—with good minds and educations—be steered by this sacred belief to raise atrocities of such towering magnitude, that they are deemed crimes against humanity? We must answer this pressing question before we can tame the violence of faith.

༃

Believers in one true god have been, and remain, divided by a deadly dispute over how to interpret and explain the moral foundations of Holy Scripture. On one side of this dispute, there are many believers on a sacred mission to terrorize and intimidate all unbelievers in their vision of god. Their solemn quest is to drive unbelievers into the temple of one true religion. Moreover, their faith is so strong that any means they employ is justified by their sacred ends. Thus, true believers see their violent actions as holy and heroic in the sight of god.

A crisis brews as believers strive to build a monopoly of religion. Their path to monopoly is to create a coercive institution founded, as noted, on this fatal theme: "For our religion to gain, your religion must be forced to lose." Trusting in the fidelity of this win-lose paradigm, believers wield the persuasion of terror to herd their neighbors into the house of god — the one true god. With faith in the sanctity of violence for the glory of god, their coercive aim is to impose their religion upon the world.

Yet, there is another side; not everyone praises or embraces this errant mission. There are those who decry all coercion in the name of god. They are an opposing faction — with no less faith in the one true god — objecting to such criminal violence. They reject the entire canon of religious monopoly through force and terror, damning it as a desecration of Holy Scripture. These men and women are the champions of religious freedom. They advance the goodwill of win-win religion for all believers of all faiths.

In grave contrast, there have always been those throughout the world who have advanced religious autocracy in the name of god. As instigators of religious oppression, they have never welcomed religious freedom.

Those familiar with the social institutions of our predecessors know that the orchestration of violence and terror to advance religious and political domination is not a new idea; it has plagued every civilization in human history. However, this plague is about to end; this ancient strategy has run its course.

With the arrival of the nuclear age in 1945, the menace of ending the human race through global devastation became a shocking reality, no longer storied fiction. By creating arms of annihilation to expand religious and political power on every continent, the potential for irreversible calamity became all too real. Unless we can identify and verify the true causes of this swelling crisis, it will bury us under an avalanche of rubble too deep to cast aside.

The origin of a durable solution to any lasting social crisis begins with the discovery of its true causes. Without this practical knowledge of cause-and-effect, solutions for the future will be as elusive as they have been for the past. Whatever the plan of action for solving a social crisis, to reach a solution, the plan has to be practical, which means it has to work. But what works, and what does not work? For one thing, the end of religious turmoil does not require the end of religious faith. Those who sanction the oppression of religious monopoly do not have to end their faith in one true god. Yet, something has to end. The faithful have to end their faith in the virtue and merit of religious monopoly through violence and intimidation.

Of course, to abandon or ignore the canon of religious monopoly requires a paradigm shift. Believers must move away from faith in win-lose religion for immoral gain, toward faith in win-win religion for moral gain. Although it takes courage to shift away from win-lose religion, such daring will create a treasury of blessings, rising beyond all experience through the moral practice of win-win religion.

∽

It is normal for humans to have faith in the truth of a variety of premises and conclusions on a variety of subjects. Unfortunately, this has included faith in the rightness of religious and political paradigms that have incited and inflamed history's most stunning calamities of social violence. This raises at least two relevant questions. What is faith?

And, can faith in the merit of violence be superseded by faith in the merit of nonviolence?

The essence of faith can be defined in a few words: *Faith is belief in the truth of premises and conclusions that have not been verified through independent observation.* Whether people have faith in the merit of violence or nonviolence depends entirely upon which premises and conclusions they accept on faith to be true.

Human experience shows that faith has spurred the greatest violence and destruction when it is founded on a lethal paradigm of cause-and-effect, still held to be true by many respected people throughout the world. By their faithful sanction, they have cloaked this paradigm with the mantle of respectability. This fatal model of social causality is defined as the win-lose paradigm: *For us to gain, they must lose through force or fraud.* The deadly power of this paradigm is derived from the fact that all who embrace it believe it to be true.

We can observe that acting on faith in the respectability of violence always poses a danger to society. This paradigm of causality—this worldview of cause-and-effect—fosters belief in the efficacy and morality of organizing violence for religious or political gain through the loss of others. The social effects are grave. Faith in the virtue of violence has proven its potential for disaster in every civilization. Yet, if faith in the merit of religious and political violence is not tamed in the near future, it poses a critical threat to human survival.

Human faith is a governor of human choice, and human choice is the source of human power. Humans can wield win-win power for mutual gain, or win-lose power for coercive gain. It is our choice.

It is no secret that the power of faith to change the world for better or for worse is in the hands of the faithful. Today, the human vision of faith is of critical importance precisely because it is crucial to the success or failure of our entire species. Men and women can adopt a nonviolent faith to unleash peace, prosperity, and freedom—or they can adopt a violent faith to unleash war, poverty, and servitude.

From the Bronze Age to the Machine Age, our ancestors proved their ability to survive the social ruination that fell upon them through their ongoing quests for religious and political domination. Yet, we can no longer afford to repeat the religious and political violence of the past, no matter how "holy" or "noble" the aim of its advocates may be. In the nuclear age, such measured coercion can ignite the process of human extinction with no chance of recovery.

To avoid the demise of our species, faith in the merit of win-lose religion for violent gain must be superseded by faith in the merit of win-win religion for nonviolent gain. Whether this is possible or impossible, practical or impractical, are crucial questions that will be addressed and answered in this treatise. As the flawed and spurious claims for the merit of win-lose religion for violent gain are refuted and repudiated, win-win religion naturally ascends as the moral and benevolent alternative. The social and spiritual gains of moving from win-lose to win-win religion are priceless. Canons of win-win theology offer an alluring path toward moral and kindly behavior. Moreover, as the equity, utility, and morality of win-win religion for mutual gain are affirmed and reaffirmed through observation, the way to applying win-win models of social action becomes ever more compelling.

The main focus of this writing is on taming the violence of religious faith. However, the violence of political faith will not be ignored. The extreme risks of advancing political faith in the merit of win-lose violence will be thoroughly examined in a later work to follow.

෨෨

The doctrine of one true god spurs human conflict by dividing humans into opposing classes. It splits the human race between those who believe in the one true god—and those who do not. It incites hostility that did not even exist before the invention of this arbitrary social division that thrives on win-lose gain.

In trusting the scriptural account of one true god, many worshipers are sure that all people must embrace the certitude of their faith—and that it is their sacred duty to advance its sole authority and dominion on earth. Not everyone, however, is convinced that such religious claims are true and tenable. Some voice their reservations, or even their outright disbelief. In reply, believers are incredulous over those who fail to see what is self-evident to them. With open chagrin, they ask how can one *not* believe in the singular supremacy of our one true god?

Believers tend to elevate themselves to an elite society of followers who are worthier than those who do not believe. Those who fail to embrace the divinity of a singular god of supreme power are commonly held in contempt as inferior human beings. For their glaring inferiority, they are damned, dehumanized, and dishonored by their "superiors" as unworthy *disbelievers*. In contrast, those who do believe are praised and honored as *true believers* in the one true god of the one true faith.

Those who have created a *superior* class of believers, unavoidably, have created an *inferior* class of disbelievers. This raises a class struggle between human superiors and their no less human inferiors. Those who reject, ignore, or are ignorant of this unique god are spurned and dehumanized with derisive labels such as infidels, heathens, heretics, apostates, and pagans. This verbal abuse goes far beyond mere name-calling when the faithful fashion a divisive theology that incites violence against unbelievers.

Where there is only one *true* religion, it follows that all other religions must be *false*. Thus, those who follow false religions are said to impede or bar the advance of the only true religion sanctioned by the only true god. With trust in the supremacy of a singular god, throughout much of history its visionaries have asserted the rectitude and virtue of a sinister model of religious faith. It assures faithful followers, *For true believers to gain, disbelievers must be forced to lose.* This deadly paradigm of social causality forms the foundation of win-lose religion. Of course, a relevant question is, "So what?" Religious turmoil is an ancient social occurrence. It has prevailed throughout civilization with few interludes or interruptions to celebrate. So why be alarmed now when nothing is new? Because there *is* something new, and it demands our attention. A final calamity is looming that trumps all experience from imminent danger.

The reality of our time is that pious followers of this ancient paradigm of win-lose religion have instigated a world crisis that threatens to delete ten thousand years of civilization. Even more appalling, it threatens to annihilate the human species without any help from errant asteroids, random comets, or volcanic explosions that could dwarf the fury of Krakatau.

Ꮽ

Win-lose religion has a long and tragic history of inciting believers to commit unspeakable crimes against humanity. Religious leaders have justified, sanctified, and deified the murder of millions upon millions of innocent people who were killed for one reason. They were held to be *disbelievers* or *unbelievers* in the one true religion of the one true god. Yet, for many victims of win-lose religion, their source of non-belief was their complete ignorance of its theology. Still others refused to believe that its spiritual leaders had found the *only* true religion led by the *only* true god. Regardless of their reasons, the risk of disbelieving in its absolute singularity was grave, indeed because freedom of worship had been banished by clerical authorities through the oppressive reign of win-lose religion.

True believers saw unbelievers as the enemy of religious truth and a menace to its faithful followers. Unbelievers were treated as pariahs who had rejected the one true god, a supernatural deity whose reality must be accepted on faith, or else. People were warned that it is forbidden to disbelieve in the supremacy of the only true god. People's lives—whether to live or die—depended on what they openly believed to be true. True believers, in their zeal to impose a religious monopoly, gave disbelievers an ultimatum: Believe in our revelation of divine truth—convert to our religion—or suffer the consequences. These included dire threats by religious and judicial authorities to imprison, torture, or kill all disbelievers.

∾

The appalling crimes of win-lose religion could have gone on forever without threatening human survival—that is, as long as humans could procreate faster than they were felled by religious brutality. However, by the mid-twentieth century, what only had been a minor crisis for our species suddenly became a major crisis. The onset of the Nuclear Age gave rise to an alarming shift in social dynamics. For the first time in human history, it became possible for religious activists to destroy every human on earth.

Since the conclusion of World War II in 1945, there have been rapid advances in both the power and production of nuclear, biological, and chemical arms—the so-called weapons of mass destruction. Thus, the possibility has continued to grow that religious rulers, religious fanatics, and religious terrorists will buy, seize, steal, or produce these weapons and, with little or no hesitation, use them to destroy their enemies. And, who are their enemies? They include every unbeliever and disbeliever in their sacred vision of one true god.

It is well known that if unconventional weapons are unleashed on disbelievers, with the genie out of the bottle, there may be no turning back. The lethal exchange of weapons that might follow a single nuclear, biological, or chemical attack could trigger a domino effect of unstoppable destruction.

During a news conference held in Hong Kong in summer 2006, world-renowned cosmologist Stephen Hawking warned that human "life on Earth is at the ever-increasing risk of being wiped out by a disaster, such as sudden global nuclear war, a genetically engineered virus or other dangers we have not yet thought of."[1]

Hawking is neither a rabid extremist nor a naive alarmist over his concern that "life on Earth" (which includes us) can be "wiped out" by nuclear or biological warfare — or by "dangers we have not yet thought of." Indeed, we could be blindsided in the future by a weapon of human destruction soon to be invented — or by one already deployed that we know nothing about. Surely, such prudent concerns by Hawking and others do not spring from naiveté or paranoia.

Forty years ago, Christian cleric and civil rights leader, Martin Luther King, Jr., gave his analysis of the crisis. "Our scientific power has outrun our spiritual power. We have guided missiles and misguided men."[2] Where men are "misguided," they are acting on false explanations of causality as if they were true. Unless they can make a paradigm shift away from their allegiance to false explanations of social causality toward true explanations, they will remain misguided. Where their misguided actions lead them to commit crimes against unbelievers in the name of the one true god, civilization is at risk of destruction, and our species is at risk of annihilation.

It is no exaggeration to stress that faith in the rightness of win-lose religion renders humans an endangered species. As noted, this human crisis is incited by pious people who believe in the truth of a deadly model of win-lose theology that for our religion to gain, your religion must be forced to lose. In short, for believers to win, disbelievers must lose.

Fortunately, this fatal paradigm is not carved in stone. If it can be shown that this win-lose doctrine is flawed, that religious believers can win more, achieve more, benefit more through the gain of others, rather than through the loss of others, then win-lose religion will fall from favor as a true and reliable guide to religious action.

∽

Many people argue that religious and political warfare is inevitable because humans, by their nature, are born to make war against their fellow humans. However, observation of human action reveals that humans are endangered not because their *human nature* impels them toward violence, but because their *human paradigms* steer them toward violence. Where humans act on false paradigms of causality and spurious models of reality — while believing they are true and above reproach — many bad things will happen to many good people. The worst of those bad things include the chilling afflictions of war, poverty, and servitude.

Furthermore, it is not our human nature that is driving us to extinction; it is our human paradigms founded on *imagination of causality* rather than on *observation of causality*. This unreliable strategy of imagining causality without observing it, without testing it, without verifying it, is steering us toward extinction and oblivion.

When religious activists seek the blessings of peace, prosperity, and freedom by taking coercive action for win-lose gain, which will only advance war, poverty, and servitude—whether they are religious or not, intelligent or not, educated or not—they don't know what they are doing!

Western libraries are filled with the history of social catastrophes, unleashed by eager activists who believed in the virtue of their sacred aims toward noble ends—ends that they were sure could only be reached through the agency of force and violence for win-lose gain. When pious Christians tortured and executed medieval "witches" for spreading the plague of Black Death across Europe, they did so not because they were malicious authorities, as most of them were not, but because they didn't know what they were doing. By misidentifying biological and social causality, they set the stage for disaster in acting on false models of causality as if they were true.

We know today that these poor witches were entirely innocent of the crimes for which they were accused and charged. Sadly, it is too late to save them from the win-lose actions of sincere people—"good guys," if you will—who believed they were doing the right thing by burning witches to death in the town square.

In our time, it is not too late to save our species from the win-lose actions of good guys who also believe that they are doing the right thing by persecuting their fellow humans for righteous and hallowed causes. When good guys with good minds and good schooling misidentify and misunderstand *which* social causes lead to *which* social effects—and thereby act on flawed paradigms of causality—a deadly die is cast. Again, many bad things will happen to many good people. At their worst, these bad things include social catastrophes and tragedies on a monolithic scale.

On the other hand, if good guys who are not malicious by nature create social crises by not knowing what they are doing, what about the danger posed by notoriously malicious bad guys like Secretary Stalin, Chancellor Hitler, and Chairman Mao? Their win-lose political policies legalized and imposed crimes against humanity. But like the good guys, the bad guys wreaked havoc by acting on false models of causality, proving that they too did not know what they were doing. A question to consider is this: Given the choice, would you rather be killed by a "bad guy" who doesn't know what he is doing, or by a "good guy" who doesn't know what he is doing?

∾

As a religious leader, Jesus was an ardent advocate of nonviolence. He scrupulously avoided involvement in either military or political leadership, which historically had been associated with organized violence for win-lose gain. Six centuries after Jesus, Muhammad flourished not only as a religious leader, but also as a military and political leader who believed in the virtue of institutionalized force as a holy means to sacred ends. Muhammad's legacy continued through the spread of his religious creed by way of the proven efficacy of military conquest for coercive gain.

Three years after Muhammad's death in A.D. 632, Damascus fell to a Moslem invasion. Their military forces soon conquered al-Barish in Iraq, Antioch in Turkey, and Jerusalem in the Middle East. By 642, Moslem armies had vanquished Alexandria and greater Egypt. Moving west, they conquered Spain in 715. The Moslem Western advance was finally arrested in 732 in France at the city of Tours by the army of Charles Martel, Prince of the Franks, and grandfather of Charlemagne. By the time of the Columbus discovery of the New World in 1492, the Moslems (Saracens) had been driven out of Spain by Christian armies.

Those familiar with religious history know of the Christian Crusaders who, in the Middle Ages, aimed to free the Holy Land of Moses and Jesus from Moslem control and domination. These warriors were guided by their belief in a sacred paradigm that launched the Crusades: *For Christians to gain, Moslems must be forced to lose.*

In 1056, Christian leader Pope Urban II demanded that Christians impose religious and political control in Asia Minor. Beginning with the First Crusade in 1095, there were nine Christian Crusades lasting several centuries until the last decade of the thirteenth century. Moreover, there were lesser Crusades that historians did not include in their main count, continuing for centuries more.

During the Crusades, Christian warriors, fighting for their one true god, were busy slaying infidels—non-Christians—throughout the Holy Land. With little or no mercy, devout Christians imprisoned, tortured, and killed Moslems and Jews. Yet, what did these Christian believers hold to be true? They believed in the rightness of persecuting disbelievers in the one true god—the omnipotent and just god of the Old and New Testaments.

Even Christians were not immune from the onslaught of Christian brutality in the name of Jesus. In the Fourth Crusade of 1201 to 1204, Christians set out to kill Moslems defending Jerusalem. Instead, they wound up killing Christians and Jews when they sacked the grand city of Constantinople, which was governed by Christian leaders of the Byzantine Empire. In brief, Christian leaders in Rome were unhappy with Christian leaders in Constantinople who headed the Eastern Orthodox Church of the Byzantine Empire.

The Roman paradigm avowed, *For Roman Christians to gain, Byzantine Christians must be forced to lose.* To their credit, many Byzantine Christians risked their lives to protect their Jewish neighbors (though not always with success) from being killed by Roman Christians as they raided Byzantine cities populated by Christians, Jews, and Moslems.

If we strip away Western justification and glorification of the Crusades, and the historical apologies for their horrific violence, what is left? Western believers in the one true god were certain that they had a sacred mission. It was to convince Eastern disbelievers (Byzantine Christians, Moslems, and Jews) to embrace the Western vision of God as ordained by the Christian Church of Rome — or else be jailed, tortured, or killed. Their holy command was to believe as we believe, or suffer the harsh punishment that you deserve. This paradigm of social causality, this model of religious brutality has guided intelligent people, educated people, and righteous people to commit outrageous crimes in the name of their one true god. In any society where the most respected people commit the most horrific crimes, such a society is a win-lose society that is seriously flawed.

℘

Led by followers of Jesus, these military crusades into the Holy Land and other Moslem territories further fueled the win-lose paradigm, "For Moslems to gain, Christians must be forced to lose." Moslems, acting on behalf of Allah — their one true god — matched the brutality of Christian Crusaders by imprisoning, torturing, and killing as many Christian infidels as they could find.

Moslems — commonly called Muslims today — often have been united in their aim to kill Christians and other unbelievers in Islamist supremacy. Since the seventh century, however, Moslems also have been killing each other with fiery passion. The ongoing conflict between Sunni and Shi`ah Muslims is incited by their ageless dispute over which contender has the sacred right to speak for Islam's holy founder, Arab prophet and teacher, Muhammad.*

---

*   In the Western world, followers of the prophet Muhammad, founder of Islam, have been known for centuries as Moslems or Mohammedans. More recently many of them prefer to be known as Muslims. I usually refer to the ancient Mohammedans as Moslems and contemporary Mohammedans as Muslims, nonetheless, they all claim they are followers of Muhammad.

To resolve their differences, both sides impose the force of win-lose religion. With utter confidence in their belief, one side insists that for Sunnis to gain, Shi`ahs must be forced to lose. With no less confidence, the other side contends that for Shi`ahs to gain, Sunnis must be forced to lose. As each Muslim sect strives to impose a theocratic monopoly throughout Islam, their win-lose actions, spur an endless cascade of violence, torture, and murder in the name of Allah.

⌒∽

The religious protests of sixteenth-century Europe—known as the Protestant Reformation—aimed to *reform* the Roman Catholic Church by ending its monopolistic authority over all Christian institutions. Since the division that followed between Catholics and dissenting Protestants, Christians have been killing each other with the same passion for religious violence as the Muslims.

For over four centuries, Catholic and Protestant authorities have been fighting over which of them is the rightful standard-bearer of Christianity, founded two thousand years ago by the apostles Peter and Paul. To resolve their dispute, each faction has imposed win-lose religion: *For Protestants to gain, Catholics must be forced to lose.* And, conversely, *For Catholics to gain, Protestants must be forced to lose.* These hostile factions have fought for centuries over which Christians represent God's true church. Their conflict of beliefs has been fueled again and again by the fury of win-lose religion.

One of the most catastrophic wars of European history was the notorious Thirty Years' War. It was fought between Catholics and Protestants over an incredible thirty years of organized butchery, violence, and destruction to decide one outcome: Who will monopolize control of all religious and political institutions in Europe, the anti-Catholic Protestants or the anti-Protestant Catholics? Prof. R. J. Rummel has related the scale of tragedy imposed upon Europe by Christian leaders and prosecutors of the Thirty Years' War.

> Probably a greater number of common folk died when towns and farms in the path of invading or marauding armies were pillaged and families killed. Moreover, many died from famine and disease caused by passing armies. The German Empire alone may have lost more than 7,500,000 people in the Thirty Years' War, most doubtless perishing from such causes. The population of Bohemia was reduced from around 4 million to possibly no more than 800,000. Putting a number of such figures together, I estimate that in this war alone from 2 million to over 11 million people were probably murdered.[3]

The conflict finally ended as a stalemate in 1648, only because the battling armies of religious and political institutions had finally run out of combatants (cannon fodder) and material resources to wage further war. Beyond the organized slaughter of war, millions more were killed by the usual famine and disease brought in the wake of such devastating violence.

After thirty years of battles, both sides were exhausted and bankrupt. Mutual bankruptcy alone has ended many of history's most infamous wars. Unfortunately, financial bankruptcy has not ended the desire to impose religious and political monopoly through coercive means for win-lose gain. In time, with the raising of new armies and the creation of new wealth to fund those armies — usually through legal or illegal seizure of wealth — the wars have continued generation after generation. As long as conventional wisdom fails to identify, clarify, and verify the fundamental and necessary causes of war, war remains a persistent and unrelenting threat to the advance of peace, prosperity, and freedom.

In Northern Ireland, Christian Catholics and Christian Protestants have been killing each other for generations. By the end of the twentieth century, 3700 men, women, and children had been assassinated with tens of thousands more maimed or seriously injured. [4] By the beginning of the twenty-first century, efforts were made by Catholic and Protestant leadership to share political power in Northern Ireland to end the religious violence. After a decade of peace, however, violence broke out again in March 2009 as members of the Irish Republican Army—in their aim to bring Catholic rule to Northern Ireland—gunned down three more hapless victims. In the long run, to reach a durable peace, Catholics and Protestants must abandon their win-lose model of religious conviction: *For us to gain, they must lose.*

༄

Persecution and murder of nonbelievers to advance religious monopoly and domination cannot go on forever. For humans to survive in the nuclear age, they must replace faith in the rightness of win-lose religion with a kind and friendly alternative. But what choices are there?

The vital alternative to the harmful effects of win-lose religion based on gain through the loss of others are the beneficial effects of win-win religion based on gain through the gain of others. There is a salient contrast—a crucial difference—between the multiple benefits of gain through gain as opposed to the multiple deficits of gain through loss. It is the difference between peace over war, prosperity over poverty, and freedom over servitude. There can be no more dramatic distinction than there is between the harmful effects of win-lose religion when compared to the beneficial effects of win-win religion.

The contrast between win-win and win-lose strategies for human gain is so extreme, that all comparative clichés fall short. Nonetheless, if we use our skills to show and confirm the dramatic gulf between the predicted effects of win-win religion in contrast to win-lose religion, inevitably, win-lose religion will lose respect among the faithful. Its coercive strategy of imposing religious monopoly and hegemony throughout the world will fall out of favor and into disuse as its image of respectability and credibility continues to tarnish and decline.

To avoid the prospect of a social catastrophe, win-lose religion must be superseded by common faith in the altruistic kindness and benevolence of win-win religion. There are no laws of nature to bar or prohibit this crucial paradigm shift. Humans can be saved from self-destruction only if religious leaders and their followers will make it their humanitarian aim to turn members of their own faith away from committing criminal violence against humanity in the name of god.

When the institution of win-lose religion threatens the lives of your family, friends, and associates, the cost of silence is high. If there is a time to remain silent on a critical issue that affects your life, this is not one of them. Silence is *not* golden; it is an inordinate risk when it threatens you, your loved ones, and everyone else with irreversible disaster.

∽

We know that six million Jews were methodically murdered across Christian Europe after 1933 by German authorities. In hindsight, few historians would deny that the Holocaust was made possible, in part, by widespread silence among European Christians on the persecution of European Jews. Yet, today, we face the real prospect of a holocaustic revival with the alarming potential to eclipse the human tragedy of those desperate years in Europe. Now, seven decades later, the crisis of human survival has risen far beyond that of World War II. There are over *six billion* people of every religious denomination who are in grave peril of becoming victims of a religious catastrophe that could become the ultimate Holocaust.

With the end of the Cold War, many breathed a sigh of relief; we had dodged the unthinkable bullet, the dreaded "Hot War" of nuclear devastation. Yet, the decline and fall of the Cold War did not lead us out of the woods of nuclear peril. American and Russian authorities still point enough weapons at each other to assure nuclear obliteration for themselves and everyone else, if they ever pull the trigger — which we know can be pulled in error or by accident, if not by design. Of course, it is not any less fatal to be killed by mistake, than to be killed by intent.

Moreover, Americans and Russians are not the only political players deploying weapons of ruination. It is well known that the French, British, Chinese, North Koreans, Israelis, Indians, and Pakistanis possess and deploy nuclear weapons, with the Iranians and others eager to join the "nuclear club." With growing danger since the end of the Second World War, this exclusive club has been losing its exclusivity over time as more nations join the club. You don't need a "war degree" to know that as "membership" goes up, the risk of nuclear disaster goes up.

India and Pakistan, for example, like others in the club, have a long history of mutual hostility. Hindus of India and Muslims of Pakistan have already engaged in three bloody wars. The first of these featured the largest and deadliest tank battles since World War II. As avid warriors, they take their warring seriously, which now include the Indo-Pakistan Wars of 1965, 1971, and 1999. What sacred paradigm spurs these holy wars? The firmness of their faith braces their devout belief in the practice of win-lose religion: *For Muslims to gain, Hindus must be forced to lose.* Of course,

Hindu faith is no-less firm: *For Hindus to gain, Muslims must be forced to lose.*

Thus far, faith in their win-lose religion has only incited *conventional* conflicts, causing the usual carnage of ancient and modern warfare. But if Muslims and Hindus ever decide that it is time to unlock the fury of their *unconventional* arms – their lethal weapons of nuclear destruction – to wage a holy and glorious "Fourth Indo-Pakistan War," the collateral damage could surpass all conflicts of human history. If they incinerate themselves by launching their own cache of fifty to sixty nuclear warheads at each other, those far from the fury may lament, "What a tragedy – too bad for them – but fortunately we are nowhere near the conflict." If you know people with a Pollyanna mentality, who cling to such chancy optimism, wish them luck. Wherever they may be there may be no safe harbor.

In the mid-1980s, international scientists including noted astronomer Carl Sagan predicted a disastrous downside to nuclear war that few had considered. A nuclear war, aside from the intended slaughter and destruction, would also loft enough smoke and particles into the atmosphere to reduce solar radiation to a dangerous level, provoking a far colder, darker, and dryer planet. Such a dramatic climate change toward global cooling would unleash a "nuclear winter," causing worldwide disruption and destruction of agricultural productivity. A global famine – clearly an unintended consequence – would disrupt production of goods and services, followed by widespread destruction from civil unrest, which could incite even more unconventional warfare. This could include launching nuclear arms, as well as biological and chemical arms in response to an attack, or fear of attack. Today, the dread of a "preemptive strike" – with weapons of mass destruction – against real or imagined enemies remains an ongoing threat.

When the nuclear-winter scenario was put forth in the mid-1980s, some authorities questioned the reliability of its scientific models. Since then, however, research has continued to determine whether this fatal hypothesis can be verified or falsified. With the remarkable advance in technology of cheaper, faster, more powerful computers, coupled with vital advances in our understanding of atmospheric phenomena — all since the mid-1980s — new research shows that not only is the original model of nuclear winter viable, but its predictions on the scope and scale of disaster, if anything, were too conservative. Americans Alan Robock, professor of climatology at Rutgers University, and Owen Toon, chair of oceanic and atmospheric sciences, University of Colorado at Boulder, and their colleagues in research have reached this grim conclusion:

> New analyses reveal that a conflict between India and Pakistan, for example, in which 100 nuclear bombs were dropped on cities and industrial areas — only 0.4 percent of the world's more than 25,000 warheads — would produce enough smoke to cripple global agriculture. A regional war could cause widespread loss of life even in countries far away from the conflict.[5]

In short, scientists have concluded that a limited "regional nuclear war...could blot out the sun, starving much of the human race."[6] With deadly implications, it turns out that launching only *one-half of 1 percent* of existing nuclear arms in some "minor" regional war may be enough to induce nuclear winter. This is not good. To be sure, some may argue, "What if the scientific model of nuclear winter is flawed?" Why worry about the possibility of a global catastrophe, when science has not verified such a dismal prediction?

Indeed, what if the models are overly pessimistic and a nuclear winter only starves half the world population. Thankfully, that would leave over three billion people still living with only three billion dead. What if the model by Robock and Toon on the danger of a regional nuclear war would miss the mark and only a billion people die in the aftermath of nuclear winter? That would be the greatest war catastrophe in human history. Yet, even without the pall of nuclear winter, Toon and his colleague Rich Turco of the University of California, "found that more than 20 million people [in India and Pakistan] could die from the blasts, fires and radioactivity" from their regional nuclear war.[7] That is not a small number of deaths. It took the Nazis a dozen years to murder twenty million Europeans (excluding battlefield causalities) using conventional weapons of the time. Today, with only a hundred warheads, the Pakistanis and Indians could kill off that many in a few hours or a few days of well-orchestrated nuclear war. However, it is uncertain whether a regional nuclear war could ever be contained without spreading to other regions. When the German army attacked Poland in 1939, it was only a regional war. Yet, it soon spread to more and more regions to become the Second World War.

In extrapolating from Toon and Robock's model, if only 2 percent of the world's nuclear weapons should be detonated by the spread of localized regional war, that would be four fold (4 times) their prediction of the explosive force needed to impel nuclear winter. What if their model exaggerates the magnitude of risk, and it would take two or three regional wars, averaging one hundred warheads, to provoke nuclear winter? What if it takes detonation of 1 percent or 2 percent of the world's 25,000 warheads to ignite nuclear winter, and not the mere 0.4 percent as predicted? If true, would this mean the crisis has faded? Could we then return to business as usual, which includes continuing to raise the risk of self-destruction through nuclear war?*

Even if we escape the ruins of nuclear warfare, we face another catastrophe through the possibility of chemical warfare. Many in the civilized world believed that the horror of chemical warfare would finally end after its tragic use in World War I. In 1925, the Geneva Protocol was signed by national leaders, who agreed to ban the use of chemical agents as weapons of war. Nonetheless, chemical weapons of increasing sophistication and power of mass destruction have been steadily developed by many nations since 1925. In March of 1988, the Kurds suffered history's largest and deadliest chemical attack against civilians, as unwary men, women, and children were ruthlessly blindsided by Iraqi military forces, killing some five thousand, and seriously injuring more than twice that number.

As destructive as nuclear and chemical weapons may be, an even more frightening weapon waits in the wings. Weapons of biological warfare could trigger a global pandemic—a worldwide plague—that could wipe out humans faster than they could procreate. Unlike nuclear weapons, biological and chemical weapons can be used as an efficient way to destroy entire populations without destroying their physical wealth, which is easy to appropriate when there is no one left to defend it.

In our time, the towering risk of a cataclysmic social failure does not have to be exaggerated. Even if we escape the disaster of political warring, we still face the disaster of religious warring. In either case, the outcome could be a global catastrophe. Through the shameful advance of religious and political folly, we are at risk of overshadowing the annihilation

---

* For details on how professors Toon and Robock developed their models on nuclear winter, see their compelling arguments in *Scientific American*, "Local Nuclear War, Global Suffering." January 2010.

of six million Jews with the annihilation of over six billion people of every faith. Now, nearly 75 years after World War II, millions march—with a spring in their step—to the drum of the leader on the road to ruin.

Something has gone wrong, but what? If we cannot identify and verify the source of social failure, the risk of human annihilation will not go away. Following the leader by default—without analyzing the equity, utility, and morality of the leadership—could be the final human folly.

No leaders of our human parade, regardless of rank or prestige, are above the challenge of this crucial question: *Can the means they employ attain the ends they seek?* This is the pragmatic question for all human action. It is the key challenge for everyone, regardless of education, intelligence, or status, namely, "Can you identify, clarify and verify, which social causes lead to which social effects?"

The most critical and urgent question is which causes lead to the beneficial effects of peace, prosperity, and freedom, and which causes lead to the detrimental effects of war, poverty, and servitude? Without this imperative knowledge of causality, our days as a species are numbered. How do we know where we going, and how do we know how to get there? We can no longer afford the complacency of taking the default path of acquiescence, which is business as usual.

Without ever saying so, many intelligent people think, "Who am I to challenge authority and question whether our social leaders know what they are doing, where they are going, and how to get there?" Thus, a vital message must be dramatized to gain the attention of decent people.

> *To follow the leader by default without verifying the equity, utility, and morality of the leadership through observational analysis is to bury our heads in the sand and to risk human extinction.*

Without acting to identify and verify social causality, there will be no escape from human extermination by human hands. As noted, this is not the Iron Age, it is not the Bronze Age or the Stone Age; it is the *nuclear age*. In earlier ages, we did not have to understand social causality and tame the violence of faith. This was because people procreated faster than they could be slaughtered with the ancient arms of iron, bronze, and stone that now grace our cultural museums. Once cherished weapons of death and mayhem, they are now outmoded.

If there are future historians, the name they may choose for our age remains to be seen. They may dub it the information age, computer age, electronic age, transportation age, nuclear age, or perhaps the "age of crisis" or the crisis age. Clearly, the magnitude of our social crisis has no historical precedent. Social failure through legitimizing, deifying, and codifying organized violence by decree is no longer an option, whether we like it or not. If humans fail to tame the violence of faith, it will doom them to self-extermination and the extinction of their once vaunted species. Again, this is not good.

The hard lesson is that it is not enough to protest the institutionalized violence that may rise from someone else's faith in win-lose religion or win-lose politics. We have to protest the institutionalized violence of all win-lose faith wherever it erupts. Furthermore, we must protest, we must speak out when any act of violence, past or present, is held to be sacred and legitimate, especially by leaders or followers of our own faith. We cannot remain silent. We can no longer afford the towering risk of acquiescence to win-lose leadership, wherever it may rise. Silence remains the common response among decent people, whenever win-lose gain is imposed by their own cherished and esteemed institutions.

We must protest the deadly paradigms of win-lose religion and win-lose politics that threaten to delete civilization and human existence.

෴

Spanish-American philosopher, George Santayana, gave us a clear warning on how to avoid social catastrophe and advance human progress.

> Progress depends on retentiveness...when experience is not retained, as among savages, infancy is perpetual. *Those who cannot remember the past are condemned to repeat it.*[8]

Memory of the past is crucial to human progress—but memory alone is not enough to ward us away from repeating past blunders. Although Santayana's much-quoted advice is true, it gives us only a partial picture of how we can avoid the social disasters that have littered our troubled history.

Europeans and Americans *remembered* World War I, but their memory of its horrible devastation was not enough to keep them out of the even greater disaster of World War II. For Americans, their memory of the global carnage of World War II was not enough to bar them from the Vietnam War. As we have seen, memory alone of the matchless horrors of war is not enough to obsolete human warfare as a strategy for resolving international disputes.

There are many grand monuments to war, and to those who died in the violence of battle. Tributes to fallen heroes grace the capitols of every nation. Unfortunately, they all have this in common: They help us remember the wars of the past without giving us a clue on how to avoid the wars of the future.

Remembering the past must be combined with *understanding* the past to be of any lasting value. Where violence rains from the force of religious or political warfare, that crucial understanding can only be derived from our ability to identify and verify its true causes. We must do better than merely *remembering* the tragedies of human conflict, or we "are condemned to repeat" them again and again. Without a verifiable understanding of social causality that transcends mere arbitrary opinion—whether expert opinion or not—there can be no cure for these social maladies of perpetual warfare that leap from the crucibles of religious and political strife.

Wherever violence is orchestrated for religious or political gain, to tame such violence, *opinions* of its causes must be superseded by *observations* of its causes—observations that can be verified to be true by independent observers. Paradigms of social causality based on popular opinion, expert opinion, or conventional opinion are dangerous and destructive whenever they govern humans toward win-lose gain. It cannot be over-stressed, opinions, opinions, opinions on causality—especially when they claim the merits of win-lose violence for peace, prosperity, and freedom—are nothing more than arbitrary beliefs without observational verification.

No matter how bright and schooled people may be, too often their opinions on social causality have been unreliable at best and catastrophic at worst. Again, for progress to flourish, *opinions* of causality must be replaced by *observations* of causality that can verify their truth. Louis Pasteur did not base his germ theory on popular opinion, conventional opinion, or even his own expert opinion; he based it on his own observations of biological causality. Astronauts did not reach the moon by following opinions of causality on how to get there. They reached the moon by following principles of causality on how to get there. These natural principles have been observed and verified to be true again and again without end.

Natural principles are not hatched from *opinions* — they are discovered from *observations*. Once discovered, these repeating principles of causality can be observed by anyone who cares to look. Where the aim is to understand causality — the foundation of progress — observation of causality trumps opinion of causality.

Whether aiming for the moon or aiming for peace, opinions of causality must be replaced by principles of causality to reach such grand aims. In a similar way, we must find observational principles that can lead us away from reliance on win-lose religion toward reliance on win-win religion.

∽

In our time, a great threat to human survival springs from an insidious paradigm of social causality that proudly proclaims the sanctity of win-lose religion. Because this threat is real, because it is critical and universal, those who see the magnitude of the menace cannot afford to remain silent. Their very survival depends on speaking out against the win-lose violence that is provoked in the name of god by their own theologies, and by their own religious leaders and their faithful followers.

Taming the violence of faith requires a paradigm shift away from faith in win-lose religion toward faith in win-win religion. This shift is crucial because our paradigms — our models of causality and reality — guide our human actions either toward win-win gain or toward win-lose gain. Those who truly believe their religious gain can only come through the loss of others, will actively seek win-lose gain, or openly sanction it, or quietly approve it by remaining silent.

Due to the power of theology to govern human action, a dramatic case is needed to show the humanity of win-win religion over the inhumanity of win-lose religion. The extreme contrast between these contrary doctrines must be revealed, advanced, and promulgated. The viability and survivability of the human species depends entirely upon the paradigm shift among the faithful from win-lose to win-win religion. One of the aims of this treatise on *Taming the Violence of Faith*, is to show how this crucial shift from win-lose to win-win religion can be made with integrity and dignity for the enrichment of all members of all denominations of faith.

ENDNOTES

1. Dennis Overbye, "Stephen Hawking Plans Prelude to the Ride of His Life," *New York Times*, Science, Mar. 1, 2007, http://www.nytimes.com/2007/03/01/science/01hawking.html (Accessed September 9, 2010)

2. Martin Luther King, Jr., *Strength to Love* (New York: Harper & Row, 1963).

3. R. J. Rummel, *Death by Government* (New Brunswick, New Jersey: Transaction Publishers, 1994), 54.

4. For fatal statistics, see *The Orange County Register*, May 5, 2007, 15, 18.

5. Alan Robock and Owen Brian Toon, "Local Nuclear War, Global Suffering," *Scientific American*, Jan. 2010, 74-75.

6. Robock and Toon, "Local Nuclear War," 74.

7. Robock and Toon, "Local Nuclear War," 77.

8. George Santayana, *The Life of Reason*, vol. 1 (New York: Charles Scribner & Sons, 1905), 284.

Chapter One

The Disbeliever

The most dangerous places on earth are where freedom of belief and opinion have been banished by religious and political authorities. The danger is so extreme that honest people who have not harmed anyone can be jailed or killed for merely questioning the authority of their oppressors — or for only being suspected of such doubt. The idea of enforcing a single way of worshiping has killed millions. The idea of enforcing a single way of governing has killed millions more. By imposing religious and political monopolies through violent means, sincere people with ideal aims have created social catastrophes without parallel. In this way, the Communist Revolution, Fascist Revolution, French Revolution, Islamic Revolution, and Christian Revolution, to name a few, became violent social movements impelled by the prospect of endless glory through win-lose gain. Their leadership aimed to crush all competition by silencing all competitors. They demanded unwavering support for their superior rulership of the people. The old adage, "He who is not with me is against me," became the creed and spur of religious and political conversion.

These ruinous revolutions were driven by a false model of social causality, a fatal idea of reality that extolled a deadly paradigm: *For true believers to gain, disbelievers must be forced to lose.* Those who did not admire and conform to the politics of Communism or Fascism, those who did not esteem and convert to the religion of Islam or Christianity ran the risk of being tortured, imprisoned, or killed as that most condemned of all humans: the *disbeliever.*

Readers of world history know that theologians proclaiming the superiority of their vision of god and his holy commandments have dominated religions. To promote their doctrines of total belief in the one true god, they have imposed religious monopolies through violent means. Clergy of nearly every faith have avowed that for their religion to gain, other religions must be forced to lose. With eager devotion to advancing the monotheism of one true god, true believers became brutal killers of millions of disbelieving men, women, and children who had offended no one. These innocent victims were killed because they did *not* believe in the one true god, or because they had abandoned their orthodox beliefs in favor of unorthodox heresies. Yet, many nonbelievers had never even heard of the one true god. In any case, whatever their source of non-belief, they were branded as dissenters, idolaters, hedonists, witches, and as already noted, infidels, heathens, pagans, apostates, and heretics. Merely being accused of disbelief could lead to ritualized murder by fire, sword, bullet, strangulation, suffocation, torture, or starvation.

Religious authority banished freedom of belief. Theologians claimed that they were commanded by god to kill all who did not embrace him as the sole creator of heaven and earth. Centuries of religious monopolies have spurred social tragedies that have only been rivaled by centuries of political monopolies. Any society where innocent people are routinely killed for expressing their beliefs — whatever those beliefs may be — is a society of terror, violence, and murder.

$\backsim$

Before the twentieth century, coercive religions had orchestrated the murder of millions of disbelievers who were killed, mainly with swords, arrows, and bullets. By the mid-twentieth century, nuclear, biological, and chemical weapons of unprecedented destruction and annihilation upstaged these conventional weapons. As we know, they have the destructive power not only to demolish civilization, but also to abolish the human race.

After decades of development, both smaller and more powerful weapons of mass destruction continue to be mass-produced. As their proliferation and pervasion continues to grow, the risk continues to grow that true believers will gain control of these weapons and gladly use them to kill as many nonbelievers as possible. This growing crisis is alarming as we face the possibility of a cataclysmic disaster. However, if we can understand how we reached this crisis of impending doom, we can learn how to attenuate (weaken) its potential for destruction, until it no longer threatens human survival.

To understand the origin of this crisis, we must reflect on the paradigms of causation that were held by our ancient ancestors, who lived in a prehistory world tens of thousands of years ago. Although most people have little interest in anything that happened before they were born, understanding the human actions of our distant forerunners is the key to understanding today's social crises. We cannot understand the present world unless we can understand the social causes that have led to both its glorious and its inglorious past.

$\backsim$

During the course of human evolution, a profound advance of human nature was reached when we gained the intelligence to ask questions — any questions — especially those concerning cause-and-effect. Asking questions on causality is the prelude to finding answers on causality. Our only pathway to human progress is through our greater understanding of the true causes of physical, biological, and social effects.

A lesson yet to be learned by many educated adults is that nothing is more crucial to human success than learning how to identify cause-and-effect. This means that a method is required to discover which physical, biological, and social *causes* lead to which physical, biological, and social *effects*. Questions of causality are the most important questions to be asked by those who aim to build solutions to the litany of problems to be solved in our quest to reach our human aspirations, whatever they may be.

Early humans, after gaining greater intelligence than their distant antecedents, were able to ask, "Where did we come from?" How did the earth and its wondrous creatures come into being? Yet, the difficulty of finding true answers was far more daunting than anyone could have imagined. Still, as they beheld a breathtaking universe with its marvels of physical and biological diversity, many continued asking what or who could have created all this?

Long before the evolvement of science, with its unrivaled power of discovering the causes of natural effects, our ancient ancestors set forth their ideas on the creation of our universe. While imagining its genesis, they formed the foundations of mythology and theology. The most compelling narrations told of a universe raised and molded by all-powerful gods. Thus, religious doctrines evolved describing the creation of a divine universe of physical, biological, and social causation. Understandably, our ancestors imagined supernatural gods creating heaven and earth for human enrichment and enjoyment.

∾

Among the grand structures of ancient Greece and Rome were magnificent temples of worship to the people's many gods. Grecian gods, with their Roman counterparts in parenthesis, included Poseidon (Neptune), who ruled the seas; Athena (Minerva), goddess of wisdom; Venus (Aphrodite), goddess of love and beauty; and Zeus (Jupiter), the chief deity. Although Greeks and Romans had their favorite gods, by tradition, they honored and respected them all. Worshipers did not insist that their god was the one and only true god that must be revered above all others — or else.

It is important to note that the polytheism of the classical world — with its many gods running the universe — was a benign theology that rarely erupted into religious violence. In his classic treatise, *The History of the Decline and Fall of the Roman Empire*, English historian Edward Gibbon stressed this point.

> The various modes of worship which prevailed in the Roman world were all considered by the people to be equally true; by the philosopher, equally false; and by the magistrate, equally useful. And thus toleration produced not only mutual indulgence, but even religious concord.[9]

During the reign of Constantine I, emperor of Rome and a converted Christian, the Edict of Milan was issued in the year A.D. 313, extending toleration to Christians in their religious worship. The edict ended all religious persecution in the empire by Roman authorities who granted all citizens freedom to worship any deity of their choice. Earlier, during the notorious rule (A.D. 284-305) of Emperor Diocletian the persecution of Christians and followers of the Persian prophet

Mani (Manichaeism) had reached extreme levels of legalized ferocity and brutality.

In time, the tolerance of Roman polytheism would eventually give way to the intolerance of Christian monotheism. With the decline of the Roman Empire and the rise of Christian nations, the polytheism of many true gods was transformed into the monotheism of one true god. This became an ominous transformation featuring one and only *one* god as the omnipotent, omniscient, and omnipresent creator of the universe. The paradigm shift from belief in many true gods to belief in one true god would soon incite social tragedies on a monumental scale.

According to Christian and Muslim scripture, every now and then God revealed Himself to certain human envoys, while giving ultimatums on how humans must behave. These divine commands set forth the actions that humans were required to take — or not take — in relation to God and their fellow humans. The Ten Commandments given by Moses to the ancient Israelites are among the most notable of these. However, the priestly authorities of religion, who arose in antiquity from a blossoming division of labor, did not always agree on how to interpret and execute godly mandates for human behavior.

As disputes arose over interpretation and execution of godly commandments, there was no way to summon the author Himself to clarify His intentions. Since the birth of civilization, religious quarrels over how to interpret and carry out divine instructions have led to thousands of years of acrimony, violence, and murder. Theological disputes over the true meaning of divine commands have incited social tragedies that defy description. They have spurred true believers — who know their god is supreme — into murdering millions upon millions of disbelievers and so-called heretics. Heretics were said to hold unorthodox opinions on the meaning of god and his commands that were contrary (heretical) to the orthodox opinions of religious authorities.

American poet and social critic, James Russell Lowell, noted a grave tragedy of social history, "Toward no crimes have men shown themselves so cold-bloodedly cruel as in punishing differences in belief."* How have millions come to be murdered over their beliefs in a universal creator and his commands for human behavior? How have believers of one religion reached such extreme intolerance for believers of other religions that they chose to murder them over their differing beliefs? How can we explain this, especially when we learn that these killers of men, women, and children were largely respected citizens with ideal aims who sincerely believed that they were doing the right thing?

∞

All societies are run by authorities whose actions are governed by their paradigms of reality. In this way, paradigms run the people who run the world. In other words, paradigms of causality govern the authorities who orchestrate social action. These authoritarian models of social causality may be true or false; they may be constructive or destructive. Unfortunately, the most dangerous paradigm in religious history has rendered nearly every believer in its truth to be a potential danger or danger to all humans on earth.

Nearly all religious leaders and their faithful followers have embraced this prized paradigm. It avows that their religion is the only true religion recognized by the only true god. Islam's holy bible, the Qur'ān (Koran), stresses this point,

---

* James Russell Lowell (1819-1891), *Witchcraft*, vol. 2. In the late nineteenth and early twentieth centuries, Lowell was a prominent poet, critic, diplomat, and an influential writer in American literary circles.

"The only true faith in God's sight is Islam... He that denies God's revelations should know that swift is God's reckoning" (Qur'ān, 3:19).

In Islamic nations, followers of Islam are quick to impose harsh penalties, including death sentences, on those who deny "God's revelations" and deny the Islamic god (Allah) as the "only true" god. The Qur'ān (Arabic for *reading*) declares, "Those that deny Our revelation We will burn in fire" (4:55). In other words, if you "deny Our revelation" of the only true god, we will burn you alive. This is win-lose theology imposing a monopoly of religion. Its paradigm of faith demands, *For true believers to gain, disbelievers must be forced to lose.*

During his 2006 address at the University of Regensburg in Germany, Pope Benedict XVI expressed alarm over Muhammad's many Qur'ānic calls for violence against disbelievers. In response to the pope's concern, outraged Muslims rioted, firebombed Christian churches, and attacked Christian missionaries. In Mogadishu, Somalia, Muslim Cleric Sheikh Abubakar Hassan Malin condemned the pope with this inflammatory demand, "Whoever offends our Prophet Muhammad should be killed on the spot by the nearest Muslim."[10] Around the world, however, many saw this lethal reaction as only confirming the relevance of papal fear of Islamist violence in the name of Allah.

In his address, Benedict quoted fourteenth-century Byzantine emperor Manuel II who wrote, "Show me just what Mohammed brought that was new, and there you will find things only evil and inhuman, such as his command to spread by the sword the faith he preached." Vatican Secretary of State, Cardinal Bertone, gave assurance that the pope only aimed to refute "religious motivation for violence no matter where it came from."[11] Yet, in the nuclear age, whether religious violence has its roots in Islamism, Protestantism, Judaism, Hinduism,

Catholicism, or any other religion, it remains a grave threat to human survival.

⚬

Archeological evidence shows that humans began building what we now call civilization some ten to twelve thousand years ago. Along with the rise of civilization came religious and political institutions, led by men who were eager to impose their authority upon the people with a heavy hand. Not everyone, however, believed in the credibility of these authorities and their win-lose oppression. Over thousands of years, authoritarian leaders have raised the question of how should we deal with *disbelievers* in the rightness of our religious and political authority. A crisis arose over what to do about skeptics who openly questioned the truth and validity of conventional wisdom that gave leadership its very authority in the first place. How should religious and political authorities reply to disbelievers in the rectitude of their dominion over the people?

There will always be those who reject or scorn the traditional dogma that is the very foundation of the authority over them. What should be done with dissidents short of silencing them with the usual Draconian methods? Should disbelievers in conventional authority be persecuted, imprisoned, tortured, executed, or all of the above? Such violent tactics have been in common use by past and present religious authorities to put disbelievers in their proper place. However, is there a benevolent alternative, a humane approach that theologians and religious leaders can embrace within the framework of their theology? Such an alternative solution is proposed in this book as the doctrine of Win-Win Theology. However, it is premature to discuss proposed solutions to critical problems until those problems can be defined and clarified. The greater the scope and scale of the problem, the less likely it will ever be solved and understood until the problem is clearly identified and articulated. Thus, a necessary prelude to a discussion of a later chapter on The Rise of Win-Win Theology is the following chapter on The Rise of Win-Lose Theology and its destructive domino effects.

ENDNOTES

9. Edward Gibbon, *The History of the Decline and Fall of the Roman Empire*, 1781, vol. 1 (New York: The Modern Library, Random House, n.d.), 25-26.

10. Jan Fisher, "Pope Respects Islam," *The Orange County Register*, Sept. 17, 2006, 26.

11. Fisher, "Pope Respects," 26.

Chapter Two

The Rise of Win-Lose Theology

Those who embrace the paradigm of religious superiority have an unshakable faith that they are favored by the one true god of the one true religion. They are certain that their religious message is the only true account of universal causality with its ultimate vision of the First Cause. Their intolerance of other religion springs from their absolute certainty that they enjoy the only authentic religion sanctioned by the only authentic god. Proof of their god's authenticity—as they perceive proof—can be found in Holy Scripture. The Judeo-Christian Bible trumpets God's command, "You shall have no other gods before me" (*New International Version [NIV]*, Exodus 20:3; Deuteronomy 5:7).*

The exclusive singularity of one true god is further emphasized in the Biblical book of Hosea 13:4, "I am the Lord your God, who brought you out of Egypt. You shall acknowledge

---

*   Unless otherwise indicated, all subsequent New and Old Testament quotations are from the *New International Version* of the Holy Bible. It remains the most widely read English language translation.

no god but me, no savior but me." God swears that not only is He the only true god, but salvation—deliverance from sin—is only available through sole allegiance to Him. Faithful believers trust in the fidelity of this model of universal causality through the hand of the Almighty. It is superior to all others because it is the only account of the Creator revealed to be true by Holy Scripture.

❧

In the Old Testament book of Numbers, Chapter 31, "The Lord said to Moses, 'Take vengeance on the Midianites'" for seducing the Israelites into worshiping a false idol. Scripture says that the Lord was furious over those Israelites who in fraternizing with the Midianites, had been seduced into worshiping the Midianite god, Baal of Peor. In so doing, they had violated God's first commandment—given to Moses on Mt. Sinai—that the Israelites must worship the Lord as their one and only true god. In a much-quoted passage of the Judeo-Christian Bible, God warns the Israelites:

> I am the Lord your God...You shall have no other god before me. You shall not make for yourself an idol in the form of anything in heaven above or on the earth beneath or in the waters below. You shall not bow down to them or worship them; for I, the Lord your God, am a jealous God, punishing the children for the sin of the fathers to the third and fourth generation of those who hate me, but showing love to a thousand generations of those who love me and keep my commandments (Exodus 20:1-6).

God had strongly rebuked certain Israelite men for being seduced by the guile and charm of Midianite women into worshiping a graven idol, namely, a carved sculpture of the ancient Semitic god, Baal. Because Jehovah, God of the Israelites, was "a jealous God," he was resentful of Baal, and any other rival deity. God flatly refused to tolerate any deified or divine competition whatsoever.

The Hebrew prophet Moses, leader of the Israelites, obeyed God's command to "take vengeance on the Midianites" not only for worshiping a false idol, but also for enchanting Israelites to do the same. Moses, standing before his Israelite people, told them to "Arm some of your men to go to war against the Midianites and to carry out the Lord's vengeance on them. Send into battle a thousand men from each of the [twelve] tribes of Israel."

"Moses sent them into battle"—twelve thousand Israelites on the attack. They "fought against the Midian, as the Lord commanded Moses, and they killed every man." These Midianites must have been easy targets for Israelite swords, because after the battle the Israelites "officers who were over the units of the army—the commanders of thousands and the commanders of hundreds—went to Moses and said to him, 'Your servants have counted the soldiers under our command, and not one is missing.'"

After massacring all the Midianite men, apparently without suffering a single loss among their 12,000 warriors, what followed is explicit in the book of Numbers:

> The Israelites captured the Midianite women and children and took all the Midianite herds, flocks, and goods as plunder. They burned all the towns where the Midianites had settled, as well as all their camps. They took all the plunder and spoils, including the people and animals, and brought the captives, spoils and plunder to Moses and Eleazar the priest and the Israelite assembly.

Nevertheless, in spite of their overwhelming victory, "Moses was angry with the officers of the army...who returned from the battle." Moses demanded answers, "'Have you allowed all the women to live?' he asked them." They had, indeed, because Midianite women and boys were part of the captured plunder. An irate Moses ordered his commanders, "Now kill all the boys," regardless of age. "And kill every woman who has slept with a man, but save for yourselves every girl who has never slept with a man." The plunder of all kinds was then divided among the victors.

After Moses, Eleazar, and other tribal authorities had taken their share of the pillage, such as "gold—all the crafted articles," and more, "the plunder remaining from the spoils that the soldiers took was 675,000 sheep, 72,000 cattle, 61,000 donkeys, and 32,000 women who had never slept with a man." In short, for God to gain, for Moses to gain, for the Israelites to gain, the Midianites must be forced to lose everything. They lost their wealth, their possessions, their lives, and even their virgin daughters who were forced into sexual servitude for the pleasure of their Israelite masters.

In our time, many would call such a merciless massacre an outrageous act of *genocide*—a term coined during World War II to describe the barbarity of the European Holocaust. An unabridged English dictionary records this usage of genocide: "The deliberate and systematic extermination of a national, racial, political, or cultural group."[12] Except for "32,000 women who had never slept with a man," and were spared as sexual prizes because of their coveted virginity, Holy Scripture makes it clear that the "extermination" of the Midianites was "deliberate and systematic."

The Lord God had carried out his threat recorded in Exodus of "punishing the children for the sin of the fathers." All 32,000 virgin daughters of Midianite fathers—mere girls who were innocent of seducing Israelite men into worshiping Baal of Peor — were forced into sexual slavery in Israel.

Moreover, the slain Midianite boys were just as innocent as were their sisters. Because the birthrate of boys to girls is nearly 50/50, we can assume that there were some 32,000 innocent boys who were massacred by the Israelites — God's chosen people. Holy Scripture tells us that God chose the Israelites to commit genocide on His behalf.

Some would argue that when the Israelites obeyed God's command to "take vengeance on the Midianites," they had committed an outrageous act of religious injustice and criminal debauchery. In any case, why take such violent vengeance against the Midianites? What was being *revenged*? Was this revenge against the Midianites for their violent acts of murder, assault, arson, battery, kidnapping, or theft against the Israelites? No, it was not.

According to Holy Scripture, God and Moses were intent upon ending the people's freedom of worship by imposing a monopoly of religion throughout the lands that they had conquered and controlled. They warned of a divine edict, a holy command. Those who bow to any idol or who worship any deity other than the one true god of the Israelites may be killed without mercy — along with their families. Then as now, the matchless horror of genocide is incited by a flawed paradigm of social causality: *For us to gain, they must lose through force or fraud.*

∽

Saint Augustine, one of Christianity's most influential theologians, writing early in the fifth century, emphasized the unique role of Roman Catholicism in opening the only gateway to salvation from sin. Augustine assures his readers, "No man can find salvation save in the Catholic Church.

Outside the Catholic Church he can find everything save salvation."*

The Augustinian message is clear that not only is there one true god, but also there is only one true church blessed by God. To escape eternal damnation in hell and avoid its endless tortures, the only path to salvation is through a firm belief in the doctrines of Christian supremacy as interpreted by Augustine and the Catholic Church. In his influential treatise on *The City of God*, Augustine defines the dichotomy of the human race.

> The [human] race we have distributed into two parts, the one consisting of those who live according to man, the other of those who live according to God. And these we also mystically call the two cities or the two communities of men, of which the one is predestined to reign eternally with God, and the other to suffer eternal punishment with the devil.[13]

Augustine divided the entire human race into two social classes of which only one will "reign eternally with God." This is the superior class of *believers* who have embraced the tenets of the Catholic Church, which will admit them to "the City of God." Everyone else is in the inferior class of *nonbelievers* who are relegated to "the City of Man" because they have rejected, ignored, or are ignorant of the Catholic dogma of salvation. As second-class citizens, Augustine assures his

---

* Saint Augustine (A.D. 354-430), Numidian Bishop of Hippo in North Africa, *Sermo ad Caesariensis Ecclesiae Plebmen.* More commonly quoted is Augustine's black-and-white assertion: *Salus extra ecclesiam non est*, "There is no salvation outside the Church" (*De Bapt.* IV. Xvii). Although writing in the late fourth and early fifth centuries, Augustine's influence continues to this day, and he is still esteemed by many Catholic and Protestant scholars as the founder of theology. In A.D. 1298, nearly a millennium after his death, St. Augustine was honored by the Church, for his revered contributions to Christian theology, with the title of Doctor of the Church.

followers that such inferiors are on track to "suffer eternal punishment with the devil."

Fifteen centuries after Augustine, Pope Pius IX, in his influential *Syllabus of Errors* (1867), strongly condemned what he called an erroneous idea of the modernists (those who would "modernize" Catholic theology). The pope sharply condemned the idea that, "Protestantism is nothing more than another form of the same true Christian religion, in which form it is possible to please God equally as much as in the Catholic Church." In other words, the doctrine that Catholics and Protestants are equal in the sight of God was an unacceptable error and a serious deviation from Church doctrine. The pope proclaimed that the Catholic Church of St. Peter is the only true church among all Christian churches. One church—the Church of Rome—has been sanctified by God to offer eternal salvation to Christians through the magnanimity of Jesus Christ.

The successor to Pius IX was the eminent scholar and statesman, Pope Leo XIII, who, like his predecessor, echoed the Augustinian theme of one true church. Heralding the superiority of Catholicism over Protestantism, as well as its preeminence over all religions, Leo XIII declared, "The Church deems it unlawful to place all the religions on the same footing as the true religion."[14] This official pronouncement from the Vatican Palace on November 1, 1885, delivered with the full weight of papal authority, asserted that the Bishop of Rome (the pope) was the one true leader of the one true church of the one true religion.

Where there can only be one true church of one true religion, it follows that all other churches and religions must be false and thereby inferior. This Augustinian division of the human race establishes a class struggle between believers and nonbelievers. True believers, from the lofty height of their superior stance, tend to dehumanize their inferiors who are disbelievers in the one true god of the one true church. Once dehumanized, disbelievers become both necessary and timely targets of win-lose aggression.

In the fall of 2000, a heading on the front page of the *Los Angeles Times* read, "Vatican Declares Catholicism Sole Path to Salvation."[15] In their, *"Declaration 'Dominus Iesus'"* (Lord Jesus), Vatican authorities declared:

> With the coming of the Saviour Jesus Christ, God has willed that the Church founded by him be the instrument for the salvation of all humanity. This truth of faith...rules out, in a radical way, that mentality...which leads to the belief that "one religion is as good as another."[16]

In short, the Catholic Church of Rome—echoing the theology of St. Augustine—is the sole channel to human salvation from eternal punishment in Hell. This Vatican Declaration was written and signed by Cardinal Joseph Ratzinger. Five years later on April 19, 2005, Cardinal Ratzinger became Pope Benedict XVI.

On July 10, 2007, while vacationing at his summer villa in the Dolomite Mountains of Italy, Joseph Ratzinger, by then writing under his new authority as Pope Benedict, released a Vatican document that reaffirmed his earlier position in *'Dominus Iesus'* that, "Christ 'established here on earth' only one church," namely, the Roman Catholic Church. Pope Benedict's edict reasserted that outside the Catholic Church, there is "no means of salvation."[17] According to Catholic doctrine, without salvation—which means deliverance from human violation of divine law—there is only endless damnation.

❧

How does belief in a singular god lead to religious violence and unspeakable crimes against humanity? A religion of monopolistic superiority cannot be created without derogating all other religions. Superior means above all others in status, virtue, and power. Anything *superior* must be in contrast to something *inferior*. When theologians preach the superiority of their religion, this implies that all other religions are inferior. Inferior religions—especially when they are deemed unrighteous or heretical by theological authorities—pose a corrupting danger; it is said, to righteous believers in the only true god.

According to faithful believers, it follows that inferior people embrace inferior religions. These unrighteous followers of false religions pose a peril to all righteous believers in the only divine religion. To remove this peril from society, many believers are certain that to advance the one true and superior religion, it is necessary to purge society of unrighteous people with their inferior beliefs—especially heretics, apostates, heathens, pagans, infidels, and dissenters. Thus is born the foundation for the matchless horrors of win-lose theology and its institution of win-lose religion, built upon this generalization of social causation:

> PRINCIPLE OF WIN-LOSE RELIGION
> *For true believers to gain, disbelievers must be forced to lose.*

The model of win-lose religion has proven to be one of the deadliest and most destructive paradigms of social causality ever conceived. It demands that all nonbelievers and disbelievers in the one true god must be forced to lose their wealth and freedom at spear point, sword point, or gunpoint. Its promoters claim that for followers of our true religion to gain, followers of your false religion must be forced to lose. In the Qur'ān, disbelievers in Allah's singular superiority are given myriad warnings to repent or be brutalized—if not in this world, then in the next.

> These are the two adversaries [believers and disbe-
> lievers] who dispute with each other about the Rabb
> (Lord or Allah): as for the disbelievers, garments of
> fire will be cut out for them, boiling water will be
> poured over their heads, which will not only melt
> their skins but also the inner parts of their bellies and
> there will be maces of iron to lash them (22:19-21).[18]
> [Translator's brackets; author's parentheses.]

Wherever win-lose religion has prevailed, the penalties for disbelief in the supremacy of a singular god have
been more than harsh. Religious brutality is not without
purpose. An overt and covert aim of all win-lose religions
has been to impose a theocratic monopoly upon society
through sanctified and legitimized force, and through the
silent power of intimidation and terror. The theological
excuse for win-lose religion has echoed a common theme,
"It is God's will." Indeed, if it is God's will, then God is unavoidably a win-lose god: *For God to gain, disbelievers in His
supremacy must be forced to lose.* Disbelievers are solemnly
warned that God and his faithful followers will not tolerate
disbelief.

As discussed, win-lose religion launched the Christian
Crusades of the Middle Ages.* The Crusades were military campaigns aimed to free the Holy Land from Moslem
domination. Over centuries of military invasions, Crusaders were inspired, as noted, by the sanctity of their win-lose
paradigm: *For Christians to gain, Moslems must be forced to
lose.* Through the bloody hands of devout Christians, Moslems lost their families, their possessions, their freedom, and
their lives. Indeed, many Moslems lost everything to the
sacred violence of win-lose Christianity. Similarly, Moslems

---

* Historians have designated the thousand-year era of the fifth to the
fifteenth century, as more or less (depending on the historian), the "Middle
Ages."

embraced their own win-lose paradigm: *For Moslems to gain, Christians must be forced to lose.*

The Crusades also were used as a pretext to hunt down alleged heretics who were said to be no longer true believers of the one true Church of Rome. In giving examples of these ritualized murders of so called heretics at the hands of Roman Catholic Christians, R. J. Rummel told of the "Catholic Church's treatment of heretics, who were hunted and when allegedly found, tortured, burned at the stake, or left to die of privation and disease in dungeons" across Europe:

> During the thirteenth-century Albigensian Crusade in France, historians count 140 heretics burned to death in Minerva, 400 in Lavaur, 60 in Cassè, 183 in Montwimer, 210-15 at Montségur, and 80 in Barleiges. In the Roman arena at Verona, Italy, 200 heretics were burned at the stake.[19]

Jesus would have condoned none of this frightful criminality; nevertheless, many hundreds of thousands of innocent victims, accused of heresy or witchcraft, have been tortured and murdered "in the name of our Lord Jesus." In today's language, Christian leaders "were not on the same page" with Jesus and his novel sermons on "love thy neighbor as thyself." Ignoring the benevolent teaching of Jesus, these prelates of the Catholic Church imposed their win-lose Christianity across Europe, Asia, the Americas, and beyond.

❧

Win-lose religion has expanded around the globe with mortal consequences. For Catholics to gain, Protestants must be forced to lose. For Protestants to gain, Catholics must be forced to lose. For Sunnis to gain, Shi`ahs must be forced to lose. For Shi`ahs to gain, Sunnis must be forced to lose. For

Hindus to gain, Muslims must be forced to lose. For Muslims to gain, Hindus must be forced to lose.

In March 2001, many watched the news in utter disbelief as Taliban Muslims blew up two towering statues of Buddha—priceless relics, carefully carved into the Bamyan cliffs of Afghanistan some fifteen hundred years ago. Whether or not one is a Muslim, why destroy such splendid monuments of religious antiquity? Taliban officials argued that these grand images of Buddha had to be destroyed because they were forbidden idols. Islamic law, they said, bans all idol worship, which is a sinful affront to Allah. On March 6, 2001, *The Times* of London quoted Islamic Mullah Mohammed Omar as proclaiming, "Muslims should be proud of smashing idols. It has given praise to God that we have destroyed them." In brief, *For Allah and his Muslims to gain, Buddha and his Buddhists must be forced to lose.*

Reporting from Pakistan in 2009, a journalist for the PBS series *Frontline,* Sharmeen Obaid-Chinoy, interviewed a Taliban commander in charge of recruiting children to become suicide bombers. She asked him, "How do the Taliban invite or convince small children to join them?" He replied, "The kids want to join us because they like our weapons. They don't use weapons to begin with. They just carry them for us. And off we go. They follow us because they are just small kids." Obaid-Chinoy then asked, "Don't you think it's wrong to use kids to attack?" With self-assurance, the Taliban commander justified and glorified training Islamic children to become assassins and suicide bombers with this reply:

> If you are fighting, then God provides you with this means. Children are tools to achieve God's will. And whatever comes your way you sacrifice it. So it's fine.[20]

But it's not so fine for anyone with even a modicum of moral scruples. To train innocent children to murder by stealth, and then to "sacrifice" them as bomb-delivery weapons to "achieve God's will," is clearly criminal child abuse beyond atonement. Only a coward enlists children to fight his battles. Moreover, only a win-lose god without any sense of equitable justice and common decency would ever sanction such nefarious crimes against humanity. Surely, a merciful and just god would rebuke such sinful and shameful action in his name as a spurious corruption of his sacred and beneficent aims. Is it not a blatant blasphemy to God for pious men to sanctify and herald a religious tenet that proclaims: *For God to gain, His children must be sacrificed — on a mission of murder — for the glory of God?* What could be more blasphemous to God and more iniquitous to righteous men and women of moral courage, whatever religion they may revere? Does this not rival criminal child abuse by Christian prelates of the Holy Inquisition? Is not such a shameless atrocity a sinful affront to Allah?

In 1992, in the city of Ayodhya, India, devout Hindus tore down a sixteenth-century Muslim mosque, reducing it to ruins. This act of wanton destruction led to several thousand deaths during clashes between Hindus and Muslims. In defending their win-lose destruction, Hindus claimed that they had to destroy the mosque because it "had originally been built on the site of a temple marking the birthplace of the Hindu deity Lord Rama."[21] Did Lord Rama encourage and condone such criminal destruction of a holy mosque? If he did, then Lord Rama is a win-lose god: *For Hindus to gain, Muslims must be forced to lose.*

A decade later, in 2002, in the Indian province of Gujarat, Hindu mobs torched a Muslim mosque and other facilities, leading to seventy deaths in the escalating violence between Hindus and Muslims. Only the day before, Muslims had firebombed a train that had departed Ayodhya carrying Hindu activists of men, women, and children. Fifty-eight people were killed in the resulting explosion and fire. *For Muslims to gain, Hindus must be forced to lose.*

In counting the fatalities of religious coercion, we cannot forget the tragedy of 1947 that followed the Partition of old British India into the Muslim nation of Pakistan and the Hindu dominated nation of India. As British authority on the subcontinent of India ended, win-lose religion exploded. Fighting between Hindus and Muslims over who should prevail, who should have what, and who should live where, led to the massacre of more than a million men, women, and children and the forced displacement of fifteen million more who were suddenly rendered homeless and with few, if any, provisions for survival.

Hindus and Muslims had failed to heed the wisdom of India's Mohandas K. Gandhi, the renowned leader for non-violence. Gandhi, an attorney, activist, and creative negotiator for win-win exchange, was admired around the world as "Mahatma," a title reserved for those of high esteem. However, esteem for Mahatma Gandhi was not universal, as he had escaped many attempts on his life. In 1948, there was no escape as Gandhi was shot and killed by a Hindu, spurred to violence by his win-lose religious beliefs.

A quarter century earlier, Gandhi set forth a rule of spiritual morality for all people of all religions to follow.

> Non-violence is the supreme law. By it alone can mankind be saved. He who believes in non-violence believes in a living god.[22]

In India, or anywhere, to practice the principle of non-violence is to reject and avoid the ill will of coercive action for win-lose gain. This paves the way for the good will of non-coercive action for win-win gain. This is the necessary and essential foundation of win-win theology, and its creation of religious freedom for all people of all denominations.

∾

The deadly intolerance of win-lose theology in defense of one true god has provoked religious violence for thousands of years. The notorious persecution of witches and heretics that plagued Europe for so many centuries was promoted by a Christian theology that ignored the humane teachings of Jesus. It converted Christianity into a religion of terror, torture, and murder. If anyone dared show that the entire doctrine of witchcraft was an imaginary concoction without merit, a heavy price would be exacted for such heresy. That price included public execution by fire. England's famed eighteenth-century jurist, Sir William Blackstone, gave this warning:

> To deny the possibility, nay, actual existence, of witch-craft and sorcery is flatly to contradict the revealed word of God, in various passages in both the Old and New Testament: and the thing itself is a truth to which every nation in the world hath in its turn borne testimony..."[23]

Part of that "revealed word" came from the hallowed pages of Exodus, Chapter 22, Verse 18: "Thou shalt not suffer a witch to live." (*NIV*, "Do not allow a sorceress to live.")

In Exodus, God demands capital punishment for all witches and sorceresses. A witch was believed to have the power to commit evil deeds that included spreading plagues; a sorceress could cast evil spells that caused crop failures or other disasters. Besides women, there were men—as well as boys and girls—accused and convicted of witchcraft.

∾

One of the most infamous books of Western Civilization was written by two members of the Christian order of

Dominicans, Heinrich Kramer and James Sprenger, in compliance with the wishes of Pope Innocent VIII. The book was published in 1486 with the Latin title of *Malleus Maleficarum*, which in English means "The Witches' Hammer." This was a textbook for righteous Christians on how to identify, torture, prosecute, and execute those accused and convicted of practicing witchcraft.

Christians believed *a priori* (prior to experience or observation) that so-called witches had had sexual intercourse with various devils, and in particular with Lucifer, also known as Satan. Holy Scripture portrays Satan as a fallen angel and the chief adversary of God. The Greek *satân* means adversary.

Although there were a few intellectuals, scholars, and even some theologians in Christendom who believed that the persecution of witches was fueled by mere superstition, most Christians embraced *The Witches' Hammer* as near-holy writ. The work enjoyed immense popularity, and English translator Rev. Montague Summers noted, "There were fourteen editions between 1487 and 1520, and at least sixteen editions between 1574 and 1669. These were issued from the leading German, French, and Italian presses." Its influence reached across both Catholic and Protestant Europe, "The *Malleus* lay on the bench of every judge, on the desk of every magistrate. It was the ultimate, irrefutable, unarguable authority. It was implicitly accepted not only by Catholic, but also by Protestant legislature."[24]

If anyone doubted the sanctity and authority of their writing in *The Witches' Hammer*, Kramer and Sprenger made it very clear that such doubt was not without risk. They gave this sinister warning to their readers in the first sentence of page one:

> Whether the Belief that there are such Beings as Witches is so Essential a Part of the Catholic Faith that Obstinately to maintain the Opposite Opinion manifestly savours of Heresy.[25]

To deny or even doubt the holy truth of the existence of witches was to commit heresy. Catholic Inquisitors Kramer and Sprenger gave a broad meaning to the capital crime of heresy in pronouncing:

> For any man who gravely errs in an exposition [explanation] of Holy Scripture is rightly considered to be a heretic. And whosoever thinks otherwise concerning these matters which touch the faith that the Holy Roman Church holds, is a heretic. There is the faith. [26]

Indeed, "There is the faith." You must keep the faith in Church doctrine, which holds that to publish or expound any contradiction of "the faith that the Holy Roman Church holds," is the sinful crime of heresy. Such heresy was duly punished by the sacred ritual of death by fire in the public square. Furthermore, those who did not have faith in the sanctity of destroying all Witch Societies, that heresy also was punishable by death. If there was any doubt among Christians, professors of theology Sprenger and Kramer made it frightfully clear that freedom of speech, freedom of the press, and freedom of religion had been banished by the Holy Inquisition and the Catholic Church, through the codified use of religious violence against all dissenters. To be a dissenter was to be a heretic. Thus, the Church had institutionalized the horror of the "thought crime," duly enforced by the "thought police," represented by the prelates, clerics, and minions of the Inquisition.

Because without warning, anyone could be charged with the hated crime of heresy, those who doubted that the satanic power of witchcraft could harm anyone at all were inclined to keep their doubts to themselves. To avoid being dragged into the dreaded dungeons of the Holy Inquisition—where under physical and mental torture even the bravest men and women would confess to any so-called crime—all in Christendom were warned to "keep the faith"—or else. But keep the faith in what? Keep the faith in the rectitude and sanctity of defending and expanding religious tyranny through the "sacred" imposition of violence, terror, torture, cruelty, incarceration, privation, and ritualized murder—all for win-lose religious gain at spear-point, sword-point, or gunpoint.

No one would have been more appalled by such institutionalized criminality than would Jesus. New Testament Scripture records how Jesus had the confidence to speak out against the lethal severity of Hebraic justice handed out by the Pharisees to those who allegedly had violated the laws of Moses. However, the leaders of the Holy Inquisition raised the bar of Draconian justice in their heinous maltreatment of witches and heretics. Christian Inquisitors made the Jewish Pharisees look like Boy Scout leaders eager to discipline their charges for swimming after dark in the camp pool. Harvard historian, George Sarton, capsulized the modus operandi of the witch-hunt as set forth by the guidelines in the *Malleus Maleficarum* by Catholic theologians and Inquisitors of the Holy Office, Sprenger and Kramer.

> When the inquisitors entered a new district they issued a proclamation calling on all people to give intelligence against suspected witches; if any persons withheld such intelligence they were liable to be excommunicated and to suffer temporal penalties. To inform was a sacred duty. The names of the informers were not divulged. Suspected persons, including those who might have been denounced by private enemies were kept in ignorance of the charges against them and of the evidence upon which these charges were based; they were presumed to be guilty and it was up to them to prove that they were not. The judges used every means, mental and physical, to force them to confess and

to name their accomplices. Promises of remission or leniency were made to them in order to encourage their confessions, but it was understood (by the judges) that there was no moral obligation to keep faith with sorcerers or heretics, except perhaps for a short while (just as long as confidence was expedient). Each knavery used against them was justified by the holy purpose. The more torture was practiced the more necessary it became. These statements can easily be confirmed and amplified by reference to the *Malleus* and other books and also more concretely by the records of actual trials, which are fairly numerous.[27]

Those accused of witchcraft were subjected to the cruelest tortures ever devised by human ingenuity. The only escape from endless torture was to confess to crimes of witchcraft—crimes that the accused knew nothing about. *The Witches' Hammer*'s guidelines on effective torture specified that torture must continue—it must not be ended—until the accused confessed to all their crimes. Not surprisingly, from the pain of torture, eventually, everyone confessed. However, before they could confess, they had to find out what crimes they were accused of, because they were never told the charges. Thus, they had to beg for this information in order to learn which crimes they should confess to.

After confessing to alleged crimes, entirely imagined by their accusers, the accused were threatened with more torture until they named their presumed cohorts in crime. In their extreme desperation, these victims of win-lose Christianity would often name everyone they knew. In turn, the newly accused were seized and tortured by the authorities until they named everyone they knew. Because this persecution of witches and heretics was legitimized and sanctified throughout Christian Europe for centuries, it is not difficult to see why there were hundreds of thousands of victims.

Here is a sample of some of the sorry citizens who were burned alive in 1598 for the alleged crime of practicing witchcraft in the West German town of Würzburg. These victims of Christian brutality were ordinary citizens; they could have been found in any town. Their final torture was death by fire.

THE TWENTIETH BURNING, SIX PERSONS:
Goebel's child, the most beautiful girl in Würzburg
A student who knew many languages, an excellent musician
Two boys from the Minster [cathedral], each twelve years old
Stepper's little daughter
The woman who kept the bridge gate

THE TWENTY-EIGHTH BURNING, SIX PERSONS:
The wife of Knertz, the butcher
The infant daughter of Dr. Schultz
A blind girl
Schwartz, canon at Hach
Ehling, a vicar
Bernhard Mark, vicar at the Cathedral[28]

These were common citizens of Würzburg who were carefully consumed by fire in the town square. Their torment became an awesome spectacle for the eyes of the madding crowd. But what did these tortured victims of ceremonial brutality do to deserve such harsh treatment by Christian and judicial authorities? Nothing!

Included in the roster of victims in the Thirteenth Burning at Würzburg was, "A little girl, nine or ten years old." She was duteously inflamed along with, "A younger girl, her little sister." Then in the Fourteenth Burning, they torched, "The mother of the two little girls before-mentioned," along with "Liebler's daughter." There is no record of what her father, Herr Liebler, thought of all this. Yet, whatever he may have thought, what crimes could these girls — mere children — have committed that would justify the brutality of a legal death by fire?

These innocent victims who were falsely accused of capital crimes were tortured, convicted, and executed by intelligent men, devout men, sincere men—all good men—but men who didn't know what they were doing. What error in their thinking could have led respected men to decree the Twentieth Burning that stole the lives of "two boys...twelve years old" along with "Stepper's little daughter?" Did Herr Stepper see his daughter through the smoke and flames crying out in desperation, pleading for his help?

What ominous threat could the little "blind girl" of the Twenty-eighth Burning have posed to the good citizens of Würzburg, who watched in awe as she was lashed to a wooden stake, after which the fagots beneath her naked feet were carefully torched? As fire engulfed her frail body, surely tears fell from her sightless eyes. Was there no compassion for her among the throng of Christians crowding around her brutal execution? Perhaps, a few, in witness to her agony, held a measure of empathy for this innocent child. One thing, however, is certain; whatever their concern, it was not enough to spare her from a cruel death beyond our darkest imagination.

By any standard of social behavior, was this not a heinous crime, an unspeakable act of child abuse? Any social system that legitimizes and ritualizes the torture and murder of innocent children is surely flawed. There are no mitigating circumstances that could ever excuse such cruel and criminal behavior. What went wrong? What was this sacred and honored *flaw*, and how can it be excised like the deadly tumor it still is from our most revered social structures?

These innocent children were all victims of *imagination* of causality without *observation* of causality. Christian and judicial authorities *imagined* that the people they had condemned were possessed with demonic powers to cause windstorms, rainstorms, ice storms, floods, droughts, crop failures, plagues, and a long list of ruinous effects.

The authorities imagined that these innocent people had fraternized with supernatural demons who had mentored them in the evil practice of witchcraft. The fatal demands of win-lose theology were written in Holy Scripture: Do not allow "a witch to live." These poor people, without any possibility of guilt, were accused and killed by true believers in the glory and righteousness of win-lose religion.

The social impact of win-lose religion has been catastrophic. French mathematician Blaise Pascal noted, "Men never do evil so completely and cheerfully as when they do it from religious conviction."[29] Although some humans may act in "evil" ways, their human nature does not drive them to commit crimes against humanity. Rather, they are misguided to do so by adopting win-lose paradigms based on flawed foundations of causality. In plain language, the avid leaders of the witch-hunts didn't know what they were doing. Yet, how can we be certain? If they had understood causality, they never would have burned innocent people at the stake for having committed "crimes" that would have been impossible to commit in the first place.

By and large, the authorities were trying to do the right thing based on their imagination of cause and effect. Like all humans, they were not born with any paradigms of causality—religious or otherwise. However, without observational analysis, their imagination of causality led them to adopt a win-lose paradigm: *For good Christians to gain, evil witches must be forced to lose.* It cannot be over-stressed, the most dangerous people on earth have proven to be those who are zealous to do the right thing, but who don't know what they are doing precisely because they have misidentified causality.

In the ancient town of Trier on the Moselle River in Western Germany, theologian Peter Binsfeld, as Bishop of Trèves, is remembered for his unflagging devotion to the sanctity of win-lose Christianity. In the latter half of the sixteenth century, the good Bishop, in carrying out his Christian duties, "ordered the death of some 6,500 people."[30] Their alleged crimes: practicing witchcraft or committing heresy. Nevertheless, Bishop Binsfeld did show a measure of empathy and compassion for his victims, "As an incentive for confession, he offered to those accused of witchcraft the option of being strangled before being burned if, under torture, they would admit to their alleged crimes."[31] In short, if you confess to your "crimes" (that are impossible to commit), we will prove our charity and kindness by not burning you to death, but by mercifully strangling you to death. Bishop Binsfeld's remarkable achievements in witch hunting, torture, and legitimized brutality might have soared to even greater heights; but in 1598, while only in his fifty-third year, this fearless slayer of witches and heretics was struck down by the Bubonic plague.

It was often more convenient for Christian and judicial authorities to accuse so-called heretics not of heresy, but of practicing witchcraft. After all, alleged heretics might have mounted a successful defense by showing that they were still true believers and had not abandoned their devotion to the truth of church dogma. On the other hand, perceived heretics who were only accused of witchcraft were more vulnerable to false testimony — especially eye-witness accounts — "proving" their criminal ties to Satan himself, or to his obedient minions.

∽

In the summer of 1971, while I was traveling through Europe to gather information on the history of religion, philosophy, and science, I visited the old German city of Würzburg in northern Bavaria to inquire about witch persecutions in the old town, but no one seemed to know anything about them. Surely, there were locals who knew of the town's witch trials. Between 1623 and 1631, Bishop Adolph von Ehrenberg, while wielding his Christian authority in the diocese of Würzburg, "tortured, beheaded, and burned 900 persons, including at least 300 children three to four years of age."[32]

It is reasonable to assume that a pious prelate like Bishop Ehrenberg could only have sanctified the horror of burning children at the stake if his models of causality were seriously flawed. Many of those flaws were revealed by a Jesuit priest of the time, Freidrich Spee von Langenfeld, in his *Cautio Criminalis* (Precautions for Prosecutors), printed anonymously in 1631. Although Father Spee believed that witches and sorcerers were real, he argued that extracting confessions of witchcraft and sorcery under torture were unjust because they were unreliable. Showing remarkable courage, Spee openly confessed that he had been entirely wrong in his own faith, namely, that torturing those accused of satanic arts could extract the truth of their wicked ways.

While Father Spee was yet a young man of only thirty, "he was asked by the Bishop of Würzburg why his hair had turned gray. Spee replied, 'Through grief over the many witches whom I have prepared for death; not one was guilty.'"[33] Such an admission of fatal error—indeed, not even one witch was guilty—required both integrity and courage within a community where devout Christians could be legally executed for even questioning the existence of witches and sorcerers. In his *Cautio*, Spee warned against the folly of applying torture to extract the names of presumed accomplices of those accused of sorcery and witchcraft.

> Many people who incite the Inquisition so vehemently against sorcerers in their towns and villages are not at all aware and do not notice or foresee that once they have begun to clamor for torture, every

person tortured must denounce several more. The trials will continue, so eventually the denunciations will inevitably reach them and their families, since, as I warned above, no end will be found until everyone has been burned.[34]

Father Spee's *Cautio Criminalis,* still in print, became an influential treatise among both Catholics and Protestants in clearing the way toward the eventual end of torture as a practical tool for protecting faithful Christians from the presumed evils of witchcraft and sorcery. His refutations of the efficacy of torture as a useful means of extracting truth from the accused are as sound today as when they were penned in 1631.

When I arrived at Würzburg, witch persecutions were no longer in vogue. Over three centuries had passed since Bishop Ehrenberg was busy burning witches in the town square. Because the fury of these persecutions had raged long ago, most locals had little or no interest in their history, even though witch hunting was once a prime focus in Würzburg. Whether twentieth-century citizens of Würzburg had learned any lessons from the false paradigms of their ancestors that led to the dehumanization and persecution of "witches" is an open question. In the same twentieth century, dehumanization of Jews and their persecution was also set off by erroneous ideas of causation that forged the Nazi paradigm of barbarity: *For Christians to gain, Jews must be forced to lose.*

The win-lose model of causality that sent the witches of Würzburg to fiery pyres in the town square, in time, would send the Jews of Würzburg to fiery ovens in the Nazi death camps. The Nazis, however, were more magnanimous than were their Christian ancestors. No evidence has surfaced to reveal that the Nazis of Würzburg — unlike earlier Christians of Würzburg — burned their Jewish victims alive.

౿

Esteemed Dominicans and Inquisitors of the Holy Inquisition, Sprenger and Kramer, in their celebrated *Malleus Maleficarum*, promulgated the merit of religious tyranny when they declared with unflinching confidence, as noted earlier, "Whosoever thinks otherwise concerning these matters which touch the faith that the Holy Roman Church holds is a heretic. There is the faith." But in the nuclear age, we cannot afford the destructive consequences of apologizing for such faith, when the apology is for win-lose religion of any kind. As already stressed, faith in the sanctity and merit of win-lose theology and religion can foster human extinction. That would be an intellectual and moral blunder from which there could be no recovery or salvation. In spite of this grave risk, not everyone agrees that respected intellectuals of the Church, such as Heinrich Kramer and James Sprenger, should be criticized or faulted for their crucial roles in expanding the coercive power and authority of the Holy Inquisition and the horror of its win-lose theology.

Translator of the *Malleus*, the Reverend Montague Summers, at the end of his "Introduction to the 1948 Edition," expresses his admiration for its authors. Summers' tribute to Sprenger and Kramer was written 462 years after the first edition of *Malleus* in 1486. This gave Summers more than four-and-a-half centuries of historical perspective with which to evaluate their contributions to Christian theology. Rev. Summers concluded:

> The Dominican chroniclers...number Kramer and Sprenger among the glories and heroes of their Order. Certain it is that the *Malleus Maleficarum* is the most solid, the most important work in the whole vast library of witchcraft. One turns to it again and again

with edification and interest: From the point of psychology, from the point of jurisprudence, from the
point of history, it is supreme. It is hardly too much to
say that later writers, great as they are, have done little more than draw from the seemingly inexhaustible
wells of wisdom which the two Dominicans, Heinrich
Kramer and James Sprenger, have given us in the *Malleus Maleficarum*.[35]

Rev. Summer's tribute to the "wisdom" of *The Witches'
Hammer,* and its illustrious "heroes," Kramer and Sprenger,
was written in 1948, three years into the nuclear age. Yet,
defense of tyranny, torture, and terror—especially since the
arrival of those chilling weapons of human obliteration—
is a dangerous cover-up of religious history. Apologies and
excuses for such immoral barbarism are fatal distortions of
historical truth that enshrine criminal behavior. Such justifications for religious tyranny blur and obscure our understanding of social causality. We can only advance beyond
the errors of the past when we can identify and verify what
they were and what caused them in the first place. Without this crucial understanding of past causality—knowing
which causes led to which effects—we are in danger of per-
petuating those errors into the future by institutionalizing
new triumphs of tyranny, torture, and terror in the name of
God, Nation, and Leader.

∽

After centuries of executing thousands (possibly 100,000
to 500,000)[36] of so-called witches by fire, it was finally realized—by too many influential critics to ignore—that these
accused women were innocent. The capital charges against
them of having had sexual intercourse with supernatural
beings (such as Satan or other devils) who had given them

supernatural power to harm their neighbors were entirely false. It was all a mistake provoked by misidentification of causality, coupled with the horrors of win-lose theology.

Some authorities give the number executed for the alleged practice of witchcraft to be as high as nine million. *The Reader's Encyclopedia* gives this account, "Pope Innocent VIII issued the celebrated bull *Summis Desiderantes* in 1484, directing inquisitors and others to put to death all practicers of witchcraft and other diabolical arts, and it has been computed that as many as nine millions of persons suffered death for witchcraft since that date."[37]

Although "witches" were hunted across Europe for centuries, causing a staggering number of victims, historians have not documented a magnitude of victims that would reach nine million men, women, and children as quoted above. However, what if the account, say, of nine million victims somehow was overstated by ten times the magnitude of deaths? What if "only" 900,000 of the accused were tortured until they confessed to crimes that they never could have committed and, thus, were bound to a stake and burned alive. Then the scale of this tragedy would defy description—as would the more conservative figure of 100,000 to 500,000 given above. Even the Nazis only tortured a minority of their victims (Jews, gypsies, homosexuals, anti-Nazis, et al.), and as noted, there is no evidence that the SS burned these poor people alive in those ghastly ovens.

We know that the legal authorities of the German state exterminated many Jews, but how many actually met such a violent fate? Not everyone agrees. Some skeptics argue that the repeated claims, by Jewish authorities, that six million Jews were victims of the Holocaust, is grossly exaggerated. R. J. Rummel's statistical research (see other chapters) on Holocaust victims gives a figure of 5,300,000.[38] However, his total is in the same statistical magnitude as the commonly quoted figure of 6,000,000.

In reply to those who believe that this figure is grossly overstated, what if the death toll of 6,000,000 Jews as given by Holocaust historians somehow was overstated, and "only" 3,000,000 Jews were murdered by German authorities? Even if this lesser magnitude of victims (one-half the reported number) could be verified, it would remain one of the great tragedies of win-lose theology allied with win-lose government. Moreover, the same would be true if "only" 1,500,000 Jews were victimized by the win-lose justice of the German state.

If this much lower number could ever be confirmed, would we then conclude, "Clearly, the Nazis and the SS were given a 'bum rap'?" They were not nearly the heinous criminals that decent people thought they were." What if the total number of European Jews who were actually murdered by German authorities did turn out to be only a quarter of what some doubters have called the "legendary" figure of 6,000,000? Would we then see the SS in a new light that would bring a new luster to its tarnished image? Would we then say that there is at least some exoneration for the National Socialists, who in the name of the Fatherland, in the name of the Lord, and in name of the Führer, only murdered 1,500,000 Jews?

ᏣᎳ

Christian persecution of witches, heretics, and Jews could have been avoided if their tormentors had followed the teachings of Jesus as told by the Apostle John. As Jewish authorities (Pharisees) were about to execute the laws of Moses by stoning to death a woman "caught in the act of adultery," Jesus challenged them, "If any of you is without sin, let him be the first to throw a stone at her." No one answered his probing challenge, and the executioners "began to go away one at a time...until only Jesus was left, with the woman still standing there." Jesus asked, "Woman, where are they? Has no one condemned you?" "No one Sir," she replied. "Then neither do I condemn you," Jesus declared, "Go now and leave your life of sin" (John, 8:3-11).

While Jesus does not condone her adultery, his actions imply that stoning this woman to death is a penalty far too harsh to fit the sin. Jesus assures the woman that her life is spared, but in return, she must "leave her life of sin." In showing the nerve to stand fast against the dominance of coercive religious authority, Jesus transformed what would have been a win-lose exchange under the strict rigidity of Mosaic Law, into a win-win exchange. Jesus proved his courage in presenting an original example of win-win justice that over time advanced the judicial principle of "let the punishment fit the crime." This principle is now a cornerstone of Western justice, whose beneficiaries have been Christians and non-Christians alike.

The theology of Moses, with its unforgiving rigidity, unmistakably sanctioned doctrines of win-lose religious gain. Remember that Moses, aiming to impose a win-lose monopoly of Hebraic religion throughout the Holy Land, ordered his military commanders, who had just slaughtered the entire Midianite army, to then, "kill all the boys. And kill every woman who has slept with a man, but save for yourselves every girl who has never slept with a man" (Numbers 31:17-18).

Even if Moses believed that it was proper and righteous to kill all the Midianite men and women for their alleged role of inspiring some Israelites to worship the Midianite god, Baal of Peor, for Moses to further order the killing of their innocent boys, and the raping of their innocent girls, was to set a menacing precedent for the pervasion of win-lose religion in the name of God. Then or now, to excuse such outrageous crimes against humanity is to condone them, which is to give them respectability as sacred paradigms of social rectitude.

If the lawful perpetration of genocide by Jewish authorities against the Midianites can be excused and condoned, then by a similar justification and validation, the lawful perpetration of genocide by German authorities against the Jews can also be excused and condoned. However, to excuse and condone the legitimatization or deification of crimes against humanity regardless of who the perpetrators may be is to perpetuate such crimes into the future. Even today, many are still certain of the efficacy (if not rectitude) of genocide as an expedient strategy to solve presumed social problems that, for them, have no other solution. Yet, in the nuclear age, systematized genocide, as a lawful or unlawful strategy for religious or political gain, must be abandoned before its win-lose domino effects inflame the extermination and demise of the human race.

ᦉ

In contrast to the benevolent sermons of Jesus, the win-lose Christianity that evolved after his legal execution provoked Christians, themselves, to become legal executioners imposing capital punishment without mercy on witches, heretics, Moslems, and Jews. *For Christians to gain, witches, heretics, Moslems, and Jews must be forced to lose.* But this false paradigm was a gross contradiction of the original teachings of Jesus as recorded by his apostles.

The merciful justice of Jesus was in sharp contrast to the unmerciful justice of Moses and the Pharisees. It was this same win-lose theology of the Pharisees that led to the crucifixion of Jesus. When the governor of Judea, Pontius Pilate, was ready to free Jesus from Roman control because he had broken no Roman laws, the Pharisees objected, "We have a law, and according to that law he [Jesus] must die, because he claimed to be the Son of God" (John 19:7). Jewish leaders were adamant; Jesus must be killed — lawfully — for telling his followers that he and his novel teachings were divine. The Pharisees saw this as a direct threat to their religious superiority and their aim to monopolize religion and its practice throughout Judea. *For the Pharisees to gain, Jesus must be forced to lose.* Jesus would soon become another victim of the deadly intolerance of a win-lose religion that had stolen freedom of speech and religion from the Israelite people.

Whether in old Palestine, or anywhere else, possession of human freedom is an intangible wealth that is priceless. Throughout history, freedom has been stolen from the people to impose religious and political monopolies. Yet, no matter how laudable the theft of human freedom may seem to many, to steal freedom is to inflict servitude and impose tyranny. Wherever you can be killed for expressing what you believe to be true, as did Jesus, clearly freedom of speech has been banished by political and religious despotism.

Jesus decried the severity of certain Hebraic laws upheld by the Pharisees. But the Pharisees viewed the originality of Jesus as a dangerous deviation from their orthodox theology. Jesus was questioning the monopoly of Jewish orthodoxy by calling for a paradigm shift away from win-lose to win-win justice. He boldly challenged every executioner of win-lose justice to stone every sinner they know — if they are without sin.

Jesus rocked the boat of Jewish authority, which in his day had already enjoyed a long history of theological tradition. After all, the ancient and lasting laws of Moses laid down the foundations of Hebraic justice thirteen centuries before Jesus and his unorthodox and, thereby "heretical" Sermon on the Mount. Yet, then as now, heresy is in the eye of the beholder. Jewish leaders judged the very heart of the seminal sermons of Jesus to be heretical. The Pharisees held the teachings of Jesus to be a criminal violation of ancient law. However, Jesus was not rejecting Mosaic Law. Instead, he aimed to minimize its overbearing violence. Jesus, rather than castigating Hebraic law, affirmed the value of the laws that were set forth by Moses in his Ten Commandments (Exodus 20:2-17).

The Decalogue of Moses warned the Israelites not to act for win-lose gain with these now familiar rules of behavior: You shall not murder, commit adultery, steal, give false testimony, or covet another's house, wife, servants, or belongings. These laws are as viable today as they were in the time of Moses. By heeding Mosaic prohibition of win-lose exchange, the door opens for the only other means to gain, which is through win-win exchange.

The Mosaic laws given above can be generalized and precisely defined as a simple principle: *Never seek gain through the loss of another by force or fraud.* This is a practical moral guide to follow. The two-sided (bilateral) gain from creating wealth through win-win exchange far outweighs the one-sided (unilateral) gain from stealing wealth through win-lose exchange.

It is observable; stealing old wealth destroys the incentive to create new wealth. However, where creative incentive is protected, humans can create more new wealth than could ever be stolen. This observation of truth trumps mere *a priori* opinion no matter how wise such opinion may seem to be. And *trump*, a variation of triumph, is the right word. What could be more socially triumphal than the creation of new wealth at a faster rate than old wealth can be stolen or destroyed? This is the foundation of social prosperity.

On the other hand, for those who spurn social prosperity because they see social poverty as the superior alternative, there is a sure path to follow: Steal old wealth at a faster rate than new wealth can be created. On a national scale, the consequences of such a win-lose policy is a steady decline into poverty that will prevail as long as this regressive policy is enforced.

∾

Win-lose religion could go on forever except for one crucial change in the last century. Advances in science made it possible to create weapons of mass destruction with enough power to destroy not just entire armies, but their civilian supporters as well. With the proliferation of these weapons since 1945, it has become an ever-growing challenge to prevent their use against global populations. As production of these weapons continue, the risk increases that religious terrorists will buy, seize, steal, or produce these deadly arms. Once in the hands of terrorists, the probability is high that they will not hesitate to use these weapons against their supposed enemies. Thus, the escalation of religious conflict threatens to engulf humanity in one final catastrophe ending in mass annihilation.

In February of 2009, the notorious black marketeer of nuclear weapons technology, Dr. Abdul Qadeer Khan, nuclear scientist and metallurgist, was released from house arrest at his home in the Islamic Republic of Pakistan where he had been detained since 2004 for hawking nuclear secrets to foreign states through an elaborate network of operatives. Revered in Pakistan as the father of their nuclear weapons program, which enabled the Pakistanis to build their own atomic bombs, Dr. A. Q. Khan confessed in 2004 to selling nuclear technology to the Islamist police states of Iran and Libya, and to the Communist police state of North Korea. Where technology and blueprints for nuclear weapons can be purchased by so-called rogue nations, police states, and various terrorist groups in quest of religious or political gain, the social crisis for all civilization continues to rise.

Dr. Khan was featured on the February 14, 2005 cover of *Time* magazine under the title of "THE MERCHANT OF MENACE: How A. Q. Khan became the world's most dangerous NUCLEAR TRAFFICKER." *Time's* cover labeling of Khan as a world "menace" does not seem to be an over-statement. At age 75, he remains a menace to humankind. In Pakistan, however, Dr. Kahn is revered as an icon in the advancement of Islamist hegemony and Pakistani political power. Khan, a Muslim, was the first to introduce nuclear weapons to an Islamic state.

In our century, coercive theology endangers survival of the entire human species. Even without religious war, religious terror can be transported anywhere in the world. A few devout fanatics armed with weapons of mass destruction can decimate populations around the globe. Islamist jihadists (holy warriors) have proven their resolve to die for their vision of religious superiority. They will use the very weapons developed by Western technology to destroy Western infidels. In any case, all paradigms of religious superiority breed the potential for disaster when they are tied to the win-lose paradigm: *For us to gain, they must lose through force or fraud.*

༻

Many Christians say they are unconcerned with the ever-growing social threat that could destroy our cities and anni-hilate our species. They argue that such cataclysmic events are inescapable because in the book of Revelation, they were prophesied by the apostle John. Writing on his revelation, John foretells of Armageddon—the last battle between the forces of good and evil. This battle will come before Judgment Day when God will assess the character of everyone living or dead. At this critical time, God will render His decision on who was good and who was evil.

Christians who believe John's revelation to be literally true are resigned to bear his prophecy of fatal warfare. In so doing, they are neutralized as defenders of the human race from self-annihilation. They are certain that nothing can prevent world cataclysm. "It's God's plan," they argue. In this way, faithful Christians become party to a self-fulfilling prophecy of ruination and doom.

On the other hand, there are Christians who interpret John's vision as a metaphorical revelation and a figurative prophecy. Thus, they believe they can influence world events to avoid social catastrophe. They only have to accept the challenge of applying win-win principles as the altruistic path toward creating a better world for all to enjoy.

∽

For millennia, key elements of religious teaching have condemned win-lose behavior. The seventh-century Qur'ān warns, "There shall be no coercion in matters of faith (2:256)."* Whether this warning against coercing anyone over "matters of faith" is a deterrent to Islamist terrorism — or to the imposition of Islamic states through violent means — is an open question. No matter, win-lose terrorists and theocrats will find God's support for their murderous violence in the same Qur'ān.

> When you meet the unbelievers *in the battlefield* smite their necks, until you [have] thoroughly subdued them, then *take prisoners of war and* bind them

---

* The familiar English translation by Abdullah Yusuf Ali reads, "Let there be no compulsion in religion (2:256)." In note 300, translator Ali comments on the meaning of verse 256: "Compulsion is incompatible with religion: because (1) religion depends on faith and will, and these would be meaningless if induced by force; (2) Truth and Error have been so clearly shown up by the mercy of Allah that there should be no doubt in the minds of any persons of good will as to the fundamentals of faith; (3) Allah's protection is continuous, and His Plan is always to lead us from the depths of darkness into the clearest light." See *The Meaning of the Holy Qur'ān* (Beltsville, Maryland: Amana Publications, 2006), 106.

firmly. Thereafter you *have the choice* whether you show them favor (*release them without ransom*) or accept ransom, until the war lays down its burdens. Thus *are you commanded* (47:4, translator's annotations in italics).[39]

Another English translation of this Qur'ānic verse reads, "When ye encounter the disbelievers, strike off their heads, until ye have made a great slaughter among them. Verily, if God pleased, He could take vengeance on them without your assistance, but He commandeth you to fight His battles" (47:4). Such inflammatory commands and divine dictates dominate much of the Qur'ān. This command is given by God — a win-lose god — to all true believers in his infinite power and wisdom to take "vengeance" against all "disbelievers" and to "strike off their heads." Although some may call such murderous actions crimes against the innocent, Islamist terrorists, by their own proud admissions, truly believe that their holy wars (jihads) are divinely inspired deeds — not crimes at all — that deserve earnest applause among true believers in the rectitude and superiority of Qur'ānic morality.

Like every terrorist, we also choose to be governed by our paradigms of causality because we believe them to be true. In simple language, our paradigms of social causality are our personal models of what we believe cause good things to happen, and what we believe cause bad things to happen. Because our human actions are governed by — steered by — our paradigms of social causality, the crucial question for all humans remains the same. Are their guiding paradigms — the very models of causality that govern their human actions — true or false, valid or invalid, moral or immoral; and are they win-win or win-lose models of causality?

In the nuclear age, we can no longer risk submission to popular opinion or conventional wisdom on social causality without the prudence of observational analysis. We must not overlook or underestimate the power of our own mind to understand the true causes of social effects. To do so is to assume the dangerous risk that goes with accepting long-held models of social causality by default. By avoiding the mental effort necessary to separate social truth from social fiction, we assume the extreme risk of inciting unintended consequences of the most destructive kind.

It is worth noting that those who have made a career out of "risk analysis" have overlooked the greatest risk that anyone can take. They have failed to include in a list of what should be named the "Top Ten Risks You Can Take," the supreme human risk. This extreme risk should crown their list without a close second. It is the blind risk, taken by respected people with good minds and educations, when without the guidance and wisdom of observational analysis they both sanction and participate in win-lose actions for win-lose gain. Moreover, they do so without ever determining in advance whether the means employed—coercion—can ever attain the worthy ends they claim to be seeking.

The question of questions for all risk analysis of human action is, "Can the human *means* employed attain the human *ends* sought?" Where the means employed can only attain the opposite of the ends sought that is high risk, to say the least. There is no greater risk that honest people can take than to assume the towering risk of creating human tragedies of monumental scale, which are derived from accepting by default, false paradigms of social causality. To do so without examining their assumed truth as models of causality for governing human action is to act on blind faith with its inherent risk of unintended consequences. A central question raised by this treatise is, "Does the violent seizure of wealth and freedom for religious gain—even if it is commanded by a win-lose deity—advance the wealth and freedom of believers, or does it advance their poverty and servitude?"

In retrospect, after more than ten thousand years of civilization, the risk of imposing win-lose coercion for seemingly worthy ends would near the top of any list of the most dangerous risks you can take. To re-emphasize, this fatal risk rises from those who provoke coercive actions for win-lose gain precisely because they have misidentified and misunderstood which social causes lead to which social effects. Most crucial to our well-being, and to those of our friends and loved ones, is the answer to this prime question, "Are our human actions the cause of peace, prosperity, and freedom; or are they the cause of war, poverty, and servitude?" Those who cannot make this critical distinction may be both intelligent and educated, but in spite of these apparent advantages, they are at grave risk of not knowing what they are doing. Therefore, such people have all too often acted toward their vision of peace, prosperity, and freedom by taking actions that have provoked war, poverty, and servitude. Because this failing is so pervasive, it cannot be over-stressed,

> *To know what you are doing is to have the wisdom to know which causes lead to which effects, and to have the courage to act accordingly.*

෨

Win-lose theology is based on the violent demands of a win-lose god—a supernatural deity who requires believers to murder unbelievers on his behalf. *For true believers to gain, disbelievers must be forced to lose.* When masked Muslims are seen on the Internet severing the heads of infidels, they rejoice in obeying Allah's command to "smite their necks" or "strike off their heads" with holy swords. For Allah to gain unbelievers in his supreme power and divine purpose must be punished; they must lose their freedom, lose their loved ones, and lose their lives.

Islamist terrorist, Khalid Sheikh Mohammed, with great pride, told American authorities exactly how in 2002 he had taken the life of a noted *Wall Street Journal* reporter, "I decapitated with my blessed right hand the head of the American Jew, Daniel Pearl, in the city of Karachi, Pakistan. For those who would like to confirm, there are pictures of me on the Internet holding his head."[40] Moreover, if a true believer like Khalid should be felled on his mission of violence for Allah, the Qur'ān assures him that not all is lost:

> As for those who are slain in the cause for Allah, He will never let their deeds be lost. Soon, He will guide them, improve their condition and admit them to the paradise which He has made known to them (47:4-6).

A win-lose god rewards his followers for their criminal violence on his behalf. When serving the "one true god," if you commit a crime against humanity, it is not a crime at all, but a holy virtue to be rewarded with everlasting life in paradise.

❧

In his 1997 film, *Deconstructing Harry*, writer Woody Allen gave his protagonist, Harry, this sardonic line, "Wouldn't it be a better world if not every group thought they had a direct line to God?" It is the believers who enjoy not only "a direct line to God" but also a monopolistic line, who spur the tragedies of win-lose theology.

This deadly doctrine of imposing religious monopoly to reach spiritual aims must fall out of favor and into disuse as a pillar of religious faith. Without a paradigm shift from win-lose to win-win religion, humans are an endangered species. We face this grave peril precisely because sincere, steadfast, self-righteous believers act on *a priori* imagination of causality without ever testing their vision of truth through the power of observation. Without observing human action, believers imagine that it is practical, equitable, and laudable to seize their neighbor's wealth and freedom as the true means of reaching their religious or political ends. However, they cannot reach worthy ends by way of atrocious means.

History shouts across the ages, no people are more dangerous than respected people who are pursuing worthy ends, but who don't know what they are doing. In acting with conviction on false ideas of causality as if they were true, they unwittingly spawn disaster after disaster. Wherever the calamities of war, poverty, and servitude prevail, they have a common source. Intelligent people are following religious and political leaders who champion or impose win-lose social policies founded on flawed models of causality. Their paradigms of which social causes lead to which social effects are derived from unverified imagination of causality, rather than on verified observation of causality. In contrast, where people have a verified understanding of social causality derived from observational analysis, their natural tendency is to choose win-win policies for mutual gain. The sum of their exchanges for win-win gain creates our most precious trilogy of assets, namely, peace, prosperity, and freedom. As will be shown in later chapters, with the advance of social progress through observational strategies that identify and verify social causality, this vital treasure of lasting peace, common prosperity, and individual freedom is within human reach on a global scale.

ᵒᵛᵓ

To create flying machines, medical cures, and skyscrapers, their creators must understand causality. In the same way, to create peace, prosperity, and freedom — that includes religious freedom — their creators must also understand causality. The prime lesson on how to identify and verify causality has been a hard lesson for people of intelligence and education to accept and embrace. This is because it is a paradigm-shattering lesson that overturns the foundations of conventional wisdom on which causes lead to which effects. It shows that imagination of causality is neither powerful enough nor reliable enough to reveal nature's principles of physical, biological, and social causality. We cannot imagine our way to the pervasion of world peace any more than we could have imagined our way to the pervasion of digital computers.

History's most ruinous model of reality stems from human imagination of the truth of the win-lose paradigm of social causality: *For us to gain, they must lose through force or fraud.* Where decent people believe this paradigm is true, they will act accordingly. Yet, they are acting on a warped picture of reality that has been passed down from parent to child, from teacher to student, from pastor to parishioner, from professional to layman — without observational analysis to verify or falsify its truth. This question must be raised again and again, "Is the win-lose paradigm true or false, valid or invalid, moral or immoral; and is it constructive or destructive?" Independent observation answers the question by verifying that the win-lose model of causality, in all of its diverse manifestations, is false, invalid, immoral, and destructive.

To reiterate, this ongoing question must be raised without end: *Which social causes lead to which social effects?* To answer this pressing question, we can imagine causality, or we can observe causality. There is no reason to fear observation of causality, but there is every reason to fear imagination of causality.

Humans, believing they were doing the right thing by relying on the truth of their imagination of causality, have imagined their way to creating every social tragedy in human history. Wherever sincere people act on their imagination that the win-lose paradigm is a reliable paradigm of social causality, the consequences of their coercive actions include the advance of war, poverty, and servitude that few will enjoy and most will deplore.

Fortunately, these historic afflictions are not inevitable. We do not have to change human nature to end these ancient barriers to human progress. We have only to change human paradigms away from reliance on imagination of causality toward reliance on observation of causality.

ENDNOTES

12. *The Random House Dictionary of the English Language,* 2nd ed., (New York: Random House, 1987), 797.

13. *The Works of Aurelius Augustine,* trans. Rev Marcus Dods (Edinburgh: T. & T. Clark, 1881), p. 49. For context, see Saint Augustine, *The City of God (De civitate Dei),* vol. 2, book 15, ch. 1.

14. Leo XIII, *Immortale Dei,* "Encyclical of Pope Leo XIII on the Christian Constitution of State," given from the Vatican on November 1, 1885.

15. Richard Boudreaus and Larry Stammer, "Vatican Declares Catholicism Sole Path to Salvation," *Los Angeles Times,* Sept. 6, 2000, 8.

16. Cardinal Joseph Ratzinger (Prefect of Congregation for the Doctrine of the Faith), "Declaration 'Dominus Iesus' on the Unicity and Salvific Universality of Jesus Christ and the Church," (Vatican, 2000), par. 22.

17. Nicole Winfield, "Pope Restates the Primacy of His Church," *Orange County Register*, July 11, 2007, 1.

18. Muhammad Farooq-i-Azam Malik (trans.), *Al-Qur'ān, the Guidance for Mankind* (Houston, Texas: The Institute of Islamic Knowledge, 1997) 382.

19. R. J. Rummel, *Death by Government* (New Brunswick, New Jersey: Transaction Publishers, 1994), 61.

20. Sharmeen Obaid-Chinoy, "A New Brand of the Talaban in Pakistan: Children of the Talaban." Frontline/World Stories from a Small Planet, Part 4 of 4, aired 9:00 to 10:00 p.m. ET, April 14, 2009 on PBS.

21. Tony Karon, "Hindu-Muslim Violence Imperils India," *Time*, Feb. 28, 2002.

22. Sarvepalli Radhakrishnan, *Mahatma Gandhi: Essays & Reflections*, (Mumbai, India: Jaico Publishing House, 2007), p. 91. See Gandhi's, "Defense against Charge of Sedition," Mar. 23, 1922.

23. William Blackstone, *Commentaries on the Laws of England*, book 4, 1765. (San Francisco: Bancroft–Whitney Co., 1916), 2230.

24. Heinrich Kramer and James Sprenger, *Malleus Maleficarum*, trans. Rev. Montague Summers (New York: Dover Publications, 1971), vii-viii.

25. Kramer and Sprenger, *Malleus*, 1.

26. Kramer and Sprenger, *Malleus*, 4.

27. George Sarton, *Six Wings: Men of Science in the Renaissance* (Bloomington, Indiana: Indiana University Press, 1957), 213.

28. Kurt Seligmann, *The History of Magic* (New York: Pantheon Books, 1948), 266-267.

29. Blaise Pascal, *Pascal's Pensées* (New York: E. P. Dutton & Co., Inc., 1958) p. 265.

30. Sarton, *Six Wings*, 213.

31. Herbert C. Corben, *The Struggle to Understand: A History of Human Wonder & Discovery* (Buffalo, New York: Prometheus Books, 1991), 217.

32. Rosemary Ellen Guiley, *The Encyclopedia of Witches and Witchcraft* (New York: Facts on File, Inc., 1989).

33. Seligmann, *The History of Magic*, 286.

34. Friedrich Spee von Langenfeld, *Cautio Criminalis* or *A Book on Witch Trials*, trans. Marcus Hellyer (Charlottesville, VA: University of Virginia Press, 2003), question 15.

35. Kramer and Sprenger, *Malleus*, ix.

36. Rummel, *Death by Government*, 62.

37. William Rose Benet, *The Reader's Encyclopedia: An Encyclopedia of World Literature and the Arts* (New York: Thomas Y. Crowell Co., 1948), 1219.

38. Rummel, *Death by Government*, 112.

39. Malik, *Al-Qur'ān*, 559.

40. Katherine Shrader, "Ambitious Planner Confesses," *Orange County Register*, Mar. 16, 2007, 6.

Chapter Three

The Rise of Win-Win Theology and Philosophy

From east to west, the ancient theologians defined a principle of human behavior for all to follow that is central to their religious doctrines. Remarkably, it turns out to be the same principle for all major religions.

Along with domestication of plants and animals in the ancient world came the erection of permanent shelters for humans and their domesticated animals. This facilitated the advance of agriculture and the revolution in food production that continues to this day. But the necessary division of labor crowded families into villages and towns, and eventually into cities. With more and more people crowded together, theologians realized the religious propriety of defining some basic rules for human interaction.

Where humans have free rein to take any actions they want, then those actions can include win-lose actions that cause disharmony, acrimony, and violence to erupt. Wherever there are human societies, social harmony requires rules of social behavior that condemn and decry coercive action for win-lose gain. Thus, ancient theologians devised a solution on how to foster harmony among crowded populations. Nearly everyone has heard of this solution, known in recent times as the Golden Rule.[41]

Historians of religion have long noted that this rule of conduct is common to all religions. A tenet of faith for thousands of years, it was innovated by theologians as a central code of religious behavior. The Persian religious teacher, Zoroaster of Babylonia (now Iraq and Iran), defined one of the earliest examples of the Golden Rule. Zoroaster also envisioned the ongoing battle between good and evil. This was some six centuries before the birth of Jesus and the founding of Christianity by his apostle Peter, and Paul of Tarsus. Here are some of the more renowned examples of the Golden Rule that evolved over thousands of years of theology:

> ZOROASTRIAN GOLDEN RULE (C. 600 B.C.)
> Whatever is disagreeable to yourself do not
> do unto others.
>> *Shayast-na-Shayast*, 13.29,
>> Zoroaster (c. 628 B.C.–c. 551 B.C.)

Zoroaster also gave us this variation of the Golden Rule that may date to the seventh century B.C.: "That nature alone is good which refrains from doing unto another whatsoever is not good for itself."[42] Out of ancient Egypt—more than a thousand years before Zoroaster—a written record on papyrus of an Egyptian Golden Rule has survived in a narrative known as *The Tale of the Eloquent Peasant*. This ancient tale has been dated by scholars as written between 1970-1640 B.C. Its anonymous author defines this principle of moral behavior,

"Do for one who may do for you, that you may cause him thus to do."[43]

Scholars of ancient history are yet to agree on many of the dates of these earliest writings on the Golden Rule. We may never know for certain, and some of these given dates may be off by centuries. Nonetheless, their chronological uncertainty does not diminish their social significance.

HINDU GOLDEN RULE (c. 500 B.C.)
This is the sum of duty: Do naught unto others which would cause you pain if done to you.
   Mahabarata, 5, 1517
   Krishna Vyasa (c. 500 B.C.)

BUDDHIST GOLDEN RULE (c. 500 B.C.)
Hurt not others in ways that you yourself would find hurtful.
   Udana-Varga 5, 18
   Gautama Buddah (563–483 B.C.)

CONFUCIAN GOLDEN RULE (c. 500 B.C.)
Is there one maxim which ought to be acted upon throughout one's whole life? Surely it is the maxim of loving-kindness: Do not unto others what you would not have them do unto you.
   Analects of Confucius 15, 23
   K'ung-tzu [L., Confucius] (551–479 B.C.)[44]

A similar Golden Rule of Confucius found in *The Doctrine of the Mean* (13:3) has been attributed to the grandson of Confucius, Mencius, by his disciples. Mencius tells us that, "Tse-kung asked, 'Is there one word that can serve as a principle of conduct for life?' Confucius replied, 'It is the word *shu* — reciprocity. Do not impose on others what you yourself do not desire.'" As will be seen, this Confucian principle of mutual "reciprocity" for win-win gain is one of the price-less discoveries of social history.

TAOIST GOLDEN RULE (C. 500 B.C.)
Regard your neighbor's gain as your own gain,
and your neighbor's loss as your own loss.
> *T'ai-Shang Kan-Ying P'ien* ("The Treatise of the Exalted One on Response and Retribution") Lao-tzu, Taoist founder

JUDAIC GOLDEN RULE (C. 30 B.C.)
What is hateful to you do not to your fellow men.
That is the entire law; all the rest is commentary.
> *Talmud*, Shabbat 31a, Hillel Ha-Babli

Hillel Ha-Babli (c. 60 B.C.–A.D. 9), was a Palestinian rabbi who became a respected and influential interpreter of Hebraic law. According to Hillel, this rule of social conduct is the centerpiece of Jewish religion, and as he said quite simply, "All the rest is commentary." The "commentary" is on how to apply this elegant principle of social behavior to all arenas of human endeavor.

The third book of the Old Testament, Leviticus, is traditionally ascribed to Moses. It was set down more than fifteen centuries before Hillel. Biblical scholars estimate it was written between c. 1146 to 1406 B.C., during the forty years that Moses and the Israelites wandered the desert. Leviticus, 19:18, records that the Lord gave Moses a crucial tenet for the Israelites to follow, namely "Love your neighbor as yourself." Jesus repeats this commandment given by God to Moses in three of the New Testament Gospels as recorded in Matthew 22:39, Mark 12:31, and Luke 10:27. Jesus reaffirms the crucial importance of God's commandment from the lips of Moses, "Love your neighbor as yourself." Clearly, both Moses and Jesus set forth a win-win theme of sacred behavior.

> CHRISTIAN GOLDEN RULE (A.D. C. 100)
> So in everything, do to others what you would have them do to you, for this sums up the law and the prophets.
> Matthew 7:12
> Jesus of Nazareth (c. 6 B.C.–A.D. c. 30)

This translation of the Christian Golden Rule is by twentieth century editors of the *New International Version* of the Protestant bible. The beginning phrase, "So in everything," that you do with respect to others does not allow for exceptions. This makes it a principle or law of social action to follow without violation. This singular principle "sums up the law" of the ancient Prophets. Jesus was saying there are not a dozen laws to follow, just one. This is it.

In similar language, the seventeenth-century version of the Holy Bible, authorized by English King James I, and published in 1611, reads, "All things whatsoever ye would that men should do to you, do ye even so to them: for this is the Law and the Prophets." The "law" refers to Judaic law, and "prophets" to Judaic prophets as described in the first five books of the Old Testament. A half century later, the Church of England's celebrated *Book of Common Prayer*, published in 1662, set forth the prime duty of every English Christian: "My duty towards my neighbor is to love him as myself, and to do to all men as I would they should do unto me." This is a clear expression of the win-win theme with its focus on the beneficence of mutual gain.

> ISLAMIC GOLDEN RULE (C. A.D. 1300)
> No one of you is a believer until he desires for his brother that which he desires for himself.

Al-Nawawi's Forty Hadiths, No. 13
Imam Yaha ibn Sharif al-Nawawi (A.D. 1234–1278)
Prophet and teacher, Muhammad (A.D. 570–632)

The Islamic Golden Rule is clearly defined as a religious principle of win-win exchange. It allows for no exceptions in proclaiming, "No one of you is a believer (in Allah and his religion) until he desires" gain through his brother's gain. On the other hand, to seek win-lose gain through a brother's loss by force or fraud would violate the Islamic Golden Rule, and render the violator a *false believer* or disbeliever. Thus, to become a *true believer*, each Muslim must "desire for his brother, that which he desires for himself" and act accordingly toward win-win gain.

❧

The ancient Golden Rules, as an overarching code of ethics for all humans, share a common theme. They directly discourage win-lose behavior while indirectly encouraging win-win behavior. Due to its priceless social value, this rule of rules for human behavior is truly "golden." The greater the number of people who follow this principle of human action, the greater will be the number of good things that will happen to good people. Those who stand fast by neither seeking nor taking win-lose action against their neighbors may or may not "love" them, but they cannot harm them by *not* acting against them.

You do not have to love people as a precondition for not harming them and, in any case, you cannot harm them without violating the Golden Rule by seizing their wealth and freedom. Of the nearly seven billion humans on the planet, you may love only a few of them, but you do not have to harm any of them.

To go beyond a general *acceptance* of the Golden Rule, toward the general *practice* of the Golden Rule, an ironclad case must be made for its universal equity, utility, and morality. To begin an effective and lasting trend away from the miseries of war, poverty, and servitude toward the blessings of peace, prosperity, and freedom, the overwhelming benefits of following the Golden Rule without compromise must be shown, especially to respected people with good minds and educations. These people wield the greatest social influence in every modern society.

The Golden Rule is an effective code of moral behavior that works because humans naturally want others to seek gain through their gain, and not through their loss. The Golden Rule is a principle of human action that generalizes a simple demand: *Do not harm others, as you would have them not harm you.* Where win-lose action is avoided by following this rule of behavior, the door opens for the only other possibility: win-win action for mutual gain. This is the necessary foundation and moral underpinning of win-win theology.

∽

Theologians were not the only intellectuals to fashion viable standards of moral behavior for everyday use. Over thousands of years, philosophers have forged the Golden Rule as a central guide to human action. In China, Meng-tzu (Mencius), the grandson of Confucius, taught a system of ethics in the fourth century B.C., which stressed the value of magnanimous behavior. He urged his students and followers to show their generosity and forgiveness to others throughout their daily lives. Mencius gave them this challenge: "Try your best to treat others as you would wish to be treated yourself, and you will find that this is the shortest way to benevolence."[45]

"Benevolence" (L., *benevolentia* meaning kindness) is the true desire to do kind things for others, which usually spawns the natural reciprocity of others doing kind things in return. This is the heart of win-win exchange. Philosophers have named this exchange, "ethical reciprocity." In brief, there is an exchange of something where, "I win, you win; we win, they win"—and there are no losers. Thus, the reciprocity of mutual kindness is mutually rewarding. It is rewarding in many profound, striking, and even subtle ways, which are not always obvious, and which will be revealed in the chapters ahead.

In his celebrated *Lives of the Philosophers* (c. 150 B.C.), Greek historian Diogenes Laertius writes, "The question was once put to Aristotle how we ought to behave to our friends; and his answer was, 'As we should wish them to behave to us.'" No philosopher has had a greater influence on molding occidental culture than Aristotle (384–322 B.C.), who is widely hailed as a prime founder of Western Civilization.

Aristotle's illustrious teacher and a student of Socrates, Plato (c. 428–348 B.C.), who became another founder of Western culture, gave his students this principle of ethical behavior to follow:*

> Dealings between man and man require to be suitably regulated. The principle of them is very simple: Thou shalt not, if thou canst help, touch that which is mine, or remove the least thing which belongs to me without my consent; and may I be of a sound

---

* In ancient Greece, nearly a thousand years before the fall of Rome, Plato's teacher Socrates (c. 470–399 B.C.), himself a key contributor to Western culture, may have implored his students, "Do not do to others that which would anger you if others did it to you." However, scholars have yet to authenticate this quotation as Socratic. Nonetheless, the value of ethical reciprocity as a prime principle of social behavior is a philosophical tenet that may have been passed on by Socrates to his "star" student, Plato. We can only surmise because no writings of Socrates have survived antiquity. It is primarily through the writings of Plato that we have any knowledge of the philosophical work of Socrates.

mind, and do to others as I would that they should do to me.[46]

Plato has defined a universal principle of social regulation with this precise caution: Do not "touch that which is mine" or seize anything "which belongs to me without my consent." This is a principle of human behavior, which like all principles does not allow for exceptions. But beyond this *negative* principle that defines what not to do, Plato gave us a *positive* principle of what to do by defining his Golden Rule of human exchange: "May I...do to others as I would that they should do to me." In other words, "I respect the integrity of your creation of wealth and freedom, as I would that you respect the integrity of my creation of wealth and freedom." For Plato, this was the social paradigm for the man of "sound mind" to follow without compromise.

Another Athenian of Plato's time, Isocrates (436–338 B.C.), was an influential philosopher, educator, and a celebrated orator. Speaking before audiences and students who were eager to learn his philosophy, Isocrates defined his Golden Rule of social behavior, "Do not inflict on the rest of the world outrages at which you are indignant when you suffer them yourselves at the hands of others."[47] As a renowned educator and professor of forensics who was in great demand, Isocrates earned his fortune in student tuitions by founding one of the most successful and influential schools of rhetoric and oration in ancient Greece.

Twenty-four centuries ago, Isocrates showed the efficacy of win-win education based on his Golden Rule of mutual gain. In defining the standard of behavior required by him to become an educated man, he asked, "Whom, then, do I call educated?" His answer, in part, was the "educated" are those "who are decent and honorable in their intercourse with all men, bearing easily and good-naturedly what is unpleasant or offensive in others, and being themselves as agreeable and reasonable to their associates as it is humanly possible to be."[48]

Furthermore, for Isocrates, the mark of an educated man was one who practiced, without compromise, the Golden Rule of win-win exchange for mutual gain. In other words, win-win gain is the aim of educated men as it transcends win-lose gain in its equity, utility, and morality.

In first century Rome, philosopher and statesman, Lucius Seneca, advised Romans to follow this vital rule of social behavior, "The essence of my teaching is this: Treat your inferiors as you would wish your superiors to treat you."[49] Seneca was a valued counselor to Nero in his early years as Emperor. Unfortunately, Nero proved that he was not a good student of Seneca's elegant ethics and his "Golden Rule" of moral reciprocity. In time, Nero would have few peers as a political tyrant of the classical world. With little reservation, he imposed the brutality of a win-lose imperial government against his rivals and subjects, all of whom he deemed to be his inferiors. Nero is especially remembered for his murderous persecution of the early Christians. In time, he would even betray his illustrious teacher, Seneca. In A.D. 65, by direct order of Nero, Seneca killed himself.

Epictetus (A.D. c. 55–c. 135.) was a Greek stoic philosopher who had been enslaved by the Romans and later freed. He taught his Roman pupils this simple rule of social action: "What you would avoid suffering yourself, seek not to impose on others."[50] In other words, never impose on others what you would not have imposed on yourself. Unfortunately, both the Greeks and Romans failed to apply these social rules of moral reciprocity—all based on the ethics of win-win exchange—to the foundational pillars of the Greek and Roman states. Over time, this proved to be a fatal error.

From the beginning, both Greece and Rome were slave states. Their political policies were patterned on the win-lose model of social action: *For us to gain, they must be forced to lose.* This included the gain of autocratic masters through the loss of their obedient slaves.

Over centuries, Greek and Roman politicians continued to expand coercive control over their citizens. They did so by enforcing ever more seizure of their citizen's wealth and freedom—at sword point. This incited a subtle social crisis that would lead to disaster and to the fatal and final end of Greek and Roman civilizations.

Something went wrong in Greece and Rome that does not take volumes to explain because it can be clarified in a sentence: *The constructive power of win-win exchange was eroded by the destructive power of win-lose exchange.* In the end, wherever destructive human action destroys constructive human action, something has to give—and it did. The once productive and creative civilizations of Greece and Rome fell into ruin, never to rise again. They were brought down by the deadly domino effects of building imperial states that glorified, codified, and amplified coercive exchange for win-lose gain.

Greek and Roman leaders used their political power to commit social suicide. As they expanded the scope and scale of win-lose gain through lawful force, there was no turning back. Without restraining coercion for win-lose gain, there was no recovery from the fatal effects of imperial self-destruction.

What oversight led Greek and Roman citizens on a certain path to self-destruction? Without oversimplifying, the explanation is *simple*. Greek and Roman leadership blundered into social calamity because they didn't know what they were doing. More precisely, they did not understand how to build a durable civilization that was impervious to self-destruction. We can infer that this was the crucial cause of their collapse because if they had known *how* to save themselves from social and physical ruin, surely they would have done so. These vibrant civilizations never would have stumbled into a "decline and fall" in the first place. If they had sustained their creative vitality, we might live in an entirely different world today. Greek and Roman civilizations might still flourish as centers of progress in art, science, technology, mathematics, medicine, education, commerce — and more. But their leaders, in failing to understand social causality, led their citizens like lemmings, to drown in the turmoil of win-lose destruction. Historians still call the aftermath of their demise the Dark Ages.

Fifteen centuries after the classical civilizations of Greece and Rome self-destructed; Europeans revived Greek and Roman culture. This remarkable revival culminated in the Renaissance, a term adopted by historians from the Latin verb *renasci*, which means, "to be born again." The European Renaissance fostered a rebirth of classical philosophy. Thus, by the seventeenth-century, philosophy as a discipline of serious study was flourishing once again — but this time in Europe. In Holland, Dutch philosopher, Baruch Spinoza, in his philosophical treatise, *Ethics*, gave this elegant moral tenet, "The good which every man, who follows after virtue, desires for himself he will also desire for other men."[51] Central to the ethics of Spinoza, this was his "proposition 37," which is the moral principle of desiring for others what you desire for yourself. Spinoza noted that those who follow this proposition are "just, faithful, and honorable in their conduct."[52]

In Great Britain, English philosopher, Thomas Hobbes, echoed the value of the Golden Rule of the Scriptures in his acclaimed *Leviathan*, "This is that law of the Gospel: Whatsoever you require that others should do to you, that do ye to them."[53] In the next sentence, Hobbes gave a universal *law of all men* to follow, "What you do not want done to you, do not to another."[54] This negative variation on the Golden Rule cautions you what *not* to do. When followed, it preempts social crises, which would naturally erupt where all human actions are permissible. In a world of such extreme license lacking social rules, Hobbes warned that humans would face, "continual fear, and danger of violent death; and the life of man [would be] solitary, poor, nasty, brutish, and short."[55] Thus, we must transcend social chaos. But just *how* this should be done is an old and still pressing issue. One approach has been to impose an autocratic police state ruled by well-groomed thugs, who repress all social dissent and protest at gunpoint—a state where all "troublemakers" and "malcontents" are jailed or shot. However, it will be revealed why all such win-lose societies—whether theocratic or political—are doomed to degrees of failure at best, and degrees of disaster at worst.

෨

Thomas Hobbes was followed by another renowned English philosopher, John Stuart Mill, who avowed the practical morality of the Golden Rule, "In the Golden Rule of Jesus of Nazareth, we read the complete spirit of the ethics of utility. To do as one would be done by, and to love one's neighbor as one's self constitutes the ideal perfection of utilitarian morality."[56] Mill stressed that this rule of morality (a win-win rule) has *utility*, which means it has practical value as the central guide to human action. The Latin *utilatus* means "useful." Furthermore, Mill asserted that this "utilitarian morality" has the greatest social and economic *usefulness* when it is gender blind. Mill believed that you could not create a flourishing society where there is one standard of morality for men, and another for women.

As an early advocate of social equality for women, J. Stuart Mill rocked the boat of gender discrimination against women in his 1869 essay on *The Subjection of Women*. He assailed the ancient tradition and oppressive paradigm that for men to gain, women must be forced to lose. Mill argued,

> That the principle which regulates the existing social relations between the two sexes — the legal subordination of one sex to the other — is wrong itself, and now one of the chief hindrances to human improvement; and that it ought to be replaced by a principle of perfect equality."*

Mill understood the social utility of applying the Golden Rule to include relations between "the two sexes." This is the basis of "social equality"; it is the engine for enriching the lives of both men and women through the creative power of win-win exchange.

In America, philosopher and founder of pragmatism, William James (1842-1910), advised his readers, "The first thing to learn in intercourse with others is non-interference with their own peculiar way of being happy provided those ways do not assume to interfere by violence with ours."[57] For James the pragmatist, the most practical thing, which is "the first thing" for humans to learn in reaching for happiness and a better life, is how *not* to interfere with others. Because humans do not inherit a "Golden Rule Gene" imbedded in their DNA, they must learn how *not* to seize the wealth and freedom of others for their own win-lose gain, just as they must learn how *not* to repulse their dinner guests from the table with offensive manners.

---

* John Stuart Mill, *The Subjection of Women*, 1869. This quotation is from the first paragraph of Mill's essay. It was written in 1861, but not published until 1869 at which time Mill thought the timing would be better for disclosing his contentious arguments for advancing the social and legal equality of women.

Good manners in exchange for good manners, is a win-win exchange that must be learned. There is no "good manners gene" to inherit from our well-mannered parents. However, once good manners are learned and used, everyone wins. In the same way, once people learn how *not* to pursue win-lose gain for themselves or anyone else and they act accordingly, everyone wins.

But before people—whether they are considered "decent" or "indecent"—can learn how *not* to pursue win-lose gain, they must first learn how to identify the human actions that always involve coercion for win-lose gain. Many decent people, by default alone, without observational analysis, believe in their "heart of hearts" that win-lose action for coercive gain is necessary, practical, and meritorious, especially when it is imposed upon society by the "proper" authorities. Thus, they truly believe that such legitimized or legalized coercion does not violate the Golden Rule. However, where this conventional wisdom is accepted as true, the Golden Rule cannot be a universal moral standard. It can only be a relative standard that only applies where it is deemed relevant and appropriate.

⁓

Moving from religion and philosophy to manners and etiquette, another American, Arthur Martine, in his 1866 *Martine's Hand-book of Etiquette and Guide to True Politeness*, gave this elegant standard for what it means to be a "gentleman."

> Gentility is neither in birth, manner, nor fashion—but in *the* Mind. A high sense of honor—a determination never to take a mean advantage of another—an adherence to truth, delicacy, and politeness toward those with whom you may have dealings—are the

essential and distinguishing characteristics of a GEN-TLEMAN.[58] [Martine's italics and small caps.]

Martine notes that because no one is born with "gentility," its virtues have to be learned as a model of social behavior. In common usage, *gentility* is the quality of being refined and well-mannered, which in a word is to be polite. Politeness in exchange for politeness is a sublime example of win-win exchange. Politeness alone, however, does not make a "GENTLEMAN."

In clear language, Martine asserted that, "the essential and distinguishing characteristic of a GENTLEMAN" is to have "a high sense of honor," which springs from his "determination never to take a mean advantage of another." This is the principle of win-win morality, which is the basis of the Golden Rule.

In defining what it means to be a gentleman, Martine implies what it means to be a lady, which is to follow the same principles of social behavior as a gentleman. Moreover, he says it is all in "*the* Mind." This makes it a win-win paradigm of social causality. One reason that *Martine's Hand-book of Etiquette* is still in print after a century and a half, is that its core principles of etiquette and ethics, gentility and politeness, never wear out or become obsolete.

Martine realized that it is not enough to be merely courteous and polite to others if you also "take a mean advantage" of them. After all, one's meanness may include a malicious aim to inflict harm upon others. The mean and malicious quest for gain through the loss of others is always harmful, and always ungentlemanly and unladylike. This was as true in Martine's time as it is true in ours. Win-win ethics and morality are built upon timeless principles. It is not a question of what standard of moral behavior or ethical action may or may not be in vogue in our time and place, or in any other time and place. Martine's social morality transcends time, place, and culture. Regardless of the social setting, meanness and gentlemanliness are always mutually exclusive, which is to say that they can never coexist.

Members of Hitler's private police force, the notorious SS, were largely men who were well-groomed, well-dressed, and who wore their politeness with a flare. But their sense of honor did not include Martine's principle of "never to take a mean advantage of another," which is to avoid harming others.

The Nazi "sense of honor" was focused on following the leadership of *der* Führer ("The Leader," viz., German Chancellor, Adolph Hitler). However, in their allegiance to the Führer, a crucial element was missing from their code of honor. As Germany's political leader, all of Hitler's commands were modeled on the win-lose paradigm: *For us to gain, they must lose through force or fraud.* And, from the Nazi perception of social causality, who were the "they" who must lose? *They* were largely Jews, gypsies, homosexuals, Slavic Europeans and Aryan anti-Nazis. This list of designated losers was eventually expanded to include nearly everyone in the Western world who was not in sympathy with Nazi aims to dominate Europe.

The point is, even if you are well-bred, well-groomed, well-dressed, well-educated, well-spoken, and well-mannered, but your win-lose belief system guides you to gain through the loss of others, it is impossible to be a "GENTLE-MAN," as defined by Arthur Martine. The members of Hitler's elite SS were not gentlemen at all; they were merely well-dressed, well-mannered thugs, and loyal killers who stole their neighbors' lives on command. To be sure, they were polite to a fault, especially when politeness spurred their plans to dominate Europe.

You cannot be both a gentleman and an instrument of systemized savagery at the same time. In short, the Nazi code of honor was *dishonorable*, precisely because it was founded on honoring and following a criminal creed: *For*

*Aryan Germans and faithful Fascists to gain, everyone else must be forced to lose.**

Both win-lose Naziism and win-lose religion have this in common: They are missing the most practical and ethical humanitarian principle ever discovered and defined as a code of conduct for human behavior, namely, the Golden Rule of social action. Faithful believers who have taken coercive action to impose win-lose monopolies of Islam or Christianity, have proven to be just as dangerous as faithful believers who have taken coercive action to impose win-lose monopolies of Fascism or Communism. The faithful practice of these coercive doctrines of social causality shows them to be unworkable systems of social organization that advance war, poverty, and servitude in the name of peace, prosperity, and freedom. As always, common wealth for common people cannot be created by legitimizing and codifying coercion for win-lose gain.

The greatest crimes of human history have been inflicted upon society by religious and political authorities through coercive institutions of win-lose gain. Either the authorities had abandoned the Golden Rule of moral reciprocity as their central rule of social behavior, or they had never adopted it in the first place. Where this rule has not been the first canon of religion and the first creed of government, the social effects of this omission have included the spread of war, poverty,

---

* According to Nazi doctrine and propaganda, an Aryan was said to be a non-Jewish Caucasian of Nordic ancestry, who thereby was born of the superior race. Thus, if you are not a member of the *superior race* ipso facto, you must be a member of an *inferior race*. Yet, even if science should ever reveal that there is, indeed, a superior race, whatever that might mean, the idea that this would give such a superior race a natural license to harm the inferior race is abominable, and would render the alleged superior race inferior by virtue of their very adoption of such a spurious, coercive, and regressive model of social causality.

and servitude. If these social afflictions continue to erode the foundation of civilization, it will collapse into ruin.

The pressing question of social history has not changed in ten thousand years. It remains, "What is the solution to the human tragedies of perpetual war, pervasive poverty, and rampant servitude?" Unfortunately, the scale of this question is so monumental that it may sound close to unanswerable. Nonetheless, part of the answer to this critical question arrives with the realization that there are not five solutions or three solutions, but *one* fundamental solution that has the practical potential for success.

The path to a successful solution begins with an understanding of the unique power of human paradigms to shape human destiny — for better or for worse. The singular escape from our age-old social afflictions requires a paradigm shift among decent people *away* from their *a priori* faith in the presumed equity, utility, and morality of win-lose institutions of religion and government, toward a new model of social causality. This elegant standard of social action is founded on *a posteriori* (after experience or observation) trust in the equity, utility, and morality of win-win institutions of religion and government.

A posteriori trust means that you have directly or indirectly observed the fairness, practicality, and ethics of religions and governments that are anchored to principles of win-win exchange for mutual gain. Such trust is pragmatic because there is no other solution that can attenuate, that can tame, the very real threat of human demise through social suicide.

The flawed paradigms of social causality that have given win-lose institutions their status and stature must be discredited and repudiated by falsifying their alleged truth. This is necessary because all people believe that their cherished paradigms of causality are true. They are confident that their personal models of reality are, indeed, *real*. But as long as the majority of respected people with good minds and good educations believe in the rectitude and efficacy of supporting institutions of religious and political coercion for win-lose gain there will always be a heavy price to pay. This price includes the consequences of war, poverty, and servitude that few people enjoy.

❧

The Golden Rule became a universal tenet of religion and philosophy because it is the key guide to creative and constructive human exchange. Regardless of its cross-cultural origins, this classic canon defines a single moral standard that is elevated to a social *principle* that guides humans to seek mutual gain, which avoids harming others through force or fraud.

GOLDEN RULE PRINCIPLE
Do not seize wealth and freedom from others, as you would have them not seize your wealth and freedom.

The diverse gains to be reaped through the operation of this principle are observable to anyone willing to look. It does not require faith to accept the truth of its moral efficacy. This is because any human, independently of any other human, can observe its mutual rewards. Rather than *imagining* it to be true, it can be *observed* to be true. Observational verification of truth is always more reliable than imaginary certification of truth. The Golden Rule Principle works because it is in harmony with our human nature. This will be clarified in Chapter Seven on The Law of Human Nature.

The focus of science is on the search for principles of nature to solve physical, biological, and social problems. Great solutions to great problems are built on great principles. Principles of nature are generalized observations that, through their consistency and simplicity, advance our understanding of physical, biological, and social causality. The Golden Rule Principle warns: Do not kill, steal, swindle, assault, kidnap, or trespass—all of which seize the wealth and freedom of others—as you would not want to suffer the same seizure yourself. This principle is a simple generalization for all humans to follow regardless of their gender, ethnicity, culture, or status. It is a governing principle for those who aim to reach ever-greater satisfaction from the experience of life.

ENDNOTES

41. "On Golden Rules," in Peter Lorie and Manuela Dunn Mascetti, eds., *The Quotable Spirit* (New York: Macmillan, 1996), 211.

42. Zoroaster, *Dadistan-i-dink*, 94, 5.

43. Also known as *The Tale of the Peasant and the Workman*, and *The Plea of the Eloquent Peasant*, it is one of only a few extant narratives to have survived from ancient Egypt. Trans. R. B. Parkinson.

44. George Seldes, *The Great Quotations* (New York: A Caesar-Stuart Book, 1960), 283. Social philosopher, Confucius, is also known as K'hung fu-tzu.

45. Meng-tzu (Latinized name, Mencius), *Meng-tzu*, VII.A.4.

46. *Dialogues of Plato*, Laws, Book XI, trans. Benjamin Jowett (Oxford: At The Claredon Press, 1892), p. 299.

47. Isocrates, *The Orations of Isocrates*, "Nicocles or the Cyprians," trans. John Henry Freese (London: George Bell & Sons, 1894), sec. 61, 49.

48. Isocrates, *Panathenaicus*, 339 B.C.

49. *The Stoic Philosophy of Lucius Annaeus Seneca: Essays and Letter*, trans. and ed., Moses Hadas. (New York: W. W. Norton & Co., Inc., 1958), p. 193, See Epistle 47:11.

50. Epictetus, *Encheiridion*, c. 100.

51. Baruch Spinoza, *Ethica*, IV, prop. 37, trans. R. H. M. Elwes (South Australia: The University of Adelaide Library), http://ebooks.adelaide.edu.au/s/spinoza/benedict/ethics/ (Last updated Aug. 29, 2010)

52. Spinoza, *Ethica*, IV.

53. Thomas Hobbes, *Leviathan; or the Matter, Forme, and Power of a Commonwealth, Ecclesiasticall and Civil*, 1651, ed. Aloysius P. Martinich (Peterborough, Ontario: Broadview Press Ltd., 2002), 99.

54. Hobbes, *Leviathan*. *Quod tibi fieri non vis, alteri ne feceris*.

55. Thomas Hobbes, *Leviathan; or the Matter, Forme, and Power of a Commonwealth*, ed. J.C.A. Gaskin (Oxford: Oxford University Press, 2008), xliii.

56. John Stuart Mill, *Utilitarianism* (Malden, MA: Blackwell Publishing Ltd, 2003), 194.

57. William James, *Talks to Teachers on Psychology: And to Students on Some of Life's Ideas* (New York: Henry Holt and Co., 1925), 130.

58. Arthur Martine, *Martine's Hand-book of Etiquette and Guide to True Politeness* (Bedford, Massachusetts: Applewood Books, 1996) 167. First published in NewYork by Dick & Fitgerald, 1866.

Chapter Four

From Win-Lose to Win-Win Principles

I n the vast arena of human affairs, nothing is more important than the discovery of principles of causality that *gov-*
ern humans toward win-win success. Our English infinitive
"to govern" is borrowed from the Latin *gubernare*, which
means to steer, as in steering a ship. The key to win-win
governing is to follow the Golden Rule Principle by steering humans away from *seizing* wealth and freedom toward
creating wealth and freedom. The key to win-win business is
to build a proprietary venture on the Golden Rule Principle
that gains market success through the creation of win-win
profit. And, the key to win-win theology that averts religious warfare and persecution is to build theology on the
Golden Rule Principle that steers the faithful away from
the *immorality* and *criminality* of win-lose exchange, toward
the *morality* and *ethicality* of win-win exchange.

Today, this does not require theological revelation or
innovation. The world's major religions already incorpo-
rate the principle of the Golden Rule as a moral cornerstone

of their theology. The human operation of this principle precludes win-lose exchange. The preclusion of win-lose exchange expands the potential for win-win exchange.

∽

Although the term *win-win* has come into popular usage in recent decades, it is rarely if ever defined. As a consequence, because this now familiar adjective has a positive ring to it, the win-win label is commonly misapplied to promote win-lose exchange, which is the very opposite of win-win exchange.

Whether the subject is religion, philosophy, politics, economics, or science, when a key term and basic premise of any discipline is not defined, those concerned are usually presuming or guessing its meaning. Most people — whether educated or not — if challenged, will have great difficulty defining the central terms that forge the doctrines and models of causality that they embrace. This is because the semantic structure of their adopted paradigms of causality is usually accepted by default without critical analysis. The probability is small that many people will surmise or assume the same meaning used by others for any fundamental term not precisely defined. For example, if everyone using the term "win-win" is merely assuming its meaning, there is no clear communication of the win-win idea. Such presumptions on the meaning of *win-win* exchange can lead to miscommunication, misunderstanding, and misapplication of win-win principles.

Where imprecise semantics prevail, no one knows precisely what anyone is talking about — all the time. Without at least some semantic precision, communication is poor at best and nonexistent at worst. Not knowing what you are talking about is the basis of not knowing what you are doing.

Much of human thinking is expressed in language. Without semantic precision, language is incoherent, and in a word, fuzzy. Fuzzy language leads to fuzzy thinking. This raises the risk of decent people taking well-meaning actions that lead to unintended consequences. Wherever people's actions lead to unintended consequences, they don't know what they are doing. And, ominously, where decent people don't know what they are doing, their well-meaning actions could accelerate the demise of civilization and the extinction of our species. To reiterate, where the aim is to communicate fundamental concepts, we must define our basic terms. We must always strive to enhance the precision of the semantic foundation of our ideas, especially for our own understanding, as well as, the understanding of others who care to communicate.

In applying win-win theory, the expression win-win implies any exchange wherein all parties aim to create mutual gain—and no one loses through force or fraud. *Win-win exchange* must be precisely defined, so that those who seek win-win exchange and would not breech its integrity will know what they are doing. Knowing its precise meaning is crucial because true win-win exchange is the creator of new wealth and new freedom. For this critical reason, win-win exchange must never be confused with win-lose exchange, which is the creator of new poverty and new servitude.

> *Win-win exchange is the act of gaining through the gain of others without gaining through the loss of others by force or fraud.*

Like any precise definition, its semantic precision or simplicity may be refined over time. However, if the key terminology of every theory on causality required semantic "perfection" before its disclosure, few theories would ever be disclosed. Of course, if there are no fundamental definitions to begin with, then their elegance and precision cannot be refined. This applies to all definitions in win-win theory.

❧

Win-Lose theology stands on an imaginary paradigm of religious faith that praises a deadly dogma: *For believers to gain, disbelievers must be forced to lose.* Those who adopt this model of religious causation have faith in the sanctity of win-lose exchange. They are certain that it is *practical* — even *moral* — for believers to gain by forcing disbelievers to lose. They believe this because they often see no other practical or sacred means to gain. They are sure that they can only reach their religious aims through the force of win-lose gain. Nonetheless, this model of religious causality is seriously flawed because it is entirely false.

How do we know it is false? Observable principles of social causality falsify this criminal paradigm of human gain: *By observing social action, we can see that the total gains of win-win exchange always exceed the total gains of win-lose exchange.* This is revealed by observing one principle of social action that is founded on independent observation. The Principle of Win-Win Exchange predicts the social effects of originating and propagating human exchange for mutual gain.

PRINCIPLE OF WIN-WIN EXCHANGE
Win-win exchange creates wealth, expands freedom, and establishes peace.

Win-win exchange is the cause of peace because it is peaceful exchange, which is free exchange. As the creation of win-win exchange rises, so the creation of peace rises. *Peace is a byproduct of win-win exchange.*

Moreover, win-win exchange is the cause of prosperity, because it is the prime creator of new wealth. As the creation of win-win exchange rises, so the creation of prosperity rises. *Prosperity is a byproduct of win-win exchange.*

Furthermore, win-win exchange is the cause of freedom because it is a mutually voluntary exchange. As the creation of win-win exchange rises, so the creation of human freedom rises. *Freedom is a byproduct of win-win exchange.* We can verify through observation that the greatest human gains flow from the win-win domino effects of creating peace, prosperity, and freedom for all to enjoy—which includes every religious believer.

These *a posteriori* conclusions are reached by observing the operation of the Principle of Win-Win Exchange. Its operation as a principle of social action can be seen by anyone willing to look. It is a key principle for revealing which social causes lead to which social effects. In our time, the acquisition of this knowledge of social causality is both critical and crucial. In the nuclear age, we cannot afford to misidentify social causality because the consequences can be tragic for all humans. No matter how well-meaning and praiseworthy their intentions, those who provoke win-lose gain to reach religious or political aims cannot control the win-lose domino effects that may lead to their very own doom and destruction.

To identify the real causes of the social devastation brought about by war, poverty, and servitude, we must rely on observational principles as true guides to understanding. Such penetrating principles show that these age-old afflictions are not driven by human nature. If they were, we could do little or nothing to avoid their ruinous effects. Human doom would then be a foregone conclusion.

The illuminating discovery that can carry us away from doom is the realization that catastrophic social effects are *not* derivatives of our human nature; they are derivatives of our human paradigms. These flawed paradigms of "reality" owe their influence to counterfeit models of social causality, widely revered as authentic or sacred—especially among the educated classes.

These counterfeit paradigms are held to be true, largely, by two pervading social classes: (1) decent people with poor minds and poor educations; and, (2) decent people with good minds and good educations. Although both of these social classes are spread around the globe, only one class has the potential to revolutionize society by replacing the tribulations of war, poverty, and servitude with the blessings of peace, prosperity, and freedom.

It is by no means elitist to note that people with good minds and good educations, in general, are more influential than people with poor minds and poor educations. It is this former class, combining good minds with good educations, who wield the greatest social influence and, therefore, the greatest potential to build prosperous and equitable communities and nations on the Win-Win Principle for the benefit of all social classes.

∽

Human progress is driven largely by people who are not bored with principles, but who are excited by the prospect of discovering new principles of causation that explain the true causes of physical, biological, and social effects. Why is this so important? Why is it so crucial to human welfare?

It cannot be overemphasized that most of the great social tragedies of human history have *not* been caused by bad guys doing bad things, but by good guys doing bad things. Where good guys are doing bad things—very bad things—it is not because they are evil by nature, it is because they don't know what they are doing. In other words, they have failed to understand cause-and-effect, and act accordingly. In more precise language, they have misidentified and misunderstood which causes—physical, biological, and social—lead to which effects.

If the good guys cannot improve upon their understanding of social causality, if they do not have the knowledge and courage to make paradigm shifts away from false explanations of causality toward those that are true, they will continue to foster and incite war, poverty, and servitude. Therefore, how can we impede the vicious cycles of win-lose domino effects that provoke war, poverty, and servitude, and impair peace, prosperity, and freedom?

There is one avenue of escape, leading in one direction. We must do a better job of educating people on the most important thing they can learn; namely, *which causes lead to which effects*. Failure to get it right will bring certain disaster. Civilization will vanish along with its teaming masses. The ultimate human loss is the loss of our species, in which case, without mourners to mourn, we will perish unlamented.

૦૦

The operation of win-win principles implies mutually voluntary exchanges (tangible or intangible) between two or more people. Conversation itself is an intangible exchange that is the foundation of human relationships. What we say to others in conversational exchange, in large part, defines who we are. Humans, for example, in their pursuit of gain can tell a lie to reach win-lose gain, or they can tell a truth to reach win-win gain. Both Moses and Jesus gave strong warnings to the faithful that they must never bear false witness by giving false testimony against another for win-lose gain in a court of law or anywhere else. Violation of this commandment is an example of win-lose cowardice to avoid personal loss.

Everyone has the same choice of how to gain. Those who tell truths for win-win gain are entirely different people from those who tell lies for win-lose gain. Our choices of how we gain define our character. More precisely, our choices throughout our lives, whatever they may be, create the very person we become. The greater our knowledge of social cause-and-effect, the greater our likelihood of prizing win-win gain, and despising win-lose gain.

The most gratifying exchanges are often *intangible*. The possibilities of gaining through intangible exchange are endless. The kindness of the stranger who saves a child from the menace of a wild beast, ready to strike, is an example of intangible win-win exchange. The child wins, the Good Samaritan wins, and everyone caring for the child wins.

In the parable of the Good Samaritan as told in Luke 10:25-37, Jesus created a win-win hero for all time. This famous parable was provoked by a scholar of Judaic law who was testing Jesus on the depth of his knowledge by openly asking him, "What must I do to inherit eternal life?" Jesus confirmed that he must, "Love the Lord your God… and Love your neighbor as yourself." The scholar then challenged Jesus with this question, "And who is my neighbor?" His question implied, are there any exceptions? Must I love *all* my neighbors and hate none of them?

Among Jews of biblical time, there was no love and much hatred for the people of Samaria who were religious rivals living in Palestine, just north of Judea. Even though both Samaritans and Jews believed that, they were truly "the children of Israel" and of God, a schism over doctrinal differences on how to worship God had erupted between Samaritans and Jews four centuries before the birth of Jesus. Now, here was Jesus teaching his fellow Jews that even the despised people of Samaria—scorned by Jewish leaders as religious outcasts—should be seen in a new light. But should the Jewish people, as Jesus said, love these unworthy Samaritans as their neighbors, even as equals in the sight of God?

In answering the Jewish scholar with his famous allegory, Jesus tells the story of a Samaritan who was traveling along the dangerous road from Jerusalem to Jericho. The seventeen-mile road was not only steep, it wound through treacherous terrain; and was a known shelter for robbers eager to prey upon their next victim. The parable was a public reply by Jesus to the scholar's challenge to his moral authority. Jesus begins his now familiar story as told by his apostle, Luke.

> A man was going down from Jerusalem to Jericho, when he fell into the hands of robbers. They stripped him of his clothes, beat him and went away, leaving him half dead with no clothes. A [Judaic] priest happened to be going down the same road, and when he saw the man [probably a Jew], he passed by on the other side. So too, a Levite [aide to a Judaic priest], when he came to the place and saw him, passed by on the other side. But a Samaritan, as he traveled, came where the man was; and when he saw him, he took pity on him. He went to him and bandaged his wounds, pouring on oil and wine.

From the superior position of the Jews of that time, the Samaritan was an inferior being, one to be despised rather than embraced as a neighbor to be loved. Yet, Jesus, himself a Jew, was not sympathetic with Jewish hostility toward their neighboring Samaritans. The Judaic priest and the Levite from the Judaic Temple, in ignoring the plight of a helpless victim of a brutal crime, reveal not only their lack of compassion as Jewish authorities, but their cowardice as well.

In sharp contrast, the "inferior" Samaritan not only proved his compassion for the unfortunate plight of a total stranger, but also showed his courage as well. He was traveling on a road known to be dangerous, and that danger would increase if he did not reach his destination before dark. He too could have become a victim of the same robbers who may have been watching him from the rocks above. Fully aware of this risk, he interrupted his journey to aid a man who would have likely died from wounds and exposure if he were not rescued from his distress. Jesus continues with his parable.

> Then he [the Samaritan] put the man on his own donkey, took him to an inn and took care of him. The next day he took out two silver coins and gave them to the innkeeper. "Look after him," he said, "and when I return, I will reimburse you for any extra expense you may have."

The Samaritan not only showed true compassion and great courage, but his generosity and kindness were exceptional. In contrast, the pious priest and the holy Levite proved by their actions that they were devoid of such virtues.

Jesus ends his parable by asking the Jewish scholar who had challenged his knowledge of Judaic law, "Which of these three do you think was a neighbor to the man who fell into the hands of robbers? The expert in the law replied, 'The one who had mercy on him.' Jesus told him, 'Go and do likewise.'"

To "go and do likewise," is to take win-win action for intangible gain. To have the valor and empathy to risk your life while helping an unknown stranger in critical distress, is an act of win-win courage. In this storied parable by Jesus, the victim wins, his family and friends win, and the innkeeper wins. Furthermore, the Good Samaritan wins the intangible wealth of self-esteem and self-confidence from his generous and daring actions. Moreover, everyone who learns the lesson of calculated *courage* in aiding an unknown neighbor reaps a priceless gain that spawns a cascade of win-win domino effects.

∽

It is important to stress that *intangible* gains are among the richest rewards of win-win exchange. One of the remarkable masterpieces for chorus and orchestra is *St. Mathew's Passion*, composed at Leipzig in 1727 by Johann Sebastian Bach. At the time, the musical creations of Bach were largely unknown outside of Leipzig, until a century later in 1829, when conductor and composer, Felix Mendelssohn, performed the *Passion* to an ecstatic audience in Berlin. Mendelssohn went on to bring the melodic genius of Bach out of obscurity. Ever since, Bach has been a "superstar" of classical music. Today, millions of listeners beyond Germany are enthralled by the win-win creations of Bach and Mendelssohn. Near the end of his brilliant career, Felix Mendelssohn wrote his *Violin Concerto in E minor, Op. 64*, which is now one of the most applauded masterpieces ever scored.

As a seminal originator of new wealth, J. S. Bach was revered by Einstein as "the god of music." If you admire the harmonic brilliance of Bach, you enjoy a new and richer wealth even though Bach has been gone for centuries. As the classical music of Bach is revered by many, so is the popular music of the Beatles revered by many more. For Beatles fans, their intangible wealth grows as they enjoy the original songs and rousing rhythms of the boys from Liverpool. In the 1960s, with their sensational rock band, the Beatles supercharged the market for "rock" music throughout the Western world.

The creation of musical wealth by Bach and the Beatles through their melodic compositions is a win-win gain that is accessible to billions of listeners throughout the world. Through the marvelous innovations of Hertz, Edison, Armstrong, and dozens more, every listener gains through the intangible creation of win-win wealth. We are, thereby, wealthier because we share in the win-win domino effects of their creative genius that every day enriches our lives.

The melodic compositions of Bach and the Beatles are intangible achievements, created in pursuit of win-win wealth. Yet, the wealth that they still produce can be either tangible or intangible. In any case, the composers win, the musicians win, the impresarios win, and the audiences win. The potential for ongoing dividends of tangible and intangible wealth through the benefits of win-win exchange is endless. For those who thrill to the music of Bach and the Beatles, their win-win gain is as intangible as it is priceless. The proof is in the bravos and ovations that still thunder across time.

In contrast to intangible gain, money tendered at a fine Italian restaurant for eggplant parmigiana and Tuscan wine is a *tangible* exchange where proprietor and customer win. However, the theft of the restaurant's cash receipts by a local thief is also a tangible exchange, where the thief gains and the owner loses. Because all exchanges can be either win-win or win-lose, it is necessary to define a line of demarcation—a sharp division—separating win-win from win-lose exchange.

Over a decade ago, noted futurist and economist, Hazel Henderson, wrote her *Building a Win-Win World: Life beyond Global Economic Warfare.*[59] This hardbound publication was printed on quality paper, with an attractive cover and some four hundred pages. However, it gives no definition of the key term, "win-win." Although Henderson gives her readers a detailed index of 29 pages, there is no reference in her index to *win-win* anything, and win-win is never defined. We can only guess what the central term of her entire treatise actually means because it is not defined. In any case, her "win-win solution" requires win-lose seizure of wealth and freedom to bring her vision of a "Win-Win World" to fruition. But no matter how earnest the effort, it is impossible to reach win-win ends through win-lose means.

The prime question to be raised in approaching any solution to any social problem is, "Can the means employed attain the ends sought?" For example, can a win-lose economics that calls for coercive elimination of win-win exchange in the market play a central role in "Building a Win-Win World," as proffered by Hazel Henderson? *Economic history confirms that it cannot.*

If the grand social aim, as many claim, is to bring about "the greatest good for the greatest number," can this aim ever be reached by seizing people's wealth and freedom at gunpoint? It is no coincidence that where win-lose economics is the most pervasive, poverty is also the most pervasive. Moreover, it is also no coincidence that, by and large, where poverty is the most pervasive, win-lose religion and win-lose government are also the most pervasive — and often the most virulent and violent.

⁊

A natural principle describes a repeating phenomenon that always operates the same way. It is this endless repeatability and, thereby, predictability of results that set principles apart from all other human conceptions of natural phenomena. The Golden Rule Principle repeats again and again: *Do not seize wealth and freedom from others, as you would have them not seize your wealth and freedom.* This is a precise principle of human action, a social rule that does not allow for exceptions.

Although natural principles are the foundations of human progress, we must never expect to be awed by any principle when we first see it. Upon seeing for the first time the world's most celebrated principle, $E=mc^2$, it is unlikely that anyone ever sprang to his feet and cried out, "Wow, $E=mc^2$! Einstein is a genius! Energy equals mass times the velocity of light squared. Wow!"

Principles of nature, as simple as they are, require examination and reflection before their significance is illuminated and clarified. After your first exposure to Einstein's principle of $E=mc^2$, you can invest a lifetime in understanding its elegant power to discover natural causality. The "WOW" comes not upon first seeing the principle, but upon first understanding it. Therefore, don't expect to be wowed by the Win-Win Principle — or any other natural principle — the first time you see it.

A corollary (easily drawn conclusion) of the Golden Rule Principle is the Win-Win Principle. It restates the Golden Rule standard of morality set forth by the ancient theologians and philosophers. Rather than defining a *negative* generalization of what actions *not* to pursue, it defines a *positive* generalization of what actions to pursue. Moreover, it enhances the semantic precision necessary for building a Science of Social Causality that can identify and verify which social causes lead to which social effects.

> WIN-WIN PRINCIPLE
> *Always seek gain through the gain of others, and never seek gain through the loss of others by force or fraud.*

We can seek gain either through the gain of others — or through the loss of others. That covers all possibilities. For all of us, before we act, it is our human nature to ask, "What's in it for me?" There is no reason to criticize those who ask this selfish question. Everyone has the same question, "What will I gain or what will I lose from taking this action?" Everyone is going for a good deal; no one knowingly is going for a bad deal. It is human nature to ask, "What's the best deal for me?"

Where the Win-Win Principle governs human action, the many benefits of win-win gain far outweigh any supposed benefits of win-lose gain. The best deal is the "win-win deal." It is created and fulfilled by the mutual rewards of win-win gain.

On a world scale where humans, if they could, would optimize peace, prosperity, and freedom, they must apply the Win-Win Principle to every arena of human exchange to reach such worthy aims. Of course, most people neither think nor care about reaching world aims because those seem too remote from their own personal experience and beyond their sphere of influence. However, this is of little consequence because where people *do not* have world aims, they most certainly do have individual aims.

On an individual scale, there is a most compelling reason to follow the Win-Win Principle. We can observe that the operation of this principle has no equal as a practical and rewarding course of social action. It works for all individuals by increasing their mutual benefits—as no other means can approach—through the power of win-win exchange. We can see for ourselves, for example, that the negative returns of hate for hate cannot compete with the positive returns of love for love. To reiterate in common language, the operation of the Win-Win Principle is both a very "good deal" and a very "big deal" because it creates a bonanza of wealth—both tangible and intangible—for the enrichment of humankind.

There is another natural principle of social causality to observe, which, like all principles, can be seen to operate always in the same way.

Operation of the win-win principle creates the greatest wealth and freedom for the greatest number.

Observation of the Win-Win Principle in operation verifies its matchless power to yield universal benefits for all humans.

If you have discovered a principle of causality, no matter how strong the observational evidence, there will always be various detractors who deride or ignore your findings. They may defend many ideas on causality that, from your view of reality, are clearly untenable. For these and other reasons, you may not care to seek gain through their gain because you would rather not deal with them on any basis. It is important to note, however, that merely to avoid them cannot harm them as long as you do not seek gain through their loss by force or fraud. To create peace and harmony among humans, we must never act to harm others over their beliefs, no matter how fallacious or faulty we may believe them to be.

All win-lose exchange—whether or not the aim is noble and laudable—diminishes the causes of peace, prosperity, and freedom, and augments the very opposite, namely, the causes of war, poverty, and servitude. These immutable laws of social causation cannot be repealed. The destructive domino effects of win-lose religious and win-lose political action—without recourse or redress for the victims—will continue to derail the advance of peace, prosperity, and freedom. By the actions that humans choose to take or not to take, they have the power to unleash win-win or win-lose action upon their neighbors. It is always their choice. In either case, they cannot take actions that are isolated from social cause-and-effect.

Christian cleric, Anglican preacher, and English poet, John Donne, warned his parishioners of the difficulty of isolating themselves from their neighbor's tragedies when in 1624 he wrote these now famous lines.

> No man is an island, entire of itself; every man is a
> piece of the continent, a part of the main; if a clod

be washed away by the sea, Europe is the less, as well as if a promontory were, as well as if a manor of thy friend's or of thine own were; any man's death diminishes me, because I am involved in mankind, and therefore never send to know for whom the bell tolls; it tolls for thee.[60]

John Donne's bold assertion that "any man's death diminishes me" because he is not "an island" in isolation of humanity is a grand generalization that allows for no exceptions. In the larger sense of this metaphor, any one's *loss* diminishes us — all of us. Donne's use of the English infinitive "to diminish" derives from the Latin *deminuere*, which means, "to make smaller." Someone else's loss "diminishes me" by making the sum of my wealth *smaller*. When my neighbor's house is shredded by tornadic winds, though I hold no interest in his deed, the wealth of our community is diminished. I own a share of my neighbor's loss, which is a community loss from which there is no escape for me or for anyone else. That I did nothing to incur his loss is irrelevant. When the bell tolls for the wreck of his home and the death of his child, as Donne argues, "I am involved." When the reality of this tragedy touches my mind, my welling eyes betray my pathos for his fatal loss. Of course, not everyone will share my empathy. Even so, those who would ignore the peal of the bell as it cries its mortal message are also involved — because all "mankind" is involved.

Donne's haunting lines speak of the inexorable and unyielding domino effects of one man's loss upon all humanity. When the death-knell sounds, it tolls for me, for you, and for everyone else. In this classic prose, however, Donne's metaphor ends on a negative note without revealing the positive corollary, which is equally profound and telling. The bell of social action also tolls for the dynamic creation of new wealth that not only does not "diminish me," but in fact, it augments me. It enlarges the material and immaterial benefits that are available to me because now I belong to a more affluent society.

When my neighbor down the road — whose name I don't even know — merely remodels his home and landscapes his yard for an alluring result, I am, thereby, wealthier, precisely because I am an integral part of a more prosperous community. Unavoidably and inextricably, as Donne relates, "I am involved in mankind," whether or not I am sensitive to the social implications and the visual enhancement on my behalf. Citizens of my city, my county, and my country are, thereby, wealthier because my neighbor, in refurbishing his home and restoring his grounds, produced new wealth — new *win-win wealth* — by fashioning a richer environment. Moreover, my far-flung neighbors, though they live thousands of miles from my unknown neighbor and are unlikely to ever pass by his house, let alone be invited in, are also wealthier by virtue of the fact that they now live in a wealthier country.

All of us enjoy a share of humankind's win-win wealth without having to appropriate it, which is to take it without permission. The Latin *appropriatus* means, "to make [something] one's own" without consent of the owner. The appropriation of wealth for religious or political gain has always been a flawed policy for creating a better world because social action shows that neither religious nor political authorities can appropriate their way to prosperity and freedom for the commonweal.

But how do we know that they cannot when they claim that they can? Because clear observation contradicts their authoritarian "wisdom" by revealing this social principle: *The less old wealth that is appropriated, the more new wealth that is created; and, conversely, the more old wealth that is appropriated, the less new wealth that is created.* To appropriate is to confiscate, and to confiscate is to seize. To seize old wealth is to seize the human incentive to create new wealth. Principles of social causality falsify the supposed truth of religious and political arguments, which claim that the coercive seizure of wealth and freedom for win-lose religious and political gain is the creator of greater wealth and freedom for the people.

∽

The confiscation of old wealth must not be confused with the creation of new wealth through the orderly operation of the Win-Win Principle. A thousand examples show the positive domino effects of creating new wealth for mutual gain. How we come to share in the wealth created by others—without appropriating it—is explained by Donne's insightful prose, wherein he puts forth a social principle that generalizes: *Every man is involved in mankind.* This means that we cannot act in isolation of society. Our social actions unleash win-win domino effects that are constructive, or they unleash win-lose domino effects that are destructive. Unavoidably, these domino effects pervade all of human society for *better* when they are win-win and for *worse* when they are win-lose.

This means that Donne's bell not only tolls for death and loss, but it also tolls for life and gain in celebration of our new wealth and greater prosperity. However, because the ring of the bell and the sound of the toll do not change in this telling metaphor, we must listen, look, and ask, "Does the bell toll for win-lose destruction of old wealth, or for win-win creation of new wealth?" Whatever the answer may be, whether we like the result or not, we are all involved in the outcome of everyone's actions.

In China, as noted earlier, Lao-tzu anticipated John Donne by a few thousand years with his elegant principle of social action, "Regard your neighbor's gain as your own gain, and your neighbor's loss as your own loss." Lao-tzu and John Donne gave us a social principle that, in other words, we can observe to be true long after their time: *As my neighbors gain, I gain; as my neighbors lose, I lose.*

∽

The Win-Win Principle, "Always seek gain through the gain of others, and never seek gain through the loss of others by force or fraud," is a simple rule of social behavior. Like all principles, however, its significance is not obvious. Thus, it has to be carefully explained to even the brightest of those with a curiosity to know causality. The importance of the Win-Win Principle becomes more apparent when the consequences of its violation are explained by applying the converse principle:

WIN-LOSE PRINCIPLE
Never seek gain through the gain of others, and always seek gain through the loss of others by force or fraud.

Although I am sympathetic to those who may object to using the term "principle" to define a negative generalization, nonetheless, it is necessary to preserve the integrity of semantic symmetry, and to emphasize opposite concepts using familiar antonyms.

Where individuals apply the Win-Lose Principle on their own volition without organizational support, the magnitude of the destruction they impose upon society, though deplorable, is also negligible. However, the scope and scale of destruction is *not* negligible when the Win-Lose Principle is institutionalized to impose win-lose violence for religious or political gain. When the Win-Lose Principle is orchestrated against individuals—whether it is deemed legal or illegal, consecrated or unconsecrated—it confiscates wealth and freedom and, thereby, diminishes the incentive of victims to create new wealth and new freedom.

The reason Communist societies fail to advance peace, prosperity, and freedom is because they violate the Win-Win Principle by imposing the Win-Lose Principle on society by legalizing seizure of wealth and freedom at gunpoint. The predictable consequences are observable: *Win-lose Communism maximizes the number of losers per capita and minimizes the number of winners per capita.*

A Communist society is an anti-incentive society that is incompatible with human nature. Marxist Communism is founded on *a priori* faith in the merit and efficacy of the Win-Lose Principle. Furthermore, it is well known that Communists have a steadfast faith in the superiority of win-lose atheism over all theological doctrines. Driven by their superior ideology, as they see it, devout Communists believe it is their duty and destiny to force Marxist atheism on all disbelievers. The atheistic religion of Karl Marx and his infamous apostles Lenin, Stalin, and Mao proclaimed: *For atheists to gain, theists must be forced to lose.*

Like all win-lose paradigms, the Win-Lose Principle is a false model of social causality. We can observe that win-lose exchange for coercive gain minimizes the benefits of prosperity and freedom, while it maximizes the deficits of poverty and servitude. In contrast, observation of social action reveals that win-win exchange for mutual gain maximizes the benefits of wealth and freedom for both theists and atheists.

Defeating the Black Death, which killed tens of millions of victims across Europe and Asia, required observation and understanding of *biological* causality. In a similar way, defeating Marxist atheism, which has also killed tens of millions of victims across Europe and Asia, requires observation and understanding of *social* causality. It is observation of the religious practice of win-lose Communism that falsifies its *a priori* claims of creating Heaven on earth—at gunpoint. Indeed, the icon of Communist China, Mao Ze-dong (Mao Tse-tung), declared at a Central Committee meeting of the Communist Party in 1938, "Every Communist must grasp the truth: 'Political power grows out of the barrel of a gun.'"[61]

The win-lose power of political gunmen has imposed atheism throughout Communist nations in the name of Marx. Led by their *a priori* faith in the superiority of atheistic Marxism over all religious and political systems, the Marxists aimed to impose a monopoly of Communism and atheism around the globe through mass intimidation, mass enslavement, and mass murder.

In using his political gun power to advance Communist control in Asia, Chairman Mao became the greatest mass murderer in human history. Before his death in 1976, he had mandated the murder of more than 77,000,000 of his fellow compatriots while Communizing China from 1923–1976 for the supposed greater good of his subjects.[62]

As the supreme tyrant of Asia, Mao upstaged the supreme tyrant of Europe, Joseph Stalin. While Communizing the Soviet Union from 1929–1953 in order to impose a Marxist-Leninist dictatorship, Stalin ordered the murder of more than 42,000,000 of his fellow citizens.[63] If we compare murders per year between Stalin and Mao, during his win-lose reign, Stalin murdered, on average, 1,750,000 of his own people every year for twenty-four years. In contrast, Mao "only" murdered, on average, 1,450,000 of his own people per year over fifty-three years. Nearly all those dutiful followers of Mao Ze-dong and Joseph Stalin who participated in these mass murders had faith—devout faith—*a priori* faith that their win-lose actions would bring about a better China, a better Russia, and a better world. Yet, things went terribly wrong because the Communists failed to determine whether the win-lose means they employed could attain the social ends they claimed to be seeking. The means they employed to build their Socialist paradises was the ruthless operation of the Win-Lose Principle — *Never seek gain through the gain of others, and always seek gain through the loss of others by force or fraud* — which became the coercive core of every codified and legalized decree.

Human history shows that the only social systems that have to be imposed upon people through force and fraud are those systems that are unworkable because they violate the laws of social causality. One of the best-kept social secrets is that Communism is the most impractical and the most criminal social scheme ever contrived by human imagination. For this reason, its perpetrators have imposed the greatest amount of force and fraud ever unleashed upon society in a futile effort to make an unworkable system work. Well over a hundred million people have been brutally murdered by Communist authorities to advance Communism around the globe. But it will never work because its political foundation of Socialism is based on false models of causality that must be accepted on blind faith without critical analysis.

Karl Marx led generations of intellectuals to believe that his Communistic Socialism was a scientific political system. However, it takes more than merely naming a system "scientific" to render it a true derivative of the scientific method. During the course of building and imposing Socialist political systems, Marx and his deluded followers did not follow the rigid steps of the scientific method set forth by Galileo and Newton. The Marxists contrived coercive political systems of Communism and Socialism that could never be more than pseudo-scientific schemes. They were always on track to fail at reaching their promise of a better world through legitimizing institutions of win-lose violence. Communism is a pseudo-science based on faith in the superiority and rectitude of the win-lose paradigm: *For us to gain, they must lose through force or fraud.* Where respected people have *a priori* faith in the equity and efficacy of the win-lose paradigm as their esteemed model for religious or political gain, the consequences are destructive at best, and catastrophic at worst.

To reiterate, whether people's paradigms of social superiority are Communistic, Fascistic, atheistic, Hinduistic, Islamic, Judaic, or Christian, it is impossible to attain the win-win ends of nonviolence through the win-lose means of violence. This lesson in social causality must be understood by our contemporaries and by our progeny, if we are to escape the peril of human annihilation by human hands.

∾

In the summer of 2007, two American university professors doing social research in Russia conducted a poll they named, "The Putin Generation: The Political Views of Russia's Youth." The poll included 1,802 Russian respondents, and was carried out by the Levada Analytical Center in Moscow, founded by Russian sociologist, Yuri Levada. Since its inception, the center has earned commendation in the West for its unbiased research—and condemnation in the East by Kremlin authorities for the same objective studies that revealed many destructive effects of Communist coercion.

Pollsters found that among Russian youth, aged sixteen to nineteen, when asked if Stalin was a "wise leader," half the respondents agreed that he was. Moreover, among the entire 1,802 respondents, "Fifty-four percent agreed that Stalin did more good than bad," and "Forty-six percent *disagreed* with the statement that Stalin was a cruel tyrant."[64] Part of the explanation for such widespread delusion among Russia's youth is that their Communist school systems have ignored, covered up, or whitewashed the bloody history of Communist tyranny throughout the Soviet Union.

Since Mikhail Gorbachev's 1985 *glasnost* that, for the first time in Soviet history, allowed open discussion of the efficacy of Soviet Communism, the Russian commissars have reduced the violence of their iron rule as a police state. A prime reason to reduce the scale of human servitude imposed by Communism—through allowing greater freedom of exchange—is that political tyranny is always counterproductive, especially where the aim is to create national prosperity. Yet, even with the greater freedom advanced by glasnost, the win-lose paradigm remains a strong doctrine of faith among Russians who would restore Russia to its former glory as a super state to be feared by everyone.

Whether people's *a priori* faith is political or religious, where true believers with good minds and educations orchestrate and participate in the murder of millions of their fellow humans, as have religious and political leaders, they harbor a steadfast belief that they are doing the right thing. Deluded by their faith in the Win-Lose Principle, and many other spurious and flawed models of social causality, they don't know what they are doing and, thereby, they will fail to reach their pretentious aims for a better world.

Again, those who know what they are doing are not busy organizing the murder of millions, or thousands, or hundreds of their fellow humans for spurning their revered models of causality. Indeed, knowing causation, they would not even punish one lone dissenter for refusing to be a cog in the tools of tyranny.

J. Stuart Mill, in his essay *On Liberty,* gave us this timeless principle of win-win justice to follow, "If all mankind minus one were of one opinion, and only one person were of the contrary opinion, mankind would be no more justified in silencing that one person, than he, if he had the power, would be justified in silencing mankind."[65]

∽

The great problem-solving principles of nature are rarely obvious to anyone. Galileo's observation of his Law of Falling Bodies, that both heavy and light objects fall at the same rate in a free fall, is not an obvious principle of nature. If it were obvious, someone else long before Galileo would have discovered it. What seemed obvious was Aristotle's imagination that heavy objects fall faster than light objects. However, as a method for discovering natural principles, Aristotle's *imagination* of "natural law" could not match Galileo's *observation* of natural law.

The scientific revolution toward discovering true principles of nature was set in motion by the paradigm shift away from *imagining* principles toward *observing* principles. (In trying to understand causality, the superiority of observation over imagination is not obvious, either.) Precisely because principles of nature—whether physical, biological, or social—are not conspicuous even to most careful observers, their operation must be carefully explained to those who are curious enough to want to understand them. Unfortunately, principles of nature only become obvious to us after we first understand them. Here is another social principle that is not obvious:

> *Operation of the win-lose principle creates the least wealth and freedom for the greatest number.*

Whether the motivation for imposing the Win-Lose Principle stems from religious faith or from political faith, the negative effects are predictable. It does not matter when or where the Win-Lose Principle is imposed. The results will be less wealth and less freedom for people to enjoy, and more poverty and more servitude to diminish their satisfaction of life. Observation of social exchange reveals that to accept the Win-Lose Principle as the overarching paradigm of social causality is to accept a false model of reality that wreaks social havoc wherever it is enforced.

The alternative to applying the Win-Lose Principle is to apply the Win-Win Principle. Again, a prime reason to apply the latter principle was explained by this social generalization: *Operation of the win-win principle creates the greatest wealth and freedom for the greatest number.*

This is an observational falsification of collectivist social schemes. In their spurious dogma, they offer faithful followers the "good life" or the "greatest good for the greatest number," through the enforcement of one win-lose decree or another. Such social schemes include win-lose Communism, win-lose Fascism, win-lose socialism, win-lose monarchy, and win-lose theocracy.

As will be shown in later chapters, the only practical alternative to these coercive schemes is to follow and apply the Win-Win Principle: *Always seek gain through the gain of others, and never seek gain through the loss of others by force or fraud.* This principle is elegant in its simplicity, ethical in its morality, equitable in its fairness, and practical in its utility.

ENDNOTES

59. Hazel Henderson, *Building a Win-Win World: Life beyond Global Economic Warfare* (San Francisco: Berrett-Koehler Publishers, 1996).

60. John Donne, *The Works of John Donne*, vol. 3, ed. Henry Alford, (London: John W. Parker, 1839), 574-575. See *Devotions upon Emergent Occasions*, Meditation XVII, 1624.

61. Mao Ze-dong, *Selected Works*, vol. 2, 1954, 272. Chairman Mao delivered his dictum during the final speech at the Sixth Plenary Session of the Central Committee of the Communist Party, China on Nov. 6, 1938. See *Respectfully Quoted: A Dictionary of Quotations*, ed. Suzy Platt (New York: Barnes & Noble, 1993), 271. This is one of Mao's most quoted political aphorisms; it

was repeated by him at various places and times, and as early as 1927.

62. R. J. Rummel updated in 2006 (from his statistics of 1996 in *Death by Government*) the fatal statistics for the number of Asians — mandated by Mao to be murdered throughout China — from 38,000,000 to 77,000,000. This increase was after Rummel included Mao's forced famine of 1958-1962, which led to premeditated mass murder by starvation and privation. See Prof. Rummel's Web site at http://www.hawaii.edu/powerkills/ (Accessed July 8, 2010)

63. R. J. Rummel, *Death by Government* (New Brunswick, New Jersey: Transaction Publishers, 1994), 8.

64. "Russian Youth: Stalin Good, Migrants Must Go: Poll," *New York Times*, Jul. 25, 2007. http://www.reuters.com/article/idUSL2559010520070725. (Accessed September 19, 2010)

65. John Stuart Mill, *On Liberty*, chap II, (Malden, MA: Blackwell Publishing Ltd, 2003), 100.

Chapter Five

The Superiority Syndrome

Whether yesterday's Christians were burning heretics, or today's Muslims are bombing infidels, such deadly actions are incited by pious believers who hold a deep faith in the superiority of their religion. Belief in the absolute truth of their theology leads the faithful to allow their human actions to be dominated by their "superiority syndrome."

A syndrome is a repeating pattern of symptoms that together indicate and characterize a specific pathological disorder or disease. This familiar medical term comes from the Greek *syndromê*, meaning a concurrence of symptoms. Those who harbor a superiority syndrome reveal their symptoms through an unending concurrence and consensus that they must act on the conviction that their paradigms of social causality are superior to all others. Whether these models of cause-and-effect are based on religious or political superiority, such believers have proven their potential to impose great harm upon their fellow humans. By sanctifying and legitimizing institutions of coercion to impose their "superior" models of absolute truth upon others, they have incited the most sinister of social crises throughout human history. Through their win-lose actions, they have shown that they are capable of committing any crime and any atrocity to reach their religious or political aims.

In explaining this repeating symptom of win-lose behavior, it is important to emphasize that nature has not saddled humans with coercive character traits; rather, humans have saddled themselves with coercive paradigms of causality. Believing win-lose paradigms to be true, and driven by their superiority syndrome, they are certain that for them to gain, those with inferior creeds must be forced to lose.

The social tragedies of every age were largely instigated by sincere people of influence who adopted false doctrines of causality as if they were true. In reaching for religious or political aims, those who committed crimes against humanity were deluded by their faulty grasp of social causation. This delusion continues today among educated and uneducated adults who adopt false paradigms of causality — usually by default, without observational analysis to verify their truth.

The most deadly paradigms praise the merit of seizing wealth and freedom for some "superior cause" — some "greater good." The superiority syndrome sets the stage for those who would seek laudable ends by way of atrocious means. In aiming for superior goals based on supreme truth, true believers have justified and glorified religious and political oppression of disbelievers. But the only "crime" of disbelievers was to ignore or reject the authoritarian dogma of the believers.

෬

The Old Testament of the Judeo-Christian Bible glorifies a win-lose theology that gives rise to the *superiority syndrome*.

Many of its chapters sanction win-lose gain through institutional force. In I Samuel, Chapter 15, God orders King Saul of Israel to take violent action against those who have offended the Israelites.

> This is what the Lord Almighty says: Now go, attack the Amalekites and totally destroy everything that belongs to them; do not spare them, put to death men and women, children and infants (I Samuel 15:2-3).

How will Saul carry out God's command to annihilate the Amalekites? Scripture says, "King Saul summoned the men and mustered them at Telaim [in Biblical Palestine]—two hundred thousand foot soldiers and ten thousand men from Judah." Like earlier armies of antiquity, Saul's soldiers were carefully trained to kill on command. Their training was funded through political seizure of wealth and freedom from the Israelites by King Saul's win-lose government. Saul's attack on the Amalekites was commanded by a win-lose god, sanctioned by a win-lose religion, and funded by a win-lose government. Through Saul's victory, the Amalekites suffered a catastrophic loss. Scripture says Saul took the "king of the Amalekites alive, all his people he totally destroyed with the sword" (I Samuel 15:8). Men, women, children, and infants were struck down by the Israelites—God's warriors for win-lose gain.

The slaughter was justified by win-lose theology: *For Israelites to gain, Amalekites must be forced to lose.* Like the one true god of the Qur'ān, the one true god of the Old Testament is a win-lose deity. He demands his followers to seize people's wealth and freedom for win-lose gain. These Holy Scriptures portray God as a supernatural deity in pursuit of win-lose gain. He implores, he commands, his children to seize the spoils of victory through their neighbor's coercive loss. In brief, for God to gain, for his favored followers to gain, the un-favored unbelievers must be forced to lose. The faithful are continually warned to be wary of the wrath of God and obey his divine commands without questioning their equity and morality.

Whatever the reason or justification for coercive action, coercion always ignites destructive domino effects. The laws of cause-and-effect operate as a constant in every human era. Whether in Biblical times, or now, god acts either as a win-win deity for mutual gain, or as a win-lose deity for coercive gain. Those who revere a win-lose god are inclined to obey his commands by taking win-lose action for coercive gain. In contrast, those who revere a win-win god are inclined to obey his commands by taking win-win action for mutual gain. As always, the difference in the social impact is dramatic. Organizing for win-lose gain fosters war, poverty, and servitude that few will enjoy. "It's the law," a law of nature with predictable results. In diametric opposition, organizing for win-win gain fosters common peace, prosperity, and freedom for common people to enjoy. It, too, is a repeating law of nature with predictable effects.

We should not be surprised to learn that as the laws of nature arrange universal order, "Ignorance of the law is no excuse." Those who would repeal or change the laws of nature, or who would merely ignore them, will suffer poor results at best, and ruination at worst. Nature rules by enforcing natural law. In the end, there is little margin for human error. If we do not obey the laws of nature, the penalties are severe. We will fail to adapt to our environment.

The dramatic evidence of natural history shows that any species failing to adapt to its environment will perish. Humans are not immune to this law. There is no escape from its operation and enforcement. If humans "don't get it," the laws of nature will neither bend nor buckle to serve human ignorance and stupidity.

In Genesis 22, God asked the founder and patriarch of the Hebrew people, Abraham, to murder his son. God was eager to judge Abraham's resolve to follow, without question, his divine instructions. Scripture says, "God tested Abraham. He said to him...'Take your son, your only son, Isaac, whom you love, and go to the region of Moriah. Sacrifice him there as a burnt offering on one of the mountains I will tell you about.'"

On reaching the mountain, as God had directed, Abraham built an altar to sacrifice his son to God. Scripture says that a submissive Abraham "bound his son Isaac and laid him on the altar, on top of the wood. Then he reached out and took the knife to slay his son." However, before Abraham could kill Isaac, an angel cried out, "Do not lay a hand on the boy."

What can we make of this? Even if we do not question the equity and morality of this fearful trial of Abraham's faith, a key issue remains. Any god who would test the allegiance of a loyal follower by asking him to kill his only son (or *any* son) to prove and affirm his loyalty, at the very least, is a win-lose god: *For God to gain, Abraham and Isaac must lose.*

Scripture leads readers to surmise that if that angel had not interceded at the very last moment, Abraham would have stabbed his son to death — however many stabs it might have taken — and incinerated his body on God's behalf. Yet, any father who has faith in the rightness of killing his own child — whatever the source of his faith — is taking a grave risk. What if his paradigms of rightness are flawed? What if they are irrational and immoral? God has required a devoted follower to dramatize his loyalty by taking win-lose action against his own son. Whether or not this is a moral issue, for a father to murder his son for any reason, is this not the ultimate paternal betrayal?

To gain God's blessing, Abraham must cause his own loss by killing his own son. If your paradigms of faith can lead you to kill your own child "in cold blood," such inflexible faith can lead you to commit any crime.* This is one of many horrid examples of win-lose theology. It provokes true believers to commit atrocities against innocent people on behalf of the Almighty. On the other hand, if Abraham had been a fearless father, he might have answered God, "I will never betray my son to prove my loyalty to you. My loyalty is steadfast. You are imploring me to commit an outrageous crime — the murder of my own son. To commit such an evil deed cannot be justified without making a mockery of divine justice."

༄

To gain a deeper understanding of how to optimize the causes of peace, prosperity, and freedom, it is necessary to understand what optimizes the causes of war, poverty, and servitude. This leads to the question, is there a generalization that is contrary to the Principle of Win-Win Exchange? There is, indeed, an opposing principle, one that we can also observe as a reliable predictor of the social effects of win-lose exchange.

PRINCIPLE OF WIN-LOSE EXCHANGE
Win-lose exchange seizes wealth, expands servitude, and fosters war.

---

* In earlier times, it was believed that if your blood was "hot," then you were out of control. But if your blood was "cold," then you were in control of your actions. Hence, "cold blooded murder" was controlled, premeditated murder.

Institutionalizing win-lose seizure of wealth for religious or political gain advances poverty by decreasing productivity and increasing the scarcity of goods and services. The more win-lose exchange, the more poverty! *Poverty is a byproduct of win-lose exchange.* Moreover, win-lose exchange imposes involuntary servitude by forcing some people to serve other people against their will. We can observe that all involuntary servants are "un-free." Even as their masters, from their seats of authority, trumpet the "liberty" and "freedom" of their involuntary servants, the contradiction is blatant. Observation reveals that it is impossible to be *free* and *un-free* at the same time. The more win-lose exchange, the more servitude. *Human servitude is a byproduct of win-lose exchange.* Furthermore, win-lose exchange fosters and imposes the conflicts of war. We can also see that coercive exchange is un-peaceful exchange due to its belligerent and bellicose nature. The more win-lose exchange, the more warfare! *Warfare is a byproduct of win-lose exchange.* These fatal effects of the Principle of Win-Lose Exchange can be seen by anyone willing to look.

These principles of win-win and win-lose exchange are essential guides to our understanding of social causality. They reveal which social causes lead to which social effects. Whether the arrest of peace, prosperity, and freedom through religious and political force is praised or not, sanctioned or not, such win-lose coercion advances war, poverty and servitude. In other words, by contracting peace, prosperity, and freedom by legitimizing coercion for win-lose gain at gunpoint, the expansion of war, poverty, and servitude is an inevitable conclusion.

∽

The perpetuation and expansion of compulsory or involuntary servitude always suppresses the incentive of involuntary servants to create new wealth and freedom. As the incentive to create wealth and freedom falls, so the total generation of wealth and freedom falls. One win-lose effect is observable.

Where wealth and freedom per capita fall, poverty and servitude per capita rise.

Win-lose theology glorifies, deifies, and legitimizes the seizure of wealth and freedom for religious gain. In justifying such coercion, it is said that this is the holy path to religious monopoly and hegemony — a path that was ordained by God in Holy Scripture. Nonetheless, whatever excuses are proffered to justify win-lose gain, there is no escaping the law of cause-and-effect. The win-lose domino effects of imposing religious and political monopolies that institutionalize and legitimize seizure of wealth and freedom will spur the spread of war, poverty, and servitude. Such organized theft provokes the social ills that may bring about the demise of *Homo sapiens*. For humans, there can be no greater loss.

It cannot be overstressed, the imaginary and fallacious belief that for us to gain, they must be forced to lose — in whatever theological or political variation it may take — is humankind's deadliest paradigm. It provoked the surprise attack by Islamist terrorists on New York and Washington that killed three thousand men and women on September 11, 2001. The terrorist strike on the World Trade Center was premeditated murder. Innocent victims were planned targets of win-lose theology. For Muslims to gain, infidels — disbelievers in their one true god — must be forced to lose. Yet, in the eyes of the terrorists, it was not murder, but a heroic defense of Islamic superiority over all other religions.

The superiority syndrome of Muslim terrorists became their holy warrant of violence against their inferiors, against all disbelievers in the primacy of their one true god.

∞

On a much larger scale, in World War II Germany, the win-lose paradigm coupled with the superiority syndrome led to the institutionalized murder of six-million Jews through the admixture of win-lose theology and win-lose politics. In German history, there was much win-lose theology that damned the Jews as inferior people and blamed them for the crucifixion of Jesus. German founder of the Reformation and Christian Protestantism, Martin Luther railed, "Jews and papists are ungodly wretches, they are two stockings made of one piece of cloth."[66]

This German tradition of win-lose theology supported anti-Semitism. It made it easy for the Reich Minister of Public Enlightenment and Propaganda, Joseph Goebbels (1897-1945), to sell the German people on the false doctrine: *For Aryan Germans to gain, Semitic Jews must be forced to lose.* Goebbels originated and instigated powerful propaganda techniques, used with great success to advance legalized tyranny in democratic Germany. During a speech to the German Press Association, October 4, 1933, Goebbels disclosed one of his key political policies in declaring, "Any sovereign state has the right at least to monitor, if not exactly to control, the formation of public opinion to ensure that it does not become a potential danger to the state, the nation, and the common good."[67]

As a fluent propagandist extolling the alleged efficacy of totalitarian coercion, and the glory of expanding German hegemony through violent means, the win-lose propaganda of Goebbels was remarkable for its scale of influence in controlling "the formation of public opinion." In the short run, Nazi propaganda swayed most of the German people to accept its false models of social causality as true. However, eventually all false models of social causality fail to meet their promised ends. One of those lofty promises was that National Socialism would build a "thousand-year Reich" of German supremacy and prosperity. But since the tyranny of the Third Reich lasted for only a dozen years, the Nazi promise of a thousand-year reign fell short of the promise by 988 years.

Widespread faith in the truth and equity of Nazi propaganda, without critical analysis, led to the destruction of the Third Reich and much of Europe as well. Again, where respected people have faith in the merit of the win-lose paradigm, and act accordingly, many bad things will happen to many good people. In the end, unbridled faith in the truth of false models of social causality—embraced by both educated and uneducated Germans—led to the rapid decline and fall of their revered civilization of Teutonic supremacy and Aryan superiority.

∞

German sociologist Alexander Rüstow—a leading opponent of Naziism before Hitler's rise to power in 1933—summarized the anti-Semitic theme of Luther's 1543 pamphlet, *Of the Jews and Their Lies*. For Jews not baptized in the Protestant faith, Luther "demands destruction of their synagogues and houses, expropriation and heavy forced labor, indeed complete expulsion from the country."[68] According to Luther's original German text, the Jews were to be persecuted through the agency of win-lose government. If anyone doubted the authority of such government, Luther called on the even greater authority of St. Paul who wrote in Romans 13:1.

> Everyone must submit himself to the governing authorities, for there is no authority except that which God has established. The authorities that exist have been established by God.[69]

In other words, wherever government authorities are persecuting innocent victims for political gain, God ordains such governmental coercion. By 1933, this would even include the Nazi authorities—"established by God"—according to St. Paul. Editors of the widely acclaimed *Zondervan NIV Study Bible* sustained Paul's position in explaining, "Even the possibility of a persecuting state did not shake Paul's conviction that civil government is ordained by God."[70]

Luther was an earnest supporter and promulgator of a win-lose society dominated by coercive institutions of religion and government. Furthermore, Luther openly declared the sanctity of feudal slavery, made necessary as he claimed by the natural "inequality" of man:

> An earthly kingdom cannot exist without inequality of persons. Some must be free, some serfs, some rulers, some subjects.[71]

Luther's "earthly kingdom" was a win-lose society where for freemen to gain, their serfs must be forced to lose; and for rulers to gain, their subjects must be forced to lose. Rüstow concluded, "The majority of the German people between 1933 and 1945 conducted themselves in accordance with this teaching of Luther's, which had become a deeply ingrained part of their heritage."[72] Indeed, Germans had a long "heritage" of win-lose theology in support of coercive government. Eventually this deadly combination of win-lose ideology led to the orchestrated murder by German authorities during World War II of over twenty million Europeans (excluding battlefield casualties) of which six million were Jews.*

The Nazi paradigm alleges that for Aryan Germans to gain, Semitic Jews must be forced to lose. Yet, had Aryans traded with the Jews instead of stealing from the Jews, they would have created more new wealth for Aryans to enjoy than all the old wealth that was stolen. The laws of social causality determine such social effects.

The promise of Nazi Fascism that win-lose exchange would bring prosperity to the German people was entirely false. Whether in Germany or anywhere else, the harmful consequences of organizing coercion for win-lose exchange are predictable. Their destructive effects can be observed and generalized as a social principle: *Win-lose exchange decreases old wealth, increases new poverty, and increases new servitude.* In sharp contrast, *Win-win exchange increases new wealth, increases new prosperity, and increases new freedom.*

It is not enough, however, for good people with good minds to be against Naziism or any other brand of state Fascism. If they do not understand the social model of Fascism — especially the win-lose coercion upon which it stands — they are always vulnerable to welcoming and embracing neo-Fascism under a different banner. To be sure, the seductive slogans and alluring symbols may ring new, but this win-lose model of society is old and unworkable. Today, in the West, nearly all educated people, if you ask them, would denounce Naziism in a heartbeat. Yet, many of the

---

* For statistical details on quantifying the magnitude of these fatalities, see R. J. Rummel's *Death by Government* (New Brunswick, New Jersey: Transaction Publishers, 1994). While a professor at University of Hawaii, Rummel directed intensive research that separated battlefield casualties from deaths due to outright murder by governmental authorities. Rummel showed that in the twentieth century, institutionalized murders by win-lose governments eclipsed the number of battlefield casualties by a significant margin.

same people embrace National Socialism (of course, under different names) as their revered model of social causality. The internal contradiction is large; National Socialism was the coercive soul of Naziism. *Nazi* is the abbreviated name for the Fascist political party: *Nationalsozialistische Deutsche Arbeiter-Partei*, which translates in English to National Socialists German Workers' Party.

The laws of social causality falsify the Nazi doctrine that for Aryans to gain, Jews must be forced lose. Moreover, these natural laws falsify all win-lose policies that may assure the people with eloquence and passion: *For us to gain, they must be forced to lose.* In the twenty-first century, decent people can no longer afford to be seduced and deluded by coercive policies that trumpet the "rightness" and "worthiness" of win-lose violence for religious and political gain.

Another social fallacy that led to the legalized murder of European Jews is the "static pie" or "fixed pie" fallacy. It has incited much coercive mischief throughout the world. The static pie fallacy presumes that the world's wealth is static, that it is fixed in size like a lone pie. Therefore, to gain your fair slice of pie, you have to appropriate it—steal it—either legally or illegally.

Where Jews were perceived to have more than their "fair share" of wealth, their wealth was targeted for confiscation by Nazi authorities. However, the static pie fallacy ignores observation. To reiterate, through the creative power of win-win exchange, more new wealth can be created than can ever be stolen through win-lose exchange—from the Jews or from anyone else.

The *superiority syndrome* led to wide acceptance in Germany of the Nazi paradigm of Aryan supremacy. It said that for the superior Aryans to gain, the inferior Jews must be forced to lose. However, this false paradigm lacked any evidential merit. It was no more true than the medieval paradigm that for righteous Christians to gain, those unrighteous witches—the ones spreading the plague—must be forced to lose.

ꙮ

The Roman Catholic Church founded the notorious Holy Office of the Inquisition in the thirteenth century to put on trial those accused of heresy. Although the noun "heretic" may have a contemptible ring for many, so-called heretics merely held different beliefs on religious doctrine than did religious authorities. English philosopher, Thomas Hobbes, described the "crime" of heresy in these few words, "They that approve a private opinion, call it opinion; but they that dislike it, heresy; and yet heresy signifies no more than private opinion." [73]

Court trials for heresy commonly involved torturing the accused into confessing their heresies, followed by execution of those convicted of the alleged crime. Italian philosopher, esteemed intellectual of the Church in Rome, and the most influential theologian of the Middle Ages, Thomas Aquinas, justified the institutionalized hunt for heretics, "If forgers and other malefactors are put to death by the secular power, there is much more reason for excommunicating and even putting to death one convicted of heresy." [74] In short, the theology of St. Thomas espoused the tyranny of win-lose religion: *For believing Christians to gain, disbelieving heretics must be forced to lose.*

In other words, Church authorities asserted that you must believe in our vision of the Creation and its lone Creator, who in his infinite wisdom has shown all men the sole path to Salvation—or we will kill you in the name of our Lord Jesus. In Christian history, this was the summit of win-lose theology.

ꙮ

The Catholic Church was not without its Christian critics, many of whom claimed that church leadership was
heretical at best and satanic at worst. Luther railed that the
pope was "the devil in disguise."[75] By the sixteenth century,
there was a grand opportunity for protestors to reform the
Roman Catholic Church beyond Rome, especially by ending
the criminal cruelty of the Holy Inquisition in its persecution of so-called witches and heretics. But famed reform-
ers of the Roman Church such as Martin Luther and John
Calvin were not about to give up their win-lose theology.
They introduced their own holy inquisitions in search of
disbelievers in the superiority of their new Protestantism,
a movement that grew in protest of some of the win-lose
theology of Roman Catholicism. Deplorably, and without
shame, their own win-lose theology demanded: *For Protestants to gain, Catholics, heretics, witches, and Jews must be forced
to lose.* Martin Luther revealed his intolerance and hatred of
heretics in declaring,

> Heretics are not to be disputed with, but to be con-
> demned unheard and whilst they perish by fire.[76]

Luther was adamant; he threatened to burn all heretics
at the stake for the alleged crime of rejecting his Protestant
vision of the only true doctrine of Christian faith. He warned
the accused not to defend themselves against charges of heresy because their accusers would not listen. There was nothing to dispute. To be accused of heresy was to be guilty of
heresy. According to Luther, all heretics deserved to "perish
by fire."

There is no more vile and iniquitous crime against humanity than when pious people—rendered "holier than thou" by
their superiority syndrome—ritualize and glorify the murder of their fellow humans. For what "divine" purpose did
Christian leaders murder their neighbors? They were killed

for their alleged *disbelief* in the claimed truth of religious doctrines based on imagination of spiritual causality.

In Geneva, Protestant theologian John Calvin was busy laying the foundations of Presbyterianism; a church governed by elders known as presbyters. But Calvin was also busy practicing win-lose theology by burning heretics at the stake and setting new standards of religious cruelty. One victim of Calvin's new win-lose theology was Spanish physician, Miguel Servetus (A.D. 1511-1553), who set forth in his "heretical" writings a nearly correct explanation of human circulation of blood. This was three quarters of a century before Galileo's student, William Harvey, published, in 1628, the complete picture of human circulation.

The prime heresy of Servetus was to argue for the unity of one god (Unitarianism) that dismissed the Christian Trinity of a three-person god in the form of the Father, the Son, and the Holy Ghost. For Calvin, this heresy was unforgivable. His instruction to the executioner was clear. Servetus would not be allowed a quick death. Thus, in 1553, Dr. Servetus was slowly roasted over flames, fueled by his own writings, deemed heretical by Calvin.[77] Through the tireless efforts of John Calvin, win-lose theology and Protestant brutality were alive and well in Geneva.

In view of the merciful and equitable justice of Jesus, we must pose this question. What tenable excuse, what acceptable apology for inflicting such vicious cruelty against defenseless dissenters could ever be raised? "Heresy" was nothing more than an expression of disbelief in the absolute trueness and sanctity of theocratic authority. What argument could ever mitigate the magnitude of the horrific crimes that these religious icons unleashed without mercy against their hapless victims? The question should answer itself. Unless the teachings of Jesus are entirely abandoned, there is no tenable excuse, no acceptable apology for such blatant and abominable atrocities in pursuit of religious monopoly and hegemony.

∽

Across the Atlantic in the Americas, the win-lose religion that was brought to the New World by Spanish, French, English, Portuguese, and Dutch explorers and settlers doomed the indigenous natives. Those who were not killed by the vicissitudes of European crowd diseases, such as smallpox and measles, were at great risk of being killed by European swords and guns. From the view of European Christians, American natives were heathens—inferior unbelievers—whose demise was no great loss.

The earliest settlers of the Western Hemisphere had arrived in various migrational waves many thousands of years before Italian navigator, Christopher Columbus, and his Spanish sponsor, Queen Isabella of Castile, were born. Professor Jared Diamond of the University of California at Los Angeles stressed that, "For the New World as a whole, the Indian population decline in the century or two following Columbus's arrival is estimated to have been as large as 95%."[78]

Not long after the North American landing of Columbus in 1492, Christians began enslaving even the most friendly and generous "heathens" of the New World. The notorious slave trade—arguably the vilest institution of human history—is sanctioned by the Holy Bible in Leviticus 25:44: "Your male and female slaves are to come from the nations around you; from them you may buy slaves." Any society where you can buy and sell human slaves—where such trade is deemed honorable by religious and judicial authorities—is a win-lose society dominated by lawful persecution and violence against innocent victims of coercive gain.

Slavery is further condoned and encouraged by the central author of Christian theology, St. Paul, who warned, "Slaves, obey your earthly masters with respect and fear, and with sincerity of heart" (Ephesians 6:5). In short: Slaves, obey your slave masters! Clearly, a theology that furthers the enslavement of humans by their fellow humans is a win-lose theology: *For masters to gain, their slaves must be forced to lose.*

It is not overstatement to note that the attacks upon and enslavement of New World natives by European Christians was tantamount to genocide. Indigenous natives — mocked as so-called heathens for their un-Christian and uncultured ways — became victims of a win-lose Christianity that was driven by the superiority syndrome of its promoters: *For superior Christians to gain, inferior heathens must be forced to lose.* Again, in benign contrast, Jesus who taught and practiced the principle of "love thy neighbor as thyself," never would have condoned such blatant atrocities on the part of his Christian followers.

∾

In January 1869, General Philip Henry Sheridan was at Fort Cobb, Oklahoma, in conversation with a Comanche chief who distinguished himself from other natives by declaring, "Me good Indian." Without hesitation, Gen. Sheridan replied, "The only good Indians I ever saw were dead."[79] Sheridan later denied making this bitter slur, although witnesses recalled that he had. On the frontier, this well-known barb was commonly phrased as, "The only good Indian is a dead Indian." In any case, it conveyed the sentiments of a great many Americans in the nineteenth century who were nearly all Christians of European heritage with full confidence in their superiority to the indigenous natives.

The superiority syndrome—especially among theologians, politicians and their followers—led to tragic consequences for American Indians. Civil War scholars have noted that after the war, federal troops played the central role in massacring Indians who refused to be banished to the submarginal lands of federal reservations. In short, Native Americans became victims of win-lose government sanctioned by win-lose Christianity.

The final massacre of indigenous people by the U.S. Cavalry took place on January 29, 1890 at Wounded Knee, South Dakota, with the slaughter of some 150 to 300 men, women, and children of the Lakota tribe. Of course, there was little sympathy for their plight. After all, the Lakota and other Indian tribes were seen as an inferior race of people who were completely lacking in the civility and sophistication that came with European culture, Christian tradition, and white supremacy. Riflemen of the U.S. Calvary were certain that slaying Indians—who were entirely outmatched by the weaponry and logistics of federal troops—was a just and honorable thing to do.

Gen. Sheridan's military superior was Gen. William Tecumseh Sherman, who remains one of America's most honored military heroes and leaders. At the main entrance to Central Park in New York City, an imposing Gen Sherman rides a gilded bronze stallion, fashioned by the illustrious sculptor, Augustus Saint-Gaudens.

Sherman's strategy on how to deal with Native Americans was explicit and blunt in this telegram dispatch of 1866 to commanding general of the federal army, Ulysses S. Grant.

> We must act with vindictive earnestness against the Sioux [Nation], even to their extermination, men, women, and children. Nothing less will reach the root of the case.[80]

Sherman's genocidal policy of exterminating the American Indians was well received by the majority of cavalry officers and men who were ordered by federal authorities to force the Indians onto federal reservations, whether they liked it or not. If they resisted forced deportation from their homelands of more than 15,000 thousand years (as confirmed by archeologists at Buttermilk Creek, Texas) onto the reservations, they ran the risk of being killed without mercy.

During the Civil War, Gen. Sherman's scorched earth tactics were used without restraint to force Confederate troops to surrender, or die. After the war, they were used again without restraint to force Indians onto federal reservations, or die. These policies were highly praised in the North, and Sherman might have been elected President of the United States had he chosen to run on the Republican ticket of 1884. However, he declined to be a presidential candidate with this famous rebuff to the Republican National Convention in Chicago, "I will not accept if nominated, and will not serve if elected." Unlike other famous generals in history, Sherman had no interest in political office. Moreover, he criticized the politics that led to the scandalous treatment of Indians by federal reservation authorities. At the same time, he also believed that the Plains Indians of the West and the African slaves of the South were inferior people who could not rise above their natural inferiority. In a letter to his brother-in-law, he revealed his win-lose paradigm on the efficacy of African slavery in America.

> I would not if I could modify or abolish slavery. I don't know that I would materially change the actual political relation of master and slave.[81]

Sherman goes on to justify his position, without any apparent reservations.

Negroes in the great numbers that exist here must of necessity be slaves. Theoretical notions of humanity and religion cannot shake the commercial fact that their labor is of great value and cannot be dispensed with.[82]

Deplorably, Sherman believed: *For white Christians to gain, black heathens must be forced to lose.* However, like all win-lose paradigms of social causality, this too was flawed, spurious, and untenable. Today, we have a truer understanding of social causality than was available to William Sherman in the nineteenth century. We know that the positive gains to be reaped by whites trading with blacks—instead of whites enslaving blacks—are beyond compare. The creative power of free exchange generates more peace, prosperity, and freedom for all to enjoy than can ever be gained by coercive exchange that generates war, poverty, and servitude. The institutions of human slavery fall into disuse as the paradigm, "For masters to gain, their slaves must be forced to lose," is refuted and repudiated as a false model of social causality.

Throughout the long history of human slavery, its origin was always the same: the failure of decent and indecent people to understand social causality. Observation shows that slave masters were not born to enslave their fellow humans; they were born to seek gain and avoid loss. However, because they embraced false models of social causality on mere faith—while believing them to be true—they blundered into the creation of institutions of human slavery. Yet, they never would have done so if they had known what they were doing in the first place. Just as decent and righteous people never would have used legal procedures to burn witches and heretics at the stake if they had understood causality, so too they never would have used legal procedures to force people into bonded slavery.

Before most American politicians had figured out that slavery was not good for America, most British politicians had figured out that slavery was not good for Great Britain. A generation before the outbreak of the American Civil War, the British tossed the entire institution of slavery right out of their sprawling empire. Parliament, on behalf of the British Empire and the United Kingdom, enacted the Slavery Abolition Act of 1833. Its long title says it all.

> Act for the Abolition of Slavery throughout the British Colonies; for promoting the Industry of the manumitted [freed] Slaves; and for compensating the Persons hitherto [legally] entitled to the Services of such Slaves.

The "manumitted slaves" had been freed of their shackles and their masters had been compensated in return. That was the end of slavery in the British Empire. It did not require a civil war in Great Britain to free the slaves. It would not have required a civil war in America to free the slaves either. The Civil War was not fought over whether or not to preserve slavery; it was fought over whether or not to "preserve the Union," that is, the coercive political Union between North and South.

⁊

The most catastrophic political disaster in U.S. history, one that devastated the nation, was the Civil War. It ended in 1865 with the ruination of the South by the federal armies of the North, of which Gen. Sherman's 1864 "March to the Sea" across Georgia was the most mercilessly destructive of Southern lives (including civilians) as well as Southern resources, private property, and public infrastructure.

Sherman deserves credit as an originator of modern warfare, which rains destruction on both military and civilian populations, assets, and resources without mercy as the path to total victory. By the war's end, the physical devastation was paled by the brutal death of some 620,000 Southern and Northern combatants.

In trying to cope with the magnitude of his own orchestration of human butchery on a grand scale, in July 1864, Sherman wrote to his wife, "I begin to regard the death and mangling of a couple of thousand men as a small affair, a kind of morning dash—and it may be well that we become so hardened."[83] Yet, here is a critical question to consider. If Sherman was not killing Southern soldiers to free black slaves, because, as he said, Negroes "must of necessity be slaves," then what was he doing? He was killing Southern soldiers for one prime reason. It was to preserve the federal power of the union of states to seize wealth and freedom from the American people whether they lived in the North or the South.

If the Northern politicians had allowed the Southern politicians to secede (Latin, *secedere*, to withdraw) from the Union, the political authority of the federal government would have been cut in half; its power would have been divided and diluted. With the Secession of eleven Southern states leaving the federal union, political authorities in Washington would have lost half of their political power to rule the people, collect taxes, and make war.

For Lincoln, this loss of political power was unacceptable, and it became the pressing issue of his administration. As president of the United States, Lincoln made his warning clear to Southern leaders: If they seceded from the coercive union of states, if they went their own way, they would be barred from escape by federal force of arms. Yet, how can we be sure that this does not overstate Lincoln's grand aim to preserve the Union? Because under Lincoln's authority as commander and chief of federal military forces some 260,000 Southerners were killed by Union soldiers for trying to secede, which was to leave or escape from the Union. In short, Northern leaders warned Southern leaders that if you try to leave our Union of states—a union bound together by blunt force—our military combatants will hunt you down and kill you, which is what they did.

The common belief that the Civil War was fought to free black slaves is the reigning mythology on the central cause of the conflict between North and South. This Civil War mythology, however, is clearly contradicted by President Lincoln in his own words. No one ever explained the truth of his political mission with more clarity than did Lincoln himself. In a famous letter penned by Lincoln at the Executive Mansion in Washington on August 22, 1862 to newspaper editor, Horace Greeley, of the *New York Tribune*, Lincoln clarified his political policy on Southern slavery by stressing, "As the policy I 'seem to be pursuing' as you say, I have not meant to leave any one in doubt." Indeed, Lincoln left few "in doubt" by clarifying his objective in waging the war.

> My paramount object in this struggle *is* to save the Union, and is *not* either to save or to destroy slavery. If I could save the Union without freeing *any* slave I would do it, and if I could save it by freeing *all* the slaves I would do it; and if I could save it by freeing some and leaving others alone I would also do that.

In this widely published letter of 1862, written to Greeley as the war was already in progress, note that Lincoln's own italics (above) give emphasis to his position that, "My paramount object in this struggle *is* to save the Union." As we know, *paramount*, as in "paramount object," means chief in importance and preeminent above all other objectives. The objective of the federal prosecution of the war was not to save the fettered *slaves* from human bondage, but to save the federal *Union* from loss of its political control over millions of Americans in the South.

In the end, 620,000 men and boys were slaughtered to preserve the political power, political authority, and political hegemony of the federal government. Now, nearly a century and a half after the end of the war, the great majority of educated Americans argue that the Civil War was necessary and justified. By 2011, 150 years after the start of the Civil War, some 50,000 books were published on the conflict between North and South. Nearly all Civil War historians embrace this paradigm of historical causality: *For the North to gain, the South must be forced to lose.* Moreover, around the globe, most war historians embrace the war paradigm as true: *For our nation to gain, your nation must be forced to lose.* Yet, unless this paradigm of social causality is shown to be false, spurious, and untenable, the eventual self-extermination of our endangered species would seem to be an inevitable conclusion.

If we are to preempt the proliferation of warfare and involuntary servitude among people, we must identify, clarify, and verify their necessary and essential causes. In any case, we can no longer afford the luxury of relying on either popular or esoteric mythology as our esteemed source of understanding social causality. Unless we can break our addiction to the romance of mythology, with its mythical explanations of social causality, it will continue to drag us down the road to social ruin.

∾

General Robert E. Lee surrendered his Confederate army to General U. S. Grant at Appomattox, Virginia on April 9, 1865. Only a little over a generation later, American military forces engaged in another conflict: the Spanish American

War, which ended in 1898 with the victory of the United States over Spain.

Historians have long noted that the American war against Spain was triggered and fueled in part by false propaganda against Spain. Spanish authorities were portrayed—especially in the influential New York press—as committing outrageous atrocities against their own citizens in their Caribbean colony of Cuba. These accusations, often greatly exaggerated, were spread by the so-called yellow journalism of celebrated newspaper publishers William Randolph Hurst and Joseph Pulitzer as they competed for circulation.

Through the persuasive power of propaganda, Hurst and Pulitzer aimed to elevate American nationalism and broaden acceptance of the war paradigm. The American military attack on Spanish colonies sprang from this win-lose model of political causality: *For America to gain, Spain must be forced to lose.*

In losing the war to United States forces, Spanish authorities lost control of nearly all of their colonies including Cuba, Puerto Rico, Guam, and the Philippines. After more than three centuries of Spanish colonization of their Asian settlement in the Philippine Islands, the U.S. Army wrested control from Spanish authorities. However, not everyone in America supported our political interventionism in the Philippines.

Many in the United States, especially the anti-imperialists, were against the federal government ruling any colonial empire anywhere. They argued that by annexing (seizing control by force of arms) the Philippine Islands, the United States would then become an imperial power just like those of Europe that were so abhorred by our founding fathers.

The anti-imperialists, however, lost the battle of ideas to those who believed that it was time to ignore George Washington's *Farewell Address to the People of the United States.* In his published and widely circulated *Address* of 1796,

Washington gave, as he said, his "great rule of conduct for us in regard to foreign nations." His "rule," as he called it, for federal leaders to follow was simple. He warned his successors to have "as little political connection as possible" with all "foreign nations." In brief, for America to flourish, never use federal political or military power to intervene in foreign affairs.

Washington's caution was clear: To avoid the ruin of war, avoid win-lose interference with all nations, whether near or far. However, by the end of the nineteenth century, Washington's "great rule of conduct" was largely ignored by his political successors. A growing number of American leaders had come to embrace the war paradigm. Again, it trumpets one theme: *For our nation to gain, your nation must be forced to lose.* Where decent people with good minds and educations embrace this false model of social causality as if it were true, war is a forgone conclusion. The only open question on war is when, where, for how long and, of course, what is the cost in money, devastation, fatalities, and destructive domino effects that may provoke more war, poverty, and servitude? The mythology of war stands upon imagination of causality without observation of causality.

രൂ

With the victory of federal military forces over Spain in the Spanish American War, President William McKinley was struggling over how to manage the territorial spoils of war. Should the Philippines be given the sovereignty to govern themselves, or should they be annexed and taken over by the federal government? Annexation would place the Philippine people—without their consent—under the control of American politicians. In addressing this question, President McKinley later recalled his vexation over this thorny issue.

I walked the floor of The White House night after night until midnight. I went down on my knees and prayed Almighty God for light and guidance. There was nothing left for us to do but to take them all, and to educate the Filipinos, and uplift and civilize and Christianize them.[84]

Newsweek writers in a May 7, 2007 article, "In God They Trust," were critical of McKinley's Western superiority and Protestant piety as revealed in his words above. They argued,

Never mind that most Filipinos were already Roman Catholic, or that they didn't want to be occupied. In a brutal insurgency that dragged on for three years, more than 4,000 Americans and half a million Filipinos died.[85]

Of course, it is easy to decry such horrific slaughter after the fact, but much more difficult to prevent it in the first place. Yet, one does not have to be a military historian to realize that if American politicians had not blundered into the Spanish American War, there never would have been a Philippine American War to follow. Again, it is not enough merely to "remember the past" as Santayana would have us do. We must *understand* the past. To understand our past, we must understand our human paradigms of causality that govern all social actions past and present.

Paradigms have the power to guide human action because all humans believe that their paradigms of causality are true. This means that for human progress to occur, false paradigms of causality must be replaced by those that are true. If we cannot make paradigm shifts away from false paradigms on the causes of war and peace, toward paradigms that are true, the advance of war will continue to preempt the advance of peace.

The signing of the Treaty of Paris in 1898 formalized the end of the Spanish American War. Spanish authorities surrendered their colonial possessions of Puerto Rico, Guam, and the Philippine Islands to the United States for $20,000,000. But, many Filipinos saw the Americans as foreign invaders and occupiers of their cherished homeland. Philippine resistance to American political domination of their islands led to the tragedy of the Philippine-American War. Yet, how did American politicians blunder into this war? After all, American sovereignty in North America was never threatened by the prospect of Philippine sovereignty in Asia.

McKinley spoke on behalf of a large segment of the American people in revealing his superiority syndrome and expressing his win-lose paradigms, "There was nothing left for us to do but to take them all," which meant to control them all by win-lose force. McKinley further expressed his strategy on how to "uplift" the Filipinos. It was to "educate," and to "civilize and Christianize them."

Those who had to be educated, civilized, and Christianized were perceived to be inferior by those who saw themselves as superior—because they, thank God, were educated and civilized Christians. William McKinley's superiority syndrome coupled with his win-lose paradigm was clear: *For American Protestants to gain, Filipino Catholics must be forced to lose.* Not only did half a million Filipinos lose their lives to United States' military power, many more were injured along with the usual destruction of property and the tragic bereavement of millions of those who lost their loved ones to the violence of win-lose government sanctioned by win-lose Protestantism.

꙰

If today's Christians can elevate their practice of the Golden Rule Principle so that it becomes the paramount principle of Christian truth, their rewards will surpass all experience. If Christian leaders and laity can raise their moral standards to reach the win-win tenets set forth by Jesus two thousand years ago, if they can find the discipline to practice win-win Christianity in their quest for human gain, this would be a profound advance not only for Christians, but for all humanity. Again, Donne's Principle is universal— "No man is an Island"; everyone gains from win-win Christianity founded on inviolable principles of mutually voluntary exchange that is the essence of human kindness.

Where the *sine qua non* of Christian integrity and fidelity is the Golden Rule Principle, the appalling desecration of Christianity by Christian leaders and laity becomes an iniquity of the past, where it belongs. Every Christian has the same choice: To follow win-win Christianity or win-lose Christianity. The former celebrates the benevolent teachings of Jesus; the latter desecrates them.

If the glaring violation of the moral tenets of Jesus by Christian clergy and their followers were primarily historical transgressions, it would no longer be a critical and pressing issue for Christendom. Regrettably, this is not always the case. Where, for example, the criminal abuse of children by Christian clergy goes from burning them in public in earlier times to molesting them in private in recent times, this is not an advance in the moral teachings of Jesus. The disciple Mark recalled an event where,

> People were bringing little children to Jesus to have him touch them, but the disciples rebuked them. When Jesus saw this, he was indignant. He said to them, "Let the little children come to me, and do not hinder them, for the kingdom of God belongs to such as these" (Mark 10:13-14).

If Jesus was "indignant" over "little children," of whom he said, "the kingdom of God belongs," being turned away as they clamored to be with him, how much more indignant would Jesus be at the prospect of criminal abuse by Christian clergy of innocent children and vulnerable minors? During a meeting at the Vatican in April 2002 on sex abuse within Catholic institutions in America, Pope John Paul II told the ten American cardinals convened in his private library, "People need to know that there is no place in the priesthood and religious life for those who would harm the young."[86]

The challenge for Vatican leadership has been how to protect the sacred image of the Church and at the same time discipline priests and prelates where the evidence is overwhelming that they have harmed, directly or indirectly, young people under their official care. Where priests are "disciplined" for sexual abuse of minors by reassigning them to a new parish, the risk of institutionalized harm to the new crop of minors under their sinister authority is extreme. We all know that sending the "wolf to watch over the sheep" will not bode well for the sheep. A pedophile priest, who has taken a sacred vow of celibacy, and to protect his charges from harm, but then acts on his pedophilic desires, is the proverbial "wolf in sheep's clothing." In both the Christian and the secular world, such duplicity is a flagrant fraud.

The sensational revelations of 2009 in Ireland, finally unveiled decades of sexual abuse of minors by Catholic clerics and decades of cover-ups by Catholic prelates. Pope Benedict XVI, according to Vatican authorities, said he was "deeply disturbed and distressed" by these scandals, and he expressed "his profound regret at the actions of some members of the clergy who have betrayed their solemn promise to God."[87] In 2002, similar scandals in America of sexual abuse of minors by Catholic clergy were disclosed, as well as cover-ups of these crimes by various prelates. In March 2011, "The Philadelphia archdiocese suspended 21 roman Catholic priests who were named as suspected child abusers in a scathing grand jury report." Earlier, "the grand jury named 37 priests who remained in active ministry despite credible allegations of sexual abuse."[88]

With irate response, some Catholics led by U.S. bishops vowed to establish a policy of "zero tolerance" for such criminal maltreatment. The time is critical for Catholic laity and clergy to inaugurate and secure such intolerance of sexual abuse not only in the U.S., but also in the Americas, Europe, Asia, Australia, and wherever Catholic authorities are responsible for supervising minors.

One does not have to be a psychologist to know that the mental damage to minors from molestation by those with authority over them, too often, is damage for life from which there may be no permanent escape. In America, perhaps, the three billion dollar payout since 1950 by Catholic dioceses to victims of sexual abuse by Catholic authorities will mitigate some of the psychological damage.[89]

To be sure, sex abuse of minors is not limited to Catholic or other religious institutions; it remains a problem in public schools as well as in many other nonsectarian institutions. Yet, it does not seem overly demanding to expect those who are successors of Jesus and his disciples to follow the highest moral standards of win-win Christianity.

The win-lose paradigm of social causality has many corollaries to its general theme. The iniquity of sexual abuse of minors springs from this win-lose corollary: *For a superior adult to gain sexual satisfaction, an inferior minor must lose sexual innocence through force or fraud.* For clerics or anyone else with superior authority in the Church who would act out this win-lose corollary, is this not heresy according to Roman Catholic tradition and canon? An act of heresy is committed when any baptized member of the Catholic Church willfully and persistently rejects Christian articles of faith. Their very actions are a rejection of Christian faith. Yet, whether heresy or not, anyone with only cursory knowledge of the Gospels knows that the sinister practice of this paradigm of sexual indulgence is a sacrilege and a barbarous breach of the principles of moral integrity set forth by Jesus.

Sexual abuse of minors is another example of the mischief unleashed by those who embrace the superiority syndrome: *For superiors to gain, their inferiors must be forced to lose.* This is the pedophile's paradigm of causality. When it is acted out through force or fraud, it becomes a tragedy, unleashing cascades of destructive domino effects.

❧

For those who would protect both children and adults from institutionalized harm, the challenge remains what can be done about it. As always, the question must be raised, "Is there a practical solution, one that transcends utopian idealism?"

At first blush, practical solutions to stubborn problems may sound impractical. If the elegant sophistication of a vital solution to a salient problem is not understood, beyond sounding impractical, it may even sound impossible. Moreover, it is common for effective solutions to unyielding problems to seem unexciting and tedious. For this reason, their significance may be overlooked and ignored. Indeed, the solution to the horror of institutionalized harm of both children and adults is a tedious solution. It is tedious because it calls for the same social action again and again. Tedium is sameness without end. The solution is in the hands of those who have the daring to make paradigm shifts away from respect for models of causation that condone or esteem coercion for win-lose gain. The strategy of the solution is both tedious and stirring.

The supposed truth and validity of the win-lose paradigm must continue to be exposed as a falsified and disgraced model of social causality, especially among the educated classes.

These educated classes include the clergy of all religious faiths who are among the social elite and influential members of every civilized society. As religious leaders advance their understanding of social causality, win-lose religion will fall from favor as it loses luster and prestige as a sacred, vital, ethical, and meritorious standard of faith.

ENDNOTES

66. Martin Luther, *The Table Talk of Martin Luther*, "Of the Law and the Gospel," trans. William Hazlitt, Esq., (Philadelphia: The Lutheran Publication Society, 1821), 275

67. English trans., Kermit L. Snelson. Goebbels original speech reads, "Es ist das souveräne Recht des Staates, die öffentliche Meinung, um nicht zu sagen, zu kontrollieren, so doch wenigstens in ihrer Gestaltung zu überwachen und dafür zu sorgen, dass sie nicht in Wege hineingerät, die Staat und Volk und dem Allgemeinwesen abträglich sein könnten." See http://books.google.com/books?id=_WCahx2G5kYC&pg=PA5. The most common English translation still to be found appeared in the October 16, 1933 issue of *Time* magazine: "It is the absolute right of the state to supervise the formation of public opinion." Although this is a loose translation of what Goebbels actually said, it is a clear description of his propaganda strategy and justification of his propaganda mission. See http://www.time.com/time/magazine/article/0,9171,746182-1,00.html. (URLs accessed June 30, 2011).

68. Alexander *Rüstow, Freedom and Domination: A Historical Critique of Civilization* (Princeton, New Jersey: Princeton University Press, 1980), 276.

69. Zondervan, *NIV Study Bible*, ed. Kenneth L. Barker (Grand Rapids, Michigan: Zondervan, 2002), 1766.

70. Zondervan, *NIV Study*.

71. Martin Luther, *Werke*, vol. xviii, 327.

72. Rüstow, *Freedom and Domination*, 275–276.

73. Hobbes, *Leviathan*, 79.

74. Thomas Aquinas, *Summa theologica*, vol. 2, c. 1265.

75. Martin Luther, *Riffel, Kirchengeschichte*, II, 9.

76. Luther, *Riffel*.

77. Stefan Zweig, *The Right to Heresy: Castellion against Calvin* (New York: Viking Press, 1936). See chapter five: "The Murder of Servetus," 115–136.

78. Jared Diamond, *Guns, Germs, and Steel* (New York: W. W. Norton, 1997), 211.

79. Edward S. Ellis, *The History of Our Country: From the Discovery of America to the Present Time* (Cincinnati, Ohio: Jones Brothers, 1900), 1483.

80. Robert Debs Heinl, Jr., *Dictionary of Military and Naval Quotations* (Annapolis, MD: United States Naval Institute, 1966), 155.

81. William T. Sherman, *Memoirs of William T. Sherman*, 1875 (Bloomington, IN: Indiana University, 1958). See "Letter to brother-in law."

82. Sherman, *Memoires*.

83. William T. Sherman, *Home Letters of General Sherman*, ed. by M. A. DeWolfe Howe (New York: Charles Scribner's sons, 1909), 299.

84. Evan Thomas and Andrew Romano, "In God They Trust," *Newsweek*, May 7, 2007, 35.

85. Thomas and Romano, "In God."

86. "The Pope's Speech to the American Cardinals on the Church Crisis," AP, *New York Times*, April 24, 2002, http://www.

nytimes.com/2002/04/24/national/24VTEX.html (accessed May 31, 2011).

87. "Pontiff 'distressed' by Irish Catholic abuse cases," Dec. 11, 2009, http://www.msnbc.msn.com/id/34377938/. (Accessed July 8, 2010)

88. "Catholic church suspends 21 priests suspected of child abuse," *The Guardian,* March 9, 2011. http://www.guardian.co.uk/world/2011/mar/09/catholic-church-suspends-philadelphia-priests (accessed March 22, 2011).

89. Nicole Winfield, "Pope sees sex scandal as test; bishops urge reform," April 1, 2010, http://thebulletin.us/articles/2010/04/02/top_stories/doc4bb5765610546620754718.txt. (accessed September 12, 2010).

Chapter Six

Win-Win Altruism for Win-Win Theology

We can observe that false models of causality beget false models of causality. The misguidance that they instill provokes more misguidance. Much of human history is the lethal record of misguided activists, oblivious to causation, creating social catastrophes on a grand scale—not because they were born evil or malevolent, but because they misunderstood, *which* social causes led to *which* social effects. As a result, most of the great social disasters of world history have been caused by sincere men, devout men, driven men who in their passion to reach noble aims, provoked actions that led to persecution, terror, torture, murder, slavery, and war—usually in the name of god, leader, or nation.

Where decent people aim for peace, prosperity, and freedom by taking actions that lead to war, poverty, and servitude, it is safe to say that they don't know what they are doing. Yet, if you want to incur the ire of respected people with good minds who are certain that their prized paradigms of causality are above reproach, try telling them simply, "You don't know what you are talking about, and worse than that, you don't know what you are doing."

Of course, your concern for the damage that they may cause by acting again and again on flawed models of causality as if they were true can be voiced in more scathing language—while avoiding the euphemisms that dull the truth. But regardless of your delivery—whether gentle or harsh, whether elegant or vulgar—any criticism of their paradigms of causality is unlikely to be well received. Humans tend to defend their paradigms of causality because they believe that they are true. Certain of their truth, they see no point in hearing any challenge to their credibility and validity. Furthermore, it is always easier to defend what is false, than to admit what is false.

∾

To persuade followers of any religion that their theology is not superior to all others would be a formidable challenge. Devout believers do not like anyone questioning the superiority of their religious faith. However, adopting paradigms of causality on faith alone—without any observational verification—is always risky. Religions founded on *a priori* faith in the superiority of win-lose theology continue to foment coercive action that can delete civilization. Happily, such destruction is not a foregone conclusion. Belief in one's religious superiority does not have to lead to endless calamity. A peaceful alternative is found in applying a principle of religious tolerance that vows, "Keep your religious superiority, but never use it to harm your religious inferiors." The altruistic alterative to win-lose religion is its converse.

PRINCIPLE OF WIN-WIN RELIGION
For true believers to gain, disbelievers must gain and never be forced to lose.

Those who avow and declare their religious superiority and moral integrity must *never* seek gain through the loss of others by way of force or fraud. This warning includes the crucial caution never to seek gain through the loss of even their religious inferiors—no matter how *inferior* they may seem to be. However, those who claim religious superiority may choose *not* to seek gain through the gain of their religious inferiors by simply ignoring them altogether. But they must never violate the principle of win-win religion by gaining through the loss of their inferiors, whose presumed inferiority stems from their non-belief.

Without giving up faith in their religious superiority, true believers can give up faith in their religious coercion wherever it demands gain through the loss of others. To reiterate, faithful followers must never take advantage of their religious inferiors (disbelievers, nonbelievers, and unbelievers) by seeking gain through their loss. To be sure, for those who would withdraw their sanction or end their practice of win-lose religion—and do so against the challenge of conventional wisdom—this will take daring and resolve. Both family and friends in their reach for moral integrity may very well damn them. Yet, the exercise of courage is a reward in itself where the aim is to advance win-win religion. Its peaceful practice of not harming others allows those whom they may never know to create more new wealth, and enjoy more new freedom than ever before. For this reason, win-win religion is altruistic. *Altruism is genuine concern for the welfare of others.*

For followers of win-win religion to gain, it must be an *altruistic* gain, which is gain through the gain of others. Where altruism advances mutual gain, the long-term benefits may even include saving civilization from destruction and the human race from extinction. Such universal benefits are profoundly large. The altruism of seeking mutual gain is a crucial cornerstone of moral theology in laying a foundation for win-win religion.

❧

Some intellectuals have condemned altruism and altruistic aims (most notably Russian-born American novelist and philosopher, Ayn Rand) for provoking religious and political gain for some through the loss of others. Nevertheless, practicing altruism for the welfare of others can be either constructive or destructive. This depends entirely on the strategy of altruism: is it win-win or win-lose? The win-win altruism of two-sided gain must not be confused with the win-lose altruism of one-sided gain that follows the seizure of wealth and freedom on behalf of *others* through religious or political coercion.

To confiscate wealth from the creators of wealth at gunpoint to provide homes for *others*, such as homeless indigents, is an example of win-lose altruism. Wherever there is social action for win-lose gain, no matter how righteous and noble the religious or political aim, the destructive effects are always harmful because they confiscate human wealth and freedom at gunpoint. Such harmful action is usually driven by well-meaning altruists, who cling to flawed paradigms of social causality. For religious or political reasons they may believe that for the so-called needy to gain, the un-needy (both "productive rich" and "idle rich") must be forced to lose. However "helping" others (in this case, the needy) by seizing the wealth and freedom of the un-needy is win-lose altruism. Its social effects are always counterproductive at best and catastrophic at worst. In any case, there are win-win solutions for housing people who are without shelter. These solutions avoid the involuntary servitude that is always imposed by usurping the people's wealth and freedom to fund win-lose altruism.

Legitimizing the seizure of wealth and freedom from those who have created it through win-win exchange has always been a false road to prosperity. The supposed virtue of such seizure is provoked by *a priori* acceptance on blind faith of the static pie fallacy mentioned in an earlier chapter. Where society's wealth is widely held to be static, many will believe that to gain their "fair share" of wealth, others must be forced to lose some or all of their wealth. But in a win-win society, the society's wealth is never static; rather, it is dynamic as the pie continually expands in size. The fact that your relative slice of the growing pie might get smaller and smaller means nothing, if your absolute slice gets larger and larger as the pie grows larger and larger.

❧

One crucial question is timeless because we must ask it forever, "Are our paradigms of causality true or are they false?" The question is pivotal to our well-being. One of the most dangerous risks anyone can take is to act on false models of causality while believing they are true. This usually leads to poor results at best and disastrous ones at worst. Clearly, this misidentification of causality is a serious impediment to reaching "the good life."

More than any other variable, the quality of human life is tied to the quality of human paradigms that govern human action. If they could, everyone would enjoy the good life, which for most people is a by-product of common peace, prosperity, and freedom for common people. Yet, where war, poverty, and servitude are common conditions for common people, the good life is hard to come by.

The mystery, however, of securing the good life is not an endless riddle if we can identify its true causes. Our potential to do so is determined by our success at discovering which causes lead to which effects. The truest guides to the good life are the truest models of physical, biological, and social causality.

One guide, easy to observe, is that the good life cannot be bequeathed, it cannot be given gratis to anyone. Even if your rich uncle bestows his sprawling wealth upon you with true love and affection, you still have to create your own good life. No one can do it for you. A thousand tales tell of wealthy heirs who never enjoyed the good life because they never solved its mystery. Often, they were inept at gaining two vital skills: How to manage old wealth, and more importantly, how to create new wealth. Some wasted their wealth some did not. However, in spite of their riches, many led miserable lives. What might have been the good life for "advantaged" heirs, has often turned out to be "the bad life" — very bad, indeed. Things went bad because, too often, they made too many poor choices in managing their wealth and their lives as well.

To create worthy ends such as good health, good food, a good living, or a good life, you have to know what you are doing. For all of us, we must not only understand causality, but we must take effective action on our understanding. There is no free pass to the good life. It is all about learning, learning, and more learning. But learning what? What is key, cardinal, and central to; and what is the *sine qua non* of the good life? It is so simple, it may sound sophomoric; but in truth, it is elegant in its sophistication. It is all about learning not mere facts, which have limited value at best, but *learning which specific causes lead to which specific effects.* This knowledge is crucial to finding the good life for people of all religious and political persuasion.

When we "don't get it," when we don't apply it, the laws of nature are blind to our failure and deaf to our excuses. Whatever our excuses may be, whether lame or not so lame, it does not matter. All excuses fall on deaf ears because nature is not listening. We are on our own; we must learn causality as a prelude to taking wise and effective action toward the good life. As will be seen, the only practical approach—one that works—is to create new opportunities for win-win success through mutual gain. This is the quiet engine of human progress.

Those who follow and apply the laws of causality create great potential for great success in fashioning the good life through win-win gain. To follow, however, any laws of causality, you first have to know what they are, and then learn how they operate. A far-reaching discovery of human history has thrown open the windows to surprising views of how the laws of causality operate. For many people, however, the magnitude of this discovery has been hard to grasp and appreciate. Nonetheless, this discovery is more than remarkable; it is more than phenomenal. It is a revolution in the strategy of how to detect and perceive the world around us. To say this is a lofty leap in our potential to advance in every field of human endeavor does not overstate its pragmatic significance.

A powerful method has been discovered on how to discern the world around us, which transcends all authority—including even scientific authority. It is this bold discovery:

> *Truth and reality are not only OBSERVABLE, but they are INDEPENDENTLY observable by anyone with the courage and capacity to look.*

Directly or indirectly, anyone can observe causality, with full independence from authoritarian doctrines, dogma, and of course, independence from the heavy weight of conventional wisdom. This is the crucial key to the revolution. It involves individuals acting to understand causality with the power of their own observations—observations, entirely *independent of all authority*. To be sure, some look, and some don't. Some get it, and some don't. In any case, no one is excluded from the discovery process due to ethnicity, status, or gender.

However, in spite of the priceless value of independent observation, many authorities have ignored its potential, minimized its value, or questioned its power to solve formidable problems; especially those volatile social crises that we all know can ignite disaster in a heartbeat. For many authorities on causality, this revolutionary discovery on how to find new truth in nature may appear to threaten the very prestige of their authority. Their concern is understandable. All authorities are prone to resist erosion and loss of their prestige as authoritarian leaders. In every field of expertise, they tend to defend the relevance of their authority, especially when it is questioned by their peers, or challenged by noisy nonprofessionals.

❧

Many authorities fail to realize that their power to guard the presumed truth and validity of their authority has been seriously weakened in a most fundamental way. The genie is out of the bottle; there is no turning back. To observe causality, you do not have to belong to a closed clique of scientific investigators. Observation of causality is not an exclusive affair reserved for a few insiders of privilege. It is a *democratic* process, which means the process is open to all people. Yes, there is a catch. It is only open to those willing to look. Those who will not look — for whatever reason — cannot see, but not because it is impossible to see.

The curt cliché is, "This is not rocket science." You do not have to be a scientist to get it. It is a question of choice, and you have to make one. The choice is "black or white." It is look or don't look, see or don't see, learn or don't learn.

What is there to learn here that is such a big deal? Learn what is crucial and paramount to human progress and the survival of our species; namely, learn *causality*, which is to understand which causes lead to which effects with the sway of independent validation.

Once we learn the critical importance of knowing causality, we have another choice. We can *imagine* causality, or we can *observe* causality. Again, the choice is black or white. We can act out our lives on imagination of causality, or on observation of causality. The advantage, however, of acting on observation of causality is significant: *There is far less risk of making fatal errors when acting on observation of causality, than when acting on imagination of causality.*

With the transition from ancient agrarian to modern industrial societies, such errors of causality have influenced human life in ever more destructive and deadly ways. It is the imagination of causality, which has fostered and furthered belief in the merit of the win-lose paradigm: *For us to gain, they must lose through force or fraud.*

From the earliest civilizations, faith in the merit of this paradigm has incited social catastrophes around the globe. In dramatic contrast, observation of causality has fostered and furthered belief in the merit of the win-win paradigm: *For us to gain, they must gain.* To be sure, some might ask, "Does it really matter to me which models of causality other people choose to govern their lives? So what if people adopt false models of causality while believing they are true."

Before the nuclear age, the survival of civilization and our species was not endangered by our failure to identify causality through observing the effects of human action. When acting on false explanations of causality led to unintended effects that ignited fatal social disasters, of course, this was unfortunate. Such lethal destruction, however, did not and could not have led to the worldwide loss of our species through self-extinction. The reason is simple. To reemphasize, in every nation, people had eagerly procreated faster than they could be killed through the brutality of religious and political violence. After all, people had been procreating for many thousands of years without fatal interruption. But by mid-twentieth century, all bets were off. We had reached a new age, an unprecedented era of human ability to harness and control physical power.

It was a spectacular breakthrough. Humans could now wield and employ massive destruction at will. A stunning power, long dreamed of by many, had arrived with little warning. It was the power not only to destroy civilization, but every human on earth. Of course, with the dawn of global ruination—if such a terminal "success" can finally be reached—there would be no one left to celebrate such a glorious and singular demise.

No one has ever walked away from the endless effects of the laws of nature. There is no escape from their operational presence in our lives. Whether reaching for the moon, or for the good life, we have to figure out how to get there. The steps on our journey are not negotiable because nature never negotiates. Because nature's laws are not going away, we must discover how they operate.

Again, this is not rocket science. From the micro world of families and communities, to the macro world of cities and nations, the prime principle of action for reaching the good life remains a social constant. The only workable, the only practical way to get there is to follow and apply the Golden Rule Principle: *Do not seize wealth and freedom from others, as you would have them not seize your wealth and freedom.* For those who obey this principle, eventually, good things happen to them and to others as well. Conversely and inevitably, for those who disobey the same principle, eventually, bad things happen to them and to others.

When this rule of nature—the Golden Rule Principle—is disobeyed, who are its violators? They include people who are decent and respected members of their community. They may be schooled or unschooled, intelligent or unintelligent, but in every case, they are people who have misidentified and, thereby misunderstood social causality. For this reason, the equity, utility, morality—and universal relevance—of the Golden Rule Principle cannot be over-explained, over-stressed, or over-sold. Note that it is *not* thugs, murderers, arsonists, bandits, or even deluded terrorists who have to be convinced. They are largely unreachable. Those who must be convinced to turn in their win-lose models of causality for win-win models are respected people with good minds and educations. The world follows their leadership. The question remains: Is it win-win or win-lose leadership? Those who employ the dynamic power of win-win leadership also possess the dynamic potential for taming the violence of faith.

∾

For those who have faith in the truth of religious explanations of causality, should the truth of those explanations be questioned before acting on them? What if religious doctrine demands coercive action for win-lose gain by forcing disbelievers to lose? Are such demands governed by true or by false paradigms of causality? In any case, for all religious followers, there is always a choice between the nonviolence of win-win religion and the violence of win-lose religion. Whether or not believers can separate true from false models of causality, nonetheless, they always choose their paradigms of reality, which when chosen, are always true and real to them.

Computer users know that in running their software, there are hundreds of "default settings" to change if they like. At any time, they can tweak the default settings, or scrap them altogether. Yet, even a default choice is still a choice. To default or not to default—to act or not to act are always your choices, whether the choices involve running your computer or running your life. Those who would avoid the stress and challenge of independent thinking can do so by accepting everything they believe to be true on authority. This is the "default setting" for a default life—for those who live by default alone—where truth by authority, on authority, through authority, and with authority is the rule. Where authority rules, the authorities rule human life, whether the authorities are living or dead.

Religious authority comes in two brands, win-win, or win-lose. Those who choose the authority of win-win religion over the authority of win-lose religion are following an altruistic creed for the well-being of others.

Who wins, who gains, from religious altruism? The answer can be observed—*independently*—by anyone willing to look. Directly or indirectly, everyone wins from those who seek gain through the gain of others—whether their motivation is religious or secular.

Win-win altruism is a crucial pillar of win-win theology. Jesus gave his followers this altruistic advice on how *not* to act toward others, "Do not murder, do not commit adultery, do not steal, do not give false testimony," all of which impose loss upon others for win-lose gain. Jesus reaffirmed the value of these Commandments of Moses. Moses himself quoted the Lord as saying, "Love your neighbor as yourself" (Leviticus 19:18). Then Jesus took a bold and revolutionary step by elevating the prominence of this Win-Win Principle to become the central canon of his teaching. It echoes the same five words of Moses, "Love your neighbor as yourself" (Matthew 19:18).

It is important to note, however, that Jesus did more than merely reiterate another Mosaic command to observe. He maintained there is a cardinal law of sacred action to follow; it is the salient principle, which transcends all others in its universal merit and value. What does Jesus mean by "love your neighbor?" If this cannot be defined, then the principle cannot be understood and, therefore, it cannot be followed.

Whatever Jesus meant by "love your neighbor" surely excluded hating your neighbors or harming them in any way. Love and hate are mutually exclusive. Loving your neighbors implies pursuing win-win exchanges with them, for there is no love to be found in pursuing win-lose exchanges with them. Loving your neighbors involves following the altruism of the Golden Rule Principle, which is a necessary cornerstone in the foundation of win-win theology.

Jesus emphasized the practical and spiritual benefits of win-win altruism as a governing principle for all humans regardless of their gender, culture, status, or ethnicity. Jesus taught a win-win theology founded on "love your neighbor." However, in sharp contrast to the altruism of Jesus, when God ordered King Saul to "attack the Amalekites" and "put to death men and women, children and infants" without mercy, this was the win-lose theology of a win-lose god: *For the Israelites and their god to gain, the Amalekites and their god must be forced to lose.* Clearly, the superiority syndrome of the ancient Jews of Israel violates the integrity of the principle of win-win altruism.

Centuries later, when Martin Luther demanded destruction of Jewish synagogues and houses and the expulsion of Jews from Germany, this again was win-lose religion requiring coercive action for win-lose gain: *For Protestants to gain, Jews must be forced to lose.* This time, the superiority syndrome of the Protestants violated the integrity of win-win altruism of Jesus. Alexander Rüstow noted, "Luther paved the way for National Socialism [Naziism] even as regards[to] anti-Semitism."[90]

Regrettably, the revered founder of the Protestant Reformation of Christian Catholicism, Martin Luther, was among Hitler's authoritarian sources for backing the so-called Final Solution on what to do with the millions of European Jews.

From the superior view of many intelligent Aryans educated in Germany, there were too many Jews corrupting the Fatherland and greater Europe. German authorities were certain that they had to find a resolution to this growing problem, that is, a "Final solution to the Jewish question."

The strategic plan for this Final Solution (*Die Endlösung der Judenfrage*) was confirmed at the Wannsee Villa Conference outside Berlin on January 20, 1942. Chairman Reinhard Heydrich of the SS told the assembly of state officials of the grand scale of the problem, "In the course of this Final Solution of the European Jewish problem, approximately eleven million Jews are involved."[91] Where "eleven million" Jews are said to be the "problem," the numbers are, indeed, breathtaking. Heydrich had called the meeting to confirm that these senior authorities of the German state were on board for the Final Solution. Military historian, John Keegan noted, "In the Berlin suburb of Wannsee, his [Himmler's] deputy Heydrich proposed and received authority to institutionalize the massacre of the Jews."[92] This *institutionalized* massacre was to be carried out by deporting, at gunpoint, all European Jews to concentration camps where they would either be worked to death or executed. In either case, the Jews would be exterminated. This was the core of the Final Solution.

The now infamous Gestapo officer Adolf Eichmann was recording secretary of the conference. Martin F. J. Luther was there as Under Secretary of the Reich Foreign Ministry. Of the fifteen Nazi officials, attending the Wannsee Conference, eight of them held doctoral degrees, and all fifteen were highly educated Germans with sharp, if not brilliant minds. However, we should ask that if they had all these worthy attributes — especially knowledge-power and brain-power — shouldn't this have prepared them to make capable and wise decisions concerning human affairs? And if so, then why would they even attend such a sinister gathering in the first place?" What went wrong? If this question cannot be answered with cogent clarity, this may not be the last conference for securing the administrative protocols for organized, legitimized genocide.

It is crucial to identify what went critically wrong. A dozen things did not go wrong. In fact, just one thing went critically wrong, which led directly to human error on a grand scale: educated Germans held tightly to their faith in the truth of false models of social causality, which they had accepted by default without critical analysis.

When good people of any nation or culture act on false models of social causality as if they were true, in time, bad things will inevitably happen to them. The Holocaust was one of many social catastrophes that happened because schooled people of intelligence and apparent respectability simply did not know what they were doing. Why didn't they? The answer is always the same. They failed to identify, clarify, and verify which causes lead to which effects. Yet, such failure was not peculiar to German National Socialists (Nazis). In earlier centuries, devout Christians hunted witches and heretics for one reason: they didn't know what they were doing either. Still earlier, Israelites hunted Amalekites and Midianites for one reason: these devout Jews didn't know what they were doing.

Those familiar with world history know that the Germans did not invent genocide, although the term genocide was coined in the early 1940s with them in mind. Thousands of years earlier, the ancient Israelites carried out God's own "Final Solution" in the Holy Land, which was to wipe out the hated Amalekites. God commanded the Israelites to "Go and completely destroy these wicked people, the Amalekites; make war on them until you have wiped them out" (I Samuel 15:18). As noted earlier, the Israelites carried out a complete and total wipeout of the Amalekites. God warned them, "Do not spare them, put to death men and women, children and infants"—which is what they did (I Samuel 15:3).

Some may argue that the Israelites were merely retaliating because the Lord Almighty said, "I will punish the Amalekites for what they did to Israel when they waylaid them as they came up from Egypt" (15:2). Yet, no equitable and ethical standard of justice would ever demand or condone the killing of children and infants who, by virtue of their age alone, would have been innocent of any alleged crime against the Israelites. Where people kill children to reach win-lose religious or political aims, they don't know what they are doing. How can we be sure? People who know what they are doing do not violate the Golden Rule Principle by killing innocent children and infants in the name of god, nation, or leader.

This is still the case even when the killing is deemed by many decent people to be legal, legitimate, righteous, meritorious, and virtuous, as was the genocide unleashed on the Jews by German National Socialists—as well as the genocide unleashed by the Israelites on the Amalekites and the Midianites. Also noted earlier, the Israelite genocide against the Midianites was provoked to punish them for worshiping a competing god, Baal of Peor. The Israelites unleashed genocide in the Land of Canaan to impose a religious monopoly of their one true religion fathered by their one true god. This was religious monopoly by sword point. Yet, observation shows that religious monopoly cannot be imposed without imposing religious tyranny at the same time.

To be sure, the orchestration and execution of genocide will always have its avid apologists. All institutionalized crimes for religious and political gain have had their share of defenders whose apologies rest on the overshadowing "merit" and "virtue" of some grand and glorious aim, as they see it. A common apology for genocide is to deny that such crimes even took place at all. It is said with authority that there was no genocide against the Jews of Europe. There was no genocide against the Armenians of Turkey. There was no genocide against the natives of North America — or of South America.

During the early1930s, it was said that there was no genocide against the kulaks of the Ukraine. The Moscow correspondent for the *New York Times*, Walter Duranty, wrote at the time, "There is no famine or actual starvation, nor is there likely to be." For his meritorious journalism on Ukrainian affairs, Duranty was awarded the Pulitzer Prize for his "scholarship, impartiality, sound judgment, and exceptional clarity."[93] Somehow, Duranty overlooked or ignored the Kremlin's perpetration of a planned famine in the Ukraine and the North Caucasus. The number of Ukrainian kulaks (wealthy peasants) who were carefully starved to death by their Soviet masters ranges from five to six million, which approaches the magnitude of the Holocaust.

No matter how eloquent, articulate, and sincere the apology for crimes against humanity may be such fatal crimes remain humanity's most shameful missions. Where the mission of decent people is to kill for god, nation, and leader — or to kill for god, glory, and gold, as did *el Conquistadores* in the Americas — many bad things will happen to many good people.

It is critical to note that, thus far, all major "crimes against humanity" have had a common origin. Invariably, they erupt from the legitimization, codification, and institutionalization of win-lose religion and win-lose politics for coercive gain. The more eloquent and persuasive the apologies for past crimes against humanity, the more likely they will pave the way for the explosion of such crimes in the future. Today, around the globe, many win-lose leaders and their obsequious minions are on track to transcend the greatest and grandest crimes of our inglorious past, and as always, crimes in the name of progress or some other meritorious aim. By any equitable and moral standard of social behavior, such criminality rises beyond barbarism.

It is not overstatement to note that win-lose religion has imposed—and still imposes, as in today's Middle East, as well as many other places around the globe—human tragedies of major magnitude without recourse to the victims. Because such violent theology is anchored to false paradigms of causality accepted on faith and by default without observational analysis, its paradigms must be refuted and repudiated by religious altruists who would preserve humanity from imminent self-destruction. What could be more altruistic?

∽

In applying the Win-Win Principle to theology, where there is a conflict between win-win and win-lose doctrines, always choose win-win theology over win-lose theology. Always favor the justice and kindness of a win-win exchange based on loving your neighbors over the injustice and unkindness of win-lose exchange based on harming your neighbors.

In Matthew 22:39, Jesus discloses the centerpiece of his theology in giving this overarching commandment to his followers, "Love your neighbor as yourself." To put this principle in perspective to all his teachings, Jesus declares this one of the two "greatest commandments" given to his followers.

In his sermons, Jesus did not distinguish between Jewish and gentile neighbors. However, the principle of love your neighbor has universal significance. The practice of love your neighbor requires win-win exchange, which is the creator of peace, prosperity, and freedom for Jews as well as all *gentiles*—which is everyone else.

For millennia, many Christians have enjoyed win-win success and reward from practicing the Golden Rule—people who might not have done so without their knowledge of and devotion to the teachings to Jesus. The social result has been positive with the advance of win-win Christianity for everyone's benefit, directly or indirectly. Yet, over the millennia, there have also been many Christians who failed to understand the principle of love your neighbor, or who failed to apply it to their daily actions.

The negative consequences have been large. The great social tragedies that were spawned by Christian leaders originated, in large part, from the failure of Christians to follow the revolutionary ideas of Jesus. Christians claiming to act in the name of Jesus have committed millions of atrocities against their neighbors. However, all these atrocities have violated the prime principle of social action taught by Jesus.

Nowhere is Jesus quoted by his apostles as asking his followers to "persecute your neighbors, torture your neighbors, imprison your neighbors, or kill your neighbors on my behalf." Nowhere does Jesus ask his followers to use the authority of his name to justify and glorify any harmful actions against their neighbors. Whatever theological justifications that Christians have devised to extol and glorify the persecution of their neighbors, such win-lose theology violates and desecrates the cardinal teachings of Jesus.

Surely, it is ironic that throughout Christian history, zealous Christians have advanced win-lose Christianity by defiling the very teachings of Jesus. While believing they were doing the right thing, earnest Christians have committed infamous crimes against humanity, "In the name of our Lord Jesus." To go from the fundamental Christian tenet of love thy neighbor to the diametric opposite of torture thy neighbor or murder thy neighbor raises hypocrisy to new levels of win-lose duplicity.

Even Jesus himself, along with millions before and after his time, became a victim of win-lose theology. The Pharisees and other Jewish authorities demanded the legal execution of Jesus because he preached to his apostles and followers that he was the Son of God. The Pharisees, to protect their divine authority as sole agents for Jehovah (God), and to advance their monopoly of divine truth in the Holy Land, ordered the execution of Jesus. The alleged crime of Jesus was his failure to preach the divine dogma of the Pharisees. According to Pharisaic authority, the teachings of Jesus were unauthorized heresies.

In contrast, in what Gospel does Jesus warn that if you do not believe that I am the son of Jehovah and born to teach his holy word, I will kill you, or my apostles will imprison you or my followers will torture you? By his actions and his words, Jesus was a *disbeliever* in the divinity of the Draconian justice of the Pharisees.* Moreover, nothing in the altruistic message of Jesus would condone the win-lose justice of his Christian followers who would flourish after his time.

၈๑

It is an observable truth that whatever your neighbor may believe or disbelieve on any theological subject cannot harm you. Thomas Jefferson saw this truth in noting, "It does [me] no injury for my neighbor to say there are twenty

---

* Draconian comes from Dracon (dray'kon) or Draco, a notorious lawgiver who flourished in Athens during the late seventh century B.C. He is remembered for the severity of his code of laws, which he enacted for the Athenian state. Dracon mandated the death penalty for nearly every offense—including the crime of idleness. Today, a professor of Western jurisprudence might ask the modern successors of Dracon, "Does the punishment fit the crime? Moreover, what is a 'crime' in the first place?" For example, can the disbelief in anything, whatever it may be, ever be a crime, especially in a free society? Whether in ancient times or now, where disbelief, per se, is a crime, this is the hallmark of an un-free society where tyranny reigns.

Gods, or no God. It neither picks my pocket nor breaks my leg."[94] Those who believe there is only one true god—whether they are Christians, Muslims, or Jews—cannot be harmed by anyone's disbelief in the singularity of their one true god.

But what is it that can, indeed, harm true believers? If believers cannot be harmed by disagreements over what is true and what is false—no matter how erroneous or outrageous these disagreements may seem to be—then what is the observable source of all harm? Their neighbors can only harm them when they confiscate their wealth and freedom through force or fraud. Whether such coercion is organized or disorganized, legitimate or illegitimate, righteous or unrighteous—in any case, believers have been harmed. However their neighbors may justify such harm, it does not lessen the harm.

Jesus was harmed by institutionalized, legitimized, and sanctified seizure of his freedom, his wealth, and his life—at sword point. Yet, neither Jesus nor his followers were harmed by those who rejected, ignored, or were ignorant of his teachings.

St. Paul, co-founder of Christianity, clarified in Romans 13:8 what he meant by taking action that is consistent with "the fulfillment of the law" on how Christians must act toward their neighbors:

> Let no debt remain outstanding, except the continuing debt to love one another, for he who loves his fellow man has fulfilled the law. The commandments, "Do not commit adultery," "Do not murder," "Do not steal," "Do not covet," and whatever commandments there may be, are summed up in this one rule, "Love your neighbor as yourself." Love does no harm to its neighbor. Therefore love is the fulfillment of the law.

Paul illuminates the meaning of *love* as in "love your neighbor as yourself" by affirming, "Love does no harm to its neighbor." It is observable that harming your neighbors involves taking coercive action against them for win-lose gain. Paul follows the example of Jesus by elevating this rule of social action to the status of an inviolable principle. Paul asserts, "He who loves his fellow man has fulfilled the law." In other words, those who apply the principle of "love your neighbors as yourself," which is never to harm them, have "fulfilled the law." *Not* to harm your neighbors is to take no action against them for win-lose gain through force or fraud. Because no love is found in harming your neighbors, and because loving and harming are mutually exclusive, loving your neighbors includes not harming them.

Everyone has the same choice: you can *harm* your neighbors for win-lose gain—or *love* your neighbors for win-win gain. With a consistent and clear message, Jesus implores his followers to love their neighbors and not harm them. This elegant principle of social action, taught by Jesus to his disciples and followers, was further clarified and emphasized by Paul as quoted above.

In contrast to Paul's plea to love your neighbors without harming them, as noted, Paul also sanctioned win-lose slavery when he warned, "Slaves, obey your earthly masters with respect and fear, and with sincerity of heart, just as you would obey Christ" (Ephesians 6:5). The difference, however, between a slave obeying his slave master and obeying his Christ Jesus is a profound and dramatic distinction. The slave is an involuntary servant, forced against his will to obey his slave master. In sharp contrast, Jesus is not a slave master. He does not force anyone to either obey him or serve him. It is the difference between win-lose involuntary obedience and win-win voluntary obedience.

It is impossible to enslave your neighbors for win-lose gain without also harming them. Those who impose involuntary servitude by force always harm the involuntary servants. However, there is a win-win solution to this theological contradiction. Christians only have to give priority to the win-win altruism of Jesus, which clearly implies:

Always love your neighbors through win-win exchange and never harm them through win-lose exchange.

Always love your neighbors by way of their gain, and never harm them by way of their loss. In other words, always choose win-win exchange founded on love your neighbor over win-lose exchange founded on harm your neighbor. Where the scriptures call for win-win action in one passage, and win-lose action in another, always resolve this contradiction by choosing the benevolence of win-win religion over the malevolence of win-lose religion.

In St. Paul's letter to Christian churches of the Roman Province of Galatia, he urges Christians to shift their paradigms away from faith and trust in laws that impose human servitude, toward faith and trust in the teachings of Jesus — teachings that encourage believers to replace their human servitude with human freedom.

It is for freedom that Christ has set us free. Stand firm, then, and do not let yourselves be burdened by a yoke of slavery (Galatians 5:1).

಄

Readers of European history know that in the Middle Ages, serfdom was a legalized and legitimized institution of involuntary servitude. In short, for the lord of the land to gain, his serf — an involuntary servant of his master — must be forced to lose. Our English word serf comes from the Latin *servus,* meaning slave. Because serfs were legally forced to serve their aristocratic overlords, whatever the supposed justification for serfdom, the serfs were still slaves.

In his book on *Freedom in the Making of Western Civilization,* Harvard University's cultural sociologist, Orlando Patterson, enumerates the influences that led to the demise of serfdom as a social institution. Patterson recalls, "That in all the peasant revolts, one of the main demands was the abolition of serfdom." Patterson stresses, "The ground for this principle of personal liberty was a radical reading of Christianity as the religion of freedom."[95] Again, St. Paul assured the Christians of Galatia, "It is for freedom that Christ has set us free."

In the 1525 revolt by German peasants against serfdom, their demands to be free of the servitude imposed by institutionalized feudalism were founded on the teachings of Jesus. In making their argument for freedom, leaders of the revolt revealed their Christian paradigm.

> It has until now been the custom of the lords to own us as their property. This is deplorable, for Christ redeemed and bought us all with his precious blood, the lowliest shepherd as well as the greatest lord, with no exceptions. Thus the Bible proves that we are free and want to be free.[96]

Peasant serfs were rejecting the superiority syndrome of aristocratic lords who claimed they were superior to everyone of lower station and thereby were born to rule and enslave their inferior subjects. According to scripture, however, in the eyes of Jesus the "greatest lord" was no more worthy, righteous or superior than was the "lowliest shepherd."

As the win-win teachings of Jesus were broadcast across Europe, they challenged the supposed wisdom and rectitude of the politically legalized institution of feudalism with its win-lose doctrines of aristocratic superiority over the inferiority of *commoners*—that is, people of common birth. These challenges to the autocratic monopoly of win-lose authority, with its legalized seizure of wealth and freedom from peasant serfs, eventually led to the fall of serfdom and the rise of freedom for common people of common birth. The win-win domino effects were profound.

The decline and fall of feudalism in Western Europe became a lavish boon not only for Christians; it also became a blessing for everyone regardless of their religious faith. It led to the erosion and demise of a "deplorable" social structure tied to the coercive theme: *For masters to gain, their serfs must be forced to lose.* The unforeseen collapse of feudalism in the Christian West moved Western Europe away from a win-lose economy toward a win-win economy and thereby the advance of common prosperity beyond all experience. This unprecedented social advance is explained by the following social principles:

> *The greater the human freedom, the greater the win-win exchange that creates the greatest prosperity for the greatest number.*

In marked contrast, there is this contrary corollary:

> *The greater the human servitude, the greater the win-lose exchange that creates the greatest poverty for the greatest number.*

The consistent operation of these social principles can be verified through the observation of social action by anyone willing to look. As extrapolations from these principles are observed to come true as predicted, this ongoing process of verification continues to corroborate their fidelity.

∞

A Christianity that is in harmony with the teachings of Jesus is a win-win religion of "love your neighbor." Conversely, a Christianity that violates the win-win teachings of Jesus is a win-lose religion of "harm your neighbor." No matter how righteous, devout, and well-meaning Christians may be, they cannot advance the win-win teaching of Jesus, which is, "love your neighbor as yourself," by harming their neighbors through win-lose violence against them. The belief that Jesus would praise them for harming their neighbors is clearly false because it violates his prime principle of loving your neighbors through the practice of win-win altruism.

In a similar way, where Mohammed says, "Let there be no compulsion [violence] in religion," Muslims cannot follow Mohammed's Principle of Islamic Nonviolence while they are attacking their fellow Muslims and assailing non-Muslims whom they openly berate as infidels. Mere usage of "infidel" as a derisive barb against nonbelievers proves their religious intolerance. Throughout religious history, this fatal paradigm of coercive intolerance has led to religious persecution and to the destruction of human freedom for win-lose gain. To free the Muslim world of such religious tyranny, Muslims must follow Mohammed's elegant Principle of Islamic Nonviolence. It is not enough to memorize and recite his holy words. They must summon the courage and integrity to follow and obey Mohammed's uncompromising command — a central canon of Islamic doctrine that cannot be overemphasized: *Let there be no compulsion in religion.*

༄

Whatever religious doctrines the faithful may follow, they must never allow the *superiority syndrome* to incite them toward win-lose religion for coercive gain. Those who are certain of their religious superiority are inclined to believe that they can do no wrong in promoting its doctrines. Such confident people are always at risk of becoming a grave danger to society. For example, when a doctrine believed to be superior declares: *For men to gain women must be forced to lose,* believers may accept this as absolute truth, with nothing to argue. Unfortunately, for women, this win-lose paradigm may have tragic consequences.

Where women would advance their understanding of causality, it is a gross violation of the Golden Rule Principle for men to impede or prevent their quests for knowledge and professional advancement. Yet, win-lose theology has long discriminated against women who would pursue a career of their own choosing. Renowned theologian, Martin Luther, defined the proper role for women in a Christian society, "To the end they should remain at home, sit still, keep house, and bear and bring up children."[97] For Luther, a Christian society was a win-lose society where women by their natural inferiority are bound to remain subservient to the preeminence of male superiority and domination. However, in a win-win society (which is a free society); women are free to create careers of their choice, which may or may not include the challenging career of mother and homemaker.

Deplorably, in much of the world, men are still guided by the win-lose paradigm, which presumes the inborn superiority of men over women. Qur'ānic translator and Dean of the Institute of Islamic Knowledge, Mohammad Malik, clarifies a prominent verse of the Qur'ān (4:34):

Men are overseers over women because Allah has made the one of them to excel the other, and because men *are required to* spend their wealth *for the maintenance of women.* Righteous women are, therefore, devoutly obedient and guard in *the husband's* absence what Allah requires them to guard (*their husband's property and their own honor*). As to those

women from whom you fear disobedience, first
admonish them, then refuse to share your bed with
them, *and then, if necessary*, beat them. Then if they
obey you, take no further action against them and do
not make excuses to punish them.[98] [Malik's italics
and parentheses.]

According to the Qur'ān, "Men are overseers over women
because" men naturally "excel" over women. Women are the
inferior gender because men are the superior gender. The
superiority syndrome of males over females fuels the win-
lose paradigm: *For superior man to gain, inferior woman must
be forced to lose.* Clearly, there is no equity in this shameful
and flawed paradigm of causality. It lays the foundation for
both voluntary and involuntary servitude, where females
are indoctrinated with a sacred duty to serve their "overseers" — their husbands.

When the innately superior husband believes his innately
inferior wife has disobeyed his demands, she is threatened,
"and then, if necessary" beaten until she obeys. To add
injury to injury, her husband may have been forced upon
her to begin with through an arranged marriage without her
consent.

Where a woman's obedience to her husband is spurred
by her fear of him, this sets the stage for a win-lose marriage.
Moreover, where the marital aim is mutual happiness, a
marriage built on force and fear will fall far short of the win-
win marriage, which is a relationship built on the priceless
bounty of mutual exchange for mutual reward. The win-win
marriage is based on four pillars of social exchange: mutual
respect, mutual friendship, mutual affection, and mutual
love.

In both Western and Eastern cultures, the superiority
syndrome of male supremacy over females, esteemed by
many men in many places, has had injurious and sometimes

fatal effects for women. In many Islamic nations where a father's daughter or brother's sister is victimized by the heinous crime of rape, the plight of the innocent victim may go beyond Draconian discipline. Governed by their win-lose models of social justice, the closest relatives of the victim herself commonly believe that the only righteous and honorable escape from family disgrace and dishonor is to shoot this poor girl in the head, slit her throat, or consume her in fire. Yet, such base brutality and malicious cruelty violates two thousand years of Golden Rules from Zoroaster to Muhammad.

There is nothing honorable about slaying your own daughter or sister for any aim no matter how righteous it may seem. Moreover, for men who would dominate women by mutilating the sexual organs of innocent girls before they blossom into womanhood, such criminal cowardice makes a travesty of righteousness only a win-lose god could condone. What could be more cowardly and dishonorable than the murder or mutilation of defenseless girls by their own fathers, brothers, or other family members? Surely, such deluded disciplinarians have fallen for the shameful lure of the superiority syndrome of male supremacy.

Where Muslims have tortured juveniles in the name of Allah, and Christians have done the same in the name of God, surely they did not know what they were doing — and surely prophets Muhammad and Jesus would condemn such cruel child abuse as a wicked transgression of sacred law. To impose chastity upon women through clitoral excision is no less criminal and barbaric than to impose chastity upon men through male castration.

To endorse and exalt sexual chastity for both women and men before marriage, and sexual exclusivity after marriage, is one thing, but to impose it through criminal violence is quite another. Wherever social justice is the norm, honor killings and genital mutilation — justified by the superiority syndrome of pusillanimous males, and often with the complacency of women—will be abhorred as crimes against humanity.

Men of courage, goodwill, and true honor will never use their greater physical strength to gain through the loss of women. Let the Golden Rule Principle prevail by avoiding these honor killings and genital mutilations, which by virtue of their lurid savagery can only be the acme of family dishonor.

Wherever men believe that for men to gain, women must be forced to lose, no woman is safe from male attack through rape, battery, violence, fraud, or economic and cultural discrimination. Where women are routinely forced through win-lose religion or win-lose government to "remain at home, sit still, keep house, and bear and bring up children," as Marten Luther demanded, such force creates a coercive society that is in stark violation of the Golden Rule Principle.

Social progress for women will be impeded or thwarted until the great majority of men seek gain through the gain of women and not through their forced or fraudulent loss. Conversely, the same rule demands that women seek gain through the gain of men, and not through their forced or fraudulent loss. The Golden Rule Principle is gender blind; it sets forth a moral guide for all humans regardless of their gender—and regardless of their ethnicity, culture, status, religion, or age.

⁊

Operation of the Win-Win Principle advances win-win exchange, which in turn leads to the spontaneous growth of peace, prosperity, and freedom. In the Middle-East conflict between Israeli Jews and Palestinian Muslims, if opposing sides would replace their win-lose paradigms of theology and government with win-win paradigms, one dramatic effect would be the replacement of war, poverty, and servitude with peace, prosperity, and freedom within the borders of old Palestine.

If Israelis follow their Judaic Golden Rule, which demands of every Jew: Do not to your fellow men what is hateful to you, and if Palestinians follow their Islamic Golden Rule, which calls Muslims to desire for their brothers what they desire for themselves, then many good things will follow in wake of their win-win exchanges. On the other hand, if they pursue win-lose exchange, many bad things will continue to happen. It is unavoidable. We cannot bend the laws of social causality to reach a more desirable outcome from our destructive human actions.

The multiple benefits of moving away from win-lose gain toward win-win gain are predicted by win-win theory and verified by observing the effects of social action. Yet, broader adoption of this Principle of Win-Win Exchange requires decent people to make paradigm shifts from win-lose to win-win models of social causality.

To be sure, few humans are quick to make paradigm shifts toward new and revolutionary explanations of causality. This is because they are confident that their old and established paradigms are true—or, at least good enough and beyond challenge. Most people believe that their worldviews of how things work, or how they ought to work, are above reproach. Whether they are educated or not, intelligent or not, it is always a formidable challenge for them to accept the idea that any of their cherished models of causality are in any way flawed. Yet, if no one ever made a paradigm shift, then, like our distant ancestors, we might still live in a cave.

Although it may have been risky for early humans to leave the natural security of the caves of their ancestors, it would have been far riskier to have stayed in the cave and remain *cavemen* forever. Yet, as perpetual cavemen, they never could have realized their human potential for ingenuity and creativity that could only flourish beyond the security of the cave.

In a similar way, humans of our time must be shown the vast scale of their unrealized potential for ingenuity and creativity, not by abandoning their caves, but by abandoning their flawed and spurious paradigms of social causality that fool decent people into believing: *For us to gain, they must be forced to lose.* Yet, the cavemen might still have survived extinction even if they had never abandoned their regressive ideas of caveman superiority. In contrast, it is certain that civilized men cannot survive extinction in the nuclear age without abandoning their regressive ideas of win-lose superiority, which incite social disaster and cultural ruination.

It took courage for early humans to change their false paradigms of causality, especially those honored by conventional wisdom. For humans today, this still takes courage. Fortunately, before we were born, there were those who had the audacity to make paradigm shifts toward truer and better explanations of causality. There are no laws of nature to bar us from emulating their brave example.

After the Salem "witches" of Massachusetts were hanged in 1692 for the alleged crime of witchcraft, the convicting jury began to have second thoughts. In fact, they made a public repudiation of their win-lose actions against the innocent:

> On further consideration and better information, we justly fear we have been instrumental, with others, though ignorantly and unwittingly, to bring upon ourselves and these people of the Lord, the guilt of innocent blood.... We do, therefore, hereby signify to all in general (and to the surviving sufferers in special) our deep sense of, and sorrow for, our errors... for which we are much distressed and disquieted in our minds.... We do heartily ask forgiveness of

you all, whom we have unjustly offended, and do declare, according to our present minds, we would none of us do such things again.[99]

This remarkable paradigm shift led to a public confession of error that was signed by all twelve Salem jurors. Their intellectual honesty helped bring an end to witch trials in North America. In England and on the Continent, opponents of witch hunting used these confessions of error as a powerful argument for ending the deadly superstition that witches, warlocks, and sorcerers can harm the faithful by fraternizing with supernatural demons. Intellectual integrity and courage were not dead then, and they are not dead now.

In a hundred centuries of building civilizations, humans have never faced a crisis wherein their win-lose religion could erase civilization and delete its people from every corner of the earth. To halt the fatal slide into oblivion, men and women must show the courage and valor to abandon their faith in the rectitude of win-lose models of causality that sanctify and glorify coercive action for win-lose gain. Instead, they must show their reliance on the rectitude of win-win models of human exchange for mutual gain. This is the only human gain that can ensure the equity, utility, and morality of win-win civilizations. The practice of win-win altruism will always be the crucial element for optimizing the causes of peace, prosperity, and freedom for the enrichment of all humans of all religions and philosophies.

ENDNOTES

90. Rüstow, *Freedom and Domination*, 276.

91. William L. Shirer, *The Rise and Fall of the Third Reich: A History Germany* (New York: Simon and Schuster, 1960), 965.

92. John Keegan, *The Second World War* (New York: Viking Penguin, 1990), 288.

93. Thomas Sowell, *Intellectuals and Society* (New York: Basic Books, 2009), 122.

94. Thomas Jefferson, *Notes on the State of Virginia*, Query 17, ed. William Peden (Chapel Hill, NC: University of North Carolina Press, 1955), 159.

95. Orlando Patterson, *Freedom in the Making of Western Culture* (New York: Basic Books/HarperCollins, 1991), 373.

96. Peter Blickle, *Revolution of 1525: The German Peasants' War from a New Perspective* (Baltimore, Maryland: Johns Hopkins University Press, 1985). See "The Twelve Articles," in Appendix 1, 197.

97. Martin Luther, *Table Talk or Familiar Discourse of Martin Luther*, trans. William Hazlitt (London: David Bogue, 1848), par. 725, 299.

98. Malik, *Al-Qur'ān*, 177.

99. Kurt Seligmann, *The History of Magic* (New York: Pantheon Books, 1948), 278.

Chapter Seven

The Law of Human Nature

When decent people believe that false paradigms of causality are true and valid models of reality, and especially if they believe: *For us to gain, they must be forced to lose,* a deadly die is cast. Such people are governed by their paradigms to sanction, promote, and execute coercive action for win-lose gain. The social destruction they unleash generates the win-lose domino effects that inflate the causes of war, poverty, and servitude, while they deflate the causes of peace, prosperity, and freedom. Fortunately, there are no laws of nature to prevent people from making paradigm shifts away from allegiance to their belief in the rightness of coercive means for noble ends. This crucial paradigm shift, if made, will remove the human race from the laundry list of endangered species. Our only escape from this danger is to advance our understanding of social causality. Our success follows our ability to identify and verify laws of nature that operate continuously and consistently without fail. The consistency of natural principles enables us to know which causes lead to which effects. For humans, nothing is more crucial and more pressing to the attainment of our happiness and well-being.

The entrance to this vital knowledge is through the discovery of natural principles of physical, biological, and social causality. We must search for repeating phenomena, definable as *principles* or *laws* of nature due to their endless repetition and their constant operation.

One of the more remarkable distinctions between humans and other animals is that only humans are highly curious about knowing cause-and-effect, and only they have the necessary intelligence to identify and verify which causes lead to which effects. However, having both the intelligence and curiosity to know causality gives no assurance that we can get it right. Getting it right is the hard part.

There are two diverse approaches to attempting to understand the true causes of any effect. One is to *observe* the causes of physical, biological, or social effects. The other is to *imagine* the causes of such effects. If religious believers have gained any blessings from modern technology, those blessings flow from the discovery of natural principles — not by imagining their operation, but by observing their operation. The spectacular advances in physical and biological science have been built upon the discovery of natural principles. These amazing discoveries of repeating phenomena in nature are the laws of reality that give us breathtaking views of physical, biological, and social causality. Understanding causality is the creative engine that converts mere information into organized knowledge to advance progress by building an endless array of human solutions to human problems.

∽

Wherever there are societies, people are making exchanges of every kind, both tangible and intangible. Some exchanges are harmful and others are beneficial. Intuitively, it would seem that intelligent people could easily differentiate between the two. Unfortunately, most people—whether intelligent or not—have failed to identify and verify, with any consistency, which human actions are harmful and which are beneficial.

Analysis of social history shows that creating wealth and freedom is beneficial—and destroying them is harmful. But isn't this obvious? No, it is not obvious. The crucial question to answer is, "How can we act to create social benefits without destroying or preventing their creation in the first place?" Because nature does not teach us how to do this, we have to figure this out on our own.

Where we aim to maximize beneficial exchanges and minimize harmful ones, it is essential to identify and verify the very nature of human beings who are making these exchanges. It is exchanges between humans that create every society. Humans enrich their lives by exchanging information, conversation, friendship, love, and a vast variety of material and immaterial products. Eliminate exchange and you eliminate society—which in turn would eliminate our species.

The dynamo of exchange is *human nature,* which remains largely misunderstood. The failure of decent people to understand how to act in harmony with human nature has led to one social disaster after another. For us to reach the next century, we must minimize the scope and scale of these disasters by attenuating their true causes before they eclipse the combined fury of every social tragedy of our coercive past.

❧

What does it mean to be human? Can the essence of humanness be discovered through observation and defined as a natural principle? Here is a law or principle of nature that is generalized from observing humans in action:*

LAW OF HUMAN NATURE
The law of human nature is the inborn drive of all
people to act toward gain and away from loss.

This natural law identifies the essence of human nature, which is the invariable focus of all human aims. We are naturally predisposed to seek gain and avoid loss. Because it is impossible to alter or repeal this natural law, we must learn to use this law to our advantage by understanding how it operates. This includes knowing the negative consequences of trying to violate the Law of Human Nature, as well as the positive consequences of obeying it.

Because the sum of individuals forms the basis of every society, the structure of a successful society must be harmonious with the human nature of its individual members, or it is doomed to certain failure. Due to their inborn nature, humans do not fit easily into a social structure that has been arbitrarily designed by autocratic overlords to repress individualism in reaching their win-lose aims. Wherever this is tried, such oppressive rulers build a society of misfits who do not fit into their ideal schemes that often include imposing so-called egalitarian societies upon the people.

Such planned societies founded on legalized coercion are always utopian. Thus, the social ideal of utopian bliss (whether in St. Thomas More's island Utopia or anywhere else) has not worked and will not work. The autocratic social planners always fail to meet their societal aims for building a better world through legitimized force. The social failure of all collectivist societies is predictable where people are

---

* "Natural laws" and "natural principles" are used here interchangeably.

compelled to be "equal." As always, such pseudo-equality and spurious equity is contrary to the Law of Human Nature, which remains constant and cannot be repealed.

On the other hand, in a truly *egalitarian* society, the opportunity to create win-win wealth and freedom for all people is equal and universal. Because such moral egalitarianism is built on the nonviolence of win-win order and exchange, it is not only progressive and constructive, but it is pragmatic, which means it works.

∽

The advance of peace, prosperity, and freedom requires a foundation of *social order*. However, if the concept of social order is flawed, it can advance war, poverty, and servitude. Thus, it is crucial to define two dissimilar approaches to devising a system of social order:

> 1. *After* observing human nature, organize (a posteriori) a system of social order wherein humans fit naturally and harmoniously.

> 2. *Before* observing human nature, organize (a priori) a system of social order wherein humans do not fit naturally and harmoniously.

The first approach fosters societies founded on win-win religions and governments that are established through the operation of win-win order by mutual agreement without the imposition of violence. The second approach has fostered oppressive societies founded on win-lose religions and governments that are established through the operation of win-lose order by coercive rule through the imposition of violence.

To render win-lose religions and governments palatable to the people, they have been glorified, deified, and legitimized throughout human history. Nonetheless, they are all flawed social schemes based on the supremacy of institutional force over individual freedom of action and expression. In short, the individual is warned, "You will fit into our social system, or else. Any questions? Good!"

Organized oppression, whether religious or political, suppresses and smothers individualism. Through ritualized seizure of wealth and freedom, the individual is sacrificed for "the greater good" of society. Confiscation at gunpoint is justified to reach some highly touted win-lose aim. The grand societal mission of the authorities is proclaimed superior to all individual aims. Autocratic collectivists resort to violence in a futile effort to force everyone into the same social mold. Wherever such social experiments have been tried, the downside is always the same: win-win exchange is repressed by appropriating—in other words, seizing—people's freedom of choice to govern their own lives. However, try as they may, authoritarian social planners cannot "force a square peg into a round hole."

The more wealth and freedom they seize from their subjects to force them into some ideal or better system of religion or government, in general, the more their subjects dislike, resent, and fear their religious and political leaders. The regressive consequences are predictable. Individual incentive to create new knowledge, new inventions, and new products is either curtailed or suppressed altogether without recourse.

But why does the growth of collectivism shrink and erode personal incentive to create better ideas and products until that incentive may be destroyed without any hope of restoration? Our human nature requires us to act toward gain and away from loss. However, if the more wealth and freedom we create the more we are punished through its illegal or legal seizure, then the more we will move away from creating new wealth and new freedom. Our very focus of life would move away from creating human gain, and move toward avoiding human loss. This forced redirection of human action is harmful and damaging in a profound way. It causes our human actions to focus on avoiding the negative effects of loss and no longer on achieving the positive effects of gain. The regressive social effects are both subtle and far-reaching.

To repress individual freedom is to repress individual aims for creative and productive gain. With such repression, individuals lose the driving incentive to assume the necessary risk to create new knowledge, new inventions, and new products in producing common wealth for common people. Would-be consumers of new wealth can no longer obtain the products of their choice—especially the diversity of products that never come to fruition in a repressive society that destroys initiative and creativity.

Consumers lose their freedom to consume as their freedom is seized to impose win-lose gain through religious and political coercion. This is why all social systems based on coercive *collectivism*—in the course of repressing *individualism*—cannot avoid creating institutions of inefficiency and incompetence on a grand scale. There can be no other outcome. This is precisely because their win-lose policies go against human nature by repressing individual aims by coercive means. The anti-individual authority of collectivism creates an anti-incentive society of followers, imbued to follow the rules of their theocratic, autocratic, and bureaucratic overlords—or be fined, imprisoned, or killed.

∽

The imposition of collectivist communism in Tibet by the Chinese Communists has been well publicized in the West. Among many coercive policies, the Communists aim to replace faith in Buddhism with faith in atheism. Communist violence in Tibet has included the destruction of Buddhist temples and the murder of Buddhist monks. The Communists aim to unleash a gun-imposed monopoly of atheism throughout Tibet. There and elsewhere, the deification of Marx into a demigod renders their Marxian Communism a quasi-theology of atheism. Inflated by the self-aggrandizement of their superiority syndrome, they are guided by one of their many win-lose paradigms: *For atheists to gain, Buddhists must be forced to lose.* In this way, they pretend to justify the organized destruction of freedom and the annihilation of their assumed inferiors. Nothing is more alien to the communist mentality than the idea of freedom of exchange for win-win gain, which fosters freedom of religion, press, and speech as natural byproducts.

It is important to point out that if applying the Win-Win Principle to solve social problems were an obvious solution, there would not have been any Communist societies in the first place. A clear picture of communist causality is unmasked by replacing *imagination* of how it ought to work with *observation* of how it does work. The Law of Human Nature, which cannot be violated or altered by Communist violence, assures the death knell of political Communism-lose gain.

Through social exchange, all humans seek gain as they see it. They do not seek gain as the coercive authority sees it, which is always his gain through their loss. Win-lose exchange by dictatorial decree is the coercive engine of communism. Its win-lose paradigm of building a better world through seizure of wealth and freedom is a false path to that noble aim. Its paradigm is fatally flawed because a better world is only reachable through the advancement of peace, prosperity, and freedom. For this critical reason, political Communism cannot work because its inherent coercion and intractable violence foster war, poverty, and servitude wherever it is forced upon its citizens.

On the other hand, if the Communist aim were to provoke war, poverty and servitude by imposing Marxian policies, they have proven for more than a century that Communism works. In the same way, win-lose theocracy — while imposing collectivist religion — has proven for centuries that it also works as an effective instigator of war, poverty, and servitude. The predictable effects of win-lose policies of religion and government can be explained by this repeating principle of causation.

Win-lose religion and win-lose government maximize human losses per capita and minimize human gains per capita.

If faithful followers of win-lose religion and win-lose government unleash weapons of mass destruction upon their proclaimed enemies, the ensuing catastrophe could bring about the ultimate human loss through the annihilation of our species. Unfortunately, the principles of human action that reveal the negative effects of win-lose religious and political gains are not obvious. In other words, the win-lose causes of human calamity are not conspicuous. If the origins of war, poverty, and servitude were obvious to respected people with good minds and educations, they would carry enough influence to avoid institutionalizing and legitimizing their win-lose causes in the first place. To impede and preempt institutionalized tyranny, it is critical to recognize that the common people — the so-called masses — have never institutionalized anything, whether constructive or destructive. Human survival depends upon the influential classes taking effective action to replace win-lose institutions of every kind with win-win institutions. Fortunately, there are no laws of nature to prevent this vital transition.

∽

The violence of religious and political collectivism springs from its utopian idealism that coercive means can create a better world. Nevertheless, the premise is false. The most dramatic example of the failure of collectivism to reach constructive goals was proven for all time by Soviet leaders of Eastern Europe who aimed to make Communism work through mass intimidation and mass murder on a scale of criminality only matched by their Communist comrades in China.

From the beginning, their paradigms of social causality were gravely flawed. The chosen means—win-lose Communism—was not only impractical, but it was an impossible strategy for reaching its promised ends. Wherever the means employed cannot attain the ends sought, failure is the unavoidable consequence.

The grand social experiment was to build a Socialist utopia in the Union of Soviet Socialist Republics (USSR), which before its collapse was a coercive political alliance of fifteen Communist states in Eastern Europe. Its stunning failure illustrates the unbending nature of social laws of causality. It is impossible to act against our human nature; try as we may, we cannot act toward our own *loss* and away from our own *gain*. The Law of Human Nature dooms the possibility of a viable and durable social structure based on the coercive force of win-lose gain.

To reiterate, the ultimate collapse and ruination of all win-lose societies is predictable, precisely because the coercive means chosen cannot attain the promised ends sought. That is, unless the promise is to bring the people more misery through the ruinous effects of war, poverty, and servitude.

The lethal legacy of Lenin and Stalin give us a profound insight into the pitfalls of social engineering at gunpoint. In claiming to forge a better society for the working classes, the Communists orchestrated the greatest social failure and political disaster since the rise of civilization. In the end, even ordinary workers—who were to be the prime benefici-aries of Communism—could not escape from the brutality of their Communist masters.

From its inception, as noted, the problem with win-lose Communism was that it never could have worked. Its coercive policies were devised to build a superior society by destroying individualism and replacing it with anti-individual collectivism. To impose collectivism throughout the Soviet Union, the Communist Party created a political police state to control the Soviet people with an iron fist. Communist police ran the Soviet Union, which was to run the people at gunpoint. Win-lose bureaucrats took coercive command. They gave the orders, including where to live, where to work, what and how much to produce, what to buy, what to write, what to think—and even what to wor-ship. Atheism became the state religion. God was out, and Marx was in—at gunpoint.

Legions of secret police, backed by eager inform-ers, swarmed over Eastern Europe to enforce compliance with every political decree of the commissars. Those who stepped out of line by refusing to comply, were intimidated, incarcerated, or executed. Millions of individuals who val-ued freedom of expression where thrown into forced labor camps. These lethal prisons and notorious gulags that stretched across the Soviet empire were a tribute to tyranny. The scale of their criminality was broadcast to the West by Russian novelist and Soviet dissident, Aleksandr Solzhenit-syn (1918-2008), in his best seller, *The Gulag Archipelago*.

We can speculate that if Karl Marx, architect of the Communist police state, were intellectually honest, and if he had understood the Law of Human Nature, he might have recognized the innate impracticality of his win-lose Communism. Thus, he might have realized that the politi-cal enforcement of his utopian Socialism would lead to a social catastrophe.

As it turned out, the criminal Communism of Marx, Lenin, and Stalin became the antithesis of their declared aim to create a better world for proletarian workers to enjoy. Tragically, for these workers and for everyone else in Communist Russia and the Soviet Union, the massive crimes of the Communists (the new good guys) eclipsed by comparison the moderate crimes of the royal czars (the old bad guys). Although the brutality of the czars never matched the brutality of the commissars, nonetheless, millions of Russians faced a dire choice. Would you rather be murdered by the new Communist "good guys," or murdered by the old Czarist "bad guys?"

～

To broaden understanding of the Law of Human Nature, it is useful to generalize a corollary principle, which further explains its meaning in different words. This corollary is an easily drawn conclusion from observing human nature:

LAW OF HUMAN ACTION
*All humans act toward their perception of gain and
away from their perception of loss.*

By observing humans acting, we can *postulate* that all humans act *toward* their view of gain, and they act *away* from their view of loss as they see it.* On the other hand, what about the apparent exceptions to this postulate? Surely, the individual who is about to end his or her own life is pursuing loss — perhaps the ultimate human loss — in violation of

---

* By tradition, *postulates* are foundational premises for systems of knowledge. Postulates are propositions that are assumed to be true without proof. They are valued because every useful system of knowledge should have a functional beginning. This starting place commonly takes the form of a self-evident truth, an assumption of a generalized truth known as a postulate.

the Law of Human Action. But, he or she is not. Distressed people who would commit suicide are acting "away from their perception of loss." In taking their own life, they struggle to avoid an overwhelming loss from extreme mental or physical pain.

❦

It is important to emphasize that the Law of Human Nature and the Law of Human Action are not generalized from *imagination* of human action, but from *observation* of human action. Their truth is *not* based on *a priori* faith without possibility of independent verification; it is based on *a posteriori* observation of human action by an endless number of independent observers who do not rely upon earlier observations. *Independent observations are neither influenced nor controlled by other observers or authorities.*

As a method of identifying the true causes of physical, biological, and social effects, *independent observation* of causality has proven to be more successful and reliable than *authoritarian imagination* of causality. The advantage of observation over imagination in the discovery of cause-and-effect is that any observation can be independently tested for truth by any other observer who is willing to look. Truth does not have to be accepted on the unverifiable authority of imagination, but on the verifiable authority of observation.

In contrast, where people imagine truth, others can never independently test their perception of truth. The mental images that form our imaginations cannot be replicated in the minds of others. Moreover, even if they could, all mental images that form our imagination are subjective to our mind's eye and relative to our human experience. For example, no matter how real our imagination of physical causality may seem, we cannot imagine our way to the creation of television sets, x-ray machines, and digital computers. This is not to say that the innovators who created these revolutionary products were without imagination. It means that they could not have been built any of these products for our enrichment without their preliminary *observation* of principles and how they operate.

The most influential paradigm shift in human history—and the most revolutionary—has been the gradual move away from reliance on imagination of causality toward reliance on observation of causality. We did not reach the "unreachable" moon by imagining celestial principles, but by discovering them through the power of observation. In a similar way, we can reach the "unreachable" blessings of peace, prosperity, and freedom not by imagining social principles, but by discovering them through careful observation. The very same observational strategy that blazed a true path to the moon can also blaze a true path to peace, prosperity, and freedom for people of all religions. Again, optimism springs from knowing causality, which shows that there are no known laws of nature to impede or to bar these true and valid means to human progress.

৵

All humans are naturally predisposed to seek gain and avoid loss, where the perception of "gain" or "loss" is based entirely on subjective value judgments. The ascetic monk, cloistered in an ancient monastery, has taken a vow of perpetual poverty. He is pursuing the intangible value of spiritual gain, while having little or no interest in the tangible value of worldly gain. Like everyone else, due to his innate human nature, he has no choice; he must pursue gain and avoid loss, as he sees it. As always, perception is everything; we believe to be true what we perceive to be true.

Beyond this natural pursuit, all humans have the volition to *choose* how they act toward gain and away from loss.

Observation of human action reveals that we have only two choices in how we act toward others. We can act to gain and avoid loss through the *gain* of others—or through the *loss* of others. If we choose to gain through the loss of others, we have two further choices. We can physically seize the wealth and freedom of others for our own win-lose gain. On the other hand, if we would avoid direct participation in physical violence—not wanting to get our hands dirty—we can authorize others by proxy to seize our neighbors' wealth and freedom for our own win-lose gain. Throughout social history, the most devastating man-made losses have come from seizing people's wealth and freedom through force or fraud—by official proxy—for religious or political win-lose gain.

The irony is that such coercive institutions of win-lose gain were largely institutionalized by respected people with good minds and educations who sought to do good things. In contrast, bad people (e.g., burglars, robbers, thugs, et al.), who may have poor minds and poor educations, have never institutionalized anything. Consequently, history shows that organized good guys who did not know what they were doing were usually more dangerous and destructive than unorganized bad guys who did not know what they were doing.

For those who would prefer more good things and fewer bad things to happen to more good people, they must go beyond wishful thinking. They must understand causality and, thereby, choose a workable means to gaining these good things; that is, choosing a means that can attain the ends sought.

All social systems, religious or secular, are utopian if they cannot attain the ends sought or promised by their leadership. For example, Hitler's National Socialism and Stalin's International Communism were utopian political schemes that promised the people prosperity and freedom by seizing their possessions and liberty. In so doing, these leaders reached the zenith of force and fraud by legitimizing and glorifying the violence of political Socialism. During the first half of the last century, their attempt to impose a utopian social order upon society led to the institutionalized, organized, and legalized murder of eighty million Europeans across greater Europe. The leaders of National Socialism and International Communism set new precedents for social failure due entirely to their adoption of flawed models of social causality.

For Germans and Russians, their intelligence alone was not enough to protect them from their fatal failure to identify social causality. Without observational analysis of social systems, whether political or religious, intelligent people — who may even be good guys — are at risk of adopting false paradigms of social causality as if they were true. Decent people, for example, who embrace and impose win-lose models of causality on the mere faith that they offer a true means to the ends sought, are assuming an inordinate risk of the highest order. They are at risk of condoning, supporting, organizing, and implementing the very coercion that incites and inflames social catastrophe. The ruinous effects of such win-lose actions have included mass intimidation, mass destruction, and mass murder. Thus, embracing false paradigms of causality by intellectual default has been the road to social ruin.

A crucial social lesson yet to be widely understood is that it is not enough merely to have worthy aims if you don't know how to reach them. Too often, good people who are trying to do the right thing, but who have misunderstood social causality, have given their support to bad people who *were* trying to do bad things. Millions of good Germans sanctioned Hitler and his win-lose Naziism because they did not understand the principles of social causality. As a consequence, good Germans who didn't know what they were doing were supporting bad Germans who didn't know what they were doing either. Naziism became a social disaster precisely because its Fascist leaders did not understand social causality. The familiar adage of social dynamics, where "the blind are leading the blind," has been the core of social tragedy throughout human history.

In Germany, respected people had *a priori* trust—blind faith—in Nazi leadership and in the supremacy and efficacy of its National Socialism. The superiority syndrome of respected Germans and their faith in the primacy of the win-lose paradigm led straight to the destruction of Germany. It caused the death of millions of decent Germans who lost everything there was to lose: their families, their homes, their jobs, and their lives.

Why was their loss so catastrophic? In cannot be overstressed, they failed to understand which social causes lead to which social effects. That failure is all it takes to kill you and your loved ones—and, in our time, everyone else.

Records of civilization show that decent people who try to do good things for society—but who don't know what they are doing—pose a grave danger to the well-being of their fellow humans. Yet, intuitively we ask, "What's wrong with good people aiming to do good things?" That depends on your means to doing good; are they win-win or win-lose? This is critical because good people—often driven to live meaningful lives—are likely to act with zeal and passion toward their honorable aims as they see them. In contrast, bad people, such as robbers and thugs, who don't know what they are doing, are unlikely to show zeal and passion for reaching their win-lose aims, which they rarely see as *honorable*. Nonetheless, organized good guys with a sincere and devout passion to control you as a presumed necessary and honorable means to their religious or political aims are a dire threat to your security. Not surprisingly, they represent a far more serious menace than the disorganized bad guys who might steal your possessions—or even kill you if you happen to be in the wrong place at the wrong time. However, confiscating your wealth and freedom for a commendable cause will not be the bad guys grand purpose of life.

∽

Throughout the violent history of religion, millions of pious followers would have avoided the slaying of their families and the destruction of their homes by their religious rivals—if they could have done so. Regrettably, they have not known how, or they would have reached this vital aim by now. Their failure is the source of civilization's titanic social disasters. It is the persistent failure of influential people to identify and verify which social causes lead to which social effects. This failure remains widespread among both educated and uneducated classes. For this reason, its potential for inciting social catastrophe cannot be overemphasized.

Where decent people continue to act on false models of causality as if they were true, they will continue to pay a heavy price for their ignorance. Nature and her lasting laws are oblivious to human ignorance of causation or of anything else. History reminds us that when humans build and exalt entire institutions of win-lose religion for coercive gain, many bad things will invariably happen to many good people. There is no escape for men, women, children, and even infants, who in their innocence have offended no one. Those who murder children to reach religious or political aims, regardless of their righteousness, intelligence, education, erudition, or patriotism have reached peerless levels of delusion that lead such respected people to sanctify, codify, and glorify crimes against humanity.

∽

The Law of Human Nature and the Law of Human Action have been explained in this chapter. Observation of human action shows that it is human nature to seek gain and avoid loss. That is nature's *given*, which means that we are predisposed to seek gain and avoid loss. However, we can postulate that humans do have a choice in *how* they seek gain and avoid loss. Again, it is observable; humans can seek gain and avoid loss through the gain of others, or through the loss of others. Their choice between these extremes is governed by their paradigms of causality.

Precisely because paradigms of causality govern all human action, human salvation from self-destruction, as well as the acceleration of human progress beyond all past experience, can be found in the replacement of false paradigms of causality with those that are true. One false paradigm of social causality that has to be shattered is the common belief among intellectuals that man is *evil* by nature and, thereby, predisposed to criminal behavior. Albert Einstein, the most influential physicist since Isaac Newton, embraced this fallacy in claiming, "It is easier to denature plutonium than to denature the evil spirit of man."[100]

To "denature" something is to deprive it of its natural character. It is true that we cannot deprive humans of their natural "spirit" or vital essence, which is always to seek gain and avoid loss. However, it is *not* true that humans are born with a natural spirit or innate character that would impel them toward evil behavior (harmful action) by seizing their neighbor's wealth and freedom.

Einstein gave his position on the "evil spirit of man" during an interview with the *New York Times* on June 23, 1946, shortly after the end of World II. The global conflict of that war had transcended all prior wars for its magnitude of political murders and its measured orchestration of brutality. The massacres of civilians during the war by political governments even eclipsed the scope and scale of battlefield casualties that killed millions of combatants. In fact, in many theaters of war, it was safer to be a soldier than a defenseless civilian. The wake of destruction from the war was so far reaching that many were certain that Armageddon had finally arrived.

Einstein, having witnessed from afar and having survived the horrors of two world wars, was sure that man's "evil spirit" had driven him to organize and perpetrate crimes against humanity. This widely accepted model of social causality, especially among the educated classes, is as compelling as it is false.

During the Middle Ages, the idea that witches and warlocks were spreading the plague across Europe was also compelling to those who were suddenly surrounded by too many bodies to bury. Yet, merely because an idea is irresistibly compelling does not make it true and valid. Respected men of the community organized the violent persecution of witches. Their vile visions of "evil" women — raining ruination upon their neighbors — were compelling figments of their fatal imagination. But without observation of causality, there is nothing to counter a prelate's imagination of the evil spirit of witches, or an Einstein's imagination of "the evil spirit of man."

In their treatise on *Man the Hunted*, anthropologists Donna Hart and Robert Sussman aim to refute the flawed model of humans as inborn predators who are predisposed to violent and brutal behavior:

> One last major point we want to make…we humans are not slaughter-prone assassins by *nature*. We often act badly, maliciously, cruelly, but that is by choice and not by our status as bipedal primates…. Let's quit accepting our spurious heritage as Man the Hunter to excuse why we start wars, torture others, and scorch the earth.[101]

Although making paradigm shifts from false models of causality to those that are true is a difficult challenge for everyone, it is not impossible. The next chapter will set forth a practical criterion to differentiate between that which is *possible* and that which is *impossible*. This will be fundamental to our understanding of which social causes lead to which social effects.

ENDNOTES

100. Otto Nathan and Heinz Norden, *Einstein on Peace* (New York: Simon & Schuster, 1960), 385.

101. Donna Heart and Robert Sussman, *Man the Hunted: Primates, Predators, and Human Evolution* (New York: Westview Press, 2005), xviii.

Chapter Eight

The Possibility Principle vs. the Impossibility Principle

Over centuries, the crushing pain of war, poverty, and servitude has caused more suffering and misery among the faithful than any other source of human adversity. A vital blessing for believers of all religions would be somehow to minimize the scale of war, poverty and servitude that still invades their temporal world. Most believers would welcome a way to maximize peace, prosperity, and freedom for their families, friends, and fellow citizens to enjoy. Unfortunately, an old barrier bars the way to these precious gains that would enrich all religious followers. These blessings are denied to those who live where there is a general failure to identify their true causes.

A false model of social causality prevents believers from learning how they can play a true role in moving society away from war, poverty, and servitude toward peace, prosperity, and freedom. This barrier is nothing more than a false idea of what causes good things or bad things to happen to good people. Where members of any faith adopt a theology that incites them to gain through the loss of others, they will sanction, encourage, and participate in win-lose religion for coercive gain. Its destructive domino effects are grave. As emphasized, they include the spread of war, poverty and servitude — which for good people, is as bad as it gets.

Where followers are sure that their faith is the only true path to peace, many hold that it is their sacred duty to widen this path by monopolizing the worship of god. In their mind, this is the holy path to "peace on earth."

Esteemed apostle of Christianity, St. Luke, warned in his Gospel that peace on earth is only available to those who believe in the divinity of Jesus. Luke wrote that, "an angel of the Lord," after announcing the birth of Jesus in Bethlehem, proclaimed, "'Glory to God in the highest, and on earth peace to men on whom his favor rests.'" (Luke 2:14). In commenting on this passage, editors of the *NIV Study Bible* explain, "Peace is not assured to all, but only to those pleasing to God — the objects of his good pleasure.[102]" Thus, those who do not believe in the divinity of Jesus are not an object of God's "good pleasure," which means they will be denied God's favor. Luke's Gospel teaches that peace is only available to the true believer. Yet, for disbelievers — without the possibility of "peace" — there is only turmoil, violence, and war.*

---

* Editors of the *Bible Knowledge Commentary* explain Luke's passage, "The *NIV*'s, 'on earth peace to men on whom His favor rests,' is preferred to the King James Version's, 'good will toward men.' God's peace is not given to those who have good will, but to those who are recipients of God's good will or favor." The editors' point is that for those who are out of favor with God, there is no "peace." See John F. Walvoord and Roy B. Zuck, editors, *The Bible Knowledge Commentary: An Exposition of the Scriptures by Dallas Seminary Faculty* (Wheaton, Illinois: Victor Books, 1983), 208.

Throughout social history, we know that religious monopolies have played a key role in spurring the causes of war, poverty, and servitude. In securing their monopolies, religious leaders have also codified, glorified, and ritualized the destruction of peace, prosperity, and freedom in the name of Almighty God.

Win-lose religion, however, has not been the only barrier to peace, prosperity, and freedom. There are those who argue that these global aims are unreachable because they are unattainable. They are certain that such ideals are either hopelessly impractical or outright utopian. Unfortunately, this pessimistic model of social causality impedes the human action necessary to *optimize* the causes of peace, prosperity, and freedom and to *attenuate* the causes of war, poverty, and servitude. Both of these models of social causality, religious and secular, are fallacious. The religious paradigm claims that there is one gateway to these earthly aims by way of a spiritual monopoly. Its leaders warn that obedience to the sacred dogma of one true god is the only path to peace, prosperity, and freedom.

In contrast, the secular paradigm holds that it is impractical, if not impossible to reach the world aims of peace, prosperity, and freedom. The secular pessimist argues that if peace could replace war, if prosperity could replace poverty, and if freedom could replace servitude, these ideal aims would have been reached long ago. However, to understand the source of this shortsighted pessimism, it is necessary to examine the model of causality behind it.

A prime question of this chapter asks is there a practical path for reaching world peace, prosperity, and freedom? Of course, many respected people believe these are unrealistic and unreachable aims. Therefore, we must determine, in truth, whether such lofty aims are realistic and reachable in the real world.

In finding a practical answer to this challenging question, it is critical to define a precise distinction between what is possible in contrast to what is impossible. The idea that everything is possible is both naive and utopian. We cannot reach, for example, such ideal aims as *perfect* peace, *ultimate* prosperity, and *absolute* freedom. By observing human action, we can see that to be human is to be imperfect. Yet, even with all their imperfect achievements, humans can move closer and closer to perfection without ever achieving that which is perfect.

Leonardo's famous portrait of Lisa del Giocondo, known as the *Mona Lisa*, is not a perfect work of art, if for no other reason than "perfect" art defies definition. Without being perfect, however, his renowned painting of the alluring lady with the "Mona Lisa smile" has enough aesthetic appeal to be praised by art historians and critics as a great masterpiece of European culture. Thus, in pursuit of perfection, it makes no sense to degrade or discard the creations of Leonardo, Mozart, and Newton, because they were not "perfect" works of art, music, and science.

In devising an effective strategy toward world peace, prosperity, and freedom, to be effective, the strategy must be practical, which means it must be possible. To separate possible goals from impossible ones is a focus of this chapter. In reaching for any lofty achievement, especially when expanding peace, prosperity, and freedom, it is critical to avoid impractical strategies. As noted, it is futile to reach for perfect peace, ultimate prosperity, or absolute freedom, all of which require win-win exchange without compromise. These aims are compromised, when through ignorance of causality, some people reach for gain through force or fraud without knowing the adverse domino effects of their win-lose actions. In time, these effects may come back to haunt them, boomeranging as unforeseen contingencies and unintended consequences, which invariably are counterproductive, damaging, or even deadly. Although these win-lose actions preempt the establishment of perfect peace, ultimate prosperity, and absolute freedom, when limited in their scope and scale, they do not prevent the advance of common peace, prosperity, and freedom for common people of all nations. These altruistic aims are attainable without ever reaching social perfection. Although we cannot avoid all coercive action for win-lose gain, eventually, we can avoid building entire institutions of force and fraud for win-lose gain.

൞

In moving from idealism to the realism of finding a practical plan for advancing peace, prosperity, and freedom, it is important to define the meaning of two strategic terms that may be familiar to many readers, namely, *attenuation* and *optimization*:

> *To attenuate is to act toward weakening the force, power, or effect of some physical, biological, or social phenomenon.*

A key point of what can be called "attenuation strategy" is that to *attenuate* something does not mean to *eliminate* it. For example, to attenuate the causes of war, poverty, and servitude is not to eliminate entirely all the causes of these age-old afflictions. Rather, it means to make these pernicious social effects weaker and weaker in their degree of virulence, severity, and destructive force by attenuating their respective causes. In other words, by continuing to diminish the scope and scale of their anti-social causes, the incidence of their harmful effects will continue to diminish over time.

In a similar way, flu vaccines are not formulated to *eliminate* world influenza, but to *attenuate* the virulence of viral agents in flu vaccines, and to *attenuate* the incidence of flu by containing or minimizing its spread. In light of present medical technology, it is impractical to try to eliminate the flu. In short, to attenuate the incidence of flu in order to minimize its spread and severity is not to eliminate the incidence of flu. Thus, to attenuate is to take action toward making the strength of some phenomenon weaker and weaker over time in its degree of force, power, or virulence.

Complementary to this *attenuation* strategy is *optimization* strategy, built on this definition:

> *To optimize is to act toward creating the greatest degree of some physical, biological, or social phenomenon.*

Reaching for the greatest degree of peace, prosperity, and freedom is an ongoing social process that never ends. Yet, to reiterate, optimizing their true causes does not bring us perfect peace, prosperity, and freedom. To optimize is not to "perfectionize." Pursuing impractical ideals of social perfection is a naive scheme of endless frustration. However, we can celebrate in knowing that we only have to *optimize* the social conditions—founded on true explanations of causality—which bring us ever closer to an elegant tour de force: creation of the greatest degree of peace, prosperity, and freedom for the greatest number. This abounding blessing will be born out of the practical and vital operation of win-win principles of voluntary exchange for mutual gain.

As will be shown, by optimizing win-win social gain and by attenuating win-lose social gain, religious followers would reap huge benefits. As their *loss* of wealth and freedom would continue to fall, so their *gain* of wealth and freedom would continue to rise.

Such a dramatic revolution from social loss to social gain would be a priceless boon to their well-being. A key part of the practical application of this strategy for attenuating destructive social effects and optimizing constructive social effects begins with this observation:

> *The laws of nature do not prevent humans from attenuating the causes of war, poverty, and servitude, or from optimizing the causes of peace, prosperity, and freedom.*

This realization allows us to move away from social pessimism toward social optimism by recognizing that we do not have to change human *nature* to move closer and closer to these lofty aims—we only have to change human *paradigms*. Thus, a crucial step in our success at building win-win solutions to our most pressing social problems is tied to our skill at distinguishing between that which is *possible* and that which is *impossible*. For example, changing principles of causality is impossible, but changing paradigms of causality, though difficult, is not only possible; it is done all the time.

ɔ

In our ongoing struggle for human advancement, it is critical to know the difference between possible achievements, which are in clear contrast to those that are impossible. If we cannot tell the difference, if there is no sharp line of demarcation between possible and impossible, we may waste our time and resources in pursuing impossible aims that are forever unreachable. Therefore, it is vital to make this crucial distinction by postulating a principle of possibility:

POSSIBILITY PRINCIPLE
All human ends are possible that do not violate the laws of nature.

As a self-educated physicist, few scientists have been more influential than Michael Faraday in enriching our lives through the discovery of natural laws. Faraday observed, "Nothing is too wonderful to be true, if it be consistent with the laws of nature."[103] Consistency with nature is the key to scientific success. However, if we believe that we must repeal or violate a natural law in order to reach our creative ends, that is impractical because it is impossible. Rather, we must determine which ends are possible to attain due to their harmony with nature. Then we have only to discover which means can attain the ends sought.

For a rocket engine to power a spaceship from earth to moon, before its fuel is spent and the engine dies, it must reach escape velocity to overcome the earth's gravitational field. We cannot repeal the law of gravity to avoid the technical difficulties and added costs of having to reach escape velocity before we can reach the moon. Some engineers, perhaps frustrated by the technical challenge, may curse Newton and decry his law of gravitation. Yet, if they would reach the moon, they must first reach escape velocity, which, like it or not, is to obey the law of gravitation.

Nature's challenge is endless: Obey my laws—or fail to reach your aims. However, before we can obey nature's laws, we first have to discover them, then define and understand them. Nature does not write out her laws of causation on stone tablets; we have to discover them on our own.

The converse corollary of the possibility principle, the impossibility principle, can also be observed to operate in nature:

IMPOSSIBILITY PRINCIPLE
All human ends are impossible that would violate the laws of nature.

If humans would accelerate the creation of significant and revolutionary achievements, they must not unknowingly block or impede their advance. Thus, where humans have grand creative aims, it is imperative to know where the possible achievement ends and the impossible begins.

∞

In the history of milestone advances in any field of endeavor, from the beginning, they were usually deemed impossible to achieve. As we know, hindsight is usually superior to foresight. In retrospect, they were not impossible, only extremely difficult to achieve. As always, the greater the human achievement, the greater the difficulty of accomplishing that achievement. If our landmark achievements were easy to create in the first place, they would not have been honored as *great*.

Historical examples are legion. A. G. Eiffel's proposal to build a 300 meter (984 feet) iron tower at the entrance to the Universal Exposition of 1889 in Paris was derided by many experts in construction and engineering as impossible to build. After all, Eiffel's tower would be nearly twice the height of the world's then tallest standing structure: the 555-foot Washington Monument. Even if the tower could be built, French artists, writers, sculptors, architects, and musicians openly denounced it as a "Tower of Babel"—an iron monstrosity that would surely mar, if not ruin, the majestic skyline of Paris.[104]

In engineering and entrepreneuring the world's first thousand-foot tower, Eiffel, his architects, and engineers had to design and build a practical structure that was stable and durable. Moreover, it had to resist the force of high winds without collapsing under its own weight. For his revolutionary tower, Eiffel also innovated building techniques that would make it both possible and safe to erect

237

such a massive structure. In creating the "impossible," Eiffel became the father of the modern skyscraper. He also designed the iron skeleton for another impossible colossus: the *Statue of Liberty*.

Although Eiffel's landmark advances in modern construction were extremely difficult to achieve, they were neither impractical nor impossible because his monumental creation did not require *violating* natural laws. Instead, it required *obeying* natural laws, which led him away from impossible and impractical aims toward those that were possible and practical.

For this crucial reason, the laws of nature have been the most valuable discoveries in human history. Because they identify physical, biological, and social causality, natural laws remain the prime movers of human progress. More than any other discoveries, they have moved humans to make paradigm shifts away from false models of causality toward those that are true.

The most practical advances toward human enrichment have come through the discovery of natural laws or principles. This has led to revolutionary achievements for unlocking the hidden secrets of our mysterious universe. The key to knowing nature has always been the discovery of principles that explain which causes lead to which effects. For this reason, all natural principles are pragmatic (L., *pragmaticus*=practical), which means they have the potential leading us to new knowledge, new inventions, and new products for human enrichment.

∾

Early in the twentieth century, two bicycle mechanics in Dayton, Ohio, Wilbur and Orville Wright, were trying to build heavier than air machines that were capable of powered flight. However, their problem was formidable because they did not know how this could be done. Nevertheless, by designing controlled experiments—which included the elegant invention of the wind tunnel—they discovered the principles of aerodynamics.

To laud the Wrights' discovery of these natural principles as merely *practical* would be a gross understatement. It was this seminal discovery that enabled them to build flying machines in a world of experts who claimed that human flight was not only impractical, it was impossible. Of course, the creation of human flight was only "impossible" to those who were ignorant of its principles. For the Wright Brothers, their learning how to fly came directly from their earlier discovery of the principles of aerodynamics. This showed them how to lift their majestic machines through the air to achieve controlled, powered flight over sustained time in a craft heavier than air.

In examining the history of the discovery of natural principles and their crucial role in human progress, their unique value is generalized below as a principle of universal utility:

> *All natural principles are practical guides to solving physical, biological, and social problems.*

For this reason, all natural principles are priceless due to their pragmatic potential to advance our understanding of universal causality. To be sure, their successful application may be delayed for decades or even centuries. Yet, over time, all natural principles provide crucial knowledge for creating solutions to human problems. These include our most critical physical, biological and social problems. However, as important as the discovery of principles may be, their value as central keys to problem solving is not obvious.

The pathway to reaching major solutions to major problems is not self-evident. Humans tend to perceive the proposal of grand inventions and revolutionary innovations, based on discovered principles, to be impossible or impractical. This is especially true when they cannot imagine how those innovations could ever be accomplished. In every civilization, bright, educated, and well-read citizens have been quick to conclude, "If I can't figure out how to do it, then it can't be done."

After the Wright Brothers had been flying over America and Europe for many years, more and more people began to lose faith in their long-held belief that human flight is *impossible!* They began to back away from their ridicule of the brothers, which included calling them the "Wright Liars" (which they were not) instead of the Wright Flyers (which they were since their 1903 flights at Kitty Hawk). Yet, even as late as February 10, 1907, a French editorial in the Paris *Herald* questioned the honesty of the brothers with this bold heading: "Flyers or Liars." The editorial charged that the Wrights "are in fact either flyers or liars." They ended their accusation with this derisive barb, "It is difficult to fly; it is easy to say 'we have flown.'"[105] Their implication was clear: Because it is easier to lie than it is to fly, the Wright Brothers had to be liars, not flyers.

At the time, some naysayers finally admitted that flying was possible, but so-called experts were quick to point out its practical limitations. As supposed experts in aeronautics, some were certain that flying machines could not ever carry much more than the weight of the pilot. Pessimism on the practicality of flying was widespread. Proposals for nearly every major advance in aviation were judged either impossible or impractical by a long list of pessimists who warned against one aeronautical folly after another.

Flying after dark was impractical due to the hidden dangers of night flying. Metal fuselages, though stronger than canvas, were unfeasible because of their extreme weight. Radar was not always reliable, and was, thereby, impractical for aeronautical navigation. Because jet engines were also unreliable, jet propulsion was unfeasible. Moreover, it was thought to be impossible to fly faster than the speed of sound. Yet, by some miracle, even if it could be done, upon entering the sound barrier at some 770 mph, the aircraft would disintegrate.

As it turned out, not one of these advances in aviation was impossible or even impractical because their creation did not require the abolition of natural law.* However, they did require innovators who were driven to discover and apply nature's principles to solve aeronautical problems. No matter how trying and difficult the creative challenge, they prevailed because they never gave up. By observing the operation of natural principles, they created the science of flight we call aeronautics. Their lasting legacy is modern aviation.

Again, nothing has had more practical value in human history than the discovery of natural principles. As principles of nature guide us to solve physical problems, so they can guide us to solve social problems. The most pressing human problem to solve is how to attenuate war, poverty, and servitude, and thereby avoid the ultimate social catastrophe of human-caused extermination, which means extinction.

ᢙ

Since the entrance of the nuclear age, more than half a century ago, win-lose religion has remained a growing threat to the longevity of civilization and to our human species. The magnitude of this crisis has already been emphasized. For the first time in human history, religious leaders

---

* An Airbus A380 weighs 1,200,000 pounds, cruises at 630 mph, and can accommodate 555 passengers. This exceeds early predictions that airplanes could never carry more than the weight of the pilot.

and their followers, by continuing to enforce their vision of heavenly cosmology, have the potential power to wipe out the human species. By gaining access to weapons of mass destruction, they can unleash the full fury of nuclear, biological and chemical warfare upon disbelievers in the divinity of their one true god. However, to identify this risk of disaster does not mean that it is certain to occur. Nonetheless, many educated people are sure that such a social disaster is inevitable due to the finality of Murphy's Law, which predicts: *Anything that can possibly go wrong with a system of human endeavor will go wrong.* For such pessimists, the certainty of religious conflict leading to a world catastrophe is only a question of time. As they see it, in our nuclear age, things will go terribly wrong for the entire human race because the advance of religious intolerance and fanaticism is unstoppable.

For many, Murphy's Law provokes extreme pessimism about the future of our human species—because if Murphy were right, humans would have no future. Fortunately, Murphy's Law is no more than a humorous, satirical saying that was never a law of nature to begin with. Thus, to avoid social catastrophe and to advance the mutual kindness and altruism of win-win religion, we do not have to repeal Murphy's Law because it is not a law. But, we do have to refute and repudiate the presumed truth of win-lose religion: *For true believers to gain, disbelievers must be forced to lose.*

This has always been a false model of social causality. It is based on the erroneous premise that win-lose exchange for the glory of God will create religious peace, prosperity, and freedom for the faithful to enjoy. Religious history shows that religious leaders cannot deliver on their promise. In fact, their pernicious paradigm of win-lose theology leads to religious war, poverty, and servitude—the very opposite of their spurious promise of religious peace, prosperity, and freedom.

Win-lose religion is based on coercive exchange where force or fraud exacts gain for some through the loss of others. Regardless of their source, all win-lose exchanges generate destructive domino effects. The diminishment of these destructive effects begins with the diminishment of their true causes. Of course, this presupposes that their true causes have been identified, clarified, and verified to be broadcast to each new generation.

ENDNOTES

102. Kenneth L. Barker, ed., *Zondervan NIV Study Bible* (Grand Rapids, Michigan: Zondervan, 2002), 1571.

103. James Hamilton, *A Life of Discovery: Michael Faraday, Giant of the Scientific Revolution* (New York: Random House, 2004) 334.

104. Joseph Harris, *The Tallest Tower: Eiffel and the Belle Epoque* (Boston: Houghton Mifflin Co., 1975), 20.

105. Fred C. Kelley, *The Wright Brothers* (New York: Farrar, Straus and Young, 1950), 193.

Chapter Nine

Principles of Social Causality

Albert Einstein gave an eloquent tribute to the value of principles, "My interest in science was always essentially limited to the study of principles."[106] Einstein's "study of principles" led to his understanding of principles, which in turn led to his discovery of principles, one of which is his paradigm-shattering principle, $E=mc^2$.

It is important to examine the unique position of all natural principles as the foundation for physical, biological, and social achievement. Human progress advances through the discovery of natural principles, which can be trusted for their reliability to repeat themselves again and again without fail. However, due to their intrinsic repeatability, many people find principles to be little more than boring and unexciting abstractions. This raises the question, "How can we expect people to be thrilled by the prospect of knowing the nature of principles, when they are perceived as mere intangibles or scholastic curiosities?" We cannot, unless their perception of principles *qua* principles shifts to a new enlightenment and understanding.

The constancy of principles to remain unchanged gives them their priceless value. To be sure, those who are bored by their perception of nature's principles may suppose them to be dull generalizations without material appeal. However, such people are yet to grasp their unrivaled significance.

To be bored is to be weary of repetition. Yet, all principles are monotonously repetitious — which is the key to their unique value. The past and present reliability of a principle continually renews our confidence in its predictability to give us a view of the future that we can count on, a reality that we can foretell to be true tomorrow as it was yesterday.

A celebrated essayist and orator, and a powerful preacher against the iniquity of institutionalized slavery in America, was the New England clergyman, Ralph Waldo Emerson, who did not miss the significance of *principles* in noting, "The value of a principle is the number of things it will explain." [107] One thing that it explained to Emerson was the evil barbarity of bonded slavery. Emerson warned those who would preserve slavery in the South as well as the North, "If you put a chain around the neck of a slave the other end fastens itself around your own."[108] You cannot impose slavery on the necks of your neighbors, and at the same time, isolate your own neck from the destructive domino effects that are certain to reach you in one vile form or another. A social system that can legitimately enslave one man who is innocent of harming his neighbors, can legitimately enslave any man who is innocent of harming his neighbors.

More than any other human discovery, the discovery of natural principles eclipses all other discoveries in significance and importance. *Principles* are the perpetual constants of nature that guide us to discover which causes lead to which effects. *Principles* are the engines of physical, biological, and social progress that enable us to understand what is going on in all fundamental fields of endeavor. *Principles* are never boring to those who sense their elegance, precisely because they are exciting to ponder for their peerless power to explain cause-and-effect. *Principles* are the clearest windows to our sweeping views of universal reality.

৩৩

A great shortcoming of contemporary education has been the failure of teachers, in general, to show their students the priceless value of natural principles, the operational rules of the universe. To understand the universe is to understand its principles, which are its natural laws of organization and causation.

A key strategy of education (as opposed to indoctrination) is to illustrate and demonstrate to students the vital utility — the endless practicality — of *all* principles of nature that have been discovered and verified through the dynamic power of *independent observation*. For students, this is a crucial introduction to their basic understanding of cause-and-effect. Where the aim is to transcend mere indoctrination with true education, nothing is more fundamental. Principles are critical keys that unlock the doorways to our discovery of universal causality.

On earth, principles reveal what's going on in our world of human exchange by showing the true causes of social effects. This is best dramatized for students by comparing the verified causes of *constructive* social effects with the verified causes of *destructive* social effects. The difference is dramatic; and dramatization of physical, biological, and social *opposites* is one of the effective strategies for bypassing indoctrination in pursuit of education through independent observation.

In the Information Age the grasp of principles is our only salvation from the scourge of information overload.

Principles remain the grand simplifiers of the complex and convoluted jungle of chaotic information that engulfs our daily lives.

In the ancient Greek tragedy, *Prometheus Bound*, attributed to Aeschylus, we are told, "Memory is the mother of all wisdom." But is it? Before the revolutionary invention of movable type for mass printing on paper (c. 1450) by J. Gutenberg of Mainz, memory was far more important as a source of information than it is today. Yet, in the Information Age, with our easy access to a glut of information on demand, the information has to be filtered because most of it has little or no value, and may even be disinformation.

The most effective filters to evaluate information are principles. Principles are the key generalizations for our memory to retain, especially *verified* principles of causality. The fact is, in our time, as well as that of Aeschylus: *Understanding causality is the mother of wisdom.* History confirms that wisdom eludes all who fail to know causation.

⌒⌒

The focus of this chapter is to identify various social principles that reveal which social causes lead to which social effects. Whether these effects are beneficial or harmful, we cannot afford to misidentify their true causes. Nothing is more critical in our efforts to tame the violence of faith. Anyone curious enough to look can observe directly and indirectly the operation of these principles. Each principle is a generalized prediction of social phenomena.

In initiating the Science of Social Causation in this treatise, one of its two most fundamental principles was introduced earlier as the Law of Human Action. It generalizes: *All humans act toward their perception of gain and away from their perception of loss.* In choosing their perception of gain, for every action chosen by every individual, he or she acts toward gain through the gain of others, or through the loss of others. That covers all possibilities.

The most common argument for seeking gain through the loss of others is that seeking gain through the gain of others is impractical, in other words, unworkable. Many decent and respected people have erroneously concluded, win-win action does not work, and win-lose action does work. Win-Win Theory, however, falsifies this pernicious and pervasive paradigm of social causality.

In the chapter on The Superiority Syndrome, the Principle of Win-Lose Exchange predicts the social effects of coercive exchange for win-lose gain: *Win-lose exchange destroys human wealth, expands human servitude, and incites human conflict.* In the case of win-lose religion, driven by involuntary exchange for win-lose gain, we can observe that it destroys wealth, expands servitude, and incites conflict, not the least of which includes the provocation of war. What could be more destructive? The Principle of Win-Lose Exchange predicts the deadly consequences of win-lose religion. Like all natural principles, it can neither be repealed nor evaded. Because the quest for win-lose gain causes destructive domino effects, true believers in the sanctity of such ill-gotten gain cannot escape the destructive consequences of their misguided actions. Some of the destructive domino effects of imposing win-lose exchange for sacred aims are explained by this anti-social principle:

Win-lose exchange causes wealth and freedom per capita to fall, and causes poverty and servitude per capita to rise.

Wherever wealth and freedom are falling, while poverty and servitude are rising, these negative social effects are nearly always caused by institutionalized coercion for religious or political gain. Throughout social history, the advance of religious and political coercion has had a common justification for a common theme: we are seizing your wealth and freedom in the name of god, or on behalf of the people, or in support of the nation, or in honor of the leader. Over the ages, the authorities have sought to assure their people that the more wealth and freedom we appropriate from you, the better off you will be. As always, many citizens are certain of the truth of this promise, bolstered by the weight of win-lose dogma.

In the short run, the true causes of poverty and servitude may be covered up by those who would distort reality for their own win-lose gain. In time, however, those who are willing to view the constancy of social principles with their own eyes can expose such cover-ups. Nature's principles of causality cannot be hidden from view, and over time, they are impervious to human cover-ups.

Here is another principle of social causality that refutes the spurious claims by institutions of autocratic authority, that they can bring their followers the blessings of wealth and freedom by way of coercive exchange for win-lose gain:

> *Operation of the win-lose principle of involuntary exchange for coercive gain creates the least wealth and freedom for the greatest number.**

Observation confirms that win-lose exchange is *not* the originator of wealth and freedom; thus, we can derive a converse principle:

> *Operation of the win-win principle of voluntary exchange for non-coercive gain creates the greatest wealth and freedom for the greatest number:*†

---

* Again, the Win-Lose Principle, as a guide to human action, generalizes: *Never seek gain through the gain of others, and always seek gain through the loss of others by force or fraud.*

† The Win-Win Principle, as a guide to human action, generalizes: *Always seek gain through the gain of others, and never seek gain through the loss of others by force or fraud.*

There is a clear divide between the social effects of win-win exchange and the anti-social effects of win-lose exchange. In common language, principles "tell it like it is." Those who want peace, prosperity, and freedom must employ the Win-Win Principle of voluntary exchange. Those who prefer war, poverty, and servitude must employ the Win-Lose Principle of involuntary exchange. A corollary of these principles of social causality is easily derived: *The greater the operation of the win-lose principle of involuntary exchange, the greater the poverty and servitude.*

૬૭

By way of win-lose tradition, those who have reaped the greatest riches from coercive gain have usually been the lauded leaders of institutionalized force. Anyone who has read a little social history knows that those who sold their followers on the glory of organizing institutions of win-lose autocracy lived in palaces and mansions — while the majority of their followers and subjects lived in huts and hovels. To be sure, there is nothing wrong with living in a palace or a mansion. The crucial question is this: Were these luxurious structures built through the creation of new wealth or through the seizure of old wealth? Wherever win-lose religion prevails, its destructive domino effects lower the general quality of life. Win-lose religion includes not only seizing wealth and freedom from unbelievers and disbelievers, but from true believers as well. *Win-lose religion increases the number of losers per capita and decreases the number of winners per capita.*

The truth of these social principles can be seen in operation by any independent observer willing to look. Where the aim is to identify physical, biological, and social truth, there is no substitute for independent observation of the principles that reveal such truth. The discovery of principles of nature has given us the most practical and effective means to identify and verify physical, biological, and social causality. Because the discovery of any universal principle has universal value, its altruistic effects are universal even if the discoverer does not have the self-image of an altruist. Principles fuel the engines of progress. Directly or indirectly, this benefits all humans whether or not they are aware of the benefits. Those who discover principles of nature may not see themselves as altruists, yet their discoveries are unavoidably and necessarily altruistic, as they reach the pinnacle of win-win altruism and human achievement.

∞

To understand better what causes good things to happen to religious people, it is also important to understand what causes bad things to happen to them. No matter how devoted the faithful may be to practicing their religious beliefs, if they and their families are the victims of war, poverty, and servitude, they are unable to partake of the good life. No matter how devout religious followers may be, where food and shelter are sparse, where religious war is rampant, where children are maimed and killed by sectarian violence, and where people are forced into involuntary servitude by religious authorities, then whatever they may think is the good life, this is not it. Where then can the good life be found, and how can it be reached?

Nothing will reap more precious gains for more pious people than for them to secure the blessings of peace, prosperity, and freedom. Yet, the question remains, are these practical aims for reachable ends, or are they merely utopian fantasies that are forever beyond human reach?

∞

The elegance of the Golden Rule Principle has been precisely defined: *Do not seize wealth and freedom from others, as you would have them not seize your wealth and freedom.* But is this principle a practical guide to social action? Is it a workable standard of social conduct for all people to follow regardless of their religion, race, culture, or status?

The Golden Rule Principle clearly defines which human actions *not* to take. Yet, some people may ignore the principle for no other reason than they believe that it is *impractical* to follow. Therefore, should decent people violate the rule by seizing the wealth and freedom of others as the only "practical" path of human action to follow?

Observation of social action reveals compelling reasons to practice the Golden Rule Principle and encourage others to do the same. To multiply the followers of the Golden Rule Principle, we must answer this universal question, what are the benefits to be gained by following and applying this principle? Before we act, our human nature requires us to ask, what's in it for us?

In answering this question, it is important to note that the rich and diverse benefits reaped by practicing the Golden Rule Principle are rarely obvious. This is because the true causes of social effects — whether constructive or destructive — are not easy to identify, especially without the intellectual advantage of observational analysis. Thus, it is vital to reveal and broadcast the treasure of community wealth created by applying the Principle of Win-Win Exchange for mutual gain. In so doing, we can incite paradigm shifts away from false explanations of social causality toward those that are true. These spectacular revelations on the true causes of common wealth for common people will turn more and more people away from win-lose action for destructive gain, toward win-win action for constructive gain. This is the crucial paradigm shift in operation. Its genesis is to identify, clarify, and verify social causation.

The Golden Rule Principle, in defining the actions that we *ought not* to take, has a complement in the Win-Win Principle, which defines the actions that we *ought* to take: *Always seek gain through the gain of others, and never seek gain through the loss of others by force or fraud.* The salient question is this: are such principles merely ideal aims that are impossible to reach in the real world? Indeed, if they *are* impossible, then they are unreachable. However, this is not the case. They are quite possible to reach precisely because there are no laws of nature to bar humans from following these simple rules of social behavior.

By applying the Golden Rule Principle of never seeking gain through the loss of others, this opens the door to the operation of the Win-Win Principle of *always* seeking gain through the gain of others. Where the aim is to advance the well-being of all humans in all societies, nothing could be more practical and effective than applying these principles. This is precisely because there are no other human actions that could lead to such remarkable effects.

Where the means employed *can* attain the ends sought, such effective means are both possible and practical. In this case, the means employed is win-win exchange for mutual gain. However, merely to say that the effects of win-win exchange are "remarkable" or even "amazing," is to understate the magnitude and diversity of its manifold blessings. To reiterate, *Win-win exchange is the act of gaining through the gain of others without gaining through their loss by force or fraud.* Given this semantic foundation, here is another social principle first introduced in the chapter on The Win-Win Principle, namely, the Principle of Win-Win Exchange. It predicts the most important and valuable benefits of win-win exchange for mutual gain: *Win-win exchange creates human wealth, expands human freedom, and fosters human peace.*

These essentials of the good life—wealth, freedom, and peace—are available for the enrichment of all religious believers who live in a free and prosperous society. In such a win-win society, even those with meager assets are far better off than those who live in an impoverished society — impoverished because it is usually a win-lose society in the first place. Observation shows, *The more win-lose exchanges in a society, the more impoverished that society will be.* The escape from societal poverty is to apply the reverse principle: *The more win-win exchanges in a society, the more prosperous that society will be.*

In today's wealthy nations with a flourishing middle class, common people often reveal their prosperity by giving away unwanted garments, not because they are worn or tattered, but because they tire of them or they are no longer in fashion — or they no longer fit. In contrast, in an impoverished nation, the common people are the poor who are reluctant to give up what little they have to those who may be even poorer than they are.

The principles of nature reveal a path of escape from the earth's *gravity* by reaching escape velocity. In a similar way, the principles of nature also reveal a path of escape from the earth's *poverty* through the operation of the Win-Win Principle. Beyond the escape from poverty, the same principle shows how to escape from the desperations of servitude and the calamities of war:

> *Operation of the win-win principle causes the greatest peace, prosperity, and freedom for the greatest number.*

Wherever peace, prosperity, and freedom are perceived to be good for people, then building society on the Win-Win Principle brings about the greatest good for the greatest number. Direct and indirect observation of the Win-Win Principle in operation verifies its truth as a repeating principle of nature.

On the other hand, those who would *not* escape from the misery of war, poverty, and servitude also have a principle to follow, namely, the Win-Lose Principle: *Never seek gain through the gain of others, and always seek gain through the loss of others by force or fraud.* It does not matter whether the Win-Lose Principle is justified and imposed by good guys or by bad guys. Those who seek to justify coercive gain may be righteous or unrighteous, educated or uneducated, and they may be intelligent or unintelligent. But in every case, the coercive domino effects of their win-lose actions are predictable:

> *Operation of the win-lose principle causes the greatest degree of war, poverty, and servitude for the greatest number.*

Direct and indirect observation of the Win-Lose Principle in operation verifies its truth as a repeating principle of social causality. By this chapter, the practical value of these principles should be evident to readers through the power of their own observation. Through understanding the operation of the Win-Lose Principle in contrast to the Win-Win Principle, we can identify and verify the most important social causes leading to the most critical social effects. It cannot be overstressed: to know what you are doing—to know how to reach your aims—you must know which causes lead to which effects. Again, this means that causality must first be *identified*, then *clarified*, and then *verified*. Then it should be applied to effective action.

Once these principles of social cause-and-effect are understood by religious followers, they can make a deliberate choice between two social alternatives: (1) They can promote and employ the Win-Lose Principle to advance the greatest degree of war, poverty, and servitude for the greatest number; or (2) They can promote and employ the Win-Win Principle to advance the greatest degree of peace, prosperity, and freedom for the greatest number. If the blessings of the latter are compelling to religious believers, then the only religion that is capable of advancing the greatest peace, prosperity, and freedom for the greatest number of religious believers is Win-Win Religion. Defined in the chapter on Win-Win Altruism, the Principle of Win-Win Religion is a central principle of social action: *For true believers to gain, disbelievers must gain and never be forced to lose.*

Win-Win Religion is the only religion that truly honors the Golden Rule Principle without compromise. The practice of Win-Win Religion is a practical means for creating the greatest wealth and freedom for the greatest number of religious believers. It is practical because it is a successful means for attaining such vital ends. *Practicality is attainability of useful ends.* The most useful and beneficial ends are reached through win-win means. For every human, life's most practical question and pragmatic challenge remain: Can the means employed attain the ends sought?

The practical means to peace, prosperity, and freedom employs the Golden Rule Principle of win-win exchange.

Nature's laws of physical, biological, and social causality determine what humans can or cannot attain. These laws explain why the theology of win-lose religion is unavoidably bellicose and why it augments war and diminishes peace. The laws of nature defy their alteration for a more desirable outcome.

છ

Survival of our species in the nuclear age requires the resolve of decent people with good minds and educations to marshal their wealth and influence to convince religious believers to shift their paradigms away from faith in the rightness and righteousness of win-lose religion. They must

257

convince religious followers to make the vital paradigm shift toward a new faith in the rightness and righteousness of Win-Win Religion, anchored to the Golden Rule Principle. If they are successful, if they can "keep the faith" in Win-Win Religion, then Win-Lose Religion will fall out of favor and into disuse as a means of reaching the promise of sacred ends. Faith in the believed equity, utility, and morality of the win-lose paradigm of social causality is the *problem*. Conversely, faith in the observed equity, utility, and morality of the win-win paradigm of social causality is the *solution*. This crucial paradigm shift is a practical and necessary means of removing humans from the Endangered Species List by allowing peace, prosperity, and freedom to flourish for the enrichment of all believers of all religions.

ENDNOTES

106. Alice Calaprice, ed., *The Expandable Quotable Einstein* (Princeton and Oxford: Princeton University Press, 2000), 245. See letter to Maurice Solovine, October 30, 1924.

107. Ralph Waldo Emerson, *The Complete Works of Ralph Waldo Emerson* (Boston and New York: Houghton Mifflin Co., 1911), 232.

108. Ralph Waldo Emerson, "Compensation," *The Works of Ralph Waldo Emerson*. (New York: Hearst's International Library Co., 1914), 73.

Chapter Ten

Science and Theology

A revolutionary advance of human history arrived with the discovery of a nonviolent means of dealing with dissidents who challenged the truth of esteemed dogma on the nature of physical reality. Before this amazing discovery, claims of physical truth were nearly always derived from the imagination of religious, political, philosophical, legal, and academic authorities. Nearly all such authorities have had this in common: They did not want to be questioned or challenged on the rightness or legitimacy of their authority; and they did not want their authority to be either lost or superseded.

Authorities of every stripe are prone to defend their authority whenever disbelievers challenge it. When this happens, as it will, the crucial question is how will the authorities protect their authority from doubters, challengers, and noisy detractors who voice their disapproval? A common approach has been for the authorities to silence such irreverent people by exiling, jailing, torturing, or killing them — with or without trial. Such authorities are motivated to quell their critics because they cling to a win-lose model of social causality, a false paradigm that demands: *For the authorities to gain, their critics must be forced to lose.*

Four centuries ago, however, an original way was evolving that would show authorities how to deal with disbelievers in the truth and legitimacy of their authority without silencing them through force, the tradition throughout most of history. During the Renaissance, an entirely new approach to understanding physical, biological, and social causality was blossoming in the Western World. It would become a revolutionary strategy for the advancement of knowledge. Remarkably, it avoided either silencing or harming those who might rock the boat of authority, especially by falsifying authoritarian explanations of causality.

The question will never go away. What should be done with those "troublemakers" who dare to challenge authority? Why not go with tradition; why not jail, torture, or kill those who refuse to embrace any dogma without question, and, worse, refuse to shut up about it? After all, over thousands of years, such expedient methods have silenced those who dared to question authority. Yet, a novel alternative to the repression of critics by force evolved. This alternative was so profound that it would eventually accelerate progress beyond all human imagination. Remarkably, it turned out to be a win-win alternative to win-lose tradition.

Since the nineteenth century, this win-win method of causality identification has been known as the *scientific method*. It is the most powerful method ever discovered and developed to identify and verify which causes lead to which effects. Whether they know it or not, all humans are enriched by the physical, biological, and social progress that follows the advance of human knowledge of cause-and-effect.

Even though the scientific method came to fruition through the discoveries of Isaac Newton in the seventeenth century, its amazing versatility as a benevolent tool for the creation of win-win wealth has not been realized or understood. Few who use this method to separate fact from fiction realize its benevolence as a *nonviolent* alternative to silencing critics of the status quo. The scientific method is a win-win strategy to identify causality by revealing truth through *observation*, rather than by assuming truth through *imagination*. In technical language, it is an *a posteriori*—after observation—method of causality identification. Its grand aim is to identify and verify the true causes of physical, biological, and social effects, not through the accepted tradition of imagining causality, but through the revolutionary method of observing causality from the viewpoint of independent observers. Without *observation* of causality, there is nothing to counter *imagination* of causality.

Whatever conclusions on cause-and-effect are reached through scientific observation are recorded and described as an open invitation to any curious persons to look and see with their own eyes. Disbelievers who refuse to see or believe that these original conclusions are true—whether they observe or not—are not harmed by anyone for their disbelief. This creates a unique path for a new liberty to be found in the "freedom of disbelief"—freedom to disbelieve in the claimed truth of anything, anywhere, at any time without fear of reprisal from believers. Without this priceless freedom of disbelief, tyranny has prevailed in the name of god, nation, or leader with little interruption.

All social communities—whether religious, political, commercial, scientific, technological, or educational—have had and still have their hardcore conservatives. The conservative aims to conserve something, which is to preserve it from change or destruction. Conservatism as a path for preserving paradigms of causality can be constructive or destructive. The strategy of conservation employed by the conservator or conservative can be either a win-win or a win-lose strategy. Whether your conservatism is constructive or destructive depends entirely upon what you are trying to conserve, and your strategy for conservation.

In trying to conserve the Socialistic ideas of Karl Marx within the coercive Union of Soviet Socialist Republics, Communist authorities murdered some sixty millions of their own people. In China, Communist authorities murdered nearly seventy-seven million Chinese to conserve Marxian Socialism. Such grand policies of orchestrated murder in the name of conserving win-lose socialism are impressive for the very scale of their oppression and brutality. They should be included in the *Guinness Book of Records* with the anticipation that such heinous records—set during the execution of win-lose conservatism—will never be attempted or repeated again.

To avoid coercive conservatism, conservatives must ask: What am I conserving and how should it be conserved? Whenever conservatives conserve win-lose ideas with win-lose oppression, their conservation can only be destructive at best and catastrophic at worst. Thus, to avoid unintended social catastrophe, a sharp line of demarcation must be drawn between win-lose and win-win conservatism.

Those who would conserve classical music through the marketing of classical concerts are win-win conservatives. Those who would conserve freedom of speech and freedom of religion by broadcasting their splendid virtues to every corner of the globe are also win-win conservatives. Thus, all conservatives are either good guys or bad guys. This depends entirely on what they are trying to conserve and, even more importantly, how they would conserve it.

There are only two strategies of conservation: win-win conservatism or win-lose conservatism. Beware of the coercive conservative who demands, "If you refuse to partake in the conservation of what ought to be conserved, either I or my agents will fine, imprison, or kill you. Any questions? Good!"

∾

There will always be conservatives who deride disbelievers who challenge the truth of their most precious paradigms of causality and the conventional wisdom behind them. Conservatism is everywhere. It even pervades scientific communities; but if now and then scientists show their intolerance of disbelievers in the scientific status quo, then what is the fate of such disbelievers? Should they too be punished with the usual win-lose repression of dissenters, which has prevailed throughout most of human history?

In 1915, the German geophysicist and meteorologist, Alfred Lothar Wegener, published a daring theory of planetary dynamics in which he proposed that the continents, far from being static, as held by most geologists at that time, have been drifting apart for more than two-hundred million years. In his book, *The Origin of Continents and Oceans*, Wegener explained how the earth's crust was originally a single mass that began fracturing, and those fractured pieces, now commonly referred to as *plates* began drifting apart. [109] Unfortunately, Wegener's theory of continental drift was not well received and even ridiculed by some geologists. In the August 1922 issue of *Geological Magazine*, a geologist slammed Wegener, charging that he ". . . is not seeking truth; he is advocating a cause and is blind to every fact and argument that tells against it."[110]

As a disbeliever in the orthodox world of static continents, Wegener was marginalized and ostracized by many in the geological community. Fortunately, he was also a first-rate meteorologist where he earned recognition for advancing the emerging science of meteorology—and especially for pioneering the use of weather balloons in the important study of atmospheric phenomena.

It took a half-century for Wegener's theory of continental drift to rise from the pit of obscurity into what it had fallen due to neglect and derision. However, by the early 1960s, new oceanic research further verified the truth of Wegener's assertion of continental drift. It was finally resurrected and acclaimed as a revolutionary and paradigm-shattering theory of the dynamics of earth history.

This was a sweeping vindication for Wegener and his theory of continental drift, which, in part, is now included in the celebrated theory of *plate tectonics*. After all the ridicule that was heaped upon him for decades by many geologists and geophysicists, the truth of continental drift would finally gain wide acceptance, and his profound contribution to a truer understanding of our dynamic earth would finally be recognized. Unhappily, it was too late for Dr. Wegener to enjoy any of the praise. In 1930, at age fifty, and three decades before he would be honored with wide acclaim for the elegance of his theory, he lost his life while crossing an icecap during a meteorological expedition in Greenland.

❧

It is important to stress that although Wegener was ridiculed by scientific authorities for his treatise on continental drift, he was never *harmed* (harm is an imposed loss) in any way for his unorthodox explanations of geological phenomena. This is precisely because the scientific method of causality identification does not rely on what is either believed or disbelieved to be true. Neither believers nor disbelievers in anything are asked to present what they imagine or believe to be true as a part of their scientific evidence. Neither beliefs nor opinions are used in science to identify or verify the true causes of physical, biological, or social effects.

It cannot be overstressed that science is not built on belief in causality; it is built on observation of causality. What researchers may believe or disbelieve to be true is irrelevant. Even what Wegener, himself, believed to be true—that continents are drifting apart over time—is irrelevant to reaching observational verification. What *is* relevant to investigators is what can they actually *observe* to be true—not what do they believe or *imagine* to be true. Like everyone else, all scientists believe their paradigms of causality to be true. However, even when they disagree on what is true, in science the disagreement does not lead to bloodshed.

Compared to scientific leaders, religious leaders have a long and violent history of persecuting those who disbelieve in the truth of their imagination of causality. In contrast, scientific leaders do not persecute those who disbelieve the truth of traditional explanations of causality. In science, it is understood that no matter how respected a traditional hypothesis or theory of causality may be—new observations may not verify it as true and, even more striking, new observations may falsify it as not true.

Note that falsification of what is thought to be true never imposes a coercive loss upon anyone. In modern science, even *falsification* is valued because it reveals one more account of causality that is either false or highly improbable. With this new knowledge, researchers can then try to find better or truer explanations of causality that can pass the rigid tests of observational science. In any case, no one is punished for getting it wrong, or for getting it right. Moreover, no one is persecuted for being a disbeliever of scientific hypotheses or theories on physical, biological, and social causality.

౫

In contrast to the methods of theology, the methods of science invite the challenge of skeptics and disbelievers who would uproot scientific tradition with new explanations of causality. Whether scientists like it or not, where the scientific method prevails, either new hypotheses of causation are verified or they are not. *The greater the verification of newly discovered principles, the greater their acceptance as true.* However, pursuit of scientific discovery is not without risk. At any time, scientific authority on causality can be trumped by the introduction of truer, simpler, or broader theories of causality. That was exactly what Wegener brought to the scientific table with his truer explanation of geologic causality, which was eventually verified through independent observation.

In religion, as in science, people believe that their paradigms of causality are true. However, there is no way to observationally verify the truth of religious paradigms of causality, whether they are said to be physical, biological, or social truths. Without independent observation to test for truth, whatever anyone claims to be religious or secular truth can never be more than individual opinion. However, knowing this limitation, we can still ask, "Are the human actions that such religious opinions provoke compatible with human nature?" Furthermore, "Do these religious opinions foster equitable, practical, and moral action for win-win gain, or do they foster inequitable, impractical, and immoral action for win-lose gain?"

The genesis of The Golden Rule can be found in religious antiquity. The Golden Rule is the precursor of the Golden Rule Principle: *Do not seize wealth and freedom from others, as you would have them not seize your wealth and freedom.* The Golden Rule Principle enjoys the power of observational verification of its equity, utility, and morality. This trio of virtues assures its pragmatic status, which means it has practical application to all human affairs. In the simplest language: It works!

As win-win action works, so win-lose action does not work. Humans have a long history of killing each other over disagreements on what is true and what is false. The classical arbiter of social truth has been, *might makes right.* However, where might is the arbiter of truth, it can never be more than a pseudo truth without merit because it would slam the door on human progress. There is a pressing question for humans in the nuclear age. Can we transcend might-makes-right as the final arbiter of social truth? Without a social advance away from win-lose methods of reaching social truth toward win-win methods, the future for *Homo sapiens* looks bleak at best, and catastrophic at worst.

ᦂ

Many educated people believe that science is against theology. On the contrary, science is a win-win strategy that is never against anything. Scientists may be against many things — as are all humans — but science is a *method* of identifying physical, biological, and social causality. Science and theology, however, differ in their approach to explaining cause-and-effect. Science is built upon *a posteriori* observation of causality, whereas religion and philosophy are built upon *a priori* imagination of causality.*

Many readers are familiar with this pair of Latin terms used in philosophy and science to explain the source of one's information and the method one uses to understand causality. As briefly discussed in earlier chapters, an *a priori* premise or conclusion is accepted before observation without

---

* I have departed from contemporary editorial convention, which is to *not* italicize the Latin terms "a priori" and "a posteriori" due to their common usage in scientific and philosophical publications. However, these terms are placed in italics throughout this treatise to call attention to their extreme importance in explaining the distinction between *a priori* imagination of causality in contrast to *a posteriori* observation of causality. Knowing this distinction is crucial to observational analysis of all claims to an understanding of social causality. Again, the general failure to understand social causality, especially among the so-called educated classes, is what misguides and misgoverns them to take and condone actions that lead to war, poverty, and servitude, while they claim to be in pursuit of peace, prosperity, and freedom.

benefit of sensory perception. In marked contrast, an *a posteriori* premise or conclusion is only accepted in science *after* being examined by many independent observers. This may involve gathering direct or indirect experiential evidence derived from observing natural phenomena.

The discovery of various laws of nature by Kepler, Galileo, and Newton was made possible by their *a posteriori* strategy to identify physical causality. Their remarkable success with this method of understanding causality originated history's most influential paradigm shift: the ongoing transition away from reliance on *a priori* imagination of causality toward reliance on *a posteriori* observation of causality. This profound paradigm shift has led to the creation of nearly all-modern technology from automobiles to airplanes, from television sets to computers.

To restate this paramount point, there are two ways to reach conclusions about our universe of causal connections. We can imagine causality prior to experience, or we can observe causality after experience. This has profound significance because the latter strategy makes it possible for anyone who is interested — *independent* of all authority — to observe with their own eyes what has been shown to be true. The researcher says that here are the steps of my experiment. Follow these steps to confirm or deny my result for yourself. If the result is the same, this verifies its truth through independent observation.

Observation of causality provided the critical knowledge that propelled the astronauts to the moon. But, if they had relied on imagination of causality, they could not have gotten off the ground in the first place. Observational strategy not only works for identifying physical causality, it works for identifying biological and social causality as well.

Knowing the difference between *a priori* imaginations of causality in contrast to *a posteriori* observations of causality is critical in our time. This is because the misidentification of social causality through *a priori* imagination without independent verification is at the root of all social problems that threaten human existence. The perennial problems of war, poverty, and servitude can only be solved when their true causes are identified, clarified, and verified. For this urgent reason, imagination of their causes must be superseded by observation of their causes.

The history of our human effort to identify physical, biological, and social causality confirms that observation of causality transcends imagination of causality. To reemphasize, humans did not *imagine* their way to the moon; they *observed* their way to the moon. In the same way, we must abandon imagination of social causality, and observe our way to peace, prosperity, and freedom.

∾

Theology is the study and systemization of *a priori* beliefs in supernatural deities and their commands for human behavior. Theology defines supernatural domains that are beyond observation. Its conclusions are not subject to independent verification through observations. As in philosophy, the epistemology of religion excludes observational verification of its imagination of cause-and-effect. The storied claims by supernatural gods that certain human actions will cause constructive effects in contrast to other human actions that will cause destructive effects cannot be verified for the fidelity of their authenticity. Without verification, the foundation is set for perpetual dispute and endless acrimony over the intent of any sacred command given to humans by any supernatural being.

In the Middle East, Muslims are murdering Muslims every day. Yet, what pressing issue calls for murder? Sunni Muslims and Shi`ah Muslims cannot agree (and have disagreed since the seventh century) on who should have been Muhammad's successor and representative for all Islamic theology. In both cases their win-lose theology, based on *a priori* imagination of Allah's commands and the record of Muhammad's teachings provoke, violence, torture, and murder. Governed by their paradigm of religious supremacy that supports their superiority syndrome, many Muslims believe that it is both righteous and honorable to torture and murder their religious inferiors, whoever they may be.

Wherever win-lose theologies are built on *a priori* imagination of causality, disputes over the meaning of divine commands cannot satisfactorily be resolved because they are not subject to observational verification — and the divine commander remains out of physical reach. Today, these bitter disputes over theology, and the violence they provoke, threaten to destroy civilization and the human race.

To be a supernatural god is to be beyond observation, beyond corroboration, and beyond the laws of nature. Belief in supernatural beings can only be accepted on faith. Thus, believers are encouraged to keep the faith, which is to affirm their confidence in their belief in the *a priori* truth of their religious doctrines.

The author of the New Testament writings in Hebrews gave his vision of faith, "Now faith is being sure of what we hope for and certain of what we do not see" (Hebrews, 11:1). The familiar expression of acting on blind faith is to be "certain of what we do not see" as our basis for action.

All faith is *a priori*; it is prior to observation and, therefore, cannot be tested for truth and validity through independent observation. However, to act without observing and verifying the cause-and-effect of your actions is to risk unintended results that may prove highly undesirable.

Nonetheless, many decent people assume this risk by acting on faith as defined in the scriptures. For many, "faith is being sure of what we hope for," such as hoping for a better world. Many people have *faith* that a better world will come by way of being "certain of what we do not see." Ominously, many believers have *a priori* faith that the means to this better world is through coercive action, which may involve forcing their religion on others at gunpoint. "To be certain of what we do not see" is the faith behind support for all win-lose paradigms that argue: *For us to gain, they must lose through force or fraud.* The supposed equity, utility, and morality of the win-lose paradigm stand upon faith without observational verification. In fact, observation falsifies and repudiates the spurious claims of all win-lose models of social causality, whether imposed by spear point, sword point, or gunpoint.

∽

Italian philosopher and Christian prelate, St. Anselm (A. D. 1033-1107), as Archbishop of Canterbury, openly and wisely opposed the Christian Crusades that led to the tragedy of Christian warriors slaughtering Moslems and Jews across Asia Minor, "in the name of 'our Lord Jesus.'" Beyond opposing the Crusades, Anselm is cited here for his method of understanding the world around us by way of belief in the superiority of *a priori* imagination of causality.

> For I do not seek to understand that I may believe, but
> I believe in order to understand. For this I believe —
> that unless I believe, I should not understand.[111]

Where presumed understanding of the physical, biological, and social world is founded only on belief, per se, "in order to understand," is such belief based on imagination of causality or on observation of causality? Is belief in established authority and faith in conventional wisdom all that is necessary to identify universal cause-and-effect?

From the birth of civilization, ten to twelve thousand years ago, until only three centuries ago, nearly everyone believed that to understand causality you must have faith in the authority and truth of conventional wisdom. If your authority on truth was the written wisdom of Aristotle, then you accepted as true what Aristotle said was true. There was nothing to question or to argue because truth came by way his authority. And, if not from Aristotle, then truth came from some other revered source of wisdom. Yet, the presumed truth of authoritarian wisdom — no matter how esteemed the authority — would not go unchallenged forever.

One of the great philosophers, researchers of natural science, and theologians of the Middle Ages was the renowned Aristotelian scholar, Albertus Magnus (1193-1280). In pursuing scientific knowledge, Albertus saw no conflict between Christian tenets and natural principles. Thus, he sought to build a peaceful coexistence between the Church and science.

Although Albertus was highly influenced by the imposing authority of Aristotle, nonetheless, Albertus was one of the earliest researchers to realize the value of the key strategy of science, one that would eventually become an essential element of the scientific method. Albertus challenged the authority of conventional wisdom on the nature of physical reality. He questioned the value of subjective opinions by any authority on the *true* causes of natural effects.

The aim of natural science is not simply to accept the statements of others, but to investigate the causes that are at work in nature.*

Albertus taught his students (including Thomas Aquinas), that the classical authority of Aristotle, which dominated the academic world of the time, should not be accepted on mere authority alone. Even if it is the weighty authority of Aristotle, nonetheless, the generalizations of the illustrious Aristotle on causality must be tested for truth through independent examination. This novel idea would eventually become a revolution in the intellectual history of Western Europe. Here was a new and powerful strategy for discovering the foundations of nature. It was to pursue an autonomous understanding of cause-and-effect, one that was *independent* of all authority on the subject.

We know now that Albertus was teaching a radical idea that in time would shake the foundations of Western knowledge. This was four centuries before Galileo and the beginning of modern science. The new strategy of independent research would become a keystone of the scientific method. By the seventeenth century, the influence of Galileo and Newton had shifted the focus of science away from ratification of authority, as Albertus advised, toward independent observation and verification of "the causes that are at work in nature." In the intellectual struggle to discover which

---

* *Scientiae enim naturalis non est simpliciter narrata accipere, sed in rebus naturalibus inquirere causas.* "De Mineralia," Lib. 2, tract II, chp. I, p. 30A. See vol. 2, p. 227 of the 1651 edition of collected works edited by Petrus Jammy. One English translation reads, "Natural science does not consist in ratifying what others have said, but in seeking the causes of phenomena." Another translation reads, "For it is [the task] of natural science not simply to accept what we are told but to inquire into the causes of natural things." For this translation see, Albertus Magnus, *Book of Minerals*, trans. Dorothy Wyckoff (Oxford: Clarendon Press, 1967), 69.

natural causes lead to which natural effects, observation of causality was superseding imagination of causality.

Saint Albertus became an influential theologian of the Catholic Church; he was beatified in 1622, declared a saint and Doctor of the Church in 1931. Yet, four centuries after he flourished, even though he was beatified twenty years before the death of Galileo, his influence in explaining the compatibility of science and Christianity was not enough to protect Galileo from the win-lose paradigms of church authorities, who had outlawed his observational conclusions through the power of naked force. Yet, the win-win ideas of Jesus could have protected a devout Catholic like Galileo from persecution by Church authorities. But Christian prelates in Rome had their own win-lose ideas, which did not include listening to Jesus and acting accordingly.

The most famous student of Albertus Magnus was Thomas Aquinas. In his chapter on "How the Omnipotent God is said to be Incapable of Certain Things" from his *Summa Contra Gentiles*, Christian theologian and Aristotelian philosopher, St. Thomas Aquinas (1225-1274; Doctor of the Church, 1567) assures his readers that they can rely on building a true and reliable science because even God cannot change the principles of nature.

> Again, since the principles of certain sciences — of logic, geometry, and arithmetic, for instance — are derived exclusively from the formal principles of things, upon which their essence depends, it follows that God cannot make the contraries of those principles; He cannot make the genus not to be predicable of the species, nor lines drawn from a circle's center to its circumference

not to be equal, nor the three angles of a rectilinear tri-angle not to be equal to two right angles.[112]

Aquinas implies that we can build science on "formal principles" of nature because "God cannot make contraries of those principles." This means we can move forward in our study of nature with the confidence that those same principles will be true tomorrow as they are true today. According to St. Thomas, in our quest to understand natural causality, God *will not* change the universal ground rules precisely because he *cannot* change them.

Three-and-a-half centuries after Thomas Aquinas wrote on the constancy of natural principles, a seminal discovery took place in Europe. Through the power of observation and mathematical calculation, German astronomer, Johann Kepler (1571-1630) discovered and defined the "laws of planetary motion" that shattered the sacred authority of Greek astronomy. In the preface to his *Rudolphine Tables*, Kepler reveals the core of his revolutionary strategy toward understanding our planetary system. It involved the "transfer of the whole of astronomy from fictitious circles [imagined orbits] to natural causes [observed orbits]" — *causes* discovered by analyzing the observed orbits of astronomer Tycho Brahe.[113] Kepler's laws not only proved there are regularities in nature, but he ignited the ongoing search for more and more of these regularities known as natural principles or laws of nature. We can surmise today that without the universal regularity and unbroken constancy of natural laws, chaos would have preempted the origination and organization of the known universe of galactic and intergalactic energy.

∽

Ten thousand years after the evolvement of civilization, and two thousand years after Aristotle, the paradigm of truth by authority, on authority, from authority, and through authority, was challenged in a way that few intellectuals had anticipated. The crucial break with the time-honored tradition of *a priori* belief "in order to understand" causality, as Saint Anselm did, was set in motion by Italian professor of physics and astronomy, Galileo Galilei. Galileo's sterling strength of character was revealed as he went against all authority by verifying his discovery of nature's laws, not through imagination of causality, but through observation of causality. Galilean scholar, Stillman Drake, described Galileo's uncommon fortitude.

> Galileo's most striking personal characteristic was his refusal to accept authority as a substitute for direct personal inquiry and observation. That refusal went counter to the whole social pattern of his time, and not only with respect to the Church. All political and most social institutions of his day were authoritarian in structure. Even in the universities, the primary centers of intellectual life, the authority of the ancient writers was sedulously preserved. Only a born fighter could hope to change such well-established tradition.[114]

Although it is now four centuries after Galileo flourished, *a priori* faith in authority is still hailed as a great human virtue. However, as a source of understanding causality, its reliability is always in doubt because it cannot be tested for truth and validity through independent observation. The crucial question for all people of faith is, "What do they have faith in?" Do they have faith in the presumed truth of *a priori* imagination of causality? If so, which causes of which effects do they *imagine* are true prior to observation, and without concern for empirical evidence?

Imagination of truth without observation of truth has been a subtle and persistent cause of social disaster. Sincere people who imagined the win-lose model of social causality to be a true and virtuous paradigm, have incited the great tragedies of human history. Whether this ubiquitous paradigm is deemed true or false, its lethality is certain and predictable because it always demands coercive action for win-lose gain. Yet, this deadly paradigm is easily falsified by observing the human action necessary to maximize human wealth, kindness, benevolence, and generosity. It is observable:

Human wealth, kindness, benevolence, and generosity are maximized by gaining through the gain of others, and minimized by gaining through the loss of others.

Win-win gain is the source of universal wealth and prosperity because it optimizes human incentive to create new wealth and prosperity for all to enjoy. The more wealth and prosperity created by win-win exchange, the greater the domino effects of kindness, benevolence, and generosity between and among humans. Yet, as long as respected and influential people have faith in the rightness of institutionalized coercion for win-lose gain, their *a priori* faith leads to tragic consequences, which include the advance of war, poverty, and servitude. Where these afflictions prevail, the potential for human kindness, benevolence, and generosity is sharply eroded, if not smothered altogether.

When devout Christians tortured and murdered their neighbors for the alleged crimes of witchcraft and heresy, Christian kindness was killed by true believers who had staunch *faith* that God not only approved of their violent actions, but that such violence would be seen as righteous and heroic. Absolute faith in the holy sanctity of religious violence has killed Catholic kindness, it has killed Protestant kindness, it has killed Islamic kindness, it has killed Hindu kindness, and it has killed Jewish kindness. Yet, when such a flawed paradigm of social causality—governed by the superiority syndrome—is so pervasive among world religions, and so universally harmful, it would seem that its present danger cannot be overemphasized. In the end, faith among good people in their belief in the truth of the win-lose paradigm may lead to the destruction of civilization and the extinction of *Homo sapiens*.*

In writing on the worldwide threat of Muslim terrorism in the twenty-first century, Sam Harris, in *The End of Faith*, gives this warning: "The fate of civilization lies largely in the hands of 'moderate' Muslims. Unless Muslims can reshape their religion into an ideology that is basically benign…it is difficult to see how Islam and the West can avoid falling into a continual state of war."[115]

Again, the crisis for the human race erupted when unconventional arms of nuclear, biological, and chemical weapons of mass destruction in part, superseded conventional arms of limited destruction such as swords, arrows, and bullets. Because unconventional weapons are more widely available today than they were during the Cold War, the crisis of human survival is greater than ever before. To end this crisis, a paradigm shift must be made away from win-lose religion toward win-win religion. However, as long as true believers have *a priori* faith that for our religion to gain, your religion must be forced to lose, there will be crisis after crisis.

Wars are still funded today, as they were in King Saul's day, by confiscating people's wealth and freedom through autocratic force. Wherever win-lose religion and win-lose politics prevail, citizens who refuse to fund religious and political wars will be fined, imprisoned, or killed. As long

---

* The complete Latin name for modern humans is *Homo sapiens sapiens* (*L. sapiēns, sapient,* present participle of *sapere,* to be wise). Thus, humans have named themselves "wise wise men." In this regard, the salient question remains, will humans be wise enough to prevent their self-destruction?

as advocates of peace have faith in the efficacy of win-lose funding for war, there will be war. All religious and political institutions of war are founded on *apriori* faith in the supposed wisdom of the win-lose paradigm *without* observational analysis of its truth and validity.

For our species to survive, the war paradigm must be rejected and abandoned altogether. The idea that for our nation or our religion to gain, your nation or your religion must be forced to lose, is a paradigm that is easily falsified by independent observation. It must be repudiated as a pernicious paradigm, or warfare will flourish until humans perish from the earth. If such a cataclysmic demise should blight the planet, there will be no one left to scold with, "I told you so"—and no one left to do the scolding. In eons ahead, if alien explorers should find our planet devoid of intelligent beings, the evidence may show that humans were not destroyed by a falling asteroid, but by their *faith*, faith in a false model of causality: the win-lose paradigm. If aliens exist, and they are smart enough to get here, they might conclude from the profusion of forensic evidence that, in the end, these strange beings fell by their own hands because they didn't know what they were doing.

ENDNOTES

109. Alfred Lothar Wegener, *Die Entstehung der Kontinente und Ozeane*, (Braunschweig, Germany: *Sammlung Vieweg*, 1915), No. 23, pp 1-94.

110. I. Bernard Cohen, *Revolution in Science* (Cambridge and London: Harvard University Press, 1985), 452.

111. St. Anselm of Canterbury, *Proslogium* (Discourse on the Existence of God), A.D. 1078, trans. Sidney N. Dean, (Chicago: The Open Court Publishing Co., 1926), ch. 1.

112. St. Thomas Aquinas, *Summa Contra Gentiles*, vol. 2 (Notre Dame, IN: University of Notre Dame Press, 1975), ch. 25, sec. 14.

113. Cohn, *Revolution in Science*, 130

114. Stillman Drake, *Galileo Studies: Personality, Tradition, and Revolution* (Michigan: University of Michigan Press, 1970), 70-71.

115. Sam Harris, *The End of Faith: Religion, Terror, and the Future of Reason* (New York: W. W. Norton, 2005), 152.

Chapter Eleven

In Search of Truth

Over the millennia of intellectual history, one of the deadliest ideas ever conceived is the concept of *absolute truth*: a truth that is ultimate, perfect, and can never be overturned. The presumed infallibility of absolute truth remains a pillar of win-lose religion. Where God was said to have authored absolute truth, true believers have defended that truth by suppressing disbelievers in its flawless fidelity. In their zeal to spread their vision of truth, believers have forced their truth on disbelievers through the persuasive power of swords, guns, and bombs. As a result, the social impact of advancing absolute truth through the violence of win-lose religion has been catastrophic.

How can we distinguish between that which is *true* and that which is *false*? This is the great intellectual challenge of human history. Who is to say that one opinion of truth is superior to another? Can we somehow improve on mere *opinion* of truth where opinion is arbitrary, relative, and subjective? Must we always depend on authoritarian opinion as our source of truth? What if such authority is undependable because its vision of truth is flawed, if not spurious and designed to deceive?

One of history's most fundamental and influential discoveries was how to bypass the intimidation of authoritarian explanations of causality. Where authorities in every arena of human endeavor claim that their paradigms of causality are true and above reproach, what if, indeed, they are not above reproach because they are not true? How can we skirt the flaws of authority and blaze the way for truer and simpler models of physical, biological, and social causality?

A formidable barrier to abating the problems of war, poverty, and servitude is the common belief that political and religious authorities are the final voices of social truth — especially where such truth extols the efficacy and rightness of coercive action for win-lose gain. Yet, as long as educated people with good minds have *a priori* faith in the equity, utility, and morality of institutionalizing the seizure of wealth and freedom for noble aims — or any aims — humans will continue to reap the tragedies of war, poverty, and servitude.

∽

The revolutionary advance of the sixteenth and seventeenth centuries was the profound discovery of a way to go beyond mere imagination of the truth of cause-and-effect. This was a seminal advance due to the inherent uncertainty of truth derived through imagination without observation. *A priori imagination of the truth of causality can be no more than subjective opinion.* Due to this fact of reality, how can we find a practical and reliable alternative to mere opinion on the truth of nature's laws of cause-and-effect?

Where the authority of conventional wisdom is based on just opinion, one question is vital to human survival. Can we bypass the prestige of authoritarian opinion, which sustains religious and political coercion for win-lose gain?

Such opinions do not have to be attacked, but to tame the violence of faith, they do have to be falsified, bypassed, or superseded. Eventually, truth upstages that which is false. However, where social crises are sustained by the weight of conventional wisdom sooner is better than later.

It is one thing to search for truth, and quite another thing to find it, just as it is one thing to claim the truth and quite another thing to prove it. Centuries before we were born, those icons of natural discovery, Galileo Galilei and Isaac Newton, taught us how to improve the reliability of truth by devising a revolutionary strategy to identify and verify reality. Their simple approach to finding truth was to replace *imagination* of truth with *observation* of truth. Using the power of observation, the scientific method is a remarkable method to lead the way in the search for truth by discovering the laws of nature. This unique approach to discovery relies on independent researchers verifying natural principles — principles that illuminate another niche in another corner of our mysterious universe.

∾

The strategy for discovering causality through observation is rarely welcomed by authoritarian leadership, because all authorities — whether philosophical, historical, legal, theological, or political — resist challenge to their authority. Unlike the imagination of causality, the observation of causality rejects all authority — even scientific authority — by demanding independent verification of all claims for discovery of truth.

It is important to stress that the scientific method of causality identification has no use for unverifiable claims of finding an absolute truth that describes causality with flawless perfection. In science, truth is never infallible; it does not wear the mantle of absolute certainty. This does not mean, however, that in science there is only uncertainty of truth and unpredictability of action.

Werner Heisenberg's famed *uncertainty principle* (1927) does not maintain that everything in nature is "uncertain." Rather, it maintains that some knowledge is *indeterminable*. Heisenberg himself called this curious phenomenon of nature the *Indeterminacy Principle*. He generalized that as the accuracy of measuring one observable quantity (e.g., position of a subatomic particle) increases, at the same time, the uncertainty (indeterminacy) of the accuracy with which another quantity (e.g., momentum of a subatomic particle) can be measured also increases. In brief, "It is impossible to make an exact and simultaneous determination of both the position and the momentum (mass times velocity) of any body."[116]

Nonetheless, indeterminacy of absolute reality in nature does not rule out predictability in nature. If a principle of nature has always held true in the past, it may be called true in the present until an exception is observed that cannot be explained. The greater the number of independent verifications of a principle, the greater its acceptance as true. Conversely, the greater the number of independent falsifications of a presumed principle, the greater its rejection as true.

Avoiding the pursuit of absolute truth in science is its strength, not its weakness. This is because if an absolute truth were ever to be found—a truth that is ultimate, perfect, and infallible—the scientific method could be abandoned as no longer necessary. But to abandon the scientific method is to abandon science itself.

Science cannot improve on an absolute truth that is perfect and true for all time. If such an immutable truth were to be found, it would be beyond scientific investigation. This means that the scientific method would then become a superfluous strategy—a needless method—for either verifying or falsifying a "perfect truth" that can never be overturned. This does not mean that absolute truth does not exist in nature; it means that we have no method of *knowing* whether it is absolute.

Nonetheless, it has been the aim of some of history's most influential men of science to search for absolute truth. In the seventeenth century, one of the prime founders of modern science, Isaac Newton, proposed the idea of *absolute space*. Newtonian *space* was an inert void wherein all physical actions were explained by the laws of nature as discovered and defined by Newton. His revolutionary idea of absolute space would hold sway as conventional wisdom for some two centuries. However, by the beginning of the twentieth century, a new idea of space was gaining currency among scientists. Acceptance of the idea of absolute space was eroded and finally superseded by Albert Einstein's Special Theory of Relativity where space was shown *not* to be *absolute*, but to be relativistic. Einstein hypothesized that although neither space nor time is absolute, the "space-time continuum" is an absolute.

Seminal experiments by Albert Michelson (1852-1931) and his successors have shown the speed of light in a vacuum to be a universal constant. Its speed of nearly 300,000 kilometers per second (over 186,000 miles per second) is not only constant, but, according to Einstein, this speed cannot be exceeded. Even in science, however, where some may accept the speed of light as a universal absolute, it is understood that if sufficient observational evidence falsifies this paradigm, it will no longer be accepted as absolute, and will lose its once vaunted prestige. In any case, neither acceptance nor rejection of a presumed absolute in science is ever forced upon anyone. This is because the discovery of causality in nature through the power of scientific observation is a win-win strategy where everyone wins, and no one is forced to lose. Again, all human progress is created and advanced through new discoveries of physical, biological, and social causation.

∽

Philosopher, mathematician, and cardinal of the Catholic Church, Nicholas of Cusa, writing in the fifteenth century, concluded, "All we know of the truth is that the absolute truth, such as it is, is beyond our reach."[117] An absolute truth, indeed, "is beyond our reach" because it is unknowable. We can envisage absolute truth through our imagination. Yet, if we reach for truth by taking the steps of the scientific method, we find that science is not built on *a priori* imagination; it is built on *a posteriori* observation.

One of the great lessons learned by scientists of the twentieth century was to avoid the pitfalls of pursuing absolute truth in favor of pursuing verified truth. The diverse benefits to be reaped by continually testing the fidelity of truth to observe again and again whether an old truth or new truth will be verified or falsified includes all the technological wonders from television sets to computers, and from airplanes to antibiotics.

Even before Nicolas Copernicus published his revolutionary treatise in 1543, *On the Revolutions of the Celestial Spheres* (De revolutionibus orbium coelestium), explaining that the sun, not the earth, was the center of the universe; a century earlier, Nicholas of Cusa, in a book published in 1440, asserted that contrary to common belief, the earth turns on its own axis as it revolves around the sun. It was unfortunate for the reputation of the Christian Church in Rome that Nicolas of Cusa was not around two centuries later to advise the pope on celestial matters and how he might deal with the revolutionary writings of Galileo on astronomy.

In his day, Nicholas of Cusa was not only an influential cardinal who advocated teaching Christianity rather than spreading it by force, he also enjoyed close papal ties. In any case, we can only speculate that had the cardinal from

Cusa (Cardinal Cusanus, as he was known) been able to do so, he might have warned the pope of Galileo's time that it was not a good idea to haul Galileo before the Inquisition and charge him with the crime of heresy for publishing his celestial observations. Moreover, the cardinal might have told papal authorities that it was both foolish and unjust to force Galileo to recant his celestial theory that removes the Earth from the center of our planetary system. Furthermore, it was inadvisable because the observational evidence gathered by Galileo showed that, indeed, the Earth does rotate on its own axis as it moves around the sun.

From the view of Christian authorities, however, Galileo had degraded and devalued all humans by removing them from their exalted place at the center of God's universe. Galileo would have to plead forgiveness for his so-called astronomical errors and heresies, or face the harsh punishment of the Inquisition.

In 1633, without the counsel of an honest intellectual like Cardinal Cusanus, church officials—guided by their superiority syndrome and acting on false premises and conclusions—forced Galileo to his knees to renounce his Copernican view that the Earth moves around the sun. Then an old man, in ill health, and nearly blind, Galileo was forced by the Holy Catholic Church to confess aloud that many of his most important and revolutionary discoveries were not only false, but threatened the sacred authority of Catholic Church dogma, which made Galileo a hated heretic:

> I Galileo...have been pronounced by the Holy Office [Inquisition] to be vehemently suspected of heresy, that is to say, of having held and believed that the Sun is the center of the world and immovable and that the Earth is not the center and moves:...with sincere heart and unfeigned faith I abjure, curse, and detest the aforesaid errors and heresies....[118]

Upon rising from his recantation and renouncing the idea that the Earth moves about the sun, Galileo is said to have muttered to a friend, "Eppur se muove," (But it still moves.). Yet, if Galileo did not speak aloud, as some say, that the Earth still moves, he most certainly thought it. Historian Colin Ronan noted, "Contrary to popular belief, Galileo did not end with the statement 'But it still moves' — he was not so foolish."[119] Ronan's argument makes sense, for we can assume that Galileo would not have spoken the truth within earshot of the Inquisitors whom he very well knew held the power to punish him with torture and death for speaking such sinister heresies.

Although Galileo may have renounced his celestial views to avoid the holy terror of the Inquisition, he could not change celestial reality. He could only show what is observable to those willing to look. For those who do *look* at the visible evidence, the Earth is not fixed; it is always moving.

Galileo's empirical arguments that the Earth spins on its axis as it revolves around the sun fell on deaf ears and blind eyes. This was because the pope, the Inquisition, and Church authorities were committed to the absolute truth of their theology, which demanded an Earth-centered — human-centered — universe created by the one true god.

Even while clinging to this theology, church authorities still could have allowed freedom of speech and religion. But because they had blind confidence in the sanctity and rectitude of their monopoly of absolute truth, they were misled by their superiority syndrome to impose their will upon others through violent means.

Christian authorities in Rome were certain that every disbeliever was inferior to every believer. This included Galileo, who did not believe in the absolute truth of a geocentric (earth-centered) universe as proposed in the second century by Claudius Ptolemy of Alexandria. Catholic authorities, as stewards of absolute truth, had confidence in the sanctity of their win-lose theology that proclaimed: *For the Church to gain, Galileo must be forced to lose.*

∾

The depth and rigidity of Christian conservatism confronting Galileo was formidable. Just how formidable was explained by one of the most influential prelates of the Catholic Church, Ignatius of Loyola. A knight of Spanish nobility, Ignatius entered the Church to pursue a career as a Christian leader. He founded the prestigious Society of Jesus (1539) whose elite members are known throughout the world as Jesuits. Fifty years after his death in 1556, he was canonized as Saint Ignatius.

In 1541, a century before Galileo's death, Ignatius of Loyola explained the depth of faith that God-fearing Christians must have in the rectitude and infallibility of Church rulings and explanations of causality:

> We should always be disposed to believe that that which appears white is really black, if the hierarchy of the Church so decides.[120]

Confidence among the faithful in truly believing that "white is really black" when proclaimed so by religious leaders gives win-lose theology and religion its fatal power to foster and incite crimes against humanity. Such paradigms of intellectual superiority were pervasive among Church authorities and its hierarchy who were accusing Galileo of heresy for his heliocentric theory of celestial reality.

When we learn the standard of Christian truth as defined by Ignatius that "white is really black," we can see why Galileo's astronomical observations failed to convince the pope and his cadre of cardinals of the fidelity of his celestial truth.

The observation of truth by Galileo could not penetrate the imagination of truth by Church authorities, precisely because they imagined their truth to be an *absolute truth*, impervious to observational contradiction. Six centuries earlier, Pope Gregory VII—revered as a saint among Catholics for his papal influence—declared the absolute truth of Church authority in his *Dictatus papae* (c. 1075), "The Roman Church has never erred, and, according to Scripture, it never shall err."

Even though Galileo was a devout Catholic throughout his life, after his death near Florence in 1642, he was denied burial in consecrated ground by Church authorities for his so-called crime of publishing heliocentric heresies, declaring the Earth moved around the sun. For earnest Catholics like Galileo, such denial of a sacred burial was a damning rebuke from the Catholic Church. Yet, Galileo was a true Catholic to the end, believing as he said, "The Bible shows the way to go to heaven—not the way the heavens go."[121]

In the meantime, Galileo's fame and influence as a key founder of modern science continued to rise in the Western world. In 1687, the significance of Galileo and the importance of his discoveries were bolstered by the publication of Newton's *Principia Mathematica*. Finally, in 1835, nearly a century and-a-half after *Principia*, and nearly two centuries after the death of Galileo, his bestseller, *Dialogue Concerning the Two Chief World Systems* (1632), was grudgingly removed from the Index of Prohibited Books, by the Holy Office of the Inquisition. Even then, its removal as a forbidden book only came about through the insistence of Pope Pius VII, who is better remembered for excommunicating Napoleon from the Catholic Church.[122]

The original title of the Inquisition was The Holy Office of the Inquisition into Heretical Depravity. Founded on the win-lose paradigm, it was conceived by devout men who were seduced by the allure of their *superiority syndrome*, which warranted their mission to monopolize absolute truth. The terror and tyranny unleashed by the Inquisition was incited by schooled men with good minds and pious aims. Yet, these assets alone were not enough to protect them from fatal blunder. What went wrong? They didn't know what they were doing because they failed to understand causality. Moreover, their dismal failure to apply the win-win teachings of Jesus was proven by their shameful atrocities for win-lose gain in the name of the Father, the Son, and the Holy Ghost.

∽

Galileo was fully aware that the Inquisitional threats to cause him great harm were far from empty if he did not renounce his Copernican view of a sun-centered universe. Galileo remembered the dreadful fate of Italian philosopher Giordano Bruno, who fell prey to the Inquisition and to the win-lose Christianity of Cardinal Inquisitor Robert Bellarmine. To Cardinal Bellarmine (1542-1621), the idea of "liberty of belief," —which is the foundation of human freedom and its priceless derivatives of freedom of speech and religion— was to be condemned and decried as an anathema. An anathema was anything that was so loathed by church authorities that it was usually held to be a hated heresy. On the anathema of "liberty of belief," Bellarmine in his *De Laicis,* (Treatise on Civil Government) made his position clear:

> Liberty of belief is dangerous to those very men to whom it is granted; for liberty of belief is nothing less than liberty of error, and of error in regard to the most dangerous of all matters; for faith is not true if it [is] not . . . "One Faith," therefore liberty of falling away from this one faith [Catholicism] is liberty of plunging headlong into the abyss of errors. [123]

Bellarmine professed, "liberty of belief is dangerous to those very men to whom it is granted," believing as he did that it leads to erroneous thinking. Thus, freedom of speech and freedom of religion are not only dangerous; they are the cause of insidious harm to believers in the "One Faith," the only true faith, which to Cardinal Bellarmine was Roman Catholicism. Yet, the idea of destroying human liberty to preempt errors of thought is the deadly dogma of the "thought police." It is their validation for the administration of terror as a sacred and legitimate policy of violence and intimidation. Bellarmine's sinister role as Cardinal Inquisitor was to supervise coercion against defenseless targets of the Holy Office. In so doing, he betrayed and confirmed his belief in the moral virtue of the superiority syndrome and the win-lose paradigm.

Bellarmine's career as a cruel persecutor — even of devout Catholics like Galileo who had harmed no one — did not seem to mar his image as an admired Christian prelate. In spite of the inequity and brutality of his win-lose Christianity — clearly violating the win-win teachings Jesus — the Cardinal Inquisitor of the Catholic Church was so influential and esteemed, that in 1931, three centuries after his death, he was posthumously elevated to the sacred status of Doctor of the Church. This prestigious honor is only bestowed upon Catholics who have first been canonized as saints, and whose influence as Catholic teachers and interpreters of Christian theology is deemed both profound and extraordinary.

Two centuries after Bellarmine's death, Pope Gregory XVI echoed the Cardinal Inquisitor's damnation of "liberty of belief" in his *Encyclical Mirari Vos*. This encyclical was a formal letter addressed to all bishops of the Church, in which Gregory railed, "The worst plague of all, unrestrained liberty of opinion and freedom of speech."

For Pope Gregory XVI, the role of the Church was to restrain the "plague" of liberty and freedom. However, then or now, wherever "liberty of opinion and freedom of speech" are restrained, liberty and freedom have been throttled through the violence of suppression for win-lose gain. But without liberty and freedom, there can only be tyranny and oppression. Believers of every religious faith should remember that freedom of religion has been the first casualty of religious monopoly. Where theocratic institutions are imposed upon people through win-lose force and fraud in the name of Almighty God, it is a foregone conclusion, many bad things will happen to many good people.

∞

Giordano Bruno's execution for alleged heresy took place when Galileo was thirty-six. Thirty-three years later, the very same Cardinal Bellarmine was accusing Galileo, like Bruno before him, of the religious crime of disbelieving Christian truth and saying so in print. That was heresy, a rejection by a baptized Christian of any Christian dogma on absolute truth. Of course, nearly everyone born into Christendom was baptized as a Christian in his or her infancy. Due to widespread baptism throughout Europe, there was no fear among Christian authorities of ever running out of those who could be accused of the Christian crime of heresy.

In brief, the Christian ultimatum from Church authorities became, "Believe as we believe or we will kill you, in the name of the Father, the Son, and the Holy Ghost." By merely being baptized as an infant—without your consent—you were vulnerable to allegations by friend or foe, of committing the capital crime of heresy and, thereby, being a hated heretic.

After Bruno was locked in a dungeon for seven years as a "guest" of the Inquisition, on February 16, 1600, he was dragged out of his cell in chains, denounced as a heretic, bound to a stake and burned alive in the Field of Flowers

(Campo di' Fiori) in Rome. But what was Bruno's capital crime?

Influenced by the innovative cosmology of Catholic intellectuals, Nicolas Copernicus and Nicholas of Cusa, Bruno had boldly pronounced in published writings that neither the Earth nor the sun was the center of the universe. In his *On the Infinite Universe and Worlds*, Bruno postulates a never-ending universe filled with endless suns and endless worlds. [124] The Earth, he said, is not the center of the universe because it revolves around the sun. This was the Copernican view. However, Copernicus stopped there, believing that the sun, not the Earth, was the immovable center of the universe. In sharp contrast, Bruno went beyond Copernicus to say that the sun is not the center of the universe either because it is merely one of an infinite number of suns in an infinite universe that has no center.

Bruno's cosmology and theology were denounced by Church authorities as heretical departures from Church dogma, a dogma that demanded the divine Creation of an Earth-centered, human-centered, and Christian-centered universe. Thus, Bruno and Galileo became victims of win-lose Christianity and the superiority syndrome of church rulers in defense of their monopoly of "absolute truth."

Upon receiving his death sentence from Catholic authorities, Bruno spoke to his accusers, "You, O judges! feel perchance more terror in pronouncing this judgment than I do in hearing it."[125] Whatever fear his Christian accusers might have had in condemning him to death for his views on cosmology was masked by the certainty of their win-lose paradigm: *For Bellarmine and the pope to gain, Bruno must be forced to lose.*

The criminality of win-lose Christianity was clearly a desecration of the win-win teachings of Jesus as recorded by his apostles. The historical irony is that Christian authorities of the Catholic Inquisition, in claiming to defend the fidelity of the moral teaching of Jesus, committed horrific crimes against humanity that reached new levels of immorality. The immorality and criminality of win-lose Christianity may have been approached by other win-lose religions, but it has never been surpassed.

It is difficult to find an apology for the disgraceful actions of these Christian prelates, when they all had access to libraries filled with the altruistic and benevolent teachings of Jesus. If the generous magnanimity and exemplary kindness of Jesus is the core of Christianity, then the Christian prelates of the Holy Office of the Inquisition were, by their own definition, the standard-bearers of heresy. Their heretical criminality and blatant hypocrisy in desecrating the moral message of Jesus has yet to be matched—not even by the notorious Nazis. However brutal the Nazis were, they rarely imposed systemized, ritualized torture on their defenseless victims. For Jews and other victims of institutionalized tyranny, murder by twentieth century Nazis was usually far less cruel than murder by sixteenth century Christians.

In remembering such appalling crimes, the aim is not to rant at the villainous behavior of sanctified and glorified criminals, which takes no courage after they are long dead and their coercive power has expired. We must not, however, lose sight of the constructive aim, which is to know causality. If we can understand and, thereby avoid the intellectual and moral errors of these most pious and avid activists, we can prevent the perpetuation of those same errors into the future. In this way, we can pay homage to the memory of their wretched victims who deserve not to be entirely forgotten—which, in a larger sense, should include all people who have been victims of institutionalized crimes against humanity, crimes for the supposed virtue of win-lose religious and political gain.

There is no more important human mission than the never-ending search for truth. There is physical, biological, and social truth to be found in the universe, but how can we find it? The strategy of observational science is to come closer and closer to discovery of universal truth by observing and verifying principles of nature. Where principles can be seen to operate with consistency and without apparent fail, there is predictability. The ability to predict future events with a degree of certainty, and to know that those predictions are likely to hold true in the future as they have in the past, is what reveals the natural order of our universe. In a disorderly universe, however, there would not only be endless chaos, but little probability of intelligent life, as we know it.

In our search for truth, absolute truth remains unreachable because of the subjective limitations of science. We can only see the universe through the subjective experience of our own eyes. We can never escape from our subjectivity to become objective observers of absolute truth. Thus, we do the next best thing. Truth in science is discovered through the peerless process of independent observation and continuing verification of theories and principles of nature. The scientific observer says, "Don't take my word for the truth of this hypothesis. You test it; you observe it; you verify or falsify my theory of causality based upon my discovery of natural principles."

Science is neither a mystery nor a menace: it is merely a method of identifying causality. In the search for truth, science identifies and verifies the causes of physical, biological, and social effects through discovery of principles that operate without fail. However, what if humans reject or ignore newly discovered principles of general truth? Then they cannot use those principles to advance their well-being.

ᘓ

When Louis Pasteur used the scientific method to discover principles of the germ theory of disease, physicians were among his most passionate detractors of its authenticity. They argued with authoritarian confidence that the germ theory was nonsense. At the time, most physicians clung to the old paradigm of spontaneous generation—that life forms were spontaneously self-generated from non-living matter. Yet, if physicians had continued to reject the truth of Pasteur's germ theory, they would have rejected what science writer and historian Isaac Asimov called, "the greatest single medical discovery of all time, for only through an understanding of the nature of infectious disease and the manner of its communication could it be brought under control."[126]

Eventually, physicians (especially young medical students) made a paradigm shift from belief in spontaneous generation to belief in Pasteur's germ theory. Without this crucial paradigm shift within the medical community, medicine would have frozen in the nineteenth century. Joseph Lister would not have founded antiseptic surgery (c. 1867), which was based on Pasteur's germ theory. Without a paradigm shift among physicians on basic biological causality, physicians would have lost, patients would have lost, and everyone else would have lost. Such a profound shift, however, in causality identification was too trying for physicians, who saw Pasteur as an outsider—outside of medicine, a mere physicist and chemist. Physicians, in the grip of their superiority syndrome, rejected the truth of the germ theory, in part, because of Pasteur's professional inferiority. After all, what could a chemist know about medicine?

Fortunately, for the advance of medicine, Pasteur had gained one influential convert in England. Among all European physicians, English surgeon Joseph Lister led the way in showing practical applications of Pasteur's germ theory by developing antiseptic procedures of cutting into the human body. His surgical techniques made dramatic reductions in the dire risk of sepsis, where the body is invaded by pathogenic germs that overwhelm the host. Lister's novel use of carbolic acid as an anti-microbial agent protected those undergoing surgery from the lethality of microbial infection. When unchecked, such fearful infections would too often kill the patient—even though the operation was a stunning success.

In an 1874 letter to Pasteur, Lister offered his respect and gratitude to him in noting, "Your brilliant researches demonstrated to me the truth of the germ theory of putrefaction, and thus furnished me with a principle upon which alone the antiseptic system can be carried out."[127] Lister had successfully applied Pasteur's principles of the germ theory to the discovery of his own principles of antisepsis and antiseptic surgery.

During surgery, applied principles of anesthesia developed by Crawford Long, William Morton, and others, kept patients from dying of shock. After surgery, Lister's applied principles of antisepsis kept patients from dying of infection. In medical as well as other fields of research, the discovery of natural principles and their effective use in solving physical, biological, and social problems are the greatest human achievements, for they blaze the widest path toward human advancement and enrichment. Patients whose lives have been spared by applying principles of anesthesia and antisepsis for a striking surgical success have gained a priceless boon of intangible prosperity. Their new affluence has arrived through the creation of win-win wealth and the advance of win-win altruism.

What could be more altruistic than the innovation of anesthesia and antisepsis for the benefit of humankind? Because humankind includes every member of every religion, this is a great boon and blessing for all religious believers. However, if for religious reasons, some believe that it is unholy or unrighteous to benefit from the medical advances of anesthesia or antisepsis, neither their originators nor their successors will force this benefit upon them. Nor will anyone else where religious freedom prevails.

The fact that a patient's newly acquired wealth and prosperity came by way of a new lease on life through the marvels of modern medicine, and that this gain necessarily takes the form of *intangible* wealth and *immaterial* prosperity, such intangibility and immateriality should not dim the luster of its priceless value. The most precious win-win wealth derives from the generosity of win-win altruism. Pasteur's revolutionary discoveries and inventions in biological research generated far more win-win wealth for others than they generated for Pasteur himself. Nonetheless, as recipients by the millions gained from Pasteur's scientific benefactions, so did their benefactor, Pasteur, also gain from the gratitude of those who saw the source of their own remarkable gain, which often came by way of a dramatic rescue from an otherwise certain death. There were no losers, as everyone benefited from the creative power of win-win exchange.

Louis Pasteur was among the first to apply the scientific method to solve biological problems. Thus, Pasteur became a founder of an entirely new science: the science of biology, which forms the basis of scientific medicine. Pasteur proved the versatility of the scientific method not only to solve physical problems, as did Galileo and Newton before him, but to solve biological problems as well. One of those critical problems was how to advance our success at identifying the true causes of human disease, which in turn expanded the foundations of truth. Such discovered truth is an invaluable advance in human welfare without having to be either an absolute or an ultimate truth.

ༀ

In search of truth, the Science of Social Causation, introduced in this treatise, applies the scientific method to identify the *true* causes of social problems as the prelude to their practical solutions. As the scientific method falsified the model of "spontaneous generation" as a true paradigm of biological causality, so the same scientific method falsifies the model of win-lose coercion as a true paradigm of social causality. Those who believe that for them to gain, they must force others to lose have accepted on faith alone — without observational verification — a false and ruinous paradigm of social causality. In contrast, without reliance on faith, it is an observational truth that win-win exchanges maximize wealth and freedom per capita, while win-lose exchanges minimize wealth and freedom per capita. Where wealth and freedom are minimized by coercive interventionism, poverty and servitude are maximized.

Because paradigms guide the people who run society, in order to solve social problems we must analyze paradigms, paradigms, and more paradigms of social causality — are they true or false, valid or invalid? Are they win-win or win-lose paradigms? Only through such crucial discrimination can we rescue decent people from following false paradigms of causality as if they were true.

A prime aim of win-win theory is to identify and verify the predictable effects of win-win gain in contrast to win-lose gain. Once such social causality is revealed and verified through the light of observation, more and more people will seek win-win gain — not because they are forced to do so, but because the evidence of its multifarious benefits is overwhelming. Social salvation from human extermination will follow paradigm shifts of social causality that lead to the maximization of win-win wealth and the minimization of win-lose wealth.

Even though the anonymous man in the street may have little interest in knowing principles of causation, he only has to know that win-win principles work. More compelling for him than the Principle of Win-Win Exchange, is the *image* of win-win exchange. He only has to know that win-win exchange is the best deal for everyone. Win-win works for him, as it works for his family and friends.

Without knowing why win-win exchange for mutual gain is a necessary means to the good life, he can accept the conclusion that its benefits for him, as well as others, are remarkable. He does not have to articulate why win-win action is a practical means to a better life. Thus, common men and women do not have to understand the sequence of steps leading to the conclusion that win-win works. It works for them with little or no comprehension of how or why it works. Furthermore, because it works as a central tenet of win-win religion, believers can have *faith* that it works. Where one's faith is founded on the truth of the benevolent altruism of win-win religion, the encouragement of believers to keep the faith creates win-win domino effects. These positive effects foster peace, prosperity, and freedom for all believers of win-win faith to enjoy.

To be sure, some skeptics may raise the question, "Is win-win faith really practical?" The answer depends entirely on one's religious aims. If the aim is to spread war, poverty, and servitude, as some would do, win-win faith is impractical because it will not work. Those who would strive for such ruinous aims must keep the faith in the rightness of win-lose religion for coercive gain.

On the other hand, where the religious aim is to spread peace, prosperity, and freedom, win-win exchange founded on the Golden Rule Principle is the only action that does work. In truth, if it is the only thing that works toward benevolent and humanitarian aims then, *ipso facto*, it is the only thing that is *practical*. Whether the Golden Rule Principle is followed on observational evidence of its power to create peace, prosperity, and freedom for all believers to enjoy, or it is followed on faith and authority without independent observation to verify its truth, the universal benefits of the operation of the Win-Win Principle will accrue for the enrichment of all humans, in all places, at all times.

∽

It has been stressed that an ominous social crisis began with the nuclear age and the ever-growing efficiency, diversity, and ubiquity of its grand weapons of annihilation. More than any time in human history, the social direction we pursue is both critical and crucial. To err is to invite doom. One direction is to follow the true principles of win-win religion and win-win government. These institutions have a vital advantage because they impede neither the advance of science, industry, and art, nor do they bar the advance of peace, prosperity, and freedom. In vivid contrast, the opposite direction is to follow the false principles of win-lose religion and government. Those institutions have a dire disadvantage because they impede the progress of science, art, and industry. Moreover, they incite and impose the causes of war, poverty, and servitude, which lead to social decline and human oblivion.

The ruination of civilization, however and the demise of our species is not a certainty. When we can identify and verify the truth of social causality through the power of observation, a new perception of reality revolutionizes human action. To say this is a profound revolution does not overstate its importance.

A revolution is something that revolves, which is to *turn around*. A key element of this turning around—this social revolution—involves an entirely new perception of social reality. It arrives quietly without fanfare by discovering and verifying the equity, utility, and morality of a simple social principle. This principle has been handed down from antiquity with only minor variations on the same theme. It is the priceless guide to human behavior defined in win-win theory as the Golden Rule Principle. Like all principles, it does not allow for exceptions. Its counsel is exact and precise without compromise: *Do not seize wealth and freedom from others, as you would have them not seize your wealth and freedom.*

This principle generalizes the Golden Rule of social action set down by theologians and philosophers in ancient times. As a rule of behavior, it has survived for thousands of years because it is both elegant and pragmatic. In common language, it works. The practical efficacy of its daily operation cannot be over-explained or over-stressed. This is of critical importance because among the educated classes, the main argument *against* their support of the Golden Rule is not that it is wrong, but that it is *impractical*.

Many readers have heard the argument raised by people who rue, "The Golden Rule may sound great in theory, but it just can't work in practice." Yet, this flawed argument not only contends that win-win religion is impractical, but it warns that win-win ethics, win-win business, win-win production, and win-win exchange, are all impractical aims for starry-eyed idealists.

In truth, this tired argument is wrong. If all these win-win relations are impractical because they cannot work in practice, then what is the alternative? The only alternative is to live with—if not support—win-lose religion, win-lose ethics, win-lose business, win-lose production, win-lose exchange, win-lose marriage, win-lose government, and win-lose everything else. If this is the alternative, it is the road to ruin. It presumes the practicality of coercive action for win-lose gain. The supposed value of this win-lose alternative is fostered by faith in a fatal model of causality: For me to gain, you must lose. Belief in its truth is rife among educated people who remain the most influential classes of our time. Yet, this model of social causality is gravely flawed; its acceptance on faith is a prelude for unparalleled disaster.

A hard lesson yet to be widely learned concerns another worldwide crisis. It has been stressed that among the most dangerous and destructive people on earth are respected people with good minds and educations who rarely set out to harm anyone, but who too often don't know what they are doing. More precisely, they fail to identify and verify which social causes lead to which social effects. This failure breeds dangerous and deadly consequences for decent people, whether they are religious or not? With passion and purpose, backed by faith in the fidelity of their knowledge of causality, they act on false paradigms of causality as if they were true.

This is due in part to the fact that it is not easy to identify intellectual errors, especially those that lead to misidentification of causality. Furthermore, the tradition of ancient and modern education has been to focus on conservation of traditional paradigms of cause-and-effect. Thus, in general, the longer people go to school, and the more books they read, the more likely they are assured of the truth and rightness of their paradigms. For this reason, they are unlikely to make pivotal paradigm shifts on which causes lead to which effects. In other words, the more schoolwork, the more book work, the more instilled and imbued people are with paradigms of causality that are anchored by the heavy weight of conventional wisdom. Thus, the more likely their paradigms are accepted without independent observation of their truth and validity. This is not a modern phenomenon. It has been true for every civilization and every culture in recorded history. However, conventional wisdom or not, which models of causality are true, and which are false? We must never stop asking this crucial question.

Moreover, for those who would choose between conflicting explanations of causality, do they have a reliable standard of causality identification and verification? For most people, these questions are never raised. Furthermore, for most people with good minds and educations, whether their models of social causality are true or false, valid or invalid, moral or immoral, this is not an issue. One reason it is not an issue is that, for everyone, it is always easier to cling to old paradigms of causality than it is to embrace new ones. Yet, in the nuclear age, to cling to old paradigms of causality by default without observational analysis is a fatal mistake and false comfort, which may very well lead to disaster without any prospect of recovery.

◦◦◦

Making paradigm shifts toward better explanations of causality and higher standards of truth and morality is not an easy exercise for timid people. It is not for those who cling to the social safety and the mental security of reliance on authority and conventional wisdom for their models of causality. Again, for everyone, it takes intellectual courage and integrity to acknowledge that any of their prized paradigms of causality are in any way flawed, let alone that they may be spurious (counterfeit) and potentially fatal when carried out. Even when this is incontrovertibly and irrefutably true, who would admit that their paradigms of causality are flawed, or even blemished, let alone untenable on any rational or moral grounds? The answer is few people, very few people — but thankfully, not zero.

For all of us, our paradigms of causality are difficult to discard. It may mean giving up some esteemed, long-held view of reality, a view that is not likely open to question as we see it. Whatever models of causality people cling to — whether physical, biological, social, philosophical, theological, political, et cetera — all believers hold them to be true and above reproach. Moreover, when the very paradigms of causality that govern their actions — their daily lives — are also their default models of reality, they tend to be immune to analysis. A constant default mode requires no action. Thus, all stress and anguish over whether their paradigms are true or false, effective or ineffective, moral or immoral can be avoided. The truth of their models of causality is not an issue.

It is not easy to escape from this closed loop. It requires a certain character trait to change old paradigms of reality, and to embrace new ones, even when the evidence of their truth is demonstrable, dramatic, and overwhelming. It takes bold self-assurance coupled with self-confidence for anyone to make paradigm shifts on their fundamental models of causality.

We are fortunate that history has its beacons of intellectual honesty and integrity. There have always been people with the courage to reach for truer and truer models of causality for their benefit and ours. If this were not so, we might still live in the canopy of a forest or in the hollow of a cave. One beacon of courage already lauded was the German Jesuit, Freidrich Spee von Langenfeld.

Father Freidrich had the daring nerve to admit his errors in torturing innocent people (in the cruelest ways) until they made false confessions to crimes of witchcraft and heresy. Spee saw that it was easy for church officials, like him, to extract false confessions from the accused, especially when they finally realized that a full confession would end their misery of torture.

Through his own experience as a Christian official conducting torture for the Church, Spee showed that confessions by torture proved nothing, neither guilt nor innocence. In refuting and invalidating the entire process of sanctified and legalized torture as a means of extracting truth, Father Spee acted at a time when it was perilous to do so in a Christian society. Christian leaders, with fierce passion and the power of coercion, defended the sanctity of their win-lose authority to hunt and destroy all witches and heretics.

Even though Spee himself believed in the reality of witchcraft, he refuted the flawed methods of identifying witches. In a Christian world where it was a grave heresy, even to doubt the truth of witchcraft, one had to be careful. To challenge the truth of witchcraft was a capital crime punishable by legal execution. Nonetheless, Freidrich Spee had the valor to reveal the injustice and failure of legalized torture as a Catholic policy for suppressing witchcraft and heresy. His remarkable courage, along with those of a few other influential Christians, led to the ultimate banishment of sanctified and legitimized torture in Christian Europe. This was a large step toward reviving the win-win teachings of Jesus. It required people with courage, coupled with better knowledge of causality, to make a paradigm shift away from their faith in the sanctify and effectiveness of human torture as a means of reaching sacred truth and judicial justice.

The pragmatic question of practical value is always can the means employed attain the end sought? Not without risk of retaliation from a win-lose church, Father Spee showed that the means employed—torture—cannot attain the end sought, namely, a reliable truth. His quiet valor has brought society ever closer to the final expulsion of torture for religious and political gain.

୬୦

The win-lose paradigm, whatever its lethal variation, cannot be mended or justified on theological, philosophical, judicial, ethical, or rational grounds without resorting to the sinister delusion of subterfuge and fraud. It is both important and significant to note that few religious believers of any faith would defend win-lose religion of any stripe, if they understood social causality. Of course, *understanding* causality is the key to cogent wisdom. To understand is to see the scope and scale of force and fraud that support the flawed foundations of all coercive institutions of win-lose gain, whether religious or secular.

All coercion is destructive, but not all coercion is equally destructive. Coercion only becomes a social crisis when it is institutionalized and organized for win-lose gain. While non-institutionalized, disorganized coercion is destructive; institutionalized, organized coercion is catastrophic.

Among decent people, regardless of their theology, the key to their rejection and abandonment of win-lose paradigms of causality can be found in their acceptance of truer and truer explanations of social causality. Yet, to do this means that some people must be in search of truth. Indeed, where they find a constant principle of truth, all people with moral and rational integrity will choose principle over popularity. Throughout history, they have been the valiant vanguard of human progress.

For believers of all religions, whether they are Christians, Judaists, Muslims, Hindus, Buddhists, Shintoists, Druids, deists, or innumerable other faiths; it is their choice to practice either win-win or win-lose religion. They can apply the Golden Rule Principle, or violate it. The line of demarcation is razor sharp. Religious believers of every faith can seek gain through the gain of others, or through the loss of others. If this appears to be a black-or-white alternative, it is.

Modern scholarship, however, often derides the concept of black-or-white alternatives, where choosers are limited to only two choices by excluding the possibility of any other choice. Nonetheless, in observing the world of human interaction, where social ethics are in question, some alternatives are necessarily black-or-white. Yet, the counter argument against this view is that in daily interactions among humans, in defining the separation of proper and improper conduct, there will always be shades-of-gray. But what is proper and what is improper conduct? Although the division on this question is longstanding, observation of random action reveals two possible courses of human conduct to compare and define.

Wherever humans interact, anyone can take win-win action for noncoercive gain or win-lose action for coercive gain. Unless some other choice is found, both observation and intuition indicate that the choice is black-or-white. Without having found the elusive absolute truth, we can observe the permanence of a constant truth. We can see the dual alternative of black-or-white morality to be a constant standard of equitable ethics—without the mischief of arbitrary variation. Human progress is founded on the discovery of constant principles of regularity in nature. In fact, the subtle prize of nature is its *constancy* of principles, always operating without variation or complaint.

Yet, could there be an alternative choice to be found in some gray area of human conduct? An area of action that contradicts the observable alternative that is limited to choice *A* or *B*, or one or the other. Out of practical necessity, could there be an area of justifiable action beyond black-or-white ethics?

If not black-or-white ethics and morality, then what alternative is there? Why not a morality in shades-of-gray, that is, from light to dark degrees of morality and ethical behavior? This could be the gray scale of social ethics for a relative morality to fit every occasion. In such a gray scale of morality, perhaps what is moral behavior should be trumped by what is practical behavior. Thus, social practicality could transcend social morality.

When Mao Ze-dong mandated the murder of over seventy million of his fellow Chinese, did all of his targets get what they deserved, or just some of them, or none of them? Did the millions of innocent children dutifully erased by

Mao's minions deserve such harsh treatment? How about their parents who were seen as obstacles to raising a Marxist state in China?

In answering the question, some might argue the old adage, "There are two sides to every story." Looking at Mao's side, his apologists said that his genius for practical politics had brought the order and glory of Marxian Socialism to the people of China. Mao was not portrayed as Communizing China for himself, but for the masses of the People's Republic of China. If we were to take an unbiased view, could we say that Chairman Mao was not all bad? Many still argue that he was not a bad guy at all but was a good guy. In fact, he has many admirers today who cherish his book, *Quotations from Chairman Mao Tse-tung*, (known in the West as *The Little Red Book*), which is still in demand at bookstores and other sources.

Even though Mao forced his people at gunpoint to read *The Little Red Book* and carry it with them it at all times — or risk punishment if caught without it — today many of his readers are eager to learn the cogent wisdom of the revered Communist Party Chairman. In the preface to the second edition of *The Little Red Book*, Marshall Lin Piao (Biao) wrote in December of 1966, "Comrade Mao Tse-tung is the greatest Marxist-Leninist of our era." Lin Piao failed to mention, however, that during the course of becoming "the greatest Marxist-Leninist of our era," Mao also became the greatest mass murder of our era — or of any era. Yet, for some, this is a lasting legacy to admire.

When Chancellor Hitler caused the murder of over twenty million Europeans, did some of them get what they deserved? Some folks still argue that at least the six million Jews got what they deserved. If they are right about the Jews, then the standard of ethics cannot be a black-or-white issue. Some would say that there must be some wiggle room for moral shades-of-gray. Like Mao, maybe Hitler was not all bad, and how about Stalin?

Even though this trio of tyrants orchestrated their loyal party members to murder over 150,000,000 people (excluding battlefield casualties) to facilitate the advance of Communism, Socialism, and Fascism, could there be a gray area of value to be found in their win-lose actions? After all, those actions were legally imposed through political authority. Does political legality count for something? Genocide was *not* illegal in Germany, China, or the USSR. The legal prosecution of genocide was the law of the land.

In defense of genocide, some might argue that in murdering 150,000,000 people, there were 150,000,000 fewer mouths to feed. Could there be some hidden value that might justify exterminating millions of innocent people most of whom have harmed no one?

English economist T. R. Malthus (1766-1834) pointed out that humans tend to increase their numbers at a geometric rate (1, 2, 4, 8, 16...), while providing for their sustenance at only an arithmetic rate (1, 2, 3, 4, 5...). Thus, a perpetual crisis springs from the natural trend of baby production increasing at a faster rate than food production. For many, over time, the natural consequence will be hunger or death by starvation.* Then, could this mean that even mass murder may have a positive side in depressing population den-

---

* There is rescue from this Malthusian crisis. Demographic studies show that as wealth production per capita rises, baby production per capita falls. For those who would take the path to an explosion of wealth production, they only have to maximize win-win exchange and minimize win-lose exchange. The result is more wealth for fewer people leading to more prosperity per capita. On the other hand, for those who would take the alternate path to an explosion of poverty, they only have to maximize win-lose exchange and minimize win-win exchange. The result is less wealth for more people leading to more poverty per capita. This is another example of a social path, which bifurcates toward either win-lose or win-win gain, where the unavoidable choice is black-or-white.

sities (defeating overpopulation) by killing off millions of people through carefully organized extermination policies? Could this be a gray area of ethical conduct? In the interest of what is practical and efficacious, should we institute a moral relativism with ethical shades of gray? Can mass murder be justified, or is it entirely wrong and immoral regardless of how "necessary" and even "just" its backers claim it to be?

Lest we forget, murder by genocide is still praised as a vital *cause célèbre* by many fluent and eloquent spokesmen. What if respected citizens through legalized, codified, and institutionalized genocide carefully organize mass murder? Is it still a crime, or merely a minor crime, or a major crime, or no crime at all?

In any case, before rushing to judgment in search of truth, should we hear both sides of the story? In pursuing moral truth, there are, indeed, two sides to every story. For those who may postulate that violence is immoral, and that nonviolence is moral, then those who practice win-win exchange for mutual gain are on the moral side, and those who practice win-lose exchange for coercive gain are on the immoral side.

If we hear Hitler's side, Mao's side, and Stalin's side, what do we hear? The tyrant's side of the story never changes, which is to justify coercion for win-lose gain. His despotic theme is to obey my decrees, or be fined, imprisoned or killed.

In the social arena of human interaction, how we interact with others is limited to two choices. Observation reveals that we can practice mutual exchange for win-win gain, or we can practice coercive exchange for win-lose gain. When we are pursuing mutual exchange for win-win gain, we cannot at the same time violate the Golden Rule Principle by either directly or indirectly seizing the wealth and freedom of others through force or fraud. Our choice of action is black-or-white precisely because there is no other choice.

There is no wiggle room for shades of gray, which would allow for the presumed rightness or equity of partial seizure of wealth and freedom for win-lose gain.

Wherever there is human interaction, the integrity of the Golden Rule Principle is either violated or respected. It is one or the other, which necessarily is a black-or-white choice. Either the sun revolves around the earth, or the earth revolves around the sun. In addition, since Kepler discovered the elliptical orbits of our planets (toppling the Greek model of circular orbits), observation continues to show that there is no gray scale of truth and no latitude for argument on planetary motion. The physical laws of nature are inflexible as are the social laws of nature.

Nonetheless, where moral fidelity is defended as an inviolable principle, there is a common counter argument. It is that although morality without compromise is a worthy aim, to excel in the real world, you have to be practical. It is argued that organizing coercion for win-lose gain is a useful policy for advancing society. This paradigm praises the utility of imposing the greatest coercion for the greatest good. Of course, no religious despot or political tyrant would ever disagree with this win-lose paradigm. They all agree that organized coercion is the only practical policy for establishing social order and social equality for common citizens.

In Europe and elsewhere, believers in Fascist superiority had faith that for Christian Aryans to dominate society, it was practical policy to murder millions of Jews to clear the way for the glory of Fascism. And believers in Communist superiority had faith that for atheistic Marxists to dominate society, the practical policy was to murder millions of non-Communists to clear the way for the glory of Marxism.

Social history shows the prevailing argument for inciting crimes against humanity to be nothing more than variations on the same practical theme: *For superiors to gain, their inferiors must be forced to lose.* Yet, the lethality of this prized paradigm of social causation cannot be exaggerated.

Through no fault of their own, most victims of genocide were born of inferior people. Though they were innocent of choosing their own parents, this is not enough to spare them from extermination by those who claim to be culturally, racially, or politically superior. In short, it is said that these inferior people have to be terminated by their betters.

Many of us have seen grave photographs of genocide victims, showing mounds of inferior people, all dead, some staring at us with vacant eyes. And it is tempting to think that it's really not our problem because it's their genocide, not ours. But it is our problem because it is everyone's problem. In the end, the superiority syndrome of ignorant people—oblivious of causality—may ruin things for everyone. The blight of ruination may reach us no matter how serene and secure our surroundings may seem to be.

Still, in spite of such gloom, there is good news. Before things go that far, we do not have to square the circle or race beyond the speed of light. We only have to show good people with good minds and good educations that win-win action is the true means to enrich humankind and to reach the noble aims they surely cherish. You really do not have to kill anyone to get there if you know what you are doing. It cannot be overstated: the end of every social crisis begins when and where we can identify, clarify, and verify the truth of which social causes lead to which social effects. As always, our choice is to *imagine* cause-and-effect, or to *observe* cause-and-effect.

Whenever we aim to find out what is really going on in our mysterious universe, human history confirms the advantage of choosing observation of causality over imagination of causality. This does not require extraordinary intelligence; it merely requires ordinary intelligence and ordinary courage, which history shows is not in short supply.

It is not that difficult; people who understand causality and have the resolve to act accordingly know what they are doing toward reaching their aims. This is the source of their win-win power to build a better world, not only for themselves, but also for those who do not understand causality and may oppose those who do. Fortunately, the long-term influence of those who do *not* know what they are doing will fade in time, because where the aim is to understand causality, observation of truth always trumps imagination of truth. This irrefutable fact will continue to gain broader acceptance among people with influence.

As the negative domino effects of win-lose exchange propel more destruction, so do the positive domino effects of win-win exchange propel more construction. The truth of these principles of win-win and win-lose domino effects may or may not be accepted on faith. In either case, the consistent reliability of their operation is observable to anyone willing to examine the cause-and-effect relationships of all human exchange. The greater the scope and scale of win-win exchange, the greater the magnitude of new wealth for all to enjoy. Donne's incisive metaphor reveals that everyone is the beneficiary of win-win wealth because *no man is an island.*

To originate, generate, and promulgate human progress in a striking way, a long-held paradigm must be falsified and repudiated. To reemphasize, the common belief that win-win principles of religion, government, commerce, and freedom merely sound great in theory, but are impractical in practice is a fallacious theme based entirely on *a priori* faith without observational verification.

The great achievements of human history were all said to be impractical before they became practical realities. Experience shows that all natural principles are practical discoveries because sooner or later they illuminate our understanding of physical, biological, and social causality. They explain which causes lead to which effects. For this precise reason, nothing in our quest for human achievement and advancement is more practical, more useful, more important, more significant, and in the end, more precious.

ENDNOTES

116. Isaac Asimov, *Asimov's Biographical Encyclopedia of Science & Technology* (Garden City, N.Y.: Doubleday & Company, 1972), 1023.

117. Nicholas of Cusa (Nicholas Cusanas; Nicholas Krebs), *De docta ignorantia,* (On Learned Ignorance), 1440, trans. G. Heron (New Haven, CT: Yale University Press, 1954), p. 11.

118. Colin A. Ronan, *Galileo* (New York: G. P. Putnam's Sons, 1974), 220.

119. Ronan, *Galileo*.

120. St. Ignatius of Loyola, *Exercitia spiritaulia* (Spiritual Exercises), (Rome: Antonio Bladio, 1548).

121. Galileo Galilei, "Fragment on Falling Bodies," 1604.

122. Heilbron, John L., *Censorship of Astronomy in Italy after Galileo* (Champlain, NY: McMullin, 2005), 279-322.

123. Robert Bellarmine, *De lacicis,* trans. Kathleen E. Murphy (New York: Fordham University Press, 1928), Ch. 18. Another translation of the original Latin, (*Libertas credendi perniciosa est…nam nihil aliud est quam libertas errandi*) reads, "Freedom of belief is pernicious, it is nothing but the freedom to be wrong."

124. Dorothea Waley Singer, *Bruno: His Life and Thought with Annotated Translation of His Work On the Infinite Universe and Worlds* (New York: Henry Schuman, 1950).

125. Coulson Turnbull, *Life and Teachings of Giordano Bruno* (San Diego, California: Gnostic Press, 1913), 57.

126. Isaac Asimov, *Asimov's Biographical Encyclopedia of Science and Technology* (Garden City, NY: Doubleday & Co., 1972), 373.

127. G. T. Wrench, M.D., *Lord Lister: His Work and Life* (London: T. Fisher Unwin, 1914), 348.

Chapter Twelve

Faith in the Glory of Genocide and the Goodness of War*

The near silence of the Christian community during the Nazi persecutions of Jews and Jewish Christians, which raged across Europe in the 1930s and 40s is well known to historians of that era. One notable exception to this dramatic silence came from the steady voice of Monsignor Bernhard Lichtenberg. As Provost of St. Hedgwin Cathedral in Berlin, built in 1773 by Frederick the Great, Father Lichtenberg

---

* The term "genocide" was coined in 1943 by international lawyer Raphael Lemkin who explained its usage: "New conceptions require new terms. By 'genocide' we mean the destruction of a nation or an ethnic group. This new word, coined by the author to denote an old practice in its modern development, is made from the ancient Greek word *genos* (race, tribe) and the Latin *cide* (killing), thus corresponding in its formation to such words as tyrannicide, homicide, infanticide, etc." Ralph Lemkin, *Axis Rule in Occupied Europe: Laws of Occupation – Analysis of Government – Proposals for Redress* (Washington D.C.: Carnegie Endowment for International Peace, 1944), 79.

routinely defied the dreaded demands of the Gestapo.* They had warned him never to express compassion for the Jews and for their lawful expulsion from Germany, or for any other police action against them. Yet, Father Lichtenberg, fully aware that police action could silence him at any time for defending the Jews, openly prayed for them in church and in public as he did for other targets of Nazi brutality.

In a police state of informers eager to spy on their neighbors, Lichtenberg's contempt for Nazi authority did not go unnoticed. After witnessing his prayers for Jews and other victims of the concentration camps, two vigilant young women from his own parish had seen and heard enough. Beguiled by Hitler's anti-Semitic leadership, they reported Lichtenberg to the Gestapo. The women, deluded as they were by the spirit of German Nationalism, denounced Father Lichtenberg for openly praying for the Jews. The Gestapo arrested him on October 23, 1941.

As a high profile prelate of the Catholic Church who could not be ignored, and who refused to compromise his Christian principles, Father Lichtenberg was accused of treason. Allegedly, he had broken German law by delivering inflammatory and incendiary prayers such as, "Let us now pray for the Jews and for the wretched prisoners in the concentration camps."[128]

At his trial, Lichtenberg was charged with the crime of "insidious activity" (Heimtücke). This was in violation of the Sedition Law, which made it a crime to incite harm against the German state. In defense of these charges, Lichtenberg calmly replied, "I submit that no harm results to the state by citizens who pray for Jews." [129] His defense was denied by a German court, entirely committed to the legal suppression of freedom of speech and religion. He was convicted of

---

* Gestapo was a German acronym for Geheimstatspolizei meaning "state secret police."

seditious acts against the state, and sentenced by the Berlin District Court in May 1942 to two years in prison.

Through his conviction — by a legal court of law — of committing a so-called crime against the German government, Father Lichtenberg became another victim of a criminal justice system without justice. His "crime" was preaching his ideals of Christian kindness to his congregation, and expressing them in public. Lichtenberg insisted that Jews must be treated with the same respect as Christians. He held that social justice could not exist in a Germany where there is one standard of justice for Christians, and another for Jews.

The judges of the District Court had acted in defense of the legal tyranny of their own coercion, leveled and exacted against the defendant, the Provost of St. Hedgwin. By their own win-lose decision for political gain, the esteemed judges of the Berlin court ruled against justice and civil liberties in the Fatherland. Where criminals don the robes of justice, there is no justice, and no one is safe.

Like the witch trials of medieval Germany, so too in modern Germany the prosecutors and plaintiffs were themselves the real criminals. The accused defendants were the real victims of legitimized crimes of the court. The criminalization of civil liberties became so systemic throughout the Third Reich that it legalized crimes against humanity. Such legal and social regression was the effect of a win-lose society where justice was banished in the name of the Lord, in the name of the Fatherland, and in the name of the Führer.

Speaking before the Reichstag in 1938, Adolph Hitler, as German Chancellor, assured the spellbound members of the German parliament, "I believe today that I am acting in the sense of the Almighty Creator. By warding off the Jews I am fighting for the Lord's work."[130] Of course, Hitler's euphemistic language that he was "warding off the Jews" on behalf of the "Almighty Creator," really meant that he was killing off the Jews in his noble and sacred role of the Führer, by doing "the Lord's work," as he said.

Hitler, as a self-appointed agent of Almighty God and the Lord Jesus, was widely seen as the heroic leader of the German people in defending them from the duplicitous and culpable Jews. A messianic Hitler was walking in the footsteps of the great Protestant leader, Martin Luther, who had proclaimed that the Jews should be expelled and driven from the Fatherland. Both Luther and Hitler claimed that, in fighting the Jews, they were fighting for the Lord's work.

The general failure of educated people with good minds to understand social causality led to the codification of a German justice system where justice was the exception, and injustice the rule, without legal recourse to the victims. Win-lose justice for political gain had become the norm and the model of respectability in Germany. When the Nazis were finally rewarded in 1933 with the political prize of privilege and coercive power, their reign was only made possible through the influence and support of Germans who, without ever joining the Nazi Party, nonetheless shared the Nazi paradigm of social causality: *For us to gain, they must be forced to lose.* Herr Hitler, however, did not invent the win-lose paradigm; he only had to appeal to those who already embraced it as their model of social causality.

After Father Lichtenberg completed his jail term, the Gestapo informed him that he would be released if he agreed to neither preach in church nor pray in public until the war ended with a German victory. This meant that he must never offer public sympathy to the Jews for their deplorable treatment by state police and other political authorities. Lichtenberg, however, refused this generous offer from the Gestapo. Instead, he asked if he could accompany and attend the Jews and Jewish Christians, being deported to the miserable ghetto at Lodz near Warsaw. Lichtenberg's request was denied, and he was ordered to be confined at the SS work camp at Dachau, outside the Bavarian capitol of Munich. But Bernhard Lichtenberg never entered the gates of Dachau. While in transport to the camp in a cattle car, he collapsed and died on November 5, 1943. Father Lichtenberg was sixty-eight. Until the end, his moral integrity remained the bulwark of his striking courage.

☙

In 1971, as many had done before, I went to see for myself the remains of the former work camp at the German town of Dachau. Even now, anyone who plans to visit Bavaria should allow the time to visit this once notorious place of horror. Dachau was built for the concentration (legal imprisonment) of victims of the political union between win-lose Nationalism and win-lose Socialism, which formed the coercive foundations of what became National Socialism, and known throughout most of the world as German Naziism.

In visiting Dachau, be prepared for a sobering experience. Yet, by merely walking through its gates, you will not see the root cause of the disaster at Dachau. Instead, you will only see a fading picture that no photograph can capture. It is the physical image of the first Nazi institution designed to dehumanize, punish, and murder victims of legalized tyranny that formed the political pillars of the Third Reich.

Dachau was the despotic effect of German authorities marshaling coercive action for win-lose political gain. Yet, fully to comprehend which social causes lead to which social effects, we have to be careful observers of human action. Social causality is difficult to observe, and is a challenge to understand because of the usually long-time lag between cause-and-effect. The outbreak of war, for example, is often caused by win-lose coercion taken generations before the first shots are ever fired. The greater the time spans between cause-and-effect, the greater the difficulty of observing which causes have led to which effects.

Dachau did not grow overnight out of a social vacuum without someone authorizing coercive action to launch its creation. Dachau was a tragic effect of National Socialism driven by its all-consuming faith. But faith in what? Faith in the rightness and efficacy of institutionalized tyranny, buoyed by fervent faith in the merit of the win-lose paradigm. However, it is not faith, per se, in the win-lose paradigm that is harmful. Rather, the harm is imposed by win-lose action taken on *a priori* faith that this false paradigm of social causality is surely true and effective. It is faith in its presumed rectitude, fairness, and necessity that render it both socially acceptable and respectable in the minds of many decent people. The noble image of the win-lose paradigm is the source of its destructive power to govern human action toward win-lose gain.

It is important to know that Dachau was not an illegitimate aberration; rather, it was the legitimate child of accepted and respected paradigms of causality. Yet, that very respectability — frozen in place by win-lose tradition — masked the reality of its paradigms that were all founded on false models of social causality. Again, to both reiterate and reemphasize the paradigmatic power of win-lose models of social causality to incite win-lose action for coercive gain rises from common faith in their truth and validity as respected paradigms of reality. Tyranny stands on a firm foundation of faith in its efficacy, if not faith in its moral virtue.

In the days of political pragmatism that dominated the Nazi rise to power and their creation of a criminalized regime in Germany, Hitler revealed his central policy of National Socialism. With open candor, Hitler writes to readers of his widely read and influential *Mein Kampf* (My Struggle), 1925:

> Only in the steady and constant application of force [violence] lies the very first prerequisite for [Nazi] success. This persistence, however, can always and only arise from a definite spiritual conviction. Any violence which does not spring from a firm, spiritual base, will be wavering and uncertain.[131]

Hitler stressed that Nazi success can "only arise from a definite spiritual conviction" in the merit and efficacy of Nazi violence. Such "conviction" was maintained by believers whose *faith* in the supremacy of the Nazi creed was unflinching. These true believers became the official vanguard of faithful followers who mastered the logistical ordeal of murdering 21,000,000 Europeans (excluding battlefield causalities). In *Mein Kampf*, Hitler and his duteous ghostwriters revealed in plain German all the strategy of faith in violence for Nazi success.

The entire Nazi movement became a political machine for the "constant application of force" for the "success" of Nazi policies. Those policies were all coercive political programs for win-lose gain. Most emphatically, Hitler stressed that the "success" of National Socialism would be built upon the "constant application" of "violence." However, success for the Nazis was always *win-lose success* because the means to success was always violent action for coercive gain.

Hitler's strategy for Nazi success was founded on violence in perpetuity—which is violence forever. His paradigm was clear. There was to be no illegitimate, no illegal, violence. The violence must be *legitimized* and *legalized* as the crucial means to political gain. This was the violent policy for enriching and empowering the Nazi Party and its "progressive" leadership.

But how could the Teutonic people of Germany—the very people who had raised a great nation on a foundation of commercial, technological, scientific, and artistic success—have fallen for Hitler's political policies of institutionalized violence? And, most remarkably, how could educated Germans with good minds have been seduced into praising and supporting a social system of compulsory servitude and codified tyranny?

To know causation, however, it is not enough merely to conclude that decent Germans sold out to a spellbinding Hitler and his cadre of eloquent assassins. Then as now, the world is tainted with would-be tyrants of every coercive stripe. We should not be surprised when such deluded people arise in the future. However, if they have worn out their welcome among decent people with good minds and educations, their dreams of tyranny will remain no more than dreams. No matter how vivid, no one was ever murdered by a dream. The social solution to tyranny is to preempt those who dream of imposing tyranny from legitimizing institutions of win-lose coercion for religious or political gain—at gunpoint.

After the ignominious death of the Third Reich, nearly everyone educated in the West would tell you they are against Naziism and those hated Nazis. But how many such anti-Nazis today can articulate the essence of the Nazi paradigm of social causality? If they cannot, then they do not know what they are against. While they denounce Nazis in a heartbeat, they are at risk of condoning and even implementing Nazi policies because they cannot identify and articulate what those policies were. A key measure of your understanding of any subject is your ability to articulate it in speech and in writing. For most people, if they can't articulate it, they don't understand it.

Throughout the Fatherland, the National Socialists fostered what had already been, long before their time, a highly praised win-lose model of social causality. It recognized two distinct classes of German citizens. Many labels could define these social classes, but their cultural distinction and social status can be separated by simply referring to them as "superior Germans" in marked contrast to "inferior Germans." Furthermore, the social dynamics of their relationship was exemplified by this win-lose paradigm: *For superior Germans to gain, inferior Germans must be forced to lose.*

It was widely accepted in Germany that for superior Germans such as Christians, Aryans, National Socialists (Nazis), and healthy heterosexuals to gain, all inferior Germans must be forced to lose, especially Jews, Gypsies, Communists (except those joining the Nazi Party), homosexuals, invalids, and, of course, anti-Nazis. These inferiors included detractors of Nazi criminality like the heroic rector of St. Hedgwin, Father Lichtenberg, who in open defiance of police coercion denounced the tyranny of a National Socialism, fully committed to crimes against humanity.

More than merely falling under the charismatic spell of the Führer, the German people fell under the spurious spell of the superiority syndrome. Its lethal potential to govern human action toward fatal ends has not been overstated. It was faith in its equity and virtue that brought ruination across Germany from the North Sea to the Black Forest and beyond. In any nation where people are swayed by the bogus appeal of the superiority syndrome, they are at grave risk of condoning and sustaining autocratic leaders whose tyranny is fueled by flawed paradigms of cultural, ethnic, and social supremacy: *For superior humans to gain, inferior humans must lose through force or fraud.*

Like all paradigms of causality, those who accept them are certain they are true. It is precisely for this reason that paradigms govern the people who govern the world. The critical question is always: Which paradigms of causality are true, valid, and moral? In contrast, "Which paradigms are false, invalid, and immoral?" This is more than a mere academic question; it is truly a question of life or death.

◌◌

Before leaving Dachau, I climbed onto a weathered wall to photograph the camp from above with my wide-angle lens. However, upon seeing behind the wall for the first time, to my sudden shock, I was now looking down onto a closed area of the camp. There, stretching before me, as if in a distant time warp, lay an abandoned road, its cracking cement now pierced by a thousand weeds. This once well-traveled road still led straight through the gates of Dachau, and into the first concentration camp of National Socialism. Opened in 1933, it was built by the Munich Chief of Police, Heinrich Himmler. Herr Himmler would become the notorious chief of the SS and overseer of the Gestapo, as well as all work camps and death camps for the legal penalization and liquidation of all inferiors throughout the Fatherland.

In the iron grill above the entrance to the camp were those ominous words that read: *Arbeit Macht Frei*, "Work will make you free." This was one of many emblematic frauds of National Socialism, which without the Nazi deceit would have to read: We will work you to death—if we don't kill you first. And, as far as the SS promise at the gate, "Work will make you free," for thousands of inmates, only death would make them free.

In the earlier years of Dachau, thousands of Jewish prisoners were released if they promised to emigrate out of Germany. Over time, however, most Jews were not so fortunate. On October 18, 1941, a state edict was issued cutting off all Jewish emigration from Germany.[132] Furthermore, when Jews were transferred from Dachau, it was usually to a death camp with an even more lethal environment.

Dachau was in operation from March 1933 until its prisoners were finally liberated on April 29, 1945. Over a dozen years, camp clerks at Dachau recorded some 35,000 registered deaths.[133] Yet, many more deaths—probably in the tens of thousands—due to murder, privation, and disease were never recorded. The total number of victims will never be known. Among the motley inmates of Dachau were captured Soviet, French, and British combatants, as well as invalids who were liquidated for their disabilities. From nearly every nation of Europe, there were victims of National Socialism, including casualties of grisly medical experiments. Jehovah's Witnesses, who refused to renounce their religion and swear allegiance to Hitler and Nazi authority, were thrown into Dachau and other concentration camps across Europe—many of them killed for the crime of religious integrity.

To end the human depravity of organizing society by forcing inferior citizens into concentration camps at gunpoint, we must understand the lethal history of such prisons as legal institutions of criminal justice. We must know much more than the dismal record of their fatal statistics, and the names of long forgotten victims. Without a clear understanding of social causality, political and religious tyranny will continue to rise. Its criminal destruction of human life, wealth, and freedom is a predictable effect of human failure to deter and erase the social blunders that lead decent people to the veneration of win-lose gain for so-called worthy ends. Humans have too often blundered their way to the legal creation of criminal institutions of win-lose gain to reach religious and political aims.

The true causes of the lethal social effects of Germany's Dachau, Poland's Auschwitz, Russia's Gulags, China's Laogai, and a thousand more prisons dedicated to forced labor and to systemized brutality, torture, and murder, must be clearly explained to each new generation. If we fail to explain social causality to our posterity, these social plagues will continue to spread without remission. New institutions of legalized criminality will rise again as macabre monuments to tyranny in the name of social justice and sacred aims.

The only practical alternative to social catastrophe is the complete refutation and repudiation of the presumed truth of the win-lose paradigm of social causality. Again, this fallacy of fallacies is generalized in just eleven words: *For us to gain, they must lose through force or fraud.* Yet, this is a spurious paradigm and a colossal scam. Its supposed truth and assumed validity is founded entirely on a false foundation of *a priori* faith without observational analysis of its truth, validity, and morality. Faith in the worthiness of social action without the due diligence of critical analysis has proven to be a paramount risk to life and limb.

A famous quote from Karl Marx boasts, "Communism is the wave of the future." Yet, one cannot believe that it really is the wave of the future unless one's faith in the efficacy of Communism stands on a solid foundation of delusion. To believe that political Communism is the wave of the future is to believe that human tyranny is the wave of the future. Marx was wrong. In the nuclear age, *human freedom* is the wave of the future, or for humans there is no future.

For those who look, it is observable: human liberty is the sum of its parts, which includes freedom of belief, freedom of religion, freedom of speech, freedom of the press, and freedom of assembly. All these priceless social gems are the natural byproducts of win-win exchange for mutual gain. To reach such sterling social aims, decent people must find the wisdom and courage to banish the win-lose paradigm as their coercive model of social causality and replace it with the generosity, moral elegance, and excellence of the win-win paradigm of universal gain. After all, for decent people, it is the decent thing to do.

❧

A timely question to consider is how important is it to keep alive the memory of the Holocaust? Can broadcasting its lethal history play a role in averting similar social tragedies in the future? Yes. If its historical causes can be explained and understood by new audiences and new scholars, this can be a crucial element in preventing the rise again of such social ruination. However, the lost lesson that must be found is that mere memory alone of the Holocaust will fall far short of ensuring us against such disasters in the future. George Santayana's famous lines were shown to be incomplete when he warned, "Those who cannot remember the past are condemned to repeat it." We have to do more, much more, than merely remembering the past. Here is why:

> *Those who remember the tragedies of the past are condemned to repeat them again and again until they identify and verify their true causes, and erase those causes from the future of human action.*

We have to delete the social causes that foster and inflame holocaustic homicide and genocidal slaughter, which means we first have to identify and verify exactly what those causes are. Because we cannot afford to fail, we cannot assume the dangerous risk of relying on mere conventional wisdom to guide our way.

How wise is conventional wisdom when its assumed truth is yet to be verified through the power of independent observation? What good does it do to remember the horrors of the Holocaust and the depravity of genocide, if their criminality is repeated and replicated all over again? We most certainly would cringe at the thought of historians ever writing volumes on the tragedy of Holocaust I. To have had a Holocaust I, implies that there was at least a Holocaust II. Not only can the Jews not afford another Holocaust, neither can anyone else.

Historians of the Great War (WWI, 1914-1918) wrote volumes on the military battles that raged between the world's most powerful nations. The promulgation and advancement of the Great War in Europe was sold to the people by their political leadership as, "The war to end all wars." Citizens were urged, encouraged, and forced to support the war effort, which they were promised would finally pay off forever by ending the tragedy of major warfare.

Finally, after more than four years of mechanized, systemized, ritualized, and glorified slaughter across the fatal battlefields of Europe, the warring politicians who had carried their nations into conflict signed an armistice treaty on November 11, 1918. The Great War had come to a not so glorious end, but at least the killing and mayhem was over. Yet, within a short time, hope for the end of war and an enduring peace was shattered. It was a social catastrophe of catastrophes. In only a generation, historians had to rename the Great War. Yet, what to name it? It might have been named the "Great War I." However, historians eventually came up with a more fluid name: "World War I." The name they chose tells us that something really did go wrong—terribly wrong.

If there was a World War I, there must have been a World War II. The world leaders did it all over again; they led their followers into another great war with only a generation to recover from the first one. Still, every national leader remembered the Great War that killed ten million people, and injured or harmed tens of millions more. Nonetheless, with the image of its full fury still frozen across their minds, politicians launched the "Great Great War," now remembered as World War II.

This became the history buff's delight. For every volume written on World War I, two or three were written on World War II. Of course, it should not be necessary to discuss the possible emergence of World War III. This is not a viable option. A World War III, if its present or future planners, either now or later, can pull it off, would be the very *first* "war to end all wars." Yet, the accolades would be sparse, because it also would be the very first war to end all people.

Historians have chronicled the tragedies of war with all the gory and heartbreaking details, which are the predictable effects of systemized slaughter for religious and political gain. However, historians have largely failed to understand and explain how to prevent the wars of the future. Memories of war and its sordid minutia may be interesting and even fascinating to some, but without first identifying and verifying the fundamental and necessary causes of war, wars will continue their assault on humanity until they bring humanity to a shameful conclusion.

Santayana's philosophical wisdom notwithstanding, those who remember the disasters of the past may recreate them in the future on an even grander scale than before until they understand what caused them in the first place. The learning lesson from the fatal fury of the Holocaust can be a powerful lesson for social advancement; that is, if we can grasp its fundamental causes and, thereby profit by avoiding the social blunders that propelled it onto the stage of human tragedy. If we can just understand how to prevent the horror of a *Holocaust II*, this will take us a long way toward understanding how to prevent an even greater horror of a *World War III*.

Perhaps the salient lesson to learn from the debacle of the Third Reich is to identify and verify the source of its criminal power. Good Germans, with good minds, and good educations, made possible the Nazis rise to political prominence. Yet, these good people failed to use their good minds and good educations to identify and verify social causality. Their failure proved to be catastrophic. It led directly to the ascendancy of Naziism and the subsequent destruction of Germany and greater Europe. Without observational analysis of social causality, the same catastrophic demise can befall any nation of good people with good minds and educations. Wherever such people of influence create a win-lose society for win-lose gain through the coercive power of force and fraud, it is predictable that many bad things will happen to many good people.

Whenever a nation of decent people follow win-lose paradigms by default without testing them for truth and validity, not only are they at risk of annihilation, but so is everyone else. More than John Donne possibly could have imagined three centuries before the nuclear age, "No man is an Island." From around the globe we are bombarded with daily reports of criminal atrocities, unleashed by eager and often fearless activists, all for the glory of religious or political gain. These activists prove by their daily delusion that they don't know what they are doing. We must not forget that whether these fatal atrocities, perpetrated in the name of god, nation, or leader, are carried out near or far, "Never send to know for whom the bell tolls; It tolls for thee."

‹♥›

As Jews became victims of organized murder by the millions, this was shocking evidence of a serious flaw in a social structure that had allowed this scourge to rise—and rise within the hallowed sphere of Western Civilization. If we cannot identify this flaw and its true causes, if we cling to conventional wisdom on holocaustic causality without verification, such a fatal catastrophe can erupt all over again. This would not be good for Jews, or for anyone else. It would not be good even for those who are openly hostile to Jewish religion and culture, that is, those who might rekindle the Holocaust if they could. A second Holocaust would unleash even more collateral damage beyond the range of the Jewish community than did the first one. Those who would instigate a "Holocaust II" would face an immediate crisis: How could they contain and suppress the spread of its destruction? It could engulf the planet with a social storm of ruination impacting everyone—whether friend or foe of the Jews.

It is important to recognize that the tragedy of German National Socialism transcended the human slaughter of the Holocaust. To advance Nazi domination of Europe, the National Socialists murdered some twenty-one million Europeans, of which over a quarter were Jews. The mass murders of the National Socialists engulfed more than three times as many people as the genocidal Holocaust itself. Many of those killed were anti-Jews felled by the collateral damage of Jewish persecution. To be sure, a Holocaust II would wreak havoc on the Jews as well as killing off many of their Gentile friends and sympathizers. Yet, the collateral damage of a Holocaust II would also kill off anti-Semites in unprecedented numbers.

Those who would shield the Jews from another political pogrom of genocide must not make the strategic error of making anti-Semitism the bogeyman of holocaustic causality. To be sure, unlike the mythical bogeyman, anti-Semitism was all too real, but it was not the sole inciter of the Holocaust.* The reality is that if your aim is to murder Jews by the millions, anti-Semitism alone is clearly inadequate.

The most destructive *pogroms* (Russian, meaning, "to wreak havoc") of Jewish persecution in Russia and elsewhere were only successful in murdering Jews by the thousands,

---

* The bogeyman was a mythical goblin with supernatural power to commit evil deeds. Among his feats, the bogeyman, with sinister glee, would carry away naughty children who had misbehaved. In your childhood, if you were taken away from your home by the bogeyman, you might never be seen again. In World War II Europe, millions of Jewish children were taken away from their homes, not by the bogeyman, but by Hitler's SS police, most of them never to be seen again.

and more often only by the hundreds. However, if you aim to kill Jews by the millions, you have to design a much more potent strategy than reliance on mere anti-Semitic hostility. It is safe to say that most of the anti-Semites in history have never killed anyone, let alone Jews, because of their win-lose model of social superiority.

Anti-Semitism as the central policy of the mass murder of Jews by the millions is both insufficient and impotent. To execute mass murder on a grand scale, you have to adopt a strategic policy that is much more efficient, effective, and fatal than reliance on mere anti-Semitism. Of course, as we know, that lethal strategy was finally brought to bear in the last century by Germany's political rulers. But what exactly was this anti-social strategy that created a catastrophe for the Jews? Can it be identified and clarified with precision, so that in the future we can avoid the social plague that this win-lose policy of political terror unleashed on Western Civilization?

It is important to know that the genocidal Holocaust was not and is not merely a Jewish problem; it is a problem for all believers of all religions. Therefore, what do believers of all religions need to know about the Holocaust that is not already known from a recorded history that can be found in Holocaust libraries and museums now open to the public in many parts of the West?

Religious believers need to know that the Holocaust was founded on *faith*—on three esteemed articles of faith—that fostered, incited, and inflamed its criminality throughout most of Europe. These articles of faith are elements of the win-lose paradigm of social causality: *For us to gain, they must lose through force or fraud.* Because the truth of this prized paradigm of causality—this esteemed model of reality—cannot be verified to be true through independent observation, it must be embraced on blind faith, it must be accepted by default without critical analysis. These are the pillars of belief—the three articles of faith—that spurred and spread the Holocaust across the tortured face of Europe.

HOLOCAUSTIC ARTICLES OF FAITH
1. Win-Lose Anti-Semitism: *For Aryan Christians to gain, Semitic Jews must be forced to lose.*

2. Win-Lose Nationalism: *For our nation to gain, your nation must be forced to lose.*

3. Win-Lose Socialism: *For the seizers of wealth and freedom to gain, the creators of wealth and freedom must be forced to lose.*

These articles of faith were the vicious vectors of the Holocaust. Our English word "vector" is derived from Latin, meaning to convey or carry something. These were the win-lose articles of faith, the vectors that conveyed and carried an uninvited guest, the Grim Reaper, over the threshold and into the living rooms, workrooms, play rooms, and school-rooms of millions of European Jews, most of whom were oblivious to their impending doom. They never saw the Grim Reaper coming. They only saw his military police.

A thousand times on a thousand stages, variations of this scene played across the continent of Europe. A rabbi, glancing out the window of a synagogue, sees one of Himmler's SS captains. He is a dashing fellow with an eerie emblem of "skull and crossbones" jutting out of his cap. The officer's men are well dressed in smart and trim uniforms. Their rifles are still shouldered as they struggle to hold their dogs at bay. The captain orders his men—their eager Dobermans still in check—to surround the temple of worship. It is spring in Westphalia, a sunny Saturday in May. And, nearby, the temple garden is bursting with a thousand cornflowers, their bright-blue petals still holding the morning dew. But there's trouble in paradise; the stage is set for tragedy.

If you would achieve mass murder on a grand scale, you cannot afford to have your killers and executioners dressing like ruffians and acting like goons. Mass murder is serious business; it must be shrewdly planned and carefully orchestrated. It can only be carried out efficiently and effectively when its executioners are not only organized, but they enjoy an image of respect, if not admiration. This means that mass murderers should be well-dressed, well-groomed, stand tall—and obey orders. And, if they have been well trained, they will kill on command without reservation, hesitation, or concern.

However, if the same would-be killers were to go off half-cocked to kill on their own, while ill-equipped, ill-prepared, ill-trained, ill-managed, and ill-groomed, they would most likely fail at mass murder. Without training and discipline, before they could kill anyone, in a heartbeat, they could be killed by their would-be victims or by their armed protectors.

While random murders here and there may be carried out without serious thought or training, mass murder is another matter. To execute mass murder it must first be legitimized, institutionalized, glorified, and, of course, amply funded. You can forget about imposing mass murder on a shoestring budget.

As a win-lose policy, mass murder must be institutionalized. It must be mandated by dedicated leaders, who clearly understand the strategy and tactics of killing in large numbers for some grand and noble aim as they see it. If genocidal leaders cannot convince their followers of the necessity and glory of legitimized genocide, their aims for such mass destruction are on track to fail. At best, they will only be successful in murdering a nominal number of victims, but mass murder on a grand and colossal scale will be beyond their reach.

∾

Without a viable theory to explain social causality, social history will remain a misinterpretation and, thereby, a misrepresentation of past human action. In this way, good men with good minds have repeated the social blunders and calamities of the past over and over again. To reemphasize, it is not enough merely to remember the religious and political plagues that have killed hundreds of millions of victims across the globe. In order to avoid their unwelcome return, we must identify, clarify, and verify their true causes.

Furthermore, it is not enough to remember the biological plagues, which have also killed hundreds of millions of sorry victims. If we would avoid the terror of bubonic plague for ourselves and loved ones, what should we do? We should begin by following the principle of "first things first." We must find out the true causes of these deadly plagues, and then attenuate them until they are eliminated. But if the best we can do is merely *imagine* their true causes, no matter how creative our imagination may be, we will miss the mark by a wide margin. Who knows, as bright as we are, and with our fertile minds, we could imagine the plague being spread through town and country by those wretched witches. Of course, if this were our imaginary model of causality, it could make sense to us, and we might very well believe the following scenario on witchcraft to be true.

Who else could be casting these evil spells? In fact, it is probably the very same women we saw down by the river near the old bridge. Only last night, our dear neighbor, Hanna, poor woman, was sure she saw the horror of these same women, prancing

337

around the fire with evil spirits. She swore they were dancing with devils and warlocks. Surely, these wicked people are Satan's minions.

Still, no matter how many witches we hunt, capture, torture, try, convict, and execute, the plague rages on without end. Nothing seems to help. Truth be known, it's almost like we don't know what we are doing. But that's not possible because we are smart, we are educated, we are well-read; and most compelling, we have reliable witnesses, who with their own eyes, saw these wretched women dancing with the Devil.

And, for those who are yet to believe that these women were capable of witchcraft, they have all confessed to being satanic witches under the steady stress of torture. It must be true, for some have even divulged their intimacy with Satan himself. To be sure, for those who lack faith in the reality of witchcraft, applying torture to reach the truth may seem harsh, especially when torturing children. Yet, in truth, we know that one's age has nothing to do with duplicity. Children may be even more duplicitous and deceitful than their parents. This is clearly the case when children are under the influence of evil spirits, and can be expected to lie until they are forced to tell the truth.

As for the propriety of torturing children, it is not like the old days when torture was unregulated, and often went too far—with many children dying before they could even confess their crimes like romping and cavorting with Devils. Praise God, torture is now only applied with compassion according to the latest legal code and divine tenets of the church. As always, reaching the truth is our legal aim and our sacred duty. We all know that torture has long proven to be the most effective means of learning the truth, especially from those who would lie to deceive us, understandably, to save themselves from eternal damnation.

∽

For the few in our century who still care about the pathetic plight of these poor "witches" of long ago, it is too late to save them from a fiery death for their alleged role in unleashing the plague as well as other capital crimes. Thankfully, we were born at a time following a revolutionary understanding of biological causality and the vectors of plague. With this advance in knowledge, we can act to protect ourselves from the mortality of bubonic plague. Its lethal causes can be explained by a simple equation that identifies its vector of death by disease.

Rats + fleas + bacillus = bubonic plague*

With a true understanding of the vectors of plague, the once urgent and pressing question of which warlocks and witches have delivered death from door to door is no longer a relevant question. What changed? In time, there was a revolution in our understanding of biological and social causality. This was followed by a paradigm shift away from the old model of causality that Gertrude and Hilda had spread the plague, toward a new model of causality that rats and fleas had spread the plague.

With the light of reality switched on, there is no doubt that Gertrude and Hilda were entirely innocent; they had

---

* The bacillus was *Yersinia pestis*.

nothing at all to do with inflicting the plague on their neighbors. This is precisely because it was never within their power to do so even if it had been their evil aim. As it turns out, these poor "witches" were burned alive by mistake. *By mistake!* It was all a mistake. But what mistake?

Their persecutors acted on mistaken models of biological and social causality as if they were true. These so-called witches were not criminals, but their persecutors were criminals who, in torturing and burning their innocent victims, committed what in our time would be called crimes against humanity.

Nonetheless, the authorities leading the charge to hunt and torment innocent women accused of witchcraft, were seen by most people as honest, pious, and educated men. They had been empowered by a win-lose society to protect faithful Christians from catastrophic storms, the doom of Black Death, and other deadly disasters. Witches were also known as "weather-makers," said to wield the satanic power to inflict fatal storms of every kind upon their righteous neighbors.

Today, however, the old concern over which evil witch had spread the plague or invoked a lethal storm is no longer an issue. Consider the once critical question that demanded an answer: Was it Hilda and Gertrude who spread the plague, or was it Hans and Gerhard? For us, the question is ludicrous—truly laughable—because a dramatic paradigm shift on causality has rendered these once vital questions no longer worthy of consideration. These questions belong within the framework of an old and discredited paradigm of causality, which thankfully has fallen out of favor. Yet, why has it lost all credibility?

There was a widespread paradigm shift to a better explanation of causality, which arose out of a revolution in pathology that was powered by observing and verifying the deadly vectors of disease. At the same time, there was also a revolution in meteorology that was powered by observing and verifying the deadly vectors of violent storms. In brief, observation of causality was superseding imagination of causality.

This became the intellectual strategy for solving a laundry list of seemingly unsolvable physical and biological problems from how to travel a thousand miles an hour to how to survive a dozen deadly diseases. Nonetheless, outside of physics and biology, a moral evolution toward the spread of win-win exchange is quietly under way. It is powered, in part, by observing and verifying the deadly vectors of humankind's most cowardly, shameless, and harmful win-lose actions. These include those notorious crimes against humanity. Yet, these horrific crimes, which threaten human survival, are not preordained. They can be attenuated and eliminated by replacing false imagination of their causes with true observation of their causes.

The persecution of witches involved crimes against humanity that sprang from *a priori* imagination of physical, biological, and social causality. In a similar way, the persecution of Jews involved crimes against humanity that sprang from *a priori* imagination of biological and social causality. As thousands of witches were killed by *mistake*, so were millions of Jews killed by *mistake*. It was all a mistake. Again, what mistake? As noted, educated people with good minds acted on mistaken beliefs of cause-and-effect as if they were true. As the witches were never a threat to faithful Christians, so the Jews were never a threat to faithful Christians. When decent people act on imagination of causality without the due diligence of observing and verifying its truth, the risk is always high that mistaken actions may cause a lot of bad things to happen to a lot of good people. Those bad things include the tribulations of war, poverty, and servitude that erode and dash the quality of life for all religious believers.

❧

Nazi promulgation and execution of crimes against humanity came to pass through wide acceptance among Germans of the truth and validity of the Holocaustic Articles of Faith, identified earlier. This political triad of Nazi faith launched the holocaustic disaster. Its lethality can be reduced to a simple equation of identifying its true vector of death by murder.

Win-Lose Anti-Semitism + Win-Lose
Nationalism + Win-Lose
Socialism = Genocidal Holocaust

Whether in the Germany of National Socialism, or anywhere else, paradigms of faith—believed to be true by those who embrace them—govern the actions of those who govern the people. In short, paradigms of social causality run the world. As always, win-lose paradigms of social causality govern people toward win-lose action for coercive gain. And, as always, the social effects are the same: A lot of bad things happen to a lot of good people.

Conversely, win-win paradigms of social causality govern people toward win-win action for mutual gain. And, as always, the social effects are the same: A lot of good things happen to a lot of good people. All efforts to change the outcome of these social laws will fail because even the brightest people with endless zeal cannot repeal the verified laws of nature.

As long as the laws of human nature and human action operate in the future as they have in the past, the reality of which social actions lead to which social effects will not change. Where there has been a constancy of causal connections—confirmed by experience—these same causal connections can be predicted to occur in the future with a high degree of certainty. This means that they are not only predictable, but the probability is extremely high that the predictions will come true, based on their prior history of unfailing consistency. When they do come true, this further verifies that we have reaped a win-win gain through a better understanding of which social causes lead to which social effects. There is no finer example of win-win achievement and progress for the universal gain of all people of all religions. In common language, we can now say with confidence earned through observation; we now know what we are talking about and, thereby, we know what we are doing.

With a better and truer understanding of causality, even if you despised the people who some say are witches, you would never act to harm them in any way, especially now that you know for certain that they cannot cause plagues, floods, droughts, earthquakes, volcanic eruptions, or any other natural disaster. In a similar way, even if you despise those who some say are Jews—and even if they are Jews—you would never act to harm them in any way. Furthermore, by learning more about social causality, you realize that Jews—like the women accused of witchcraft—were also falsely accused of harming their neighbors. In post-World War I, the Jews of Germany were no more responsible for unemployment, riots, shortages of goods and services, rising poverty, and a declining quality of life—as claimed in anti-Semitic propaganda—than was anyone else in Germany. Moreover, many Jews who were raising the standard of living beyond their non-Jewish neighbors were not responsible for those social adversities.

When Jews were obeying the Ten Commandments of Moses, at the same time they were neither stealing nor destroying old wealth. In obeying Mosaic laws, if Jews were deterred from seizing old wealth for win-lose gain, then what is the only other course of action that they could have followed? Other than doing nothing, the only alternative for the Jews was to create new wealth for win-win gain. The creation of new wealth per capita by the Jews or anyone else reduces the social adversities of poverty, shortages, and unemployment, while raising the quality of life. Thus, there is no rational reason for anyone to riot over diminishing social adversities, especially where the creation of new wealth per capita is rising at a faster rate than the destruction of old wealth per capita, and is, thereby, steadily erasing those adversities.

Where Jews have followed these principles of wealth creation, and their neighbors have not, those neighbors who survived on the seizure of wealth have often envied those who survived on the creation of wealth. But the true cause of the disparity of wealth has not been generally understood.

Over time, the creators of new wealth accumulate more wealth than the seizers of old wealth, thus creating the disparity in wealth accumulation. For those who are concerned over the disparity, namely, that some have more wealth than others do, there are only three paths to greater wealth: (1) Steal old wealth; (2) beg for old wealth; or (3) create new wealth.

Those who are deceived by the allure of the win-lose paradigm believe that the practical and expedient means to their gain is through the loss of others. Having reached this false conclusion, they have two choices: They can gain through the loss of others through either (1) legal or (2) illegal means. However, whether the seizure of old wealth is legal or illegal, the social effects are always the same. Seizure of old wealth impedes or destroys the creation of new wealth. *As wealth per capita falls, poverty per capita rises.*

In the Middle Ages, legions of Jews were killed across Europe for the alleged crime of spreading the plague. If you really believed, whether then or now, that the Jews were culpable, you would fear them, and your fear could lead to hatred.

Nearly all humans dislike certain members of their own species for either rational or irrational reasons. Where the dislike is extreme, it is called hatred. Yet, extreme or not dislike alone can do no harm.

If neither dislike nor hatred alone for others can harm them, then what can harm them? To answer the question, what is "harm"? To understand the meaning of *harm*, it must be precisely defined. *Harm is any imposed loss through force or fraud.*

All harm has a single source: the attainment of tangible or intangible gain through force or fraud. For example, to seize the wealth and freedom of innocent people for religious gain imposes harm upon them. In contrast, to create win-win wealth and freedom for religious gain, everyone wins, and no one is forced to lose. Consequently, no one is harmed. Again, people are harmed by the stealing their wealth and freedom, which is the opposite of creating their wealth and freedom.

No doubt there are many educated people who would build what they believe is a better world by launching a Holocaust II. There are those who would emulate the Final Solution of German National Socialism by raising neo-fascism to renew the glory of genocide. Decades after Hitler's death in 1945, he has many admirers who revere him for his anti-Semitic leadership. A March 2005 article in the *The Guardian* on Hitler's *Mein Kampf* reaching the bestseller list in Turkey noted, "The dreams of creating a master race are being snapped up by young Turks. Its publishers believe that more than 100,000 copies have been sold in the past two months."[134]

The future risk to human life of renewing a pernicious pogrom of Holocaustic violence does not seem to be fading. Once begun, the legitimization of genocide initiates an instant crisis. How could the perpetrators of a new Holocaust rein in the scope and scale of its fury? How could they contain it? It is hard to imagine how such avid activists could ever unleash a Holocaust II, without serious collateral damage. Their anti-Semitic rage could even ignite the outbreak of World War III. Indeed, that would be serious collateral damage. The lethal pollution of another global war would inflict an ever-widening waste of collateral damage itself. In addition, it could destroy every anti-Semite from east to west—of course, along with everyone else.

Coercive action for win-lose gain is a sure and reliable generator of win-lose domino effects; they can boomerang with deadly force and catastrophic destruction. One unforeseen and unintended effect of the Holocaust in Germany was that it along with other win-lose policies of the Nazi regime, created destructive domino effects, which eventually amplified destruction to the ruination of Germany. This led to a death toll of millions of Nordic Aryans. Some of these people had been decent Germans who were never anti-Semitic. Of course, after the fact, we know that there were not enough of them who might have acted along with Lichtenburg and others to prevent the legal orchestration of the Holocaust.

The collateral damage unleashed by the Holocaust and German hegemony led to the institutionalized murder of fourteen million Europeans—excluding battlefield casualties from the war. Some fourteen millions of these victims of organized murder were not Jews; they were gentiles, which included largely Catholics and Protestants. For every Jew the Nazis murdered, they murdered three who were not Jews. Once win-lose policies for religious and political gain are enforced, there will be the unintended and unforeseen consequences of collateral damage.

 confty

The articles of faith that inflamed the Holocaust were not original to the Nazis. The Nazis did not even invent the horror of the concentration camp. British military forces invented it, during the Anglo Boer War of 1899 to 1902. The concentration camp was developed as a cheap and effective weapon to crush Dutch settlers in South Africa — the Boers — who were reluctant to give up their wealth and freedom to the coercive agents of British Colonialism. The concentration camp became an instant success as an efficient way to imprison and punish the wives and children of the Boers, who were fighting to defend their lands from British imperialism. Tens of thousands of mostly women and children died of malnutrition and disease in British concentration camps.

The Nazis, following the innovative leadership of the British military, outdid them by putting the concentration camp on the political map of organized tyranny. The British invention of the concentration camp had unintended consequences. It ultimately led to the spread of these deadly camps across Europe. The concentration camps became a central element of logistical support for the legal execution by the SS of the Holocaustic tragedy. Again, it is called collateral damage, which is a predictable effect of win-lose action for religious and political gain.

Germany's National Socialists — the Nazis — did not even invent modern political Socialism. Win-lose Socialism is a pseudo-science based on *a priori* faith in its equity and utility as a win-lose social system. German economist and philosopher Karl Marx (1818-1883) invented it. Marxian Socialism (also known as political Communism), when stripped of its fraudulent mantle of decency and its spurious image of social equity, is nothing more than a win-lose political strategy designed to build a better world through legitimized, legalized, and codified seizure of people's wealth and freedom at gunpoint. Whether Marxian dogma is called

National Socialism or International Communism, these are minor variations on the same theme, which was said to create an equitable and prosperous society through the practical politics of mass intimidation, mass punishment, and mass murder. However, where the means employed cannot reach the ends sought, that paradigm of causality is falsified and repudiated through the power of independent observation.

Hitler and his cadre of well-groomed thugs and assassins, who ran the Third Reich at gunpoint, did not invent anti-Semitism, a reality well known among the Jews. Anti-Semitism was in vogue in much of Europe long before the Nazis were born. The Nazis, however, improved on the efficiency of earlier pogroms for crushing the Jews. These pogroms were either state coordinated or riotous attacks on Jews that took place throughout much of Eastern Europe, especially in the nineteenth century. But the Germans went way beyond the localized and often random terror of the old Russian pogroms. Nazi leaders not only legitimized anti-Semitism, but they raised it to a new level of organization by codifying, nationalizing, institutionalizing, and glorifying the persecution of Jews.

For the Nazis, this was a practical policy to gain prestige and to fund the advance of Nazi hegemony, first in Germany, and then throughout Europe. The fact that Nazi Party members despised the Jews was not the only reason for attacking them. As important to the Nazis was the expedient political strategy of making Jews the ideal scapegoats for Germany's failure to impose a crushing victory over its enemies of the Great War. Moreover, because the Jews had created much commercial wealth throughout Germany and Europe, it was expedient for the Nazis to seize that wealth through the legal power of the German state, which is what they did.

Furthermore, as a practical policy for launching a new war across Europe the Jews could be pressed into forced labor to manufacture munitions and other assets to reach a successful German Victory. Jews who refused to cooperate with the legal seizure of their wealth and freedom could be imprisoned or executed as a dramatic lesson to other resisters of Nazi authority. Historian John Keegan noted, "Hitler needed to rule his conquered subjects scarcely at all. The knowledge of the concentration camp system was in itself enough to hold all but a handful of heroic resisters abject during five years of terror."[135]

In any case, to blame anti-Semitism as the central progenitor of the Holocaust is an oversimplification, that obscures the larger picture of its essential causes. These social causes are set forth here as the three Holocaustic Articles of Faith, which drove the lethal fury of the Holocaust across Europe.

It is critical for social historians to identify and clarify the multiple causes of the Holocaust, especially those causes that transcend anti-Semitism. The significance of the Nazi integration of the Holocaustic Articles of Faith must be revealed and explained to the educated classes. This identification of social causality is crucial to the potential defense of Jews and others from another genocidal disaster. Without a comprehensive understanding of Holocaustic causality, those who would deter neo-genocide and scuttle the launching of a Holocaust II, could be hindered or thwarted in their eminent defense.

At the root of the Jewish Holocaust was the failure of decent Germans with good minds and educations to understand which social causes lead to which social effects, and thereby preempt the tyranny of National Socialism (Naziism). In a similar way, in medieval times, if decent Germans with good minds and educations had only known what they were doing in the first place, they never would have organized witch-hunts, ending in the ritualized murder by fire of innocent men, women, and children. Moreover, in modern Germany, if decent Germans had known what they were doing, the Nazis never would have come to power in the first place; and they never would have organized Jew hunts ending in murder by gas, bullet, and privation. Of course, forced privation leading to death by starvation and disease is no less than premeditated murder. It just takes more time than more sensational methods of murder. We do not have to see the agony of hungry families to know that there is nothing sensational about death by starvation.

Because kulak peasants in the Ukraine were difficult to Communize, the Soviet authorities overcame their resistance by mandating the measured murder of some five million of them through the guise of an agricultural program (1932 to 1933) that was nothing more than forced famine.[136] Wherever it is imposed, death by famine is not a spectacular event, and though it is clearly a cowardly crime of the highest order, it makes little news and few headlines. Today, who even remembers the pathetic plight of the Ukrainians, if they ever knew about it all? Ukrainian peasants who refused to give up their family farms for the grand collectivization of Soviet agriculture were starved to death in order to carry forward the Communization of Eastern Europe.

By the way, for every European murdered by German Nazis three times as many were murdered by Russian Communists. In addition, the Chinese Communists murdered even more. The most efficient and effective murder weapon in the Chinese arsenal was death by starvation through famines imposed by the Communist Party. Mao's infamous famine of 1958 to 1962 — orchestrated and forced on his own people at gunpoint — took the lives of some 38,000,000 Chinese men, women, children, and infants.[137]

Murder by starvation remains one of many cruel forms of institutional criminality for win-lose political gain. One of history's consummate murderers and eloquent criminals, Mao Ze-dong, is still lauded as a great hero and political leader of his people by a disgusting number of fawning admirers in both the East and the West. Unless these faithful fawners acted themselves to ignite or fuel these crimes against humanity, some of them are no doubt decent folks. Yet, decent or not, they continue to set new standards of deluded detachment from reality. Their monumental delusion stands on their firm and enduring faith in the supposed efficacy and rectitude of political Communism for win-lose gain—at gunpoint.

If to end holocausts and genocides forever is social progress, then that aim can only be reached when honest people are driven to improve their ability and success at identifying social causality. In discovering new truth, people with intellectual integrity will be self-driven to make critical paradigm shifts away from *a priori* faith in false models of causality, toward models that continue to be verified as true through the power of observation. Although this takes intellectual courage, the scale of courage required to make this crucial shift is not insurmountable. It requires only a small measure of the valor that it took for Bernhard Lichtenberg to stand alone in Berlin—in the heart of Nazi tyranny and anti-Semitism—and to proclaim in public, that in honoring the teachings of Jesus, the Jews remain our brotherly neighbors. He avowed that it is our Christian duty to respect the Jew as equals in the sight of God.

On the day the Gestapo arrested Father Lichtenberg, the police intruders, while searching his house, found a proclamation amongst his papers, which he intended to read aloud from his pulpit at the next Sunday service at St. Hedgwin Cathedral. It said in part:

> An anonymous slanderous sheet against the Jews is being distributed to Berlin houses. This leaflet states that every German who supports Jews...be it only through friendly kindness, commits treason against the people. Let us not be misled by this un-Christian way of thinking but follow the strict command of

Jesus Christ: "You shall love your neighbor as you love yourself."[138]

The daring of Lichtenberg's win-win courage is communicable as it travels across time with a life of its own. His courage transcends his temporal death, as it can be communicated from place to place, and from generation to generation. It is a powerful example of win-win action for mutual gain. It is a model of win-win altruism that all people of all religions can emulate to enrich their lives and the lives of others.

To be sure, it is unrealistic either to ask or to expect many people to rise to Lichtenberg's lofty level of steady courage. With open and vocal indignation, he stepped forward to defend victims of organized tyranny within a Draconian police state that had legally outlawed civil liberties. His measured valor was truly extraordinary and, thereby, beyond the reach of ordinary men and women. In Berlin — the very center of Nazi power — every day, he put his security, his liberty, his comfort, and his very life at risk in order to broadcast his principles of win-win altruism for mutual gain. This was the altruism of Jesus, which was the antithesis of religious intolerance for win-lose gain.

From the view of Germany's National Socialists, Lichtenberg had a long history as a troublemaker, one who was discordant with Nazi policies for police and military domination of Europe. In 1931, a decade before his arrest by the Gestapo, Father Lichtenberg invited and encouraged Catholics to attend screenings of the anti-war film, *All Quiet on the Western Front*. It had been adapted by Hollywood filmmakers at Universal Pictures from the best-selling German novel of World War I, *Im Westen nichts Neues*, written by Erich Maria Remarque, a German veteran of World War I. *All Quiet on the Western Front* won the Academy Award for Best Picture in 1930.

By openly promoting this now classic anti-war film, with its powerful images for peace over war, Lichtenberg's endorsement was in direct conflict with the belligerent aims and bellicose plans of Nazi leaders for German domination of Europe through military conquest. Lichtenberg's promotion of the Universal film sparked a vicious verbal attack upon him by Nazi propagandist, Dr. Joseph Goebbels, in his daily newspaper, *Der Angriff* (The Attack). Because this silent film was based on a popular anti-war novel written in German by a German soldier who had survived the Great War, it was especially offensive to Nazi propagandists and warmongers like Goebbels.

After the Nazis took power in 1933, Goebbels became the imposing Minister of Enlightenment and Propaganda for the Nazi government. A key founder of modern propaganda, Goebbels was a creative, if not brilliant innovator in the art of enlightening the German people with false propaganda. One aim of their propaganda was to justify and dignify the win-lose paradigm of social causality. The polished propaganda pouring out of Goebbels' ministry gave political credibility to the criminal policies of National Socialism. Its noble language was carefully crafted to enshrine the institution of legalized servitude throughout the Fatherland.

Modern tyrants, elevated and sustained by the marvel of modern propaganda, should honor Joseph Paul Goebbels with a central place in their pantheon of heroes. After all, Dr. Goebbels' Ministry of Propaganda was an undeniable success—a *win-lose* success—in developing effective strategies for the exaltation and glorification of tyranny.

George Orwell's foreboding novel *Nineteen Eight-Four*, published in 1949, dramatized the power of false and dishonest propaganda to found and sustain the institution of social servitude. In Orwell's fascist province of Oceanian, institutionalized tyranny was revered by its victims through the mastery of propaganda by the supreme national leader,

"Big Brother," and his sinister agents. Through steady indoctrination of citizens by the Ministry of Truth, citizens were easily controlled as they came to accept as true, entirely false propaganda. The result was breathtaking. Those who accepted coercive doctrines of social organization to be true and valid prized their involuntary servitude; they cherished their very own condition of slavery.

Widespread belief in the truth of that which is false fuels the engines of tyranny not only in Orwell's novel, but in the real world as well. To love and revere Big Brother, wherever he reigns, is to love and revere your slave master. Without observational analysis of social doctrines by independent observers acting to verify or falsify all explanations of cause-and-effect, everyone — whether educated or not — is vulnerable to indoctrination with flawed and spurious models of reality.

Nazi propaganda did not merely influence the mass of common Germans. Its compelling message inspired many of the elite in science, technology, medicine, education, law, and the arts to cling to their faith in the nobility of their superiority syndrome. Moreover, they were influenced to keep the faith — faith in the truth of their win-lose models of social causality, which were skillfully sanitized, justified, and glorified by the ingenuity and flair of Nazi propagandists.

Wherever religious and political leaders of the world would sustain the violence of faith, they must firmly establish the supposed necessity and virtue of violence as an effective means to some worthy end. It must be continually validated through false propaganda and convincing indoctrination in the presumed merit of win-lose models of causality. To sustain such win-lose success, the most able and eloquent propagandists are enlisted to hail these false paradigms to be true, valid, and virtuous. As the targets of their propaganda begin to praise the truth and relevance of false paradigms, the propagandists are victorious.

Through the genius of compelling propaganda projecting the virtue of win-lose gain by religious or political decree, in time, educated people with good minds will condone—if not participate in—crimes against humanity. This is the crowning achievement in propaganda for win-lose gain; it is propaganda in its "finest hour."

Whether in Germany, Italy, Russia, China, Japan, or in any other nation, the people vulnerable to indoctrination with false paradigms of social causality have included both the educated and the uneducated classes. Such vulnerability can only be parried and foiled by finding and revealing truer and better models of social cause-and-effect. For every Chancellor Hitler, Premier Mussolini, Secretary Stalin, Chairman Mao, or Prime Minister Tojo who has grabbed despotic power, hundreds are eager to seize the day by legitimizing and glorifying force and fraud. In aiming to further his despotism, it is essential for the would-be despot to delude decent people with good minds and educations into embracing win-lose paradigms of causality as efficacious and meritorious models of social organization.

Wherever the very brightest people cannot identify and verify which social causes lead to which social effects, they are susceptible to being duped into accepting the most deadly delusions of social causality as if they were true. Without this crucial knowledge of cause-and-effect, good people with the presumed advantage of good minds and educations have become faithful Nazis, faithful Fascists, faithful Communists, or have embraced the new party of institutionalized violence under a new banner of social progress—but always "social progress" at gunpoint. Such devotion is always the prelude to social debacle. To be a Nazi, Fascist, or Communist—or collectivist of any ilk, whether religious or political—is to be devoted to the enforcement of tyranny to reach the "excellence" and "virtue" of organized coercion for win-lose gain.

These win-lose social systems are all founded and approved on faith without observing social causality to either verify or falsify their social equity, utility, and morality. Thus, they are based on faith, accepted on faith, and followed on faith—faith in the virtue of the win-lose paradigm: *For us to gain, they must lose through force or fraud.* True believers—educated and uneducated—have devout belief in the merit of confiscating wealth and freedom for worthy and meritorious ends. This has been the ideological foundation for all religious and political crimes against humanity. The salient lesson is that taming the violence of faith is problematic, if not impossible, without knowing the source of the violence in the first place—which is to identify, clarify, and verify its true causes.

Not every German was fooled by the bogus image of National Socialism. Others like Lichtenberg saw through the fraud of Nazi propaganda, with its eloquent worship of legitimized violence for the coercive triumph of Teutonic supremacy. Another Christian leader in Germany, a Protestant who proved his mettle by also speaking out against religious and political persecution of the Jews and others, was Lutheran pastor, Dietrich Bonhoeffer. He condemned German devotion to the Führer's "misleadership," as he dubbed it with disrespect and disdain. Moreover, Bonhoeffer risked harsh reprisal from the Gestapo when, with brazen daring, he violated German law by conspiring with his brother-in-law to smuggle more than a dozen Jews out of Germany, to find freedom from persecution in Switzerland. However, when his role in this bold escape was uncovered in 1943, Bonhoeffer was arrested by the Gestapo for his involvement in spiriting Jews out of the prison that Germany had become. Under the heavy hammer of National Socialism, the whole of Germany was a virtual prison patrolled by official assassins, smartly parading as wardens of the Reich.

Germany, which had seen happier days, was once the home of world-renowned poet, dramatist, novelist, and natural philosopher, Johann Wolfgang von Goethe. Over a century before the National Socialists came to power, Goethe warned his German readers.

> We are never further from our wishes than when we imagine ourselves in possession of what we wished for. No man is more enslaved than the man who believes himself to be free and is not:[139]

Little more than century later, in the crusade to drive the Jews out of Germany, Aryans were swayed and steered by the passion of Nazi propaganda, which assured them freedom in the blossoming Eden of the Third Reich. Nevertheless, German freedom was merely a mirage, suspended by a clever cult of illusionists in Dr. Goebbels' Reich Ministry of Public Enlightenment and Propaganda. Yet, independent observation of social action would have revealed that where the Jews were not free, the Aryans were not free. Freedom for every Aryan was no more than faith in the freedom to follow every command of the National Socialists, who were enshrined as a monolithic autocracy of political and bureaucratic overlords of the Reich. Another translation of Goethe's warning reads, "None is more hopelessly enslaved than he who falsely believes he is free."

Nazi propaganda was as rousing as it was bogus. Nonetheless, it worked, as deluded Aryans were "hopelessly enslaved" by the win-lose elegance of Nazi authority. The Gestapo released Dietrich Bonhoeffer, himself a victim of this authority, after serving a year and a half in prison. However, further police investigation of his illegal activities implicated him in the failed plot of July 20, 1944 to assassinate Hitler. Bonhoeffer was arrested again, and sent to the notorious Flossenburg concentration camp where he was hanged on April 9, 1945. Before his execution by German authorities, Pastor Bonhoeffer proved his strength of character. Sober and without malice, he spoke to his killers and to his posterity, "This is the end—for me the beginning of life."[140] Dietrich Bonhoeffer was thirty-nine.

Just three weeks later on April 30, 1945, after marrying his mistress the day before, the leader of the Third Reich—a Reich in ruins—Chancellor Hitler, and his comely bride killed themselves in the study of their Berlin bomb shelter, der Führerbunker. Hitler's failure was the failure of all Nazis; they did not understand the consequences of what they were doing. It is not enough to be intelligent, educated, dedicated to a purpose, courteous, and well-groomed if you don't know what you are doing. Because this common failure is the central source of our global crisis, it must be clarified repeatedly: *To know what you are doing is to know which causes lead to which effects, and to act accordingly.*

☙

After the blitzkrieg victory of the German *Wehrmacht* over French forces during World War II, some five thousand refugees of religious and political persecution made their escape from capture by Nazi authorities to the quaint village of Le Chambon, on a peaceful plateau in Southern France. There, and in surrounding villages, the refugees—largely Jewish children and their families—were hidden and protected from abduction by the Fascist regime at Vichy, France. The Vichy government was established in June 1940 in the "unoccupied" zone of Southern France in collaboration with the Nazi Party in Berlin. In 1942, French Vichy authorities—fully committed to Fascism, anti-Semitism, and acting as agents of the German Reich—began deporting Jews out of France to concentration camps in Germany and Eastern Europe. In these secure camps, bulging with the political prey of Fascism, Jews and other prisoners could be worked to death or killed without interference or constraint. This bolstered the political policy of National Socialism to rid Aryan Europe of all Jews and, thereby, bring the "Final Solution of the Jewish question" to a noble conclusion. Yet, not everyone in France was acquiescing to these criminal aims of French and German Fascists.

In the South of France, a daring intrigue to shield Jewish refugees from legal arrest by French Fascists of the Vichy government and the German Gestapo was under way. It was organized and conducted by Pastor André Trocmé and his wife Magda, of the Protestant congregation of the Reformed Church of France at Le Chambon-sur-Lignon. Under their active leadership, the scale and success of the scheme continued to grow. But so too grew the grave risk of Fascist reprisal against the greater community of some five thousand French citizens. Nevertheless, in spite of the peril to themselves, their own families, villagers and farmers, the entire community continued its protection without betraying a single Jewish refugee — or turning one away. However, even with the growing support of the Protestant community of Huguenots (Calvinists), and the smaller minority of Catholics, Quakers, Jews, and various other faiths, it became impossible to keep such a large-scale operation concealed from the Fascist authorities. It finally grew in size to nineteen boarding houses, many private residences, and farmhouses throughout the countryside.[141]

On August 15, 1942, Vichy minister, Georges Lamirand, arrived in Le Chambon along with Vichy Prefect Bach to investigate and ferret out the "nest of Jews" on the plateau above the Lignon du Velay river. Prefect Bach, asserting his coercive authority, demanded that Pastor Trocmé turn over the names of all Jews in Le Chambon. Ignoring the prefect's threat, Trocmé's reply was blunt, "We do not know what a Jew is. We know only men."[142]

Such bold defiance of Fascist authority was not well received. A few weeks later, a chief of police arrived from the Vichy government, demanding that Trocmé turn over a list of all "illegal aliens" for their legal deportation to SS camps. Again, the pastor stood firm, insisting, "But even if I had such a list, I would not pass it on to you. These people have come here seeking aid and protection from the Protestants of this region. I am the pastor, their shepherd. It is not the role of a shepherd to betray the sheep confided to his keeping." Angered by this disregard for his authority, the police chief clarified his position, "What I said to you is not advice, but an order. If you oppose authority, it is you who will be arrested and deported." [143] The threat was real. Deportation to the camps was usually a death sentence, executed by SS officers eager to savage the next cattle train of victims.

After weeks in search of Jews, the police captured one young Austrian Jew. Finally, the buses, driven in for the roundup, drove away with their lone victim in tow surrounded by police. The town's defense had worked. It was devised to scatter Jews into the woods and other shelters where they could be hidden from the police. Trocmé called this prearranged and orchestrated maneuver the "disappearance of the Jews."[144]

Pastor André's wife, Magda, also played a crucial and heroic role in securing safety for "the people of the Old Testament" within the town, in farming communities, and across the border in Switzerland. However, Vichy police and the Gestapo, true to their vile mission, would not tolerate resistance to their authority. On February 13, 1943, the police, brandishing submachine guns, arrested Pastor Trocmé, and rushed him off to a prison camp for incarceration and interrogation. During internment, the camp commandant pressured him to sign a commitment to obey all government orders from the Fascists at Vichy. Yet, to obey such orders would have betrayed innocent Jews who were being hidden and sheltered from deportation by Vichy police and the

Gestapo. A firm Trocmé refused to betray the Jews saying, "We will not bind ourselves to obey immoral orders." [145]

After five weeks in prison, Trocmé along with two colleagues arrested with him were ordered, without explanation, to be released. They were fortunate that the camp commander and his superiors did not mirror the barbarous brutality of a typical SS commander and his cadre of thugs. Even so, Trocmé was forced to go underground with his mission of saving Jews from the fatal death camps in the east. André's wife, Magda, took over the daily operation of sheltering the refugees of Le Chambon, sparing them from the barbarity of crimes against humanity.

Until the liberation of France from German authorities in August 1944, the threat by the police force against the Trocmé family and other guardians of Jewish refugees was real enough. André's cousin, Daniel Trocmé, was a director of two Protestant schools in Le Chambon and a teacher of physics and mathematics. Under cover of his schools and other safe havens he had established, Jewish students were sheltered from capture by Fascist authorities. Nonetheless, on June 29, 1943, the Gestapo arrested Daniel Trocmé and a number of his Jewish students, who later were killed at Auschwitz. Daniel "could have escaped through the back door...to the woods, but he felt responsible for the children in his houses, and so he let them take him."[146]

After confinement at various camps, Daniel was transported by cattle car to the Majdanek concentration camp at Lubin in eastern Poland where he was killed in an SS gas chamber on April 4, 1944.*[147] School director and science teacher, Daniel G. Trocmé, was thirty-two. But what was his crime? In following the Golden Rule of Jesus, he

---

* By happenstance, Daniel was killed on the very day of my eighth birthday, celebrated safely in California. Would that Daniel could have joined us as an honored guest and safe from harm.

put his life in peril by sheltering Jews and other refugees from the violence of French and German Fascists who were enforcing legitimized crimes against innocent people who had done no harm. The moral question is as old as civilization. When you are ordered to commit crimes against innocent people, should you obey all of the orders, some of the orders, or none of the orders? Well-groomed, literate sons and fathers, dutifully obeying orders, legally murdered Six million Jews.

The risk of Fascist reprisal against these courageous villagers was real and potentially fatal if they were ever caught in the crime of aiding the Jews. Before coming to Le Chambon, the town's respected physician, Dr. Roger Le Forestier, had worked in Africa with legendary physician, musician, humanitarian, and Nobel laureate, Dr. Albert Schweitzer. Roger's win-win altruism had taken him from caring for poor natives in Africa, to caring for poor refugees in France. To shield defenseless refugees, the doctor took many daring risks, including the forgery of false documents for Jewish refugees. This effective ruse saved hundreds of innocent children from the terror of Nazi death camps. Yet, in the end, the risky scheme was too widespread and successful to hide from the police. Finally, Dr. Le Forestier was arrested. On orders from the Gestapo, this kind physician and brave humanitarian was shot and killed on August 20, 1944 at the Montluc prison shortly before its prisoners of Fascism could be liberated.[148]

A society where esteemed physicians and teachers can be murdered by the legal authorities for sheltering innocent children from the same murderous authorities has reached the pinnacle of barbarism. People of win-win integrity and the measured courage of Daniel Trocmé, his cousin André Trocmé, Magda Trocmé, and Roger Le Forestier, and many other brave people of the plateau, were misfits in a society where win-lose leadership at gunpoint was the norm.

The win-lose society, no matter how noble or ignoble the aims of its originators, always has unintended consequences with harmful, if not ruinous potential. The more win-lose the society, the more outcast and outlawed are men and women of win-win integrity. People with the daring nerve to uphold and defend the moral integrity of win-win exchange for mutual gain are routinely imprisoned by the criminal wardens of a win-lose society. In a penal system where the moral character of incoming prisoners continues to rise, the moral character of prison officials continues to fall. In other words, the more win-lose a society, the more likely the highest quality people can be found in prison, and the lowest quality people can be found running them. This travesty of justice can happen in any society, where smart people, literate people, ambitious people, and ingenious people fail to understand which social causes lead to which social effects.

Bolstered by the win-win courage of Jesus, Pastor Trocmé, his wife Magda, and his cousin Daniel, resisted the menace of armed police marshaled to force their betrayal of the Jews. In resisting this real threat, they proved their Christian integrity — as well as their striking courage — by showing the Golden Rule of Jesus to be an inviolable principle. For them, it was a principle *not* to be violated even when the cost could be high. This Win-Win Principle of Christian action did not exclude Jews, or anyone else deemed inferior by the Nazis.

After the Vichy government agreed to use violent force to abduct French Jews at gunpoint and turn them over to the Nazis, André Trocmé swore to his congregation, "We appeal to all our brothers in Christ to refuse to cooperate with this violence.... We shall resist whenever our adversaries demand of us obedience contrary to the orders of the Gospel. We shall do so without fear, but also without pride and without hate."[149]

Pastor André appealed to his congregation to join him in an organized resistance to authoritarian crimes against the innocent. With Trocmé's leadership, this became an effective resistance "without hate" and without violence, in harmony with the example of Jesus. The packed congregation responded by proving their daring resolve over four long years of nonviolent resistance to the crimes of French and German authorities. Their legitimized Fascism involved humankind's most horrific and heinous crime—the institutionalized murder of innocent children and juveniles who never harmed anyone.

Like the good Christians who tortured and murdered witches and heretics by the hundreds of thousands, so the good Christians who murdered Jews and other undesirables by the millions can share the same apology: *They didn't know what they were doing.* In July 1942, when word reached Pastor Trocmé of Christians abducting and deporting Jews out of Paris to work and die in the SS camps, he delivered an angry sermon to his Christian congregation saying, "The Christian Church should drop to its knees and beg pardon for its present incapacity and cowardice."[150]

For centuries, the people of Le Chambon had been offering protection to desperate people fleeing religious tyranny. Writing on the history of Le Chambon, Philip Hallie noted some of the havoc wreaked by the Catholic Church while imposing its win-lose monopoly of institutionalized Christianity to extinguish the advance of Protestantism in France. "For three centuries, with only a few tiny cases of toleration, those who were found to be loyal to the Protestant Reformation were often stripped of their property, their liberty, and even their lives" by Catholic authorities.

> Le Chambon was an old village when Protestantism came to it in the first half of the sixteenth century. During hundreds of years of persecution, her pastors and its people were arrested by dragoons

[musket-armed cavalry] of the [Catholic] king and then hanged or burned either in Le Chambon itself or in Montpellier to the south.[151]

Trocmé and his Protestant neighbors were fully aware of their own history as victims of religious persecution by Catholic Christians. The people of Le Chambon stood their ground in defense of the Jews from persecution by baptized Christians of Catholic France, or Protestant Germany.

When Trocmé referred to following "the orders of the Gospel," those orders came from Jesus himself. The supreme orders of Jesus are familiar to every literate person, namely, "So in everything, do to others what you would have them do to you." The phrase, "So in everything" you do, does not allow for exceptions. This elevates the orders given by Jesus to be an inviolable principle, which is the Christian Golden Rule. It is not to be violated in Le Chambon or anywhere else. Help your neighbor in crisis, as your neighbor would help you in crisis.

For Jewish families in the sanctuary of Le Chambon, without the help of the surrounding villages of neighbors, it would have been perpetual crisis as Jews, French or foreign, would have faced constant danger of being kidnapped by French authorities and turned over to be murdered by German authorities. During the German occupation of France from 1940 to 1944, French Fascists, who were largely baptized Catholics, "turned over 76,000 Jews, roughly 25% of the Jewish population [of France] (1/3 of whom were their fellow citizens and 10,000 of whom were children) to be" deported to the east where the majority of them were methodically murdered by German Fascists. [152]

In the wake of such tragic criminality — in glaring violation of the Golden Rule — by citizens of two of the most advanced nations in science, industry, engineering, mathematics, fine arts, philosophy, and theology, a pressing issue must be raised: Is the altruism of the Golden Rule Principle, a practical strategy for human interaction? Is it a robust guide to social exchange; does it have a viable resilience?

Challenges on the practical relevance of the Golden Rule do not come only from the mouths of tyrants and despots. They come from decent people who accept this ancient rule as an esteemed principle. But with tragic implications, they also see it as a principle with little or limited practical value for everyday use, especially in the domain of national and international affairs. This contention, however, is as flawed as it is common. Pragmatism and morality are *not* mutually exclusive. There is an overarching practical reason not to violate this ancient rule of social action. Its violation always has a destructive downside at best and a catastrophic one at worst.

The blatant violation of the Golden Rule, for example, by decent Germans with good minds and educations — who were largely baptized Christians — gave rise to the Third Reich and its faithful and fatal prosecution of genocide for the glory and grandeur of Aryan supremacy. Moreover, we must not miss the historic irony; good Christians either sanctioned or participated in the rise of one of the deadliest Antichrist movements in two thousand years, in legitimizing the institution of National Socialism under the ensign of Naziism. If that example is not serious enough, war and its multifarious miseries is an outgrowth of various violations of the generalized Golden Rule Principle: *Do not seize wealth and freedom from others, as you would have them not seize your wealth and freedom.* The penalty for violating this law is universal: many bad things will happen to many good people.

In examining the history of Fascist states, Communist states, military states, dictatorial states, theocratic states, or states of any ilk where legalized tyranny was institutionalized, they never could have risen without the support and sanction of honest, literate, socially concerned, God-fearing citizens — but tragically, citizens who didn't know what they were doing, because they didn't understand social causality.

Father Lichtenberg and Pastors Bonhoeffer and Trocmé were among the few Christian clergymen in German-occupied Europe, actively to resist Nazi tyranny. Their daring actions proved that beyond the mythology of Western heroism, in the real world, there are true heroes of extraordinary courage. We are fortunate, indeed, that it takes people of only ordinary courage to defeat tyranny wherever it rises. It requires people acting with only a parcel of the bold bravery of Lichtenberg, Bonhoeffer, and Trocmé, in order to delete the criminal causes of win-lose religion and win-lose government.

We can celebrate the fact that humans are not without the courage to protest and resist the legitimization of tyranny wherever it rises. Ordinary people of Le Chambon — while denying they were heroes — were protesting the *legitimization* of tyranny and injustice by a despotic French government in close collaboration with a despotic German government. Such courage is a crucial and capital character trait because if humans lacked the valor to defend the defenseless against those who would nationalize and deify despotism, then tyranny would forever dominate society in the name of the leader, in the name of the nation, or in the name of god.

In aiming for win-win progress away from war, poverty, and servitude, toward peace, prosperity, and freedom, two questions should be raised: (1) is the strategy practical?" In addition, (2) is the aim possible? The answer to these critical questions is a resounding "Yes," precisely because win-win strategies are *practical*, and win-win aims are *possible*. In proving their win-win courage, Lichtenberg, Bonhoeffer, Trocmé and his wife, Magda, broke no laws of nature. We do not have to overturn nature to save our species from extinction. Indeed, repealing the laws of nature is impossible. We only have to observe and obey the laws of social causality, which reveal the moral utility and moral power of win-win action for mutual gain in every arena of human endeavor. With ordinary courage and common valor, we can act in harmony with these reliable laws of nature. In so doing, we create an ever-swelling source of wealth and freedom to enrich all believers in the rectitude and justice of win-win religion and win-win government for universal gain.

∾

The difference between prejudice and social discrimination against any class of people, in contrast to persecuting and killing them, is both an extreme and a profound distinction. Where people, for example, express their *hatred* for Hindus, Christians, Muslims, Jews, or any other religious group, such hatred can be driven by either true or false information. Hatred for people accused of witchcraft was driven by false testimony condemning them as agents of the Devil who routinely harmed their neighbors. In contrast, hatred for the Inquisitors of the Holy Office was entirely different. These errant Christians took pride in torturing men, women, and children accused of witchcraft and heresy. Hatred of Inquisitors was spurred by true information on the cruelty of their pious persecution of innocent people. If you were witness to the torture of children by members of any faith, and you understood the abomination of the torture, whether your children or not, it would be hard to quell your hatred of such agents of child abuse.

Hatred is a human emotion that indicates extreme dislike for something or someone. It can be driven by true or false inputs; but, in either case, even the most intense hatred alone, whether rationally or irrationally conceived, has never killed anyone. Human hatred does not kill, but human action does. Killing means to take physical action to destroy something living in the form of animals, plants, or microorganisms.

Social tradition has named the most serious and heinous killing to be the crime of murder, wherein one or more humans kill one or more other humans. All murder involves coercive action for win-lose gain through violent means. Whether a given killing is deemed by society to be an act of murder, where there is social equality and equity, such an important distinction will have nothing to do with the victim's religion, culture, ethnicity, or status. Those who are legally executed for their religious and political views are still victims of murder, even though their murders are duly legitimized for religious or political gain. In win-lose societies, the legitimization of murder by religious and political authorities is an ancient win-lose policy to terrorize the people into submission to coercive authority.

Members of every religion have been murdered for their religious convictions by those acting on the win-lose paradigm: *For our religion to gain, your religion must be forced to lose.* The victims of win-lose religion have been Protestants, Catholics, Muslims, Jews, Hindus, Buddhists, Mormons, Druids, atheists, and agnostics, along with those from a diversity of religious denominations too numerous to mention.

However, as long as human actors murder their fellow humans over contempt for their religious views, but at the same time their win-lose actions are neither organized nor institutionalized, the number of such murders will be negligible. As regrettable as even one murder may be, if the number of Jews who were murdered in the 1930s and '40s due to their Judaic faith was a fatality rate that could be labeled "negligible," today there would not be any Holocaust libraries and museums, precisely because there never would have been a Jewish Holocaust across Europe. Although it is unlikely that all win-lose religious and political murders can ever be eliminated, what can and must be eliminated are religious

Holocausts and political genocides. To clarify further the causal factors that incited the European Holocaust, here in still other words, is a restatement of its triadic causes:

HOLOCAUSTIC EQUATION
Win-Lose German Nationalism plus Win-Lose State Socialism plus Win-Lose Anti-Semitism equaled Nazi Genocide of Jews

The scope and scale of the tragedy of the European Holocaust was incited by the lethal synergy of German Nationalism, state Socialism, and anti-Semitism. Yet, without even diminishing the scope and scale of anti-Semitism, if the scope and scale of German Nationalism and state Socialism had been negligible, there never would have or could have been a Holocaust.

For Jews and Gentiles who remain appalled by the horror of the genocidal annihilation of Jews, it would be prudent to smash the triadic pillars of the Holocaust; namely, win-lose Nationalism, win-lose Socialism, and win-lose anti-Semitism. These crucial tenets of the Holocaust provoked the enforcement of win-lose social policies all of which were founded on flawed paradigms of causality. They were all based on one theme, which translates into common language: We are seizing your wealth and freedom at gunpoint. If you refuse to comply with our demands, we will enforce the rule of law; you will be fined, imprisoned, or killed. Any questions? Good!

Although truth can be seen through the power of independent observation, the truth may not always be popular or well received, even when it is incontrovertible and irrefutable. Whether well received or not, this observation is true: All political rule is backed with a gun. History's greatest mass murderer and political gunman, Mao Ze-dong, made this curt observation, "Political power grows out of the barrel of a gun." Mao's political truth would not have been denied by the world's second greatest mass murderer, Joseph Stalin, or by his political rival, the world's third greatest mass murderer, Adolph Hitler. They would not have disputed Mao's win-lose wisdom on the source of political power, which was their very own source of political power. However, some detractors argue that their political power was misused; but if so, how much was it misused?

Today, in retrospect, many historians would agree that the magnitude of political murders imposed by Stalin, Mao, and Hitler was excessive. To reach their utopian schemes of globalizing Communism and Fascism, Mao mandated the murder of 77,000,000 Asians, Stalin mandated the murder of 42,000,000 Europeans, and Hitler mandated the murder of 21,000,000 Europeans. However, what is not agreed upon among those who sanction win-lose societies is how far did these notorious dictators go beyond what might have been an otherwise "acceptable" magnitude of mass murder in reaching their oppressive aims?

If the scale of their murders could have been reduced by a staggering 90 percent, with Mao only murdering 7,700,000, Stalin only murdering 4,200,000, and Hitler only murdering a mere 2,100,000, today their image as world leaders might be much more positive, and they might not even be branded as mass murderers and despotic tyrants. What if they had been even less tyrannical, and each of them had "only" murdered a million or so decent people? By comparison, to the real numbers, a million murders is a nominal number that could be passed off as "collateral damage" — the necessary fallout of progressive political leadership in trying times.

For decent people, what should be an acceptable level of mass murder by their national leaders? Where murders have been legally mandated, are they no longer "murders," but instead merely legitimized executions? Should we conclude that millions of Jews were *not* murdered at all during the genocidal Holocaust because, instead of being murdered, they were legally executed under the legitimate authority of German law? Where killing innocent men, women, and children is legitimized, codified, and glorified, it is not said to be murder, but merely "legal execution."

Again, if you were going to be killed, would you rather be executed legally by a good guy, or murdered illegally by a bad guy? In human history, for every innocent person murdered by disreputable bad guys, hundreds of innocent persons were executed by reputable "good guys" who were deemed reputable by a win-lose society. Good guys who didn't know what they were doing have proven to be far more dangerous than bad guys who didn't know what they were doing.

Murder involves win-lose stealing of a human life. A victim of murder can no longer enjoy wealth and freedom. Access to these assets is stolen when a life is stolen. Where wealth and freedom can be legally stolen, so can human lives be legally stolen. In every nation, those who care about the well-being of their friends, associates, neighbors, and loved ones cannot afford the default attitude of asking, "But what's this got to do with me?" Besides, I have to drive the kids to the soccer game, prepare our taxes, and get ready for the birthday barbecue.

History shows repeatedly that when decent people fail to understand which social causes lead to which social effects and, thereby, either ignore or are oblivious to the detrimental expansion of institutionalized coercion for win-lose gain, they may not escape the pall of destructive domino effects. If respected people will not denounce autocratic oppression, whatever its source, at the very least, they must consider three possibilities. Should our religious and political leaders: (1) seize *more* of the people's wealth and freedom at gun point, (2) seize *less* of the people's wealth and freedom at gun point, or (3) are they seizing just about the right amount of the people's wealth and freedom at gun point?"

In response to these questions, those who revere religious autocracy have faith in the merit of theocratic rule and oppression through seizure of wealth and freedom at gunpoint. Those who esteem political Communism have faith in the efficacy of party authorities seizing *all* the people's wealth and freedom at gunpoint. Those who admire the Fascism of National Socialism are certain that it is laudable for the authorities to control nearly all of the people's wealth and freedom, of course, at gunpoint.

When Nazi goons released rats into movie houses to disrupt screenings of *All Quiet on the Western Front*, this was a small example of seizure of wealth and freedom. Should decent Germans have allowed this to happen without recourse to the victims? If Fascist Nazis can get away with crimes against moviegoers and theater owners, who knows, someday they may get away with crimes so extreme, so outrageous, and so massive, they may be deemed crimes against humanity. No matter, the Nazis soon realized that it was more effective just to ban all showings of the offensive film. Those who violated German law by screening banned films could then be fined, imprisoned, or killed. That any German citizens would even have wanted to see an anti-war film would make them suspect of opposing Nazi aims for military aggression. In any case, a police state like the Third Reich had no use for troublemakers who might challenge their despotic authority. It was decreed that all books critical or disrespectful of National Socialism should not only be banned, they should be burned, which is what the German authorities did. And it was more than mere Nazi goons prosecuting the book burnings. German professors and their students played a central role in the malicious destruction of intellectual property. Historian Timothy Ferris noted, "By 1931, university support for Hitler was twice that of the German population at large. The Nazi book burnings of 1933—where the works of Einstein, Thomas Mann, and H. G. Wells went up in flames—were staged by students and professors out to shape up Germany's youth for the trials ahead."[153] Such trials would eventually include facing the grim challenge of murdering 21,000,000 of their fellow Europeans.

గు

Whatever people believe ought to be the legitimized or legalized limit on the seizure of their wealth and freedom by religious and political authorities, the limitations or ceilings on such seizure is known as delimitation. To *delimit* the power of religious and political authorities to use police force against their own people is to fix the boundaries on the scope and scale of deified or legalized violence.

Wherever there are governments, whether theocratic or political, with delimitations on coercion that are precisely defined and implemented, the scope and scale of institutionalized violence is contained. However, if the delimitation on coercion for win-lose gain cannot be maintained, and the codified limits are exceeded, the delimitation has been violated. If the violation cannot be reversed, then the delimited government becomes an undelimited government with undelimited theocratic or political power to confiscate wealth and freedom. That was the plight of the undelimited governments of Nazi Germany, Communist China, Communist Russia, and scores of other despotic states. In the end, the critical crisis for the people of every religious or political government is always the same salient issue and the same pressing question. How can the scope and scale of institutionalized violence against the people be restricted and confined? Moreover, how can organized violence be attenuated before it reaches the levels of tyranny that prevailed unlimited and unchecked in Mao's Marxist Communism of China, in Hitler's National Socialism of Germany, and in Stalin's Leninist Communism of Russia and the greater Soviet Union?

Since the outbreak of civilization a dozen millennia ago, every civilization has written records and forensic evidence of a similar fatal crisis, which led straight to social disaster. Invariably, a key element of social vitality and durability has been missing. Without suitable, sufficient, and effective delimitation of the win-lose power of religious and political leaders to force their people into submission to their authority, one ruinous effect has always been the banishment of human freedom. The religious and political justifications for the legalized theft of freedom have usually been the same. Freedom of belief, freedom of religion, freedom of speech, and freedom of assembly were stolen from the people at spear point, sword point and later gunpoint in the name of the supreme god, nation, or leader.

Where there never were delimitations on religious and political authority in the first place or where earlier delimitations were either eroded or lost, the grave effects have been fatal. They have included institutionalized organization of murder, mayhem, slavery, starvation, torture, imprisonment, rape, and every other cruelty conceived by human imagination. And, for what insidious purpose has institutionalized tyranny been venerated and glorified? One purpose has been to shower the most shameful win-lose violence with respectability in every community of decent men and women. With the advantage of respectability, its nefarious purpose can be concealed to encourage decent people to advance the imposition of win-lose religion and win-lose government for coercive gain—again, as always, by spear point, sword point, or gunpoint. Institutions of win-lose religion and win-lose government can only be instituted and maintained where their presumed respectability is guarded through the power of *a priori* faith.

The grand crimes against humanity could have gone on forever without endangering the survival of our vaunted species. The virility of human fecundity has always assured that people of ordinary sexual prowess could procreate and propagate at a faster rate, than they could be killed off by the legitimized agents of institutionalized violence. Without end, crimes against humanity could have had a continuous and glorious run. Without fear of running out of cannon fodder and clueless victims to decimate, the grand reach for religious and political power could have been sustained forever. However, by the middle of the twentieth century, everything changed. After twelve thousand years of experimenting with multiple models of civilization and dozens of variations on organized confiscation of wealth and freedom, by the twentieth century, institutionalized crimes against humanity were in danger of reaching their zenith through the prospect of fatal overkill beyond all experience.

No one predicted this sudden crisis for the wielders of religious and political tyranny. Almost overnight, humans became smart enough to do something that they had never been able to do before. As already stressed, they gained the amazing power to slaughter their fellow humans at a faster rate than they could propagate. For the first time in social history, humans could achieve the annihilation of civilization, and complete the grand extermination of their own species. The potential for the ultimate crime against humanity has become an ominous reality. Human extermination followed by human extinction remains a possible consequence of widespread faith in the truth of a false model of social causality. This fatal paradigm is founded on *a priori* faith in the merit of legitimizing and glorifying a social invention that is as ancient as civilization itself. It is institutionalized violence for religious and political gain—win-lose gain without adequate defense of civil liberties through effective delimitation of the coercive power of religious and political authority.

In the nuclear age, unless we tame the violence of faith by *delimiting* the violence of religious and political action for win-lose gain, for *Homo sapiens sapien;* i.e., for "wise wise man," (as we have humbly named ourselves) the future is bleak at best for our endangered species, and at worst, unthinkable.

For decent people whose canons of social causality esteem the elegant tenets of win-win altruism, win-win compassion, win-win exchange, and win-win ethics, what should they do? The urgent thing to do, the decent thing to do, and the daring thing to do is to play some role, any role, in the moral mission of taming the violence of faith among the good people on earth. These are the very people who have *a priori* faith in the merit, efficacy, and rectitude of violent action for win-lose gain, as the cornerstone of their religious and political paradigms. Those who call themselves Christians cannot afford to fall into this anti-Christian trap.

We know that the Latin prefix *anti-* means against or opposed to. All anti-Christians are against the teachings of Christ Jesus. To be against the teachings of Jesus is to be an anti-Christ. Millions in Christendom proudly call themselves Christians, but by ignorance or by design they take actions that are *against* the central teaching of Jesus, which makes them anti-Christians.

What is the central teaching of Jesus? It is what Jesus himself told his disciples that it was. It is defined in this treatise as the Christian Golden Rule, identified by Jesus in Matthew, 7:12: "So in everything, do to others what you would have them do to you, for this sums up the law and the prophets." As Jesus implied, the prime prophet was Moses, the prime law was Mosaic Law, and the prime tenet of Christianity was the Golden Rule of Jesus. Jesus clarifies this again in a corollary when he says in Matthew 19:18, "Love your neighbor as yourself."

To be a Christian who is against the teachings of Jesus is to be a Christian against Christianity, or in brief, to be an anti-Christ. Many Christians believed that Adolph Hitler was *the* Anti-Christ. Yet, Hitler maintained that he was a disciple of Jesus doing the "Lord's work." As noted earlier, Hitler assured the Reichstag, "By warding off the Jews, I am fighting for the Lord's work." To be sure, this was a towering lie that Hitler was applying the kindly works of Jesus. The entire Nazi strategy for success through violence was based on outrageous lies. The political lie was a cunning propaganda tool of Nazi power for win-lose gain.

Of course, the Germans were not the only people vulnerable to win-lose schemes of a better world through fraud and violence. Literate people of any nation who either avoid or fail at observational analysis of authoritarian promises are assuming a grave risk. Where win-lose policies to fill such promises are imposed upon the people, eventually those policies provoke unforeseen calamities. When the history of authoritarian promises of a better world through violence is examined in depth, what can we learn? It turns out that those promises were based on flawed paradigms of social causality commonly believed to be true by both decent and indecent people. When political and religious violence (the means employed) cannot attain the promises (the ends sought), the promises have been broken.

Although it may be disturbing to look, it is observable that every political promise, whether to the Germans, Russians, Chinese, Japanese or to the people of any other nation, is a promise ultimately backed by the violence of guns. To be sure, libraries are filled with arguments on why this is necessary. Yet, social history confirms that where promises of good things for the people have been forced upon them at gunpoint, the long-term value of those promises has been disappointing at best and disastrous at worst.

Anyone who looks can observe that you only have to force something upon people when they don't want it. If they truly want it, they will go after it with desire and even passion. The new bromide applies, "This is not rocket science." In other words, where people long for something, it does not have to be imposed upon them. Yet, every religious and political autocrat gives his subjects the same decree backed by legitimized force: Obey the rules or else be fined, imprisoned, or killed.

Can any people of any nation afford the risk of bringing tyranny upon themselves by default? The question must be answered, not by unverified imagination of causality, but by verified observation of causality. What will be the price of a Holocaust II or World War III? Just one of these disasters would blight our planet through our own failure to identify and verify social causality.

To reiterate, all prudent citizens must raise these critical questions: (1) Should the authorities of win-lose religion and politics seize more wealth and freedom from the people, or (2) Should they seize less wealth and freedom from the people, or (3) Are they seizing just about the right amount of wealth and freedom from the people? Moreover, whatever the scale of coercion may be, can this win-lose strategy accomplish the ends sought? In other words, is autocratic coercion a practical and viable means to reach the worthy ends that all win-lose authorities claim to be seeking?

Of course, the common reply of all coercive authorities has been the same: Legitimized win-lose coercion is the effective, practical, and necessary means to worthy ends for the benefit of the people. This time-honored reply is more likely to be accepted where people perceive the prevailing authorities to be educated and intelligent, and who present what appears to be compelling arguments for expanding the seizure of wealth and freedom—at gunpoint. If the authoritarian leaders of win-lose religion and win-lose government are persuasive enough, they will convince people with good minds and educations of this promise: The more wealth and freedom that we confiscate from you, the better off you will be—if not in the short run, then in the long run."

What is missing? Without the due diligence of analyzing the equity, utility, and morality of all social schemes through the power of observation, you can fool most of the people most of the time. Where there has been a void of observational analysis to reveal and verify which causes lead to which effects, throughout human history, the two social classes that have been the easiest to fool have been those who went to school—and those who didn't.

ENDNOTES

128. Michael Gerson, "A Holocaust Denier at the Church Door," *The Washington Post*, Feb. 6, 2009, A 17.

129. The Righteous Among the Nations, "Bernhard Lichtenberg," Vad Vashem, the Holocaust Martyrs' and Heroes' Remembrance Authority, http://www1.yadvashem.org/righteous_new/germany/germany_lichtenberg.html. (accessed September 12, 2010).

130. George Seldes, *The Great Quotations* (New York: Caesar-Stuart, 1960), 319.

131. Adolf Hitler, *Mein Kampf*, trans. Ralph Manheim (Boston: Houghton Mifflin, 1998), 171. In the first sentence of same paragraph of the 1935 *British Foreign Policy Association* translation of *Mein Kampf*, it reads, "The very first essential for success is a perpetually constant and regular employment of violence."

132. Browning, *The Origins of the Final Solution: Evolution of Nazi Jewish Policy, September 1939–March 1942* (London: Heinemann, 2004), 197.

133. Stephen P. Morse and Peter LandJ, "Searching the Dachau Records," http://www.stevemorse.org/Dachau/intro.htm. (accessed September 12, 2010).

134. Helena Smith, "Mein Kampf sales soar in Turkey," *The Guardian*, March 29, 2005, http://www.guardian.co.uk/world/2005/mar/29/turkey.books (accessed June 1, 2011).

135. John Keegan, *The Second World War* (New York: Viking Penguin, 1990), 289.

136. R. J. Rummel, *Death by Government* (New Brunswick, New Jersey: Transaction Publishers, 1994), 80.

137. Since his scholarly and seminal publication in 1991 of *Death by Government* (see other citations) on the demographics of politically orchestrated murder in the twentieth century, Rudolph J. Rummel, has amended his statistical data on China. See his Web site listed below. Under the heading, "Chinese Bloody Century," Rummel gives this, "IMPORTANT NOTE: Among all the democide estimates appearing in this book, I have revised two upward. I have changed that for Mao's famine, 1958-1962, from zero to 38,000,000. And thus I have had to change the overall democide for the PRC [People's Republic of China] (1928-1987) from 38,702,000 to 76,702,000." Prof. Rummel also gives the details and reasons for his update on Chinese democide, originally disclosed in *Death by Government*. See http://www.hawaii.edu/powerkills/NOTE2.HTM. (accessed July 8, 2010).

138. The Righteous among the Nations, "Bernhard Lichtenberg," Vad Vashem, the Holocaust Martyrs' and Heroes Remembrance Authority, http://www1.yadvashem.org/righteous_new/germany/germany_lichtenberg.html (accessed July 8, 2010).

139. Johann Wolfgang von Goethe, *Elective Affinities*, trans. David Constantine (New York: Oxford University Press, 1999), 151. Goethe's original German from his third novel, 1809, reads: *Wir sind nie entfernter von unsern Wünschen, als*

wenn wir uns einbilden, das Gewünschte zu besitzen. Niemand ist mehr Sklave, als der sich für frei hält, ohne es zu sein.

140. Eberhard Bethe, *Dietrich Bonhoeffer: A Biography* (Minneapolis: Fortress Press, 2000), 927.

141. Rev. Dr. Jack McDonald, "The Town that Defied the Nazis," *Church Times*, Issue 7622, January 22, 2010. http://www.churchtimes.co.uk/content.asp?id=87920/. (Accessed July 4, 2010)

142. Philip P. Hallie, *Lest Innocent Blood Be Shed: The Story of Le Chambon and How Goodness Happened There* (New York: Harper & Row, 1979), 103.

143. Hallie, *Lest Innocent*, 108

144. Hallie, *Lest Innocent*.

145. Hallie, *Lest Innocent*, 39.

146. Hallie, *Lest Innocent*, 208.

147. Hallie, *Lest Innocent*, 216.

148. "Le Chambon-Sur-Lignon," United States Holocaust Memorial Museum, 3, http://www.ushmm.org/wlc/en/article.php?ModuleId=10007518/. (accessed June 30, 2010).

149. Dave Andrews, "André Trocmé," *Target Magazine*, Issue 1, 2010, http://www.tear.org.au/target/articles/andre-trocme/2010-1. (accessed June 30, 2010).

150. "Le Chambon," Jewish Virtual Library, American-Israeli Corporation Enterprise, 2010, http://www.jewishvirtual-library.org/jsource/Holocaust/Chambon.html (accessed July 12, 2010).

151. Hallie, *Lest Innocent*, 25.

152. Patrick Henry, "Daniel's Choice: Daniel Trocmé (1912-1944)" in *The French Review* 74/4 (4 March 2001) 728, http://www.jstor.org/stable/398477. (accessed August 16, 2011).

153. Timothy Ferris, *The Science of Liberty: Democracy, Reason, and the Laws of Nature* (NewYork: HarperCollins, 2010), 258.

Chapter Thirteen

From Win-Lose Faith to Win-Win Faith

What if religious leaders and their followers ignore the Golden Rule Principle? What if they continue assailing disbelievers for their ignorance or rejection of the one true god? What if they terrorize men, women, and children to spread their vision of the only true religion ordained by the only true god? What if believers commit crimes against humanity to advance their faith while believing their actions are holy and above reproach? If this is the case, then the laws of social causality predict that such win-lose religion will inflate the causes of war, poverty, and servitude and deflate the causes of peace, prosperity, and freedom. The win-lose domino effects will be destructive. The laws of cause-and-effect may be ignored, but they cannot be repealed. Even when observers of social exchange discover the laws of social causality, they may neither be understood nor be appreciated. Humans may or may not use this priceless knowledge to enhance their well-being, and to advance the intellectual and spiritual wealth of civilization.

Human history gives endless examples of losses humanity has suffered by indifference to or rejection of newly discovered laws of nature—especially those laws that are revolutionary explanations of cause-and-effect. When Catholic monk and researcher on the nature of inheritance, Gregor Johann Mendel, published his laws of inheritance in 1865, the revolutionary value of his discovery was unrecognized by the few scientists who read his work. In time, discouraged over lack of interest in his theory of inheritance, he gave up his research. In 1868, Mendel was named abbot (director) of his Augustinian monastery, where he presided until his death in 1884. Tragically, his crucial work was so little appreciated that, shortly after his death, the new abbot of the monastery tossed all of Mendel's manuscripts, correspondence, and experimental records into the courtyard and set them ablaze. It was not until 1900 that scientists doing research on inheritance came across Mendel's forgotten publications of 1865 and 1869 and realized their profound importance.

Mendel's discovery of the laws of inheritance is a cornerstone of biological science. Yet, if the importance of his crucial discoveries had been recognized near the time of his publications, public disclosures, and his letters to scientists, it is quite likely that the biological sciences would have enjoyed a much more rapid advance. Biologists might have built on the Mendelian Laws of Inheritance thirty-five years before their belated acceptance in 1900 by the scientific community. And, if Mendel had received a little recognition and encouragement for his seminal discoveries, he might have continued his invaluable research, perhaps making even greater progress in understanding the laws of nature.

Few advances in biological science rival the discovery in 1953 of the double helix structure of the DNA molecule, achieved through the landmark research of Francis Crick, James Watson, Maurice Wilkins, and Rosalind Franklin.

Building on the work of Mendel and his followers, they identified and defined the genetic code: the very "blueprint" or recipe of life. It is likely that nothing in the near future will be more fundamental to the advance of biological and medical science. This profound breakthrough in genetic theory may bring about the greatest advances in the prevention and cure of human disease since Pasteur's germ theory.

The revolutionary discovery of DNA molecules might have arrived a generation earlier if Mendel's Laws of Inheritance had been understood and appreciated by the scientific community of his time. By the close of the twentieth century, if there had been a much earlier advance of genetic research driven by Mendel's discoveries, there might already have been a medical solution for the prevention of cancer, as well as a host of other fatal maladies yet to be cured. Unfortunately, this grand goal of medicine has not been reached by the second decade of this century. However, when this revolution in the prevention of cancer and other fatal diseases is finally realized, it will become an unparalleled boon for billions of people across the globe. And, an even greater boon is on the horizon for humankind — one that will most certainly follow in the wake of a broader acceptance and operation of the Golden Rule Principle of win-win exchange for mutual gain.

In pursuing solutions to physical, biological, and social problems by trying to unlock the mysteries of natural phenomena, researchers, in reaching their aims, may discover new laws of nature. But whether or not these laws are used to advance human progress is a matter of human choice. In the short run, these invaluable laws of nature may be ignored, misunderstood, denounced, or cast aside and forgotten. However, not all is lost. In the long run, even forgotten laws (like Mendel's) will be rediscovered at a time when they may find greater acceptance. As they do gain currency, they provoke paradigm shifts toward truer explanations of physical, biological, and social causality. Again, to reiterate, to reemphasize, and to underscore, the paradigm shift toward truer and better explanations of causality is the engine of human progress.

To advance our understanding of causality is to advance human progress. Even Michelangelo had to discover the artistic causes that enabled him to create an esthetic masterpiece like his *David*, poised to slay Goliath. Beethoven had to discover the melodic causes of a harmonic triumph that enabled him to compose his *Symphony Number Five in C Minor*. Within a generation after it was first performed and conducted in 1808 by the composer himself, it became the most performed and revered symphony of classical music. It influenced the musical compositions of Bruckner, Brahms, Tchaikovsky, and many others who studied Beethoven's symphony to identify the causal elements behind his revolutionary musical inventions. Again, progress in music, art, science, and industry is a direct derivative of advances in our understanding of cause-and-effect.

෨

As always, paradigms govern the people who govern society. To govern is to *steer* human action toward either win-win or win-lose gain. There are no other choices. For this reason, it is necessary to know whether religious or secular governors are following paradigms of causality that are true or false — that are win-win or win-lose.

Where worshipers truly believe that their win-lose model of religion is right, their support of its coercive actions spur a cascade of destructive domino effects. It is predictable; win-lose religion — no matter how praiseworthy it may seem to many believers — fosters war, poverty, and servitude. When these afflictions arrive, as they will, and unleash their devastation and ruination, the reality of their causation is obscured by believers who have *a priori* faith that god, in his infinite wisdom, has orchestrated another calamity to fulfill his divine purpose. Believing their imagination of the causes of social disasters to be true and indisputable, they take no action to identify and verify cause-and-effect through the unrivaled power of observation.

Because the social laws of cause-and-effect cannot be repealed, we must discover and learn how they operate. The solution to all physical, biological, and social problems begins by identifying their true causes. This may seem obvious, but it is not. In general, the more important the solution to a problem, the less obvious it is. One of the great problem-solving equations of physical science, namely, $E=mc^2$, was not an obvious solution even to Einstein. The history of science shows that the more important the discovery, the less obvious it is even to tireless explorers with brilliant minds.

❧

Over thousands of years, leaders of win-lose religion have fostered and incited violent action that has led to war, poverty, and servitude throughout the world. Yet, these fatal effects, largely, have not been imposed through design or malice but through belief in the rightness of their false paradigms of causality, paradigms that have been held to be true without possibility of contradiction.

For those who would abandon their allegiance to win-lose religion, it is important to identify exactly how it has spurred so much destruction in pursuit of spiritual aims. Thus, to reach a cure for these social afflictions, the source of their social pathology must be identified with clarity and precision. In a similar way, to reach a cure for the biological afflictions of malaria, heart disease, and cancer, the source of their biological pathology must be identified and verified.

To gain a deeper understanding of how to optimize *constructive* ends, it is necessary to understand how to optimize *destructive* ends. What steps, therefore, must we take to optimize the causes of war, poverty, and servitude? By observing social action, we can see the operation of this social law.

> *To optimize the causes of war, poverty, and servitude, maximize involuntary exchange for win-lose gain, and minimize voluntary exchange for win-win gain.*

This principle sets the stage for understanding its converse corollary.

> *To optimize the causes of peace, prosperity, and freedom, maximize voluntary exchange for win-win gain, and minimize involuntary exchange for win-lose gain.*

The operation of these social principles can be verified through the power of independent observation. Their effective application rests on the fact that they are not articles of *a priori* faith. Where the aim is to find objective truth through the discovery of cause-and-effect, *a posteriori* observation of causality has been shown to trump and supersede *a priori* imagination of causality.

❧

Religious freedom is indivisible. Where freedom of religion is divided by stealing it away, it is no longer freedom. To divide the integrity of freedom is to destroy it. We can observe that to seize freedom is to impose servitude. However, where win-win religion prevails, all people are free to express their religious ideas to anyone willing to listen. Religious doctrines would never be imposed upon anyone, especially disbelievers. Those who disbelieve, for whatever reason, would never be commanded to accept a supreme vision of creation, or else be punished. Where religious freedom prevails, no one is threatened with violence for rejecting religious dogma, no matter how vocal his or her rejection may be.

Human freedom has always been hard to preserve, because those who prize it the most are usually those who have lost it through win-lose control over their actions. Where innocent people, for example, are herded into prisons for religious or political reasons, they quickly learn the value of freedom. Unfortunately, they are too late for defensive action, which might have prevented their loss of freedom in the first place, loss imposed upon them through violent force.

Without religious freedom, there is religious tyranny. As already stressed, religious tyrants have led the faithful in the institutionalized and ritualized murder of millions of innocent victims in order to please and honor their one true god. These righteous killers obeyed what they believed to be God's coercive commands, which they were sure would earn them God's approval and blessing.

Religious tyranny is tied to a false paradigm of causality: *For faithful believers to gain, unfaithful disbelievers must be forced to lose.* Of course, this win-lose paradigm destroys freedom of religion, where freedom is a byproduct of win-win exchange. Win-win exchanges advance freedom because they are free and mutually voluntary exchanges. Win-win exchanges promote peace because they are peaceful exchanges. Win-win exchanges raise prosperity because they are prosperous exchanges that multiply mutual wealth.

❧

The checkered chronicles of civilization tell us that not everyone wants international peace or domestic freedom. Libraries of every nation are crammed with voluminous works on the history of autocrats, eager to institutionalize violence, terror, and slavery as they legitimize and expand their absolute power. However, reading volumes on the history of absolutism is little more than historical entertainment, unless we can learn how to avoid such tyranny in the future. With this aim in mind, the necessary means to imposing tyranny must be clearly exposed through the light of observation. This critical question must be answered, "What human actions must be taken not only to increase tyranny, but to *optimize* tyranny?"

The term "optimize" applies toward reaching some positive aim, such as optimizing the efficiency of heat engines or computer programs. Yet, the term also can be applied in explaining how to reach negative or destructive aims, such as, optimizing the causes of religious and political tyranny. For humans to identify which social causes lead to which social effects, it is crucial to this aim to know when tyranny is being optimized. Optimum tyranny cannot be reached, for example, through disorganized attacks at random on the populace or by seizure of their wealth and freedom through mob violence—as destructive as these may be from a local perspective. Optimizers of tyranny must be organized; they must legitimize and legalize institutional force that can maximize coercive exchange for win-lose gain. Throughout world history, the most notable of such institutions have come in the form of win-lose religion and win-lose government. Those who would optimize tyranny for coercive gain must enforce the Win-Lose Principle: *Never seek gain through the gain of others, and always seek gain through the loss of others by force or fraud.*

Knowledge of both positive and negative principles of social causality is necessary to prevent honest people from taking win-lose actions toward peace, prosperity, and freedom, when in fact such actions can only lead to war, poverty, and servitude. Like all true principles, operation of the Win-Lose Principle is efficacious, which means it works. If one were to aim for the ruination of society and its culture, the most effective strategy would be faithful and steady operation and application of the Win-Lose Principle for religious or political gain. Organized operation of this principle has had no peer in blazing the way to social disaster. Win-win aims cannot be reached through win-lose means.

What is the time-honored justification for organizing and glorifying religious and political violence? André Trocmé observed, "To my knowledge, all the religious, philosophical, and political doctrines that affirm the inevitable use of violence also acknowledged that it is secondary. Violence is [said to be] only a means of reaching a desirable end: justice and peace." Trocmé concluded, "But peace is nonviolence. In this sense, all agree that nonviolence is their final aim."[154]

When religious, philosophical, and political leaders employ "violence" as their means to "nonviolence," can violence attain the ends sought? No! The question answers itself. Trocmé observed, "Peace is nonviolence." Anyone can observe that without nonviolence, there is no peace. By observing social action, we can confirm that peace and violence are mutually exclusive. Trocmé continued,

> Consequently, those who abandon nonviolence — the supreme goal of human endeavor — by participating in certain "necessary" violent actions in order to fulfill their human duty, are not exhibiting a genuine sense of history. In fact, they are bypassing history, freezing history, betraying history insofar as they abandon its supreme goal. Woe to humanity on the day when Christians give up being the salt of the earth and capitulate to the violent ones! Christ's followers are to draw history out of the mire by proving that nonviolent action, the visible expression of redemption, is the only means by which to bring about peace and justice.[155]

The Hindu, Mahatma Gandhi, was adamant, "Nonviolence is the supreme law." The Christian, Trocmé, was adamant, "Nonviolence is the supreme goal of human endeavor." Their moral principles of nonviolence apply to all religions. Indeed, Trocmé continued, "Woe to humanity on the day when Christians give up being the salt of the earth and capitulate to the violent ones!"

For Christians, Jews, Hindus, Muslims, and every other faith, capitulation to violence is no longer an option. All apologies for violence—whether esoteric or prosaic—must be refuted, falsified, and repudiated as flawed models of social causality without redemption. To practice nonviolence is to practice the Christian, Hebrew, Hindu, and Muslim Golden Rules. In contrast, *violence* as the central means to peace, when proposed by religious, philosophical, and political doctrines, is an oxymoronic contradiction. Independent observation reveals that violence is the engine of violence, not the engine of peace. Peace and justice are natural derivatives of nonviolence. More precisely, peace and justice are created out of the nonviolence of win-win exchange.

For anyone willing to look, this social phenomenon is observable: Where there is peace and justice, there is necessarily nonviolence, which is the derivative of creating win-win exchange for mutual gain. Win-win exchange is the causal creator of win-win peace, of which nonviolence is a natural and spontaneous social effect.

Violence can only be tamed, however, by showing people who are not direct participants in violence—but who vocally or tacitly condone violence—that violence is always a false means to worthy ends. Whether they themselves or their agents are violent, the destructive result is the same. Even when violence is unleashed by good guys, it remains a false means to a worthy end. No matter how erudite, sophisticated, and compelling the arguments for the virtue of violence may be, observation refutes all arguments, which trumpet that war and servitude create peace and freedom.

Win-win theory identifies and verifies which social causes lead to which social effects. Therefore, it is essential that we also understand how to optimize social disaster. Which human actions must be taken to bring about the greatest human catastrophes? To reiterate, how can we optimize the causes of war, poverty, and servitude, any one of which is a catastrophe by itself? Observation, observation, and more observation of human exchange reveals that coercive actions result in win-lose gain. In esoteric language, sanctified and legitimized coercion is the *sine qua non* of religious and political tyranny.

The operation of the Win-Lose Principle works for those who would impose tyranny on their fellow humans. This principle identifies the human actions necessary to increase and maximize the causes of war, poverty, and servitude. The crucial point is that before we can lessen the impact of these age-old adversities—or prevent their occurrence—we must identify what causes them. Where the Science of Social Causality confirms the positive effects of win-win gain, in contrast to the negative effects of win-lose gain, those who know causality are more likely—much more likely—to take those actions that will actually attain the positive ends they are seeking.

It is important to reemphasize that the greatest social disasters have been caused by the general failure of decent people, whether intelligent or not, educated or not, to understand the true causes of physical, biological, and social effects—especially those effects that they most *like* and *dislike*.

Most humans like the effects of peace, prosperity, and freedom, and dislike the opposite effects of war, poverty, and servitude. Yet, neither the liking nor the disliking of any effect—whether physical, biological, or social—teaches us how to gain the effects we like, or how to avoid the ones we dislike. Having an extreme dislike for the destructive effects of floods, plagues, and droughts does not explain to anyone how to prevent their destruction in the future. In the same way, having an extreme dislike for the destructive effects of war, poverty, and servitude does not explain to anyone how to prevent these destructive effects in the future. The secret to understanding physical, biological, and social *effects* is to identify, clarify, and verify natural principles that reveal their true *causes*. As disclosed earlier: *The greater the operation of the win-lose principle, the greater the poverty and servitude for the greatest number.*

Where decent people act on false paradigms of causality, their actions betray their failure to foresee the full effects of what they are doing. Thus, the long-term consequences of their actions are nearly always unintended. Critical examples of such failure have been explained. Because of the monumental magnitude of the destruction that flawed models of causation incite, it cannot be overemphasized: As long as respected citizens seek peace, prosperity, and freedom by taking win-lose actions, the social effects of their actions will continue to be disastrous. However, when these same citizens understand how to optimize peace, prosperity, and freedom, they are much more likely to endorse and pursue win-win exchange. This is the only means to nonviolent ends, which are the only worthy ends.

Another truth of social causality cannot be overstressed: Most people who impose harm on their fellow humans do not take win-lose action against them because their motives are malicious, but because they don't know what they are doing. In the Middle Ages, judicial and religious authorities tortured and burned "witches" at the stake because they were certain that these evil sinners had conspired with unearthly devils to spread plagues and other miseries across Europe. Yet, it is hard to imagine that the authorities would have imposed such fatal punishment on innocent people if they had known, for example, the true causes of disease transmission. If those same authorities had known that the Black Death was not spread by witches and warlocks, but by rats and fleas, they might have burned rats and fleas at the stake rather than old women and young girls.

Surely, they would not have tortured men, women, and children into confessing their role in spreading the plague, all the while knowing that they could not possibly have done so, even by intention. Dramatic proof of innocence of the accused is the impossibility of their ability to commit the alleged crime in the first place. Burn the guilty rats at the stake, but not blameless men and women; and not mere children who should be playing with friends, doing their chores, or learning a skill for survival.

The persecution of witches prevailed over centuries for one prime reason. Their persecutors were largely sincere people who believed the absolute truth of their *a priori* imagination that they were doing the right thing. They were certain that truth was on their side, but tragically, they continued their fatal blunders without solving any problems.

The Salem jurors deserve respect for their public confession that they had erred in convicting innocent women of witchcraft. As they said, "We confess that we ourselves were not capable to understand." "To understand" what? The necessary insight into positive human action through verifiable knowledge of *cause-and-effect*. In addition, the jurors emphasized, "On further consideration," we should have acted on "better information...." To be sure, but "better information" about what? Again, cause-and-effect. In plain language, they were saying that we are guilty of shedding "innocent blood" because we didn't know what we were doing. In more precise language, they had misidentified cause-and-effect. This error led directly to unintended consequences: They became legal and holy agents for the execution of innocent people who had done no harm to them, or to anyone else.

In short, the tragedy at Salem was due to the failure of true believers to know causality. Indeed, if they had known what they were doing, they never would have accused the Salem witches of so-called crimes that were impossible for them to commit.*

The courage of these Salem jurors—all twelve of them—in confessing their guilt in the legal lynching of these poor women who had done no wrong was a memorable display of intellectual honesty. It is fitting for us to remember them. In naming these repentant jurors, historian Kurt Seligmann noted, "We have enumerated all the undersigned, not with the intention to divulge once more the names of those responsible, but in order to honor these men. They have by their insight, honesty and modesty rendered a service to humanity."[156]

> Thomas Fisk (Foreman)
> William Fisk
> Thomas Pearly, Senior
> John Peabody
> John Bachelor
> Thomas Perkins

---

* The author of *Taming the Violence of Faith* is a direct descendent of Thomas Putnam, Sr., a central instigator of the Salem Witch Trials. His daughter, Ann Putnam, Jr., along with others made false accusations in court, which resulted in the jailing of more than two hundred Salem residents who were charged with practicing witchcraft. In 1692, fourteen were hanged on Gallows Hill, and one man who refused to enter a plea over the absurdity of the charges was carefully pressed to death under a pile of stones. My Salem ancestors and other mistaken and misled accusers were not bad people. They believed they were good Christians. But tragically, they didn't know what they were doing because they failed to understand the equitable teachings of Jesus and act accordingly. It takes more than *aiming* for good deeds to know which causes lead to which effects.

Thomas Fisk, Junior
Samuel Sayer
John Dane
Andrew Eliot
Joseph Evelith
H. Herrick, Senior

The Salem jurors have shown that intellectual honesty is available to anyone with the courage to admit error, no matter how painful it may be. These jurors were models of integrity that any of us can emulate without having to repeal the laws of nature to do so. Although it is human nature to seek gain and avoid loss, how we do so is always our choice. At any time, we are free to choose intellectual honesty over intellectual dishonesty—which is to choose win-win gain over win-lose gain.

The courage of humans to admit error in their basic beliefs on causality is essential for human progress to occur. Only through this means can paradigm shifts be made toward truer and simpler explanations of physical, biological, and social causality. The paradigm shift from false models of causality to true models turns out to be the necessary foundation of human progress. Having the nerve to act on truer and better discoveries of causality than earlier accounts—regardless of the potential for such action to provoke tangible or intangible loss, such as detraction of one's reputation—is an admirable example of win-win altruism. Such altruistic action leaps far beyond mere lip service for the virtue of altruism and the integrity required to reach its worthy aims.

∽

Win-lose religion in our time has provoked an alarming crisis. Where it incites win-lose religion, it threatens

397

not only the destruction of civilization, but also the extinction of the human race. Yet, such a fatal end is by no means certain. Not everyone's *a priori* faith is firm enough forever to defend theologies that kindle crimes against humanity. Buoyed by their greater knowledge of causality, some will find the courage to suppress the lethality of their religion by abandoning its win-lose theology. This courage can be raised by remembering that win-lose religion violates the Golden Rule of ancient and modern theology. Moreover, it is a flagrant transgression of the Win-Win Principle, which generalizes: *Always seek gain through the gain of others, and never seek gain through the loss of others by force or fraud.** The faithful practice of this vital principle of altruistic action is the operational foundation of win-win theology. Such a magnanimous theology can only rise from the kindness and goodwill of win-win exchange for mutual gain.

Those who practice the altruism of caring for others and their well-being must summon the strength to move away from their support of win-lose theology that, by its coercive nature, raises and fosters a religion that is the antithesis of altruistic benevolence. Parishioners and practitioners must move toward approval and patronage of a win-win theology. They must embrace an altruistic religion that prospers through the mutual benefits of win-win exchange. This crucial paradigm shift provides the only avenue of escape from a global crisis that is fueled and ignited every day by the lethal tenets of win-lose religion.

To be sure, the paradigm shift from win-lose to win-win theology is a difficult shift though not impossible. The same can be said for the paradigm shift from trust in win-lose government to trust in win-win government: a difficult though not impossible shift. However, without these crucial

---

*   A transgression is a violation of a law, from the Latin *transgressio*, the act of going across; in this case, the act of crossing a forbidden boundary.

paradigm shifts, all humans are in grave danger of reaping the tribulations incited by coercive institutions of win-lose gain.

In our century, the scope and scale of our present social crisis cannot be overstated. It is not mere paranoia, fantasy, or science fiction to observe that our favorite species *Homo sapiens* is an endangered species. Such endangerment has two real sources: (1) win-lose religion and (2) win-lose politics. Both dangers are supported by false paradigms of social causality — largely accepted by default without observational testing to verify their truth and validity.

The minimization of this danger begins with the exposure of these false paradigms to the light of critical analysis. The brightest light is the impartial light of the scientific method to identify cause-and-effect. Only through better identification of social causality can we find salvation by way of our deliverance from self-extermination and extinction.

This vital salvation must be earned through broader application of the marvelous rule of human action defined long ago by the ancient theologians: namely, the Golden Rule. This rule simply says, "Do not harm others as you would have them not harm you." In following the Golden Rule, individuals must not authorize anyone — openly or in secret, lawfully or unlawfully — to seize the wealth and freedom of others for their own win-lose gain, or for anyone else's win-lose gain.

∿

In building a Science of Social Causality, it is necessary to define its principles with exact phrasing toward semantic precision, which sharpens the clarity of communication. Without benefit of semantic precision, communication is poor at best and impossible at worst. Yet, the Golden Rule of religious antiquity is remarkably clear considering it originated before the evolution of modern science. Nonetheless, to enhance communication and advance science, this ancient rule with its various wordings has been generalized and precisely defined as the Golden Rule Principle: *Do not seize wealth or freedom from others, as you would not have them seize your wealth or freedom.*

This vital rule of avoiding win-lose action retains the essence of the ancient Golden Rules, while defining a basic principle of win-win theory. The rule of avoiding win-lose action will naturally and spontaneously further win-win action, the only other human action available.

The Science of Social Causation verifies the fairness, practicality, and ethicality of the Golden Rule Principle for all people, in all places, at all times. This is why it is both a big deal and a good deal to adopt and apply this principle of altruistic exchange, which fosters the diverse blessings of win-win gain.

The shift away from win-lose to win-win exchange is profound. It creates peace where there was war, prosperity where there was poverty, and freedom where there was servitude. Unlike supernatural or metaphysical laws that must rest on faith because they cannot be observed, the natural laws that support win-win theory can be verified through independent observation.

A prime reason that science has made such amazing discoveries of causality is that its peerless strategy of discovery, the scientific method, marginalizes all authority, including even scientific authority. The scientific method enables us to escape the domination of all *a priori* authority through its endless challenge of all principles. This means that you can outflank all authority by looking for yourself: You test the principle, you verify it, and you sanction it only when it meets your standards of observational approval and verification.

This democracy of observational science is open to all those who are willing to search for the true causes of physical, biological, and social effects. With the discovery of new-found principles that broaden our understanding of nature, observers must decide for themselves whether the empirical evidence justifies making paradigm shifts toward new and better explanations of causality.

∾

For everyone, it takes courage to make paradigm shifts. This is especially true when their paradigms are supported by the heavy weight of tradition and conventional wisdom. Fortunately, the human characteristic of finding courage in the face of risk is not a human quality that we have to invent. Long before we were born, men and women of bold resolve turned away from popularity, safety, and comfort to make paradigm shifts away from false explanations of causality toward those that are true. In brief, they had the courage to adopt newer and better descriptions of reality. Because they were trailblazers for greater truth, our task is easier. We only have to follow their brave example of blazing trails toward truer explanations of physical, biological, and social causality. As advocates and activists for new truth, they did not remain silent; rather they broadcast truer models of causality, while risking the ire of defenders of the status quo and the eminence of authority.

In her poem *Protest*, Ella Wheeler Wilcox urges every silent witness to religious and political injustice to cry out against its authoritarian oppression.

> To sin by silence, when we should protest,
> Makes cowards out of men. The human race
> Has climbed on protest. Had no voice been raised
> Against injustice, ignorance, and lust,

The inquisition yet would serve the law,
And guillotines decide our least disputes.
The few who dare, must speak and speak again
To right the wrongs of many....[157]

With civilization at risk and our species endangered, we cannot afford to "sin by silence." We must speak out against injustice wherever we find it "to right the wrongs of many." And, where can injustice be found? Wherever there is violence and coercion for win-lose gain, there is injustice.

Wilcox praised Christians who protested the crimes of the Inquisition during their deadly rule of Christendom. Without the courage to protest, Christians would be forever ruled by theocratic tyrants.

Brave citizens of France protested the wisdom of killing every critic of the Revolution, as well as every detractor of its despotic leadership. Without someone to denounce the Reign of Terror that sent thousands to the guillotine on false, frivolous, or inequitable charges, tyranny would have continued to reign in the Republic of France.

Wilcox stressed, "The human race has climbed on protest." Although this is true, protest also has its dark side. *Protest* is like the two-edged sword: its razor cut may be useful, or it may be lethal. To protest human action without a standard—without a criterion—of what is worthy of protestation or condemnation, raises the risk of social calamity and ruination. In our ignorance of causality, we might protest constructive social action while applauding destructive social action. Therefore, it is essential for humans to devise a criterion of protest that is consistent with, and not counter to, their worthy aims, whatever they may be.

By observing human nature, we can see that all humans can act toward their fellow humans in one of two ways. They can seek gain through the gain of others, or they can seek gain though the loss of others. Through observation of social action, we can identify and verify which social causes lead to which social effects. Wherever the means employed are incompatible with the ends sought, the results are poor at best and ruinous at worst.

Both Catholic Inquisitors and French Revolutionaries had faith in the virtue of their ideal aims. Tragically, their models of social causality were gravely flawed because noble ends cannot be reached by atrocious means. French Revolutionary leader, Maximilien Robespierre, and Dominican priest and Inquisitor General of Spain, Tomás de Torquemada, shared the same win-lose paradigm: *For us to gain, they must lose through force or fraud.*

As a Catholic prelate, Torquemada raised the level of legal cruelty and Christian brutality, especially through his unspeakable torture and murder of Jews and Moslems who were accused of the unholy crime of heresy. Some of his accused victims even included devout Christians who had the temerity to decry the persecution of Moslems and Jews.

Leaders of the Holy Inquisition, like Torquemada, had one warning for those who embraced the heresy of disbelieving in church dogma, "Believe or die." And, die they did. One social historian noted, "Torquemada, may have burned 10,220 heretics in total; 125,000 possibly died from torture and privation in prison."[158] Although in recent centuries, Torquemada was finally vilified as a Christian tyrant by various novelists and playwrights, this was not so in his time. In the eyes of Queen Isabella (he was her confessor) and other admirers across Iberia, Torquemada was seen as the heroic defender of Spain and the Catholic Church from the criminal danger of heretics and their nefarious heresies.

Because in our day there are true believers who still live in fear of those who may commit religious and political heresy, we must always protest the intrinsically flawed paradigm of heresy itself. It is impossible to harm your neighbors by rejecting or refuting the basis of their religious or political dogma, no matter how esteemed or revered its canons may be. Whatever I believe to be true or false—regardless of how unorthodox or irrational it may seem from your view—my belief alone cannot harm you.

But, one *can* harm you by taking win-lose action that seizes your wealth and freedom through force or fraud. You are harmed whether I take the win-lose action against you in person, or I authorize or appoint others to act against you on my behalf. And, you are still harmed even if one can somehow justify the seizure of your wealth and freedom.

Every tyrant in history has justified his tyranny against the people. In France, Robespierre defended his win-lose crimes against his own people with an old win-lose proverb, "You can't make an omelette without breaking eggs." Over a century later, V. I. Lenin used the same proverb to justify the murder of millions of his fellow Russians who failed to embrace his *a priori* vision of the meritorious efficacy of win-lose Communism, on faith alone.

It is imperative to recognize and reemphasize that although these religious and political leaders murdered their fellow humans through institutions of violence, it was not because they were necessarily malicious by nature; it was because they failed to understand social causality. This led them to believe that by imposing monopolies of religion and government through legal force, they could reach their utopian ideals for a better world. Nonetheless, wherever the coercive means employed cannot attain the social ends promised, we must openly protest and protest such impossible social policies. By observing and verifying social causality, we can define a standard of social protest, and one of social approval that is compatible with reaching peaceful and prosperous ends for a better world.

∽

In the twenty-first century, the most critical and necessary paradigm shift for spiritual leaders and their followers to make is for them to move away from their trust in win-lose theology toward trust in win-win theology. Here is a key verse from the Qur'ān that leads the Muslim faithful toward win-win exchange for mutual gain. It defines, in part, what it means to be a "righteous" follower of the one true god as revealed by the prophet Muhammad:

> The righteous [are] those who...restrain anger, and pardon (all) men—for Allah loves those who do good (3:134; author's brackets; translator's parentheses).

This Qur'ānic verse does not say pardon some men, or most men, or nearly all men, it trumpets, "pardon all men." It does not allow for exceptions. This makes it a rule of Islamic theology defined in this treatise as the Principle of Islamic Forgiveness.

To pardon all men is to forgive them for any perceived offense that violates some social rule or moral code. Where believers in one true god are offended by those who do not believe—because it is said that they are ignorant of the supreme god or that they reject the supremacy of god—the Qur'ān sets forth this command for every Muslim to "pardon all men, for Allah loves those who do good."

If to pardon unbelievers and disbelievers for the presumed offense of not believing in the one true god is to "do good" and, thereby, earn Allah's love, then it follows that to kill those who do not believe—whatever their reasons may be—would be to "do bad" by violating Allah's explicit command. It also follows from the scripture above that to do bad is to lose Allah's love. Yet, "those who do good" by following the Principle of Islamic Forgiveness in this Qur'ānic creed would expand the potential for freedom and prosperity for all Muslims through the enriching power of win-win exchange.

In our time, there is no greater challenge for theologians who can play a crucial role in this paradigm shift from win-lose to win-win religion. Theologian and Qur'ānic translator, Abdulla Yusuf Ali, comments on the above verse, which defines the character of righteous Muslims:

> They do not get ruffled in adversity, or get angry when other people behave badly, or their own good plans fail. On the contrary they redouble their efforts. For the charity — or good deed — is all the more necessary in adversity. And they do not throw the blame on others. Even where such blame is due and correction is necessary, their own mind is free from a sense of grievance, for they forgive and cover other men's faults.[159]

Where the "good deed" is founded on the altruistic Principle of Islamic Forgiveness, no one is harmed, and everyone wins. Christians are urged to follow the same principle taught by Jesus and stressed by St. Paul in his epistle to Christians of the ancient city of Ephesus:

> Get rid of all rage, bitterness and anger, brawling and slander along with every form of malice. Be kind and compassionate to one another, forgiving each other, just as in Christ God forgave you (Ephesians, 4:31).

Paul's central message is clear and elegant in its simplicity, "Be kind and compassionate to" others. This is the core of win-win exchange for mutual gain, which in turn is the heart of win-win religion. Where kindness and compassion are in vogue, they supersede the "rage, bitterness and anger, brawling and slander," and "malice" that Paul would have us avoid. The way to avoid all of these negative attitudes and actions is to create win-win strategies for maximizing win-win gain in all human endeavors. By creating more and more opportunities for win-win exchange, the demand for win-lose exchange will fall out of favor as an acceptable and respectable means for human gain.

Both good Christians and good Muslims, as defined by their Holy Scriptures, are those who have the resolve and fortitude to forgive, to pardon those who have offended them, whether such offense is real or imagined. Christian and Islamic forgiveness preempts the violence and criminality of win-lose exchange while furthering the benevolence and blessings of win-win exchange.

If our species is to survive, true believers must have the courage to abandon their win-lose religion in favor of win-win religion. Moreover, they must show their nerve to resist those who would preserve the status quo through intimidation.

Where the faithful would advance wealth and harmony for all, pursuit of win-win gain is always superior to that of win-lose gain, which only fosters turmoil and poverty that few will enjoy. To optimize peace, prosperity, and freedom,

> *True believers do not have to abandon their faith in the virtue of win-win religion; they have to abandon their faith in the virtue of win-lose religion.*

It is not enough, however, for the faithful follower to say, "But I would never encourage or commit a crime against my neighbors or against humanity to please our one true god—or to please anyone else." Even though such a strong assertion may be true for many believers, it is inadequate because it falls short of the crucial action that must be taken.

Those who would optimize the social causes of peace, prosperity, and freedom, must *protest*, they must speak out against the immorality and criminality of win-lose religion that unavoidably leads to war, poverty, and servitude. Only when we understand which social causes lead to which social effects can we act accordingly and thereby reach noble aims.

All humans act on their perceptions of causality, which become their paradigms of reality. Those who are sure that witches are spreading the plague will take entirely different actions than those who are sure that witches are only imaginary inventions. Perception is everything. Those who understand social causality must take action to diminish and demolish the deadly perception that win-lose religion is heroic, righteous, and moral.

Behind every human action, the wise human actor asks, "Can the means employed attain the ends sought?" The answer to this question requires an understanding of cause-and-effect. To understand what causes positive effects is to understand what causes negative effects. For example, for those who would optimize the negative effects of war, poverty, and servitude, what can they do to reach their aim? They can begin by protesting against win-win exchange. Thus, they would be on track to reach their win-lose aims.

We can observe that win-win exchange for mutual gain is the direct and indirect cause of peace, prosperity, and freedom — which is the very opposite of despotic designs. In short, if religious believers desire the universal losses of war, poverty, and servitude, then they must protest and obstruct win-win exchange for mutual gain. However, few would desire such fatal losses. Instead, if believers prefer the universal gains of peace, prosperity, and freedom, then there is one human action to protest. They must protest and protest wherever win-lose exchange rises to impose unilateral — one-sided — gain through the coercive loss of others.

Those who understand social causality must protest the inequity and iniquity of win-lose gain; they must broadcast its predictable failure as a means to beneficial ends. Those who would multiply the diverse benefits of win-win religion for all believers must take positive action. They must protest win-lose religion for coercive gain and praise win-win religion for mutual gain. The payoff is large. To protest win-lose exchange and praise win-win exchange is a key action toward shattering the positive image of any win-lose paradigm that promises: *For us to gain, they must lose through force or fraud.*

As the win-lose paradigm of social causality loses both its credibility and respectability—especially among the educated classes—a natural consequence is the advance of win-win religion. Where win-win religion flourishes, the altruism of voluntary exchange for win-win gain is naturally and spontaneously advanced. A noteworthy outcome of such win-win action is to create the greatest freedom and prosperity for the greatest number of believers to enjoy.

∾

Every prominent religion has a Golden Rule that extols the sanctity and relevance of this moral principle: "Do not harm others as you would have them not harm you." But what causes harm to others? We can observe that win-lose action aimed at unilateral gain through force or fraud always harms the victims of such coercive gain.

Religious believers who truly care about the well-being of their fellow humans—who would not harm them in any way—must not only follow the Golden Rule Principle, but they must speak out against those people, whether in or out of their religion, who violate its ethics of behavior by harming others in the name of god, nation, or leader. Noted translator of the Qur'ān, Muhammad Asad, explains the meaning of this Qur'ānic warning noted earlier, "there shall be no coercion in matters of faith."

> On the strength of the above categorical prohibition of coercion in anything that pertains to faith or religion, all Islamic jurists, without any exception, hold that forcible conversion is under all circumstances null and void, and that any attempt at coercing a nonbeliever to accept the faith of Islam is a grievous sin: a verdict that disposes of the widespread fallacy that Islam places before the unbelievers the alternative of "conversion or the sword."[160]

The Qur'ān is explicit on the evil criminality of "coercion in matters of faith" that may lead to the killing of one person or to the massacre of many:

> That if anyone slew a person—unless it be for murder or for spreading mischief in the land—it would be as if he slew the whole people: And if anyone saved a life, it would be as if he saved the life of the whole people (5:32).[161]

This argues that one individual life is precious and cannot be sacrificed for the supposed good of the many. It stands against the proverbial saying, "life is cheap," especially in poor nations where widespread poverty is the common condition. This is a win-lose fallacy that says that the lives of a few must be sacrificed for the good of the many, which is the heart of win-lose collectivism. This flawed argument says that for the *collective* (collection of people) to gain, the individual must be forced to lose at spear point, sword point, or gunpoint. When it is alleged that you are a disbeliever in the one true god, the one true religion, the one true state, or in the one true leader, then without question you must be forced to lose. The superiority syndrome has sealed your fate: *For superior believers to gain, inferior disbelievers must be forced to lose.*

In commenting on the Qur'ānic verse above ("That if anyone slew a person,") Muhammad Asad argues:

> To kill or to seek to kill an individual because he represents an ideal is to kill all who upheld the ideal. On the other hand, to save an individual life in the same circumstances is to save a whole community. What could be a stronger condemnation of individual assassination and revenge?[162]

In the nuclear age, the fate of the world is in the hands of true believers. Without renouncing their religious superiority, believers must renounce their religious violence against their presumed inferiors. These include those whom they have dehumanized as infidels, heretics, heathens, pagans, apostates, and dissenters. By tradition alone, they are all decried as unbelievers in divine truth who will not be tolerated. Thus, win-lose tradition spurs win-lose intolerance, inciting win-lose action for coercive gain.

To end this vicious cycle, true believers must abandon their intolerance of disbelievers, whatever they may disbelieve. One's disbelief, non-belief, or unbelief in whatever believers are certain is true, as a belief, per se, can never harm anyone.

Honest people have imposed worldwide destruction upon society merely because they have held fuzzy ideas on what it means to harm their neighbors. To end such destruction, *imagination* of what is harmful must be replaced by *observation* of what is harmful. The real cause of harm can be identified through direct observation of human action. Harm is the coercive effect of win-lose seizure of wealth and freedom — whether directly or by proxy — through force or fraud. In building a Science of Social Causation, the key term *harm* is defined. In fewer words, here again is the precise definition of harm: *Harm is any imposed loss through force or fraud.*

Beyond science, semantic precision is rare. Where it is rare, precise communication is also rare. As noted, without precise language, there is little precise thinking. Without precise thinking, decent people are in grave danger of not knowing what they are talking about. This leads to their not knowing what they are doing. As always, such people—especially if they are respected, intelligent, and schooled—are a potential danger to society.

While never calling it *harm*, religious leaders have glorified and deified human harm to render it acceptable and respectable. As long as devout believers have faith in the respectability of harming others to advance their win-lose religion (or win-lose politics), they will continue to do so with passion and resolve. Furthermore, they will go on imposing such harm as long as they harbor their win-lose models of religious sanctity and superiority.

There is only one salvation from the perpetual crisis of religious violence: Faithful believers must be convinced to abandon their devotion to harming others for the glory of religious gain. They must be shown that whatever the presumed gain from win-lose religion, that gain is dwarfed by the rich and diverse gains of win-win religion for mutual gain.

Regardless of their religious preference, believers will be rewarded by making paradigm shifts away from win-lose to win-win religion. This model of spiritual integrity follows the Golden Rule of Holy Scripture. To show their religious superiority, believers can follow the principle of win-win religion: *For believers to gain, disbelievers must gain—or never be forced to lose.* Moreover, to prove their superiority, they can follow the Golden Rule Principle and its corollary the

Win-Win Principle. There is no other path of salvation from human extinction.

∽

Certain Muslims who are appalled by Islamist violence have come together to write, produce, and perform a song that sends a strong message against terrorism. It rejects Islamist violence as a ruinous hijacking of the virtues of Islam. Its producers inspired the most popular singing artists in the Islamic Republic of Pakistan to record the five-minute song *Yeh Hum Naheen* (This Is Not Us).

On their Yeh Hum Naheen website, the song's Islamic producers announce their anti-terrorist theme with this blunt message in video graphics, "Terrorism is murder. Murder is haram [forbidden by Islamic law]. Countless innocents are being murdered by terrorists claiming to fight in the name of Islam."[163] With lyrics by Ali Moeen, his compelling song gives assurance that they as true and faithful Muslims are neither terrorists nor murderers.

> Yeh Hum Naheen (This is not us.)
> This story that is being spread in our names is a lie
> These stamps of death on our forehead are the signs
>   of others
> The name by which you know us - we are not that
> The eyes with which you look at us - we are not that
> This is not us - this is not us...
> As with the coming of night one loses one's way
> We are scared of the dark so much that we are
>   burning our own home
> What is this rising all around us...
> The stories that are being spread in our names are
>   lies
> This is not us...
> We have lost on the way the lesson of living together

We are now even scared of each other.
They are others whose faces are on your hands
Your hurts are a deep sea - our wounds are deep.
The stories that are being spread in our names are
 lies
Yeah Hum Nahi. Yeah Hum Nahi, Yeah Hum Nahi.
Yeah Hum Nahi,
This is not us...

The Chairman of the Yeh Hum Naheen Foundation, Waseem Mahmood, stressed, "The objective of the foundation is to build on the essence of Islam as a faith that promotes tolerance, peace, and harmony, removing prejudices within the community and amongst non-Muslims around the world." As the Yeh Hum Naheen Foundation "promotes tolerance, peace, and harmony" among Muslims and non-Muslims, it is encouraging to note the success of their highly effectual song, *Yeh Hum Naheen*. While focusing on these lofty aims, their song has earned a win-win market success as a leader on the popular music charts in Pakistan where Islam is the state religion.

Where Islamist terrorism is condemned by popular artists who are admired by a multitude of Islamic fans, everyone wins. Where win-lose action for coercive gain is abandoned for whatever reason, the only other option is to pursue win-win action for mutual gain. Those who have faith in the equity, utility, and morality of mutual gain—without resort to win-lose coercion—must have the courage and resolve to always "keep the faith" in the sanctity of win-win religion.

ᔕ

Islamic Theologian, Shaykh-ul-Islam, Dr. Muhammad Tahir Ul-Qadri (former legal adviser on Islamic Law to

Pakistan's Supreme Court), has ruled on the illegitimacy and immorality of Islamist terrorism in his six hundred-page fatwa: *Introduction to the FATWA on Suicide Bombings and Terrorism* (2010). Ul-Qadri strongly condemned all Islamist terrorists and suicide bombers as "unbelievers" in Islam.

In an interview with CNN correspondent, Christiane Amanpour, Ul-Qadri made his position clear in issuing a new fatwa (legal ruling by Islamic scholar) against Islamist terrorism. With no concessions to Islamist radicals, he charged, "Terrorism is terrorism; violence is violence. It has no place in Islamic teachings." Without compromise, Ul-Qadri pressed home his judicial conclusion that you "cannot legalize an act of terrorism. Terrorism and violence cannot be considered to be permissible in Islam on basis of any excuse." As an Islamic scholar using the Qur'ān as his guiding authority, Ul-Qadri reaffirmed that, "Allah does not like mischief and violence" (2:204-206).[164]

In announcing his fatwa at a March 2, 2010 news conference in London, Dr. Ul-Qadri explained:

> This fatwa is an absolute condemnation of terrorism without any excuse, without any pretext, without any exceptions, without creating any ways of justification. This condemnation is in its totality, in its comprehensiveness, and in its absoluteness. I will say total condemnation of every act of terrorism in every form and manifestation of radicalism and terrorism, which is being committed, or which has been committed, for the last one or two decades in the name of Islam.

In her interview, Amanpour asked him, "But who do you think is going to listen? Is it the committed extremist, the committed suicide bomber? In other words, some are complaining that your fatwa is only going to reach like-minded

Muslims, such as yourself and not the people who need to hear this." Ul-Qadri replied without hesitation:

> No, this is not the case. I would divide these people whom I have addressed, those who this fatwa is going to reach, into three categories. I would exclude just a very little number of those radicals who have already been brain washed and are not ready to listen to any reasoning. [Yet] hundreds of thousands of youths who are on the [wrong] path...have the potential to be radicalized. But they have not yet reached the stage of being brain washed. They are going to listen to this fatwa. This fatwa is going to change their mind.

Ul-Qadri pointed out the risk if nothing is done to influence Muslim youth in a constructive way:

> And then millions of other Muslim youth, they can be reached by the extremists. They can be misguided by the wrong interpretation of Islam. They can be put on the wrong track by putting the wrong concept of Jihad in their minds. Although they are not radicals and they are not suicide bombers now, but they can be misguided in [the] future; so this fatwa is going to change their mind.

Continuing her interview, Amanpour questioned Ul-Qadri, "I want to ask you a personal question. A friend of yours—a cleric, Mr. [Sarfraz] Naeemi, who also spoke out against extremism and terrorism, he was assassinated [June 16, 2009] after issuing a verbal fatwa on national television. Are you afraid, now that you have come out and made this very powerful statement; are you afraid for your own life?"

I'm not afraid of any human being on the surface of Earth.... I am working for a peaceful atmosphere of humanity. I am working to bridge up the East and West, and the Muslim World and the Western world to remove the hatred — to remove all misunderstandings.... I'm not afraid of this situation. Anybody who is afraid of this situation, they would never write this kind of fatwa. He would never declare this kind of truth. Truth is truth. One has to live for truth — or die for truth.[165]

From the beginning of this treatise on *Taming the Violence of Faith*, it has been emphasized that the dire crisis incited by the advance of win-lose religion cannot be overemphasized, and its true causes cannot be over-explained. Where ordinary people have access to world news on television, radio, Internet, and by newsprint — and where at least some freedom of the press is allowed by religious and political authorities — there is usually some coverage of the religious atrocities of the year, of the week, and of the day. It is not necessary to exaggerate reality or to use scare tactics to grab people's attention. The crisis of win-lose religion threatens to destroy civilization along with its teeming masses. The crisis is real, and it is growing on an annual basis. Its potential for disaster transcends all past experience. The outcry of many anxious observers that this is scary does not seem to be "over the top."

Our English infinitive "to scare" means to provoke sudden fright. If you just learned that a man-eating tiger has mauled one of your near neighbors, that would grab your attention in a heartbeat. You don't need a degree in feline biology to know that the tiger's appetite for human flesh will soon return.

It is natural to be scared for the safety of you and your family. And, it's OK to worry about the security of your neighbors who are at grave risk of meeting the same fate. Thus, it is timely to forego Sunday's backyard barbecue with the Johnsons until this deadly cat is captured or killed.

If this were our neighborhood, we would be scared. The risk of sudden death from the fatal fangs of a leaping cat would be all too real. Knowing the tiger kills by stealth, we would imagine it stalking us from behind every bush and tree. As concerned parents, our neighbors would not think we were paranoid for warning our kids, "The weather may be great, but this is not a good time for potluck in the park; and boys, don't ask me again if you can play in the woods."

The menace of a hungry tiger has caused a crisis that locals can respect and react to because they fear their closeness to a lethal threat, which has suddenly shattered the tranquility of their peaceful community. By understanding cause-and-effect, locals can take positive action to find protection from the real peril of a man-eating tiger on the prowl for its daily catch.

However, when the threat to our security is worldwide and so universal that everyone's life is in jeopardy, it is natural to be psychologically overwhelmed by the colossal size of the threat. The common reaction is one of resignation, "Well, what can we do?" Furthermore, we are less likely to react when the threat is out of sight and, thereby, out of mind.

The nuclear missiles that target us are hidden in underground silos or shrouded in the hulls of submarines. The chemical weapons that can reach us are stored in concealed bunkers. The microbes, carefully designed to unleash a pandemic of universal death, can be hidden and stored almost anywhere. However, even though these horrific weapons of mass destruction are out of sight, we know that their invisibility does not diminish the magnitude of the crisis imposed by their very existence.

Because the threat to human existence is real, there does not seem to be any relief without abandoning a prime cause of the peril, namely, win-lose religion. For example, when Muslims of the world follow the teaching of Mohammed who said, "Let there be no compulsion [violence] in religion," they are advancing win-win Islam, which can be defined as a principle of religious action:

PRINCIPLE OF WIN-WIN ISLAM
Always seek gain through the gain of believers and nonbelievers in the primacy of Islam, and never seek gain through their loss by force or fraud.

If asked, some may disagree on how they might define win-win Islam. Yet, however it is defined, if its definition and canons included acceptance and approval of win-lose violence against those who do not believe in Allah's divine singularity, then Islam would be a win-lose religion. It would aim to thrive on the criminality of ritualized violence for win-lose gain. But such a spurious interpretation of its religious doctrine would be a slap in the face to Islam's prophet and teacher, Mohammed. To stress once again, Mohammed gave this central command to his followers, "Let there be no compulsion [violence] in religion."

Mohammed's explicit warning is a fundamental teaching that deserves semantic elevation, generalized earlier as the Principle of Islamic Nonviolence. Muslims who would honor Mohammed, must accept this principle as an inviolable tenet—one not to be violated for any reason, especially by Islamic fundamentalists. What could be more *fundamental* (meaning a basic essential) to Islamic integrity than Mohammed's elegant Principle of Islamic Nonviolence? "Let there be no compulsion [violence] in religion."

As soon as Sunnis, Shi`ahs, or members of any other Islamic sect violate Mohammed's sacred canon of Islamic nonviolence with, say, another unholy atrocity, they will have just provoked another unholy crisis, which they will justify by the certainty of their superiority syndrome. Direct observation shows that their win-lose faith is ratcheting up the risk of exterminating Muslims around the world, as well as non-Muslims. This is not good.

༄ઐ

There is one escape from this social crisis. Muslims who would preserve the integrity of Mohammad's principle of nonviolence must marshal their influence, energy, and assets to convince those Muslims who foster and condone win-lose Islam to make the crucial paradigm shift toward the nonviolence of win-win Islam for mutual gain. Overnight, Sunnis and Shi`ahs could end centuries of mutual brutality by following Mohammed's Islamic Principle of Nonviolence.

In the nuclear age, the primacy of this inviolable principle cannot be overstressed. It must be followed not only by Sunnis and Shi`ahs, but by Muslims of every sect. Muslims, who do not have the resolve to follow the teaching of Mohammad, cannot become faithful Muslims. To become faithful, they must honor Mohammed by giving their allegiance to the Principle of Win-Win Islam and to the Islamic Golden Rule, "No one of you is a believer until he desires for his brother that which he desires for himself."

What do all Sunnis and Shi`ahs desire for themselves? Like all Muslims, they desire to gain the rich and diverse blessings that can only flow from the fountains of social peace and economic prosperity. When Sunnis desire for Shi`ahs what they desire for themselves and, conversely, when Shi`ahs desire for Sunnis what they desire for themselves — and they act accordingly — there will be no win-lose conflict between them.

Where Muslims follow Mohammed's Principle of Non-violence and they practice his Islamic Golden Rule, all mutually destructive conflict among Muslims, all sectarian violence, ends through the natural pacification of win-win exchange. Again, all win-win exchanges are peaceful exchanges that preempt and dampen human conflict.

Those who may argue that these win-win tenets of Islamic behavior set forth by Mohammed are impractical, are prejudiced by their false pessimism. Where the aim is to maximize peace and prosperity for the enrichment of all Muslims, it is the *only* practical action to follow. This is because win-win action is the only workable means to the creation of such beneficial ends as durable peace and lasting prosperity.

The infamous and shameful conflict among Jews and Muslims cannot rage on forever without engulfing the Middle East and beyond in endless crises and violence. Yet, in spite of the growing scale of this conflict, there is an irrefutable solution that can be verified through the power of observation. The only long-term solution to perpetual war is perpetual peace. This is true in the Middle East, or anywhere else. This simplification may sound sophomoric to many erudite scholars who would plead that the idea of creating perpetual peace is naive and utopian. Yes, indeed, it would be utopian if the perpetual presence of peace required changing the laws of nature. However, it does not require the impossible, as already explained.

To fashion perpetual peace and to make it a *fashionable* social condition over time, we do not have to change human nature; we only have to change human paradigms. As always, *difficult* does not mean *impossible*. It is only necessary to make paradigm shifts away from false models of causality toward those that are true. In the Middle East, this means that religious believers of every denomination who practice and support win-lose religion must make the crucial paradigm shift toward win-win religion. After all, there is much at stake, including the very survival of our species.

There is nothing more pressing today than the preservation of human custodianship of the Earth, which remains in grave risk as long as pious people cling to their belief in the sanctity and rectitude of win-lose religion for coercive gain. It is incumbent upon all believers in the equity and morality of win-win religion to focus their influence on bringing down the coercive and corrosive pillars of win-lose theology and religion. Those who have the fortitude to embark upon this sacred mission are setting exemplary examples of win-win altruism in its finest hour.

᠙

One prominent theologian who does not claim the exclusive superiority of his faith over all others is His Holiness the Dalai Lama of Tibet. He does not say that Buddhism is the only path to Nirvana or Paradise, rather he says:

> For me, Buddhism remains the most precious path. It corresponds best with my personality. But that does not mean I believe it to be the best religion for everyone any more than I believe it necessary for everyone to be a religious believer."[166]

As a Buddhist, the Dalai Lama proclaims that religion and win-lose intolerance are *not* inseparable because they *can* be separated. Although the noun *intolerance* has gained a negative image by way of the destruction it has unleashed on humankind, intolerance can be constructive or destructive. To be intolerant, for example, of coercive religion is constructive because it condemns religion for win-lose gain, which opens the door to religion for win-win gain.

∽

When Christians of the world emulate the win-win actions of Jesus, who gave them the keystone of his teaching in these simple words, "Love thy neighbor as thyself," they are advancing win-win Christianity. St. Paul, in a passage from Romans quoted earlier, made it clear that, "Whatever commandments there may be, are summed up in this one rule, 'Love your neighbor as yourself.' Love does no harm to its neighbor. Therefore love is the fulfillment of the law."

This principle of social action set forth by Jesus, that our rewards will be profound if we love our neighbors — which means *never* harm them whether they live near or far — is the elegant theme of win-win Christianity. However, there are those who argue that this centerpiece of Christianity is impractical, if not foolish. At the same time, they accept the win-lose paradigm as the reigning model of practical social action. But in reality, it is hopelessly impractical. The truth cannot be hidden; it is a flawed model of causality that guides respected people to harm their neighbors for religious gain. It remains the most destructive and thereby the most *impractical* paradigm in the history of social causality. Humans, no matter how grand their repute and prestige may be, cannot reach worthy ends by way of coercive means — not this year, next year, or in any year.

On the other hand, those who would follow a creative Christianity rather than a destructive one must refute and repudiate the win-lose paradigm as spurious and untenable on any practical, rational, and moral grounds. Jesus was right. His call to transform win-lose exchange into win-win exchange is the only means of maximizing the well-being of his followers. Love your neighbors, because if you harm them, many bad things will happen to many good people — Christians, and everyone else.

∽

The failure of win-lose Christianity to build a better world for Christians and non-Christians to enjoy, in part, stems from the failure of Christian leaders to create, codify, and promote a rigid and uncompromising standard of Christian ethics, morality, equity, and decency that was and is consistent with the kindly teachings of Jesus. Although two millennia have passed since Jesus gave his famous Sermon on the Mount as recalled and recorded in the Gospels by his apostles, Matthew and Luke, it is not too late for present day Christian clerics to rectify this potentially lethal and still sinister omission.

The great majority of Christian leaders, most of whom are Catholics and Protestants, must have the resolve to raise their canonical standards of morality to eliminate the potential for win-lose Christianity, and to lay foundations for win-win Christianity by setting moral standards that are compatible with and complementary to the cardinal teachings of Jesus. An example of such a moral criterion for Christian theology can be found in the essence of this social principle:

PRINCIPLE OF WIN-WIN CHRISTIANITY
Always seek gain through the gain of believers and nonbelievers in the primacy of Christianity, and never seek gain through their loss by force or fraud.

Whether Christians are Roman Catholics, Protestants, Anglicans, Mormons, Eastern Orthodox, or whatever their denomination may be, if they practice the principle of win-win Christianity, they will never commit crimes of force and fraud against one another for win-lose gain. Moral consistency was precious and paramount to Jesus. Any violation

424

of this moral principle where one Christian initiates a win-lose attack upon another Christian—or non-Christian—in the "name of our Lord Jesus," is a flagrant transgression. He or she has perverted the win-win Gospel of Jesus into the wicked and criminal practice of win-lose Christianity. Such transgressors by their own win-lose actions have revealed themselves to be anti-Christ in their behavior. By their own actions, those who practice win-lose Christianity—regardless of their claims of devotion to Jesus and his teachings—are using anti-Christ action for win-lose gain.

Win-lose Christianity, in whatever seemingly righteous and sacred form it may take in the eyes of some, nevertheless, is an overt desecration and repudiation of the teachings of Jesus. One does not have to be a Biblical scholar to recognize the sharp distinction between the win-win teachings of Jesus and the win-lose teachings of misguided "Christian" leaders who over millennia sanctified and codified win-lose Christianity in the name of Jesus.

All who call themselves Christians have a clear choice. They can practice either win-win or win-lose Christianity. To be sure, following the win-win teachings of Jesus may be a difficult challenge for many Christians, but it is not an impossible challenge. Again, difficult merely means not easy; it never means impossible. In any case, history shows that the more difficult the challenge to reach win-win gain, the greater the potential reward. One of those rewards may be the salvation of humankind from extinction through the hands of believers who have the courage to shift paradigms away from false worship of win-lose Christianity toward true worship of win-win Christianity. As noted, this would not be a small reward. Christians with the resolve to follow the win-win teachings of Jesus can play a key role in the quest for human salvation and the creation of wealth and freedom beyond all Christian experience.

Pope Paul VI took the leadership in convening the Second Vatican Council, out of which was issued the "Declaration on the Relation of the Church to Non-Christian Religions," October 28, 1965. It gave this explicit warning to all Catholics to end discrimination against anyone based on their respective "race, color, condition of life, or religion."

> No foundation...remains for any theory or practice that leads to discrimination between man and man or people and people, so far as their human dignity and the rights flowing from it are concerned. The Church reproves [rebukes], as foreign to the mind of Christ, any discrimination against men or harassment of them because of their race, color, condition of life, or religion. On the contrary, following the footsteps of the holy Apostles Peter and Paul, this sacred synod ardently implores the Christian faithful to "maintain good fellowship among all nations" (1 Peter 2:12), and if possible, to live for their part in peace with all men, so that they may truly be sons of the Father who is in heaven.

This papal declaration of the Church clearly "implores the Christian faithful," to follow — without compromise — the tenet defined earlier as the Principle of Win-Win Christianity, which is founded on the Golden Rule Principle of win-win reciprocity. The practical utility and efficacy of this principle is demonstrably true because its operation is the only course of social action capable of optimizing the causes of peace, prosperity, and freedom for all religious believers of all faiths. For those who would reach the sublime aims of any religious faith, win-win religion always trumps win-lose religion. In the endless quest for human gain, win-win gain works because it works in harmony with human nature. We can observe all humans acting out their human nature: *The Law of Human*

Nature is *the inborn drive of all people to act toward gain and away from loss.* By observing the nature of humans—defined by their inborn predispositions—we can observe that humans would not want their wealth and freedom to be seized through force or fraud. The ancient Golden Rule works as a practical guide to human interaction precisely because it is in accord with human nature, which is to always seek gain and avoid loss.

Again, as a simple principle of human action, nature's rule can be summarized with semantic precision as the Golden Rule Principle: *Do not seize wealth and freedom from others, as you would have them not seize your wealth and freedom.* Observation continues to verify this truth: many good things happen to both good people and bad people where they follow this rule of human action. In dramatic contrast, where they violate the rule, many bad things happen to both good people and bad people.

Donne's Principle prevails, "No man is an Island." Win-win action provokes win-win domino effects. Win-lose action provokes win-lose domino effects. There is no escape from the cascade of effects. The laws of nature prevail whether we like it or not. The best we can do is to discover these laws, and then observe and obey them accordingly. When and where we do, the rewards are large. They include the proliferation of peace, prosperity and freedom for the greater wealth of people of every race, religion, and creed. Nearly all of these people would agree this is good for me, and it is good for my friends and family. To attain these reachable aims, they only need to know which causes lead to which effects, and act accordingly.

༄

Many in the West are familiar with the Serenity Prayer. It gained wide circulation after 1942 when it was first used as a group prayer during Alcoholics Anonymous meetings designed to rescue addicts from the ordeals of alcohol abuse. Since then, it has gained currency in many languages. Authorship of the Serenity Prayer is disputed and has been attributed to various writers including twentieth-century theologian, Reinhold Niebhur. Here is a common variation on the theme of this celebrated prayer:

> God, grant me the serenity
> To accept the things I cannot change;
> Courage to change the things I can;
> And wisdom to know the difference.

If you aim to accept with serenity and dignity all the undesirable conditions and circumstances of human life that you "cannot change," then it is essential to raise this pressing question: Just what is it that you *cannot* change—today, tomorrow, or at any time?

For all of us, it is vitally important to find a true answer to this question because all of our efforts to change the unchangeable will go without reward. On the other hand, if there are human actions, for example, which can destroy the human species, and many believe they *cannot* be changed—when in truth, they *can* be changed—that could prove to be a fatal error without recovery.

As noted earlier, observation shows that humans cannot change the laws of nature. If to replace the ordeals of war, poverty, and servitude with the blessings of peace, prosperity, and freedom, we must first violate the laws of nature, then such aims would be impossible. And, nothing is more impractical than aiming for the impossible. To reaffirm the Impossibility Principle: *All human ends are impossible that would violate the laws of nature.*

If warfare erupts among men because it is their inborn nature to be warlike, then to wage war would be both natural and unavoidable. But war as a religious or political policy to settle human quarrels is neither natural nor is it unavoidable. However, the belief that war is *natural* and, thereby, *unavoidable* remains a false paradigm of social causality that is widely accepted to be true, especially among the educated classes. This dangerous fallacy gives pseudo-credence to the war paradigm: *For our nation to gain, your nation must be forced to lose.* Moreover, we hear respected people lament, "Of course war is regrettable, but it's unavoidable. So what can we do?" They are resigned to the inevitability of war because they have failed to identify, clarify, and verify the true causes of war and peace. In other words, they do not know how to attenuate the causes of war and optimize the causes of peace.

Yet, no matter how dark the passage to world peace may seem, nonetheless, at the end of a long tunnel, the light shines brighter than ever before. As the war paradigm is shown to be spurious and untenable, optimism trumps pessimism. This means that war can and must finally be rendered obsolete as an acceptable and respectable means to human gain. The social die is cast to shape our future. Legalized, organized, and glorified battles for coercive gain must be set aside before they spur global ruination, before they delete human life with the flick of a finger or the click of a mouse. Yet, it would be impossible to tame the violence of faith if to do so we also had to tame human nature.

Again, it is *not* human nature either to make war or to commit crimes against humanity. If it were so, the human race would have perished long ago. It *is* human nature to seek gain and avoid loss as revealed by the Law of Human Nature. Furthermore, the Law of Human Action reveals that it is human nature to choose *how* we seek gain—and *how* we avoid loss.

Everyone has the same choice: to seek gain and avoid loss through the gain of others—or through the loss of others. To reemphasize, in order to prevent our self-destruction, we do not have to change human nature. We only have to change human paradigms. Again, this knowledge of social causality transforms social pessimism into social optimism. Indeed, if our salvation from self-destruction required a new set of natural laws, entrenched pessimism would prevail without any hope of relief.

The Serenity Prayer—also known as The Courage Prayer—asks for the "courage to change the things I can." "To change" is to replace one thing with another thing. But what things *can* be replaced and what things *should* be replaced?

Pursuit of change for the sake of change is the genesis of folly. The classic example is replacing old win-lose policies with new win-lose policies. However, that changes nothing. The "change" is a deceitful display of bogus window dressing, nothing more than a pseudo-change. It is a false alternative sold to the people as a true model of social progress toward constructive change. Yet, wherever the win-lose paradigm remains the reigning world model of religious and political causality, nothing has changed, and there will be crisis after crisis.

Read the history books; a growing social crisis drives the demagogues and rabble-rousers out of the shadows and into the limelight. Seizing the stage, they mesmerize their audiences with eloquent deceit. They always shout the same slogan, "It's time for a change." Yet, a familiar warning should remind us, "Be careful of what you wish, because your wish may come true." Where unhappy people have wished for social change, the fulfillment of their wish has often proven to be destructive—or even catastrophic. The largely unappreciated history lesson is that if you wish for social change, you had better understand social causality, or in time, you may live to regret it.

The Nazis offered social change to wishful Germans who got that change through the tyranny of Naziism. The Communists offered social change to wishful Russians; and they got that change through the cruelty of Communism. And, the Fascists offered social change to wishful Italians. They got that change through the oppression of Fascism.

The demand for *change* is an old theme of political outsiders. The age-old slogans of "It's time for a change" and let's "throw the rascals out" are the tired sayings of those who would wrest the seats of power from religious or political authorities for their own win-lose gain. This was the lofty theme of Stalin, Hitler, Mao, Mussolini, Napoleon, as well as every other despotic leader. They all thrived on the expansion and enlargement of legalized coercion for their own win-lose gain. In demanding social change, the salient question is *always* social change in what direction, and for what purpose?

In Tunisia, Egypt, Libya, Yemen, Bahrain, in Syria and elsewhere, citizens are demanding social change away from tyrannical dictatorships and the oppression they impose. The open question remains, do the influential people of these nations know how to go from war, poverty, and servitude to peace, prosperity and freedom? It cannot be over-stressed, to do so they must know which social causes lead to which social effects. Without this understanding, they are doomed to perpetual dictatorship and the misery of organized despotism.

Change always goes in a destructive direction when that change is imposed upon society by force or fraud for win-lose gain. Chronicles of human history can only reveal the truth of social causality when there is a theory that can identify and verify which social causes lead to which social effects. It has been the destructive social changes that have followed greater demand for win-lose gain through religious and political action that has brought about the demise of civilizations. Observation shows that one direction of social change is always destructive because it is the social change *away* from win-win exchange for bilateral gain, *toward* win-lose exchange for unilateral gain.

Throughout human history, this regressive change from win-win to win-lose exchange has fueled the decline and fall of civilizations. To avoid such costly error, activists for change have to know what they are doing. The ardent activist, racing to douse the fire with fuel oil, will get poor results, especially when he aims to extinguish the flames. To go from regressive to progressive social action demands knowledge of social causality to get you there safely. The truest compass to human progress is to observe and identify the true causes of physical, biological, and social effects. However, where activists for a better world have failed to identify the causes of constructive change, in contrast to destructive change, they have failed at critical analysis. They are cannons on the loose, inclined to choose means that cannot attain the ends sought.

If a shopkeeper buys a bull to protect his precious china from thieves, he will soon be overrun by unintended consequences. The bull, in pursuing the thieves, shatters every shelf in his path. The shop is soon littered with shards of fine china. When the fury of the bull passes, the few unbroken pieces are still at risk as the bull is now in search of his mate. And, although she is grazing in the nearby park, there is bound to be trouble when he senses her presence.

You don't have to be a "bullologist" to see what went wrong. If the shop owner knew what he was doing, he never would have used a bull to guard his precious wares. Moreover, the brightest bull cannot separate thieves from buyers. Clearly, the means employed could not attain the ends sought, which was to protect the china. Whether his china is stolen by a thief, or shattered by a bull, this false alternative will bring no joy.

In a similar way, when social activists aim to guard something, to improve something, or to change something for the better, one question reigns supreme, "Do they have a true and valid understanding of social causality?" Without critical analysis of the equity, utility, and morality of their strategy of change, they are at high risk of doing more harm than good. Like the good merchant whose "bull in a china shop" is the guardian of his delft, things will go terribly wrong wherever good people act with honest aims, without knowing what they are doing.

In the end, there are only two kinds of social activists: (1) those who know what they are doing through understanding causality, and (2) those who do not know what they are doing though misunderstanding causality. The entire future of humanity depends upon the social application of a reliable standard that can separate one class of activists from the other.

In a world of wall-to-wall experts on every subject we know, the crucial question will always be the same, "Whose expertise is reliable; which experts know what they are talking about? Which models of causality are the most avid activists actually following in their pursuit of change?"

Every activist who cannot separate true from false models of causality is a loose cannon who may sink our ship of *Humanity,* in the next social storm. And, if the ship should plunge beneath the sea, defenders of the crew will surely rationalize, "Let's not be too harsh in blaming those selfless sailors, who ran the ship for all of us. They were intelligent, educated, virtuous leaders dedicated to running a tight and secure ship. Lest we forget, they never intended to sink the ship."

To be sure, all this may be true, but still the ship is gone. Moreover, a few still clinging to a lifeboat can be heard to lament, "It's too bad our eminent officers, in setting the course for *Humanity,* didn't know what they were doing, or they never would have sunk the ship."

It is clear that we stand at a crucial crossroad where social change is imperative. As noted, however, without a reliable and verifiable standard to distinguish between progressive social change and regressive social change, we are at risk of following an endless cycle of the blind leading the blind toward an unintended direction. In the end, we may be led on a grand march back to the Dark Ages, of course, in the revered name of god, nation, or leader.

What lasting lessons can we learn from observation without reliance upon the esteemed authority of conventional wisdom? Direct and indirect observation of human action shows that without a revolutionary change in direction toward voluntary exchange for win-win gain, we face certain demise.

We know that most of the species that have lived on earth are now extinct. But our species could be the first to perish by *self-extinction*, brought on by the hazards of following false paradigms of causality as if they were true. If our resolve does not give us the "courage to change the things" we can, and if our false paradigms of causality are bound by the chains of conventional wisdom, the long-term outlook is for certain doom.

Allegiance to convention has never changed paradigms away from false explanations of causality toward those that are true. Such progressive paradigm shifts always require a break with tradition. This takes human courage in the face of criticism or even ridicule from friend or foe.

To avert social obliteration and human oblivion, we must raise the quality of our paradigms of social causation; we must make paradigm shifts away from false models of causality that support win-lose gain, toward true models that support win-win gain. The equity, utility, and morality of voluntary exchange for win-win gain, is observationally true and valid without a foreseeable end to its ongoing confirmation and verification.

Of course, it will be difficult for people who believe in the rectitude and efficacy of win-lose coercion for religious or political gain to make paradigm shifts away from their cherished, but flawed, models of social causality. Nonetheless, decent people must have the courage (or find the courage) to break with win-lose tradition, win-lose dogma, win-lose authority, win-lose politics, and win-lose religion. These all bear one common denominator: They sanction legitimized gain through fraud or force to reach political or religious aims.

The Serenity Prayer also asks for courage—and courage is the master of difficulty. All major paradigm shifts have been difficult for humans to negotiate to a successful change. The difficulty stems from the reality that all people believe their paradigms of causality are true and above reproach. It takes courage for strong people to admit doubt of the veracity of any of their instilled models of causality. Yet, doubt comes easier when it is backed by the power of observational evidence that is overwhelmingly and consistently true.

Observation of social causality shows again and again, that those people who employ win-lose coercion to build their vision of a "better" world are governed by false models of social causality. Their idea of a positive social "change" is to expand institutional coercion to advance win-lose political or religious gain. In the end, this deadly social change will bring us down.

The Serenity Prayer asks for the wisdom to distinguish between what can and cannot be changed. That wisdom, in part, comes from an understanding of the contrast between the Possibility Principle and the Impossibility Principle. "Difficult" does not mean impossible. "Extremely difficult" does not mean impossible. Of course, "extremely, extremely difficult" does not mean impossible either.

All great achievements of humankind have been extremely difficult to accomplish, which is why we honor them as *great*. Greatness through the advance of win-win achievement has always been built upon the relentless courage of men and women to make paradigm shifts toward truer and truer explanations of physical, biological, and social causality. Because Donne's Principle assures us that "No man is an Island," these rewards accrue to everyone aboard our ship of *Humanity*. Neither negative nor positive domino effects of human action can be entirely contained as they travel throughout human society. As the sum of society is poorer for win-lose gain, so, too, is the sum of society richer for win-win gain.

∽

Theologians of the ancient world took the leadership in setting forth the invaluable Golden Rule. Today, theologians can assume the leadership in applying the Golden Rule as a sacred and inviolable principle toward its crucial role: to advance the paradigm shift away from win-lose toward win-win religion. This is the key to taming the violence of faith. As a consequence, the human race will flourish as never before. In the long run (which may not be that long) the alternative for humans is to flourish or perish. Where humans flourish, they know what they are doing—and they can prove it by eliminating violence from their faith, and through their advance of win-win exchange for mutual gain. As humans improve their basic knowledge of which causes lead to which effects, the win-lose paradigm of social causality will fall out of favor and into disuse, especially among the influential members of society. In its place, the win-win paradigm, which fosters win-win religion, win-win altruism, and win-win exchange, will initiate naturally and spontaneously, the blessings of peace, prosperity, and freedom for all.

ENDNOTES

154. André Trocmé, *Jesus and the Nonviolent Revolution* (1961), ed. Charles E. Moore (Farmington, PA: Plough Publishing House, 2007), 157.

155. Trocmé, *Jesus and the Nonviolent*.

156. Kurt Seligmann, *The History of Magic* (New York: Pantheon Books, 1948), 278.

157. Ella Wheeler Wilcox, "Protest," *Poems of Problems*, (Chicago: W. B. Conkey Company, 1914), 154.

158. R. J. Rummel, *Death by Government* (New Brunswick, New Jersey: Transaction Publishers, 1994), 62.

159. Abdullah Yusuf Ali, trans., *The Meaning of the Holy Qur'ān* (Beltsville, Maryland: Amana Publications, 2006), 161, note 453.

160. Muhammad Asad, *The Message of the Qur'ān* (Bristol, England: The Book Foundation, 2003), 70.

161. Ali, *The Meaning*, 257.

162. Ali, *The Meaning*, 257, note 737.

163. http://www.yehhumnaheen.org. (accessed date July 1, 2010).

164. Christiane Amanpour, CNN correspondent. Amanpour Interview of Dr. Muhammad Tahir Ul-Qadri (also, Former special adviser, Pakistani Education Minister on Islamic Curriculum). Program aired on CNN, Sunday, March 13, 2010.

165. Amanpour, Interview of Dr. Ul-Qadri.

166. His Holiness the Dalai Lama, *Ethics for the New Millennium* (New York: Riverhead Books, 1999), 21.

Appendix

Our world is in crisis because too many citizens in too many nations have faith in the truth of false paradigms of social causality — paradigms that provoke violence for religious and political gain. Although in every literate nation, news of the crisis is broadcast daily, the news fails to show the fundamental source of the crisis. Moreover, too often, news reports are riddled with misinformation, or they present flawed explanations of social causality, especially concerning the fundamental causes of war, poverty, and servitude, as well as peace, prosperity and freedom.

The subtitle of this book, *Win-Win Solutions for Our World in Crisis*, proposes that this crisis can be diminished and eventually ended through the pragmatic power of win-win solutions for mutual gain. It is important, however, to know that such solutions do not stand out as vivid insights that grab our attention. We are unlikely to cry out, "This is a remarkable and workable solution." The history of invention and innovation shows that if they are truly spectacular solutions to profound problems, then they are also subtle solutions that arrive without fanfare to announce their significance.

As noted earlier, the greater the solution to a persistent problem, the more likely the solution has gone unnoticed by the great majority of people, or if noticed at all, it has been disparaged as impractical. One vital solution to our world crisis is knowing how to distinguish between *possible* aims that are *practical*, in marked contrast to *impossible* aims that are *impractical*.

Observation shows that it is impossible to change nature's *principles* of cause-and-effect. All attempts have failed. Thankfully, to build practical solutions to major social problems, we only have to change human *paradigms* of cause-and-effect. Though always a challenge, paradigm shifts come easier with the discovery of new knowledge and greater experience with laws of nature. The proof is in the historical record of human progress.

Another element of the solution arrives with an understanding that building major solutions to major problems on natural principles is not an obvious path to success. Again, humans tend to view the proposal of innovations founded on natural principles to be impractical or impossible. This is especially true when they cannot imagine how they could ever be accomplished. In every civilization, bright people have been quick to conclude, "If I can't figure out how to do it, then it can't be done."

Durable solutions to social problems begin as we identify and verify their true causes. Without this practical knowledge of cause-and-effect, solutions are seldom created, if ever. This may seem obvious, but human history shows that the more elegant, the more significant the solution to a critical problem, the less obvious it is.

A dozen win-win solutions are identified below. In addition to these, there are many other social solutions that have been discussed in earlier chapters. Each solution below is a component of the larger solution on how to *minimize* the causes of war, poverty, and servitude and *maximize* the causes of peace, prosperity, and freedom, all of which contribute to taming the violence of faith.

☐ Defining the terms and principles of a social theory with *semantic precision* is an essential foundation for building practical solutions to our most critical social problems.

☐ In assessing the practical value of any proposed solution to any problem, the key test is can the means employed, attain the ends sought?

☐ The advance of human progress follows crucial paradigm shifts toward truer and better identification and verification of physical, biological, and social causality.

☐ In the search for workable solutions to physical, biological, and social problems, verified *observation* of causality supersedes unverified *imagination* of causality.

☐ Peace, prosperity, and freedom advance where win-lose paradigms of their *imagined* causes are superseded by win-win paradigms of their *observed* causes.

☐ To tame the violence of faith, respected people must make the paradigm shift away from faith in the equity, utility, and morality of the win-lose paradigm toward faith in the equity, utility, and morality of the win-win paradigm.

☐ In solving physical, biological, and social problems, great solutions to great problems are built on the constancy of universal principles.

☐ The flawed assumption that humans are predisposed to seek gain through force and fraud is countered and falsified by The Law of Human Nature.

☐ The greater the harmony of a social system with the Law of Human Nature, the greater its potential for creating peace, prosperity, and freedom.

☐ Those who apply the Golden Rule Principle are the creators of peace, prosperity, and freedom.

☐ Key to the solution of our social crisis is the falsification and repudiation of the invalid and specious argument that the Golden Rule Principle is impractical.

☐ Unverified faith in the equity, utility, and morality of the win-lose paradigm is the global *problem*; verified observation of the equity, utility, and morality of the win-win paradigm is the global *solution*.

The overarching key to solving the world social crisis follows a single paradigm shift away from respect for the win-lose paradigm toward respect for the win-win paradigm. When this paradigm shift enjoys common acceptance among the educated classes, peace, prosperity, and freedom will prevail over war, poverty, and servitude; and violence as a seemingly necessary policy for religious and political gain will fall out of favor and into disuse.

Observation of social cause-and-effect verifies the equity, utility, and morality of creating gain through the gain of others in all arenas of human endeavor. In stepping away from the coercion of win-lose gain, the perennial pall of destructive domino effects can be averted and avoided. The military maxim, "the best defense is a good offense" also applies to nonmilitary strategies. Wherever there is social exchange, the best defense against the destruction of win-lose gain is to marshal a moral offense of creating endless opportunities for win-win gain in all social exchange. This strategy is practical because it works; and it works because it is in harmony with the Law of Human Nature.

About the Author

J ay Stuart Snelson was raised and educated in Los Angeles, graduating from the University of California at Los Angeles in 1959. He attended L.A. schools in the early 1950s where students were required to execute, "drop drills." Classroom teachers, without warning, would suddenly shout at their students to "Drop!" In an instant, students dropped under their wooden desks, covering their heads with their arms. This was intended to protect them from the blast of a nuclear bomb. However, because a ring of critical defense plants surrounded the school, it was a "ground zero" target. Few students had confidence in the value of the drills. In this atmosphere of impending doom, at age fourteen, Snelson wrote his eighth-grade poem titled "A Losing Fight" (see frontispiece). It ends with this ominous line, "If countries shall make war again, I promise you no one will win."

Snelson's teenage concern for human survival motivated him to study social history, philosophy, theology, economics, and scientific epistemology in search of an answer to history's most critical and pressing social problem, namely, "How can the scope and scale of organized violence— whether religious or political—be limited to a level of destruction that no longer threatens to destroy civilization and the human species?" Lecturing on these issues for more than four decades, Snelson has shown that through observational analysis and verification, a greater understanding of social causality reveals a practical solution to the endless crises unleashed by war, poverty, and servitude.

His focus on finding workable strategies for resolving crucial social problems led to his development and presentation of proprietary seminars on a Science of Social Causation that identifies and verifies which social causes lead to which social effects. Causality identification and verification confirms the practicality and efficacy of win-win structures of social organization that maximize the causes of peace, prosperity, and freedom and minimize the causes of war, poverty, and servitude.

Over the past three decades, Snelson has created and presented seminars on Optimization Theory and Win-Win Theory through his Institute for Human Progress. His seminars showed the rich rewards available to believers of all faiths who apply the principles of win-win exchange for mutual gain. His Win-Win Theory revealed and verified the equity, utility, and morality of mutually voluntary exchange for win-win gain in every arena of social interaction and human endeavor.

Jay Stuart Snelson passed away peacefully on December 21, 2012 at home in San Clemente, California shortly after finishing the final edits of this book. His wife and business associate of 25 years, Nancy Rhyme Snelson, was by his side. His work to expand the exposure of Win-Win Theory to a world-wide market will be carried on by the Sustainable Civilization Institute, LLC (www.suscivinst.com).

Intellectual
Acknowledgments

D uring the course of intellectual history, even the most original and revolutionary advances in physical, biological, and social progress were built upon elements of knowledge that were developed by earlier explorers who were dedicated to discovering the *nature* of reality by understanding the *reality* of nature. To simplify this endless quest, our search can be divided into three broad areas of discovery involving the pursuit of physical, biological, and social causation. No course of human action is more crucial or more relevant to the advance of human progress than the discovery of cause-and-effect. The primary intellectual challenge is always formidable and never changes. How can we both identify and verify which physical, biological, and social causes lead to which corresponding effects?

In the study of biological action, if we fail to identify the true causes of our most deadly biological pathologies, such as cholera or the Black Death, our potential for reaching a cure is problematic at best and impossible at worst. In the study of social action, if we fail to identify the true causes of our most deadly social pathologies, such as perennial war and widespread servitude, our potential for discovering a cure is also problematic at best and impossible at worst.

To attempt to acknowledge our intellectual antecedents who have advanced the human condition is a worthwhile, but challenging aim. The publishing of elements of Win-Win Theory for the first time outside of my proprietary seminars will follow this treatise on *Taming the Violence of Faith: Win-Win Solutions for Our World in Crisis*. There I will include a broader and more detailed acknowledgment of my intellectual antecedents and sources. In this short work on the primacy of win-win religion over its social antithesis, win-lose religion, I will mention three intellectual precursors in particular who have made important advances in our understanding of social causation. These are Ludwig von Mises, for his science of human action on the efficacy of free exchange of tangible wealth; Andrew J. Galambos, for his cogent expositions on epistemology, and on the social technology of securing tangible and intangible wealth through proprietary ventures; and Robert LeFevre for his original commentary on maximizing social freedom.

Personal Acknowledgements

I t is fitting to recognize thousands of my lecture and seminar enrollees who over many decades provided a crucial forum out of which *win-win theory* evolved. They came from diverse backgrounds including engineering, medicine, education, entrepreneurship, physics, chemistry, business, proprietorship, dentistry, computer science, and from many other fields of endeavor. They all brought their curiosity to the table of inquiry with a shared interest in expanding their knowledge of social causality to build viable solutions to social problems. In part, because they were tuition-paying students, I was motivated to innovate and communicate compelling seminars on the principles of social causation. It was out of this vital crucible that the Science of Social Causation evolved, which in turn gave birth to Win-Win Theory. The scientific method of direct and indirect observation was used to identify the human exchanges necessary to maximize the causes of peace, prosperity, and freedom, while minimizing the causes of war, poverty, and servitude.

The skills necessary to create and present original seminars on social causality that gain market success are not entirely the same skills necessary to create a prose on social causality that is forceful enough to garner a growing readership. In any case, most writers cannot fashion the "good read" without someone reading and analyzing their work. The following readers were students who attended my seminars and lectures and they have all shared an interest in expanding the market for Win-Win Theory and the Science of Social Causation.

David L. Wood, M.D. of Southern California is a physician and surgeon with exceptional editorial skills whose recommendations on simplifying text for greater grammatical clarity and easier reading have been most useful. David has generously examined various chapters on win-win theory to reach greater simplicity and intelligibility. One of those chapters became the foundation for this treatise on the universal benefits of replacing win-lose religion with win-win religion.

David Carroll Woodward of Northern California is a consummate wordsmith, striving for impeccable usage against the growing tide of bastardizations of American English. In reading my manuscripts, David has not hesitated to apply Mark Twain's elegant principle, "The difference between the almost right word and the right word is really a large matter — it's the difference between the lightning bug and the lightning." Of course, finding the "right word" — or a better word — is not always easy. At times, David has fetched a volume from his unabridged edition of *The Oxford English Dictionary*, to ferret out the right word with the right meaning and the right shading. David's generous efforts on my behalf have been invaluable.

John A. Pugsley (deceased) of Southern California was a professional writer with experience in the communication of ideas on economics, markets, and social issues — all of which are a challenge to present, as he skillfully did, in non-academic, non-esoteric language that is both effective and instructive. John offered valuable suggestions on converting my lectures into effective prose and in formatting a manuscript that can reach for the literary aim of the "easy read." As air travelers who must strip away the excess baggage or the plane won't fly, in his writings, John carefully crafts the parsimonious sentence by stripping away the excess verbiage. In this regard, John was a valuable influence. Those of us who are verbose in our pursuit of semantic precision may be forced by the computer revolution to reach new levels of semantic simplicity — without the loss of precision — as a means to reaching a broader readership.

Lyle D Jacobson, D.D.S, (deceased) of Southern California was an outstanding doctor of dental surgery until he retired to pursue his dream of building a steel-hulled ketch to sail the Caribbean Sea. Beyond dentistry and sailing, Lyle was a philosopher. He showed the importance of understanding the universe in terms of its opposite elements of "empty space" and "solid matter" — and the necessary and integral relationships between these extremes. Because Lyle was focused for decades on explaining the universality of this fundamental relationship in nature, he prodded me to reflect on its significance. Consequently, I extended some of its epistemological underpinnings to the evolvement of win-win theory.

Nicole Carbone Harris of New Zealand honed her grammar and proofreading skills while attending college and editing academic papers for her fellow students. Nicole has been generous with her examination of my manuscripts, leading to various suggestions for fine-tuning grammar and punctuation, as well as enhancing brevity and clarity.

John Richard Boren of Arizona is an entrepreneur and businessman who, along with his wife, Pauline, first attended my lectures in 1975. He was fortunate to be raised in a family where literacy and learning were prized. After several careful readings of the manuscript as it evolved, Richard provided many useful suggestions on continuity, clarifying copy, and sharpening the accuracy of the exposition.

Sigmund Snelson, Ph. D., of Washington, my brother, and a retired geologist, offered useful editorial commentary on the historicity of the section on German geologist A. L. Wegener.

Nancy Rhyme Snelson of Southern California has been my beloved wife for twenty-five years. She has played an invaluable role in the successful presentation of my seminars on win-win theory and optimization theory. Nancy's enduring dedication to advancing the win-win foundations of peace, prosperity, and freedom has been a continuing source of encouragement and inspiration.

෬

Any errors or omissions on my part are not the responsibility of the helpful people recognized in these personal acknowledgments, and naming them here does not necessarily imply their agreement with the premises and conclusions proffered in this treatise. The following, who have not enrolled in my proprietary seminars, have made valuable suggestions for the preparation of this work.

John Xavier Evans, Ph.D., of Arizona is professor emeritus of English literature and a key promulgator of the Phoenix Institute Program given annually at the University of Notre Dame. His Phoenix Program focuses on broadening an understanding and appreciation for the unique and original contributions of Western Civilization for the enrichment of all humans. After a careful reading of the manuscript, Jack Evans offered valued suggestions on broadening the interest in win-win theory, especially among Christian readers.

Yassir M. Fazaga of Southern California is Imam and Religious Director of the Orange County Islamic Foundation in Southern California. Yassir is a rare student and scholar of both Islamic and Christian theology. His recommendations of Islamic source material and specific Qur'ānic passages have been most useful and have enabled me to present a much clearer picture of Islamic faith.

Kermit Lee Snelson of Northern California, my nephew, is a software designer with a scholarly interest in religious history and political philosophy. His research along with his foreign language skills, have ferreted out of the archives of history, important data on the chronology of ancient religious and philosophical information used in this treatise, as well as other historical information that I might not have found on my own.

I wish to extend my appreciation to the following: **Stanley K. Simon** retired adjunct professor of English and publishing vice president, who has read several drafts of the manuscript followed by his useful commentary. **Karin Lee Snelson**, my niece, is a professional editor, reviewer, and writer. She kindly offered various editorial suggestions in fine-tuning this treatise. **Lewis Lane, M.D.,** a neuropsychiatrist in Dana Point, California, for his insightful comments. Others who have attended my seminars include, **Donald Taylor**, retired businessman and real estate executive, and his daughter, **Marci Taylor**, advertising consultant. They have kindly read different drafts of the manuscript and offered various suggestions on the writing. **Betty Boehr Derrick** is a retired English teacher with exceptional skills as a grammarian. Her suggestions have included useful principles of effective writing.

Index

16301159R10277

Made in the USA
Lexington, KY
16 July 2012